Simone de Beauvoir

For Geir Arne

SIMONE DE BEAUVOIR

The Making of an Intellectual Woman

Toril Moi

BLACKWELL
Oxford UK & Cambridge USA

First published 1994

Blackwell Publishers
238 Main Street
Cambridge, Massachusetts 02142
USA

108 Cowley Road
Oxford OX4 1JF
UK

Library of Congress Cataloging-in-Publication Data

Moi, Toril.
Simone de Beauvoir: the making of an intellectual woman/Toril Moi.
p.   cm.
Includes bibliographical references (p.) and index.
ISBN 0–631–14673–3. – ISBN 0–631–19181–X (pbk.)
1. Beauvoir, Simone de, 1908–86.   2. Women and literature –
France – History – 20th century.   3. Women authors, French – 20th
century – Biography.   4. France – Intellectual life – 20th century.
5. Women intellectuals – France – Biography.   I. Title.
PQ2603.E362Z855   1994
848'. 91409–dc20   93–1101
[B]   CIP

British Library Cataloguing in Publication Data

A CIP catalogue record for this book is available from the British Library.

Typeset in Bembo 11 on 12½ pt by Best-Set Typesetter Ltd, Hong Kong
Printed in Great Britain by T. J. Press Ltd., Padstow, Cornwall

This book is printed on acid-free paper

Contents

Acknowledgements

This book is an old project: in one sense, I have always wanted to work on Simone de Beauvoir. Since I started serious work on the book in the spring of 1988, I have benefitted from the conversation and advice of a great number of people. First I would like to thank the Meltzer Foundation at the University of Bergen and the Norwegian Research Council for the Humanities (NAVF) for giving me travel grants to go to Paris on two occasions. The Maison des Sciences de l'Homme (MSH) in Paris made me *directeur d'études associé* from April to June 1988, and again from March to July 1991. I thank M. Clemens Heller for his invitation, and Mme Elina Almasy for her invaluable support at the MSH. To help me fund my trips to Paris, I also got a travel grant from Norsk Faglitterær Forfatterforening (Norwegian Association of Non-fiction Writers). The University Library in Bergen helped me with the initial bibliography. I would like, too, to thank Mme Liliane Phan of the Gallimard Archives and the patient staff at the Bibliothèque Marguerite Durand and the Bibliothèque Nationale in Paris. I also received much assistance from the Sterling Memorial Library at Yale University and the Perkins Library at Duke University.

During my work on this manuscript I have received particularly thorough critical advice on individual chapters or sections from Simon Blackburn, Penny Boumelha, Malcolm Bowie, Peter Brooks, Dianne Chisholm, Elizabeth Fallaize, Stanley Fish, Abigail Solomon Godeau, Rakel Christina Granaas, Julia Hell, Dana Polan, Siân Reynolds, David Rodowick, Monique de Saint Martin, Regina Schwartz, Martin Stone, Vigdis Songe-Møller, Kjell Soleim, Jennifer Wicke and Jane Winston. M. Maurice de Gandillac kindly replied to my questions about the Ecole Normale Supérieure in the 1920s. Over a number of years, Sarah Beckwith, Terry Eagleton, Diana Knight and Geir Arne Moi ended up reading most of the book in bits and pieces: I would like to thank them for their critical sense, energetic encouragement and immense patience. In the spring of 1993, Sara Danius, Stefan Jonsson and Eva Lundgren-Gothlin took the time and trouble to give me detailed comments on the whole manuscript. Their careful feedback saved me from many blunders. Nathalie Duval not only read the whole manuscript, but also provided lots of bibliographical references, and much up-to-date information on the French scene: I am deeply grateful for her support.

At Duke University my various research assistants over the years helped me organize my teaching and saved me many trips to the library: for this I am grateful to Barbara Will, Deborah Chay, Jane Winston, Faith Smith and Jack Murnighan. At various times students at Bergen, Yale and Duke have been exposed to my views on Simone de Beauvoir: they made me think more clearly than I would have done without them. I have lectured on Beauvoir in too many places to list them all here. In terms of my own work, I felt particularly inspired by my visit to Concordia University in Montreal, where I spoke about Beauvoir on the International Women's Day in 1989. My seminars on Beauvoir at Ormond College, University of Melbourne, in May 1990 made me believe that there are many men and women in the world who still care about Simone de Beauvoir and the situation of intellectual women. I would particularly like to thank Jenna Mead, Marion Campbell and Hazel Rowley for making my stay in Melbourne such a friendly one. From 1990 to 1992, Ralph Cohen at the Commonwealth Center of the University of Virginia invited me to give what seems an unseasonably high number of lectures and seminars on Beauvoir. Libby Cohen's enthusiasm encouraged me at just the right time.

Some people have provided me with different kinds of support. Michèle Le Doeuff proves by her brilliant example that feminist philosophy is still alive in France. She introduced me to Mme Hélène de Beauvoir. I am grateful to Mme de Beauvoir for her hospitality and for sharing with me her sister's unpublished letters. Thanks to Michèle Le Doeuff, I also met Mme Simone Martinet (*née* Keim) who was a student at the Ecole Normale Supérieure in the rue d'Ulm in the 1930s. Mme Martinet generously gave of her time and energy to discuss her experiences at the Ecole Normale with me. Mme Chantal Duval and Mlle Claire Bazin provided crucial books at the last minute. By lending me a beach house to write in, Diane Elmeer and Julian D. Newman allowed me to escape from the relentless pressure of everyday life in May 1992: chapter 7 owes a lot to them. My British publisher, Philip Carpenter, consistently supported this project, even when it looked as if it were never going to be completed.

I feel a special gratitude to two persons who, quite independently of each other, supported my project by taking it seriously and by encouraging me to find my own voice in relation to Simone de Beauvoir. For many years now Julia Kristeva has been consistently supportive of my work. Her generous and immensely suggestive comments on the completed manuscript deepened my understanding of Simone de Beauvoir's darker side. I am also grateful to her for being such an independent and inspiring intellectual woman in her own right. Pierre Bourdieu read early drafts of chapters 1, 2 and 5: his quick, careful and detailed responses were immensely helpful to me. His advice on where to go and whom to meet made my research in Paris far more productive than it would otherwise have been.

Several sections of this book have been previously published. A brief excerpt from an earlier version of chapter 1 and a longer section from chapter 2 appeared as 'Simone de Beauvoir: The Making of an Intellectual Woman' in *The Yale Journal of Criticism* 4.1 (Fall 1990): 1–23. An earlier version of chapter 3 was published as 'Politics and the Intellectual Woman: Clichés in the Reception of Simone de Beauvoir' in my *Feminist Theory and Simone de Beauvoir*, The Bucknell Lectures, ed. Michael Payne (Oxford: Blackwell, 1990): 21–60. A much abbreviated version of chapter 4 was published as '*L'Invitée*: An Existentialist Melodrama', in *Paragraph* 14.2 (July 1991): 151–69. An excerpt from chapter 6 appeared as 'Ambiguity and Alienation in *The Second Sex*' in *boundary2* 19.2 (Summer 1992): 96–112. A slightly abridged version of chapter 7 was published as 'Simone de Beauvoir's Utopia: Politics in *The Second Sex*', in *South Atlantic Quarterly* 92.2 (Spring 1993): 311–61. In chapters 7 and 8 I have also used material from my introduction to Simone de Beauvoir, *The Prime of Life* (New York: Paragon House, 1992) and from my introductions to volumes 1 and 2 of Simone de Beauvoir, *Force of Circumstance* (New York: Paragon House, 1992). I gratefully acknowledge permission to reprint all the material listed here.

I also gratefully acknowledge permission from the following to reprint extracts from the works of Simone de Beauvoir:

HarperCollins Publishers Ltd for *She Came to Stay*, translated by Yvonne Moyse and Roger Senhouse (Fontana); Random Century Ltd, Random House Inc. and the Estate of Simone de Beauvoir for *The Second Sex*, translated by H. M. Parshley (Jonathan Cape); and Penguin Books Ltd for *Memoirs of a Dutiful Daughter*, translated by James Kirkup (Penguin, 1963, *Mémoirs d'une jeune fille rangée*, first published in France 1958, translation first published André Deutsch and Weidenfeld & Nicolson, 1959), copyright © Librairie Gallimard, 1958, translation copyright © The World Publishing Company, 1959, for *All Said and Done*, translated by Patrick O'Brian (Penguin, 1977, *Tout compte fait*, first published in France 1972, translation first published André Deutsch, Weidenfeld & Nicolson, G. P. Putnam's Sons, 1974), copyright © Librairie Gallimard, 1972, translation copyright © André Deutsch, Weidenfeld & Nicolson, G. P. Putnam's Sons, 1974, for *The Prime of Life*, translated by Peter Green (Penguin, 1965, *La force de l'âge*, first published in France 1960, translation first published André Deutsch and Weidenfeld & Nicolson, 1962), copyright © Librairie Gallimard, 1960, translation copyright © The World Publishing Company, 1962, for *A Very Easy Death*, translated by Patrick O'Brian (Penguin, 1969, *Une mort très douce*, first published in France 1964, translation first published André Deutsch and Weidenfeld & Nicolson, 1966), copyright © Librairie Gallimard, 1964, translation copyright © André Deutsch, Weidenfeld & Nicolson, G. P. Putnam's Sons, 1966, for *Force of Circumstance*, translated by Richard Howard (Penguin, 1968, *La force des choses*, first published in France 1963, translation first published André Deutsch and Weidenfeld & Nicolson, 1965, copyright © Librairie Gallimard, 1963, translation copyright © G. P. Putnam's Sons, 1964, 1965, and for *Adieux: A Farewell to Sartre*, translated by Patrick O'Brian (Penguin, 1985, *La cérémonie des adieux*, first published in France 1981, translation first published André Deutsch and Weidenfeld & Nicolson, 1984), copyright © Éditions Gallimard, 1981, translation copyright © Patrick O'Brian, 1984.

Finally, I would like to thank my parents for believing in a book that made me a less frequent guest in Norway than they would have liked. This book is dedicated to Geir Arne Moi. His patience, fortitude and courage are exemplary: no sister could have a better brother.

Toril Moi

Key to Abbreviations

Page references to frequently quoted texts by Beauvoir and Sartre appear in brackets in the text preceded by the abbreviations listed below. The editions used are those listed in the 'Works Cited' section. In the case of texts by Beauvoir, and of Sartre's *Being and Nothingness*, I always refer first to the published English translation and then to the French original. In order to save space I do not use the abbreviation 'p.' in such double references. 'TA' means 'translation amended'. Thus (PL345; FA388; TA) means '*The Prime of Life*, p. 345; *La force de l'âge*, p. 388; translation amended'. References to other French texts are *either* to the original, and in that case the translation is mine; *or* to the published translation. In such cases the final list of works cited contains only the relevant reference.

AF	*Adieux: A Farewell to Sartre*
AMM	*All Men are Mortal*
ASD	*All Said and Done*
BN	*Being and Nothingness*
BO	*The Blood of Others*
CA	*La cérémonie des adieux*
DSa	*Le deuxième sexe*, vol. 1
DSb	*Le deuxième sexe*, vol. 2
EA	*The Ethics of Ambiguity*
EN	*L'être et le néant*
FA	*La force de l'âge*
FC	*Force of Circumstance*
FCa	*La force des choses*, vol. 1
FCb	*La force des choses*, vol. 2
I	*L'Invitée*
JG	*Journal de guerre*

LMa	*Les mandarins*, vol. 1
LMb	*Les mandarins*, vol. 2
LS	*Letters to Sartre*
LSa	*Lettres à Sartre*, vol. 1
LSb	*Lettres à Sartre*, vol. 2
M	*The Mandarins*
MA	*Pour une morale de l'ambiguïté*
MDD	*Memoirs of a Dutiful Daughter*
MJF	*Mémoires d'une jeune fille rangée*
PL	*The Prime of Life*
SA	*Le sang des autres*
SC	*She Came to Stay*
SS	*The Second Sex*
TCF	*Tout compte fait*
TH	*Tous les hommes sont mortels*
UM	*Une mort très douce*
VE	*A Very Easy Death*

Introduction

Simone de Beauvoir is the emblematic intellectual woman of the twentieth century. Whatever their differences, the great intellectual women of previous generations – Madame de Staël, George Sand, George Eliot, Virginia Woolf – had one thing in common: they were all excluded from the major educational institutions of their day. Simone de Beauvoir, on the other hand, belonged to the first generation of European women to be educated on a par with men. Entering into previously all-male institutions of higher education, she had to compete with men both at university and in her subsequent professional life. In these respects her career as an intellectual represents a radical break with the trajectories of her illustrious elder sisters. A pioneering woman in her own time, Simone de Beauvoir was only the ninth woman in France to pass the prestigious *agrégation* examination in philosophy, and the youngest *agrégée* ever in that discipline, regardless of gender. Given her unique opportunity to develop herself fully as an intellectual in a country and at a time when intellectuals were considered important members of society, Simone de Beauvoir became more *purely* an intellectual, as it were, than any other woman of her era. Precisely because of that unique position her experiences gain in intensity and sharpness of focus: in her texts, the conflicts and contradictions experienced by intellectual women in a patriarchal world emerge with unusual clarity.[1]

Born in 1908, Beauvoir belongs to the generation of intellectual women who came of age in the 1920s and 1930s, that is to say to the generation of Hannah Arendt (1906–75), Alva Myrdal (1902–84), Åse Gruda Skard (1906–85), Mary McCarthy (1912–89) and Margaret Mead (1901–78), just to mention a few. At least in relation to their education and intellectual careers, these women believed that they were being treated as equals in an egalitarian system. On the whole, they tended not to be conscious of the social significance of their own femaleness. Referring to herself at the age of 23, Beauvoir writes that 'I did not think of myself as a "woman": I was *me*' (PL62; FA73). Luckier than the true pioneers of the early 1900s (represented in this book by Léontine Zanta), some women of this genera-tion were able to pursue spectacular, albeit often slightly unorthodox careers. They were indeed what Pierre Bourdieu would call the *miraculées* – the miraculous exceptions – of the Western educational systems. By the time they reached middle age, however, the weight of their experience spurred many of them to wonder about the significance of being female in a male-dominated society.[2] It was only in 1946, if we are to believe her memoirs, that Beauvoir realized that to be an educated woman is not, after all, quite the same thing as to be an educated man. With a rare sense of moral and political integrity she faced the consequences of that insight: the very moment she realized that she was an intellectual *woman*, she started to write *The Second Sex*.

The situation of Simone de Beauvoir and other intellectual women of her generation, of course, was not like that of educated women in the 1990s: they were still relative pioneers, still part of a small elite. While they did not themselves have to storm the barricades of male intellectual privi-lege, they were often among the first handful of women to be allowed entry into previously all-male institutions. In the following decades, the situation of women in higher education did not change much. Universities and colleges did not experience a massive increase in the numbers of female students until the 1960s. Through the struggle of the women's movement in the 1960s and 1970s, women's access to all levels and types of education was finally guaranteed: today Western women take their right to pursue the education and career of their choice for granted.

Paradoxically, however, that very fact has led to a new egalitarian mystique: just like the young Simone de Beauvoir, many women today believe that they are being treated as equals in their schools and universities. Unfortunately, statistics do not always bear this out. In 1992, for instance, women taking exams at British universities were still only half as likely to get a First Class degree as men: 'While 10.3 per cent of men get Firsts, only 6.2 per cent of women do', Katharine Viner writes in the *Guardian*.[3] In spite of loud claims to the contrary in the United States, by 1990 women had not made serious inroads in American intellectual institutions: 'Women, feminists or otherwise, account for a mere 10 per cent of the tenured faculty at all four-year institutions (and a mere 3 to 4 per cent at Ivy League colleges)', Susan Faludi informs us (p. 293). In January 1993, *The New York Times* tells us, 'women make up only 11.6 per cent of full professors nationwide and have made their greatest inroads at community colleges where the pay is lowest' (DePalma, p. 11). In 1990, US census figures show, the income of women holding doctorates was 36 per cent lower than that of their male counterparts.[4] In Norwegian universities, where only about 9 per cent of all full professors are women, the situation is hardly better.

Even in the 1990s women who set out to become intellectuals have to face personal, social and ideological obstacles not generally placed in the way of aspiring male intellectuals. This is why I am convinced that Simone de Beauvoir still has much to teach us, for better and for worse. Intellectual women today cannot afford to ignore her experiences. In this context, I take 'intellectual woman' to mean any woman who has ever taken herself seriously as a thinker, particularly in an educational context. Whether or not they choose to turn their intellectual interests into a profession, such women know what it means to take pleasure in thought. More often than not they also know that powerful strands of patriarchal ideology hold that such pleasures are not made for them: one does not have to have a PhD to fear that an active interest in intellectual matters will label one a blue-stocking or a dried-up schoolmarm. Nor is it unusual for intellectual women to have a difficult time with their mothers, or to develop what Michèle Le Doeuff has called 'erotico-theoretical transference relations' with male intellectual figures.[5] In these and many other respects, Simone de Beauvoir's experiences are far from unique.

But I am not studying Simone de Beauvoir only because she is an emblematic intellectual woman. Precisely because she occupied a unique position in relation to the intellectual discourses of her time, she also became the greatest feminist theorist of our century. Long before the emergence of the women's movement *The Second Sex* posed every one of the problems feminists today are still working to solve. The book literally changed thousands of women's lives: I can think of no other work of similar effects in the twentieth century. Historically the reception and effects of *The Second Sex* remind me of the responses to Harriet Beecher Stowe's *Uncle Tom's Cabin*, or perhaps, in a different register, to Richardson's *Clarissa*. To write about Simone de Beauvoir without taking *The Second Sex* seriously is to refuse to take her seriously as a philosopher, as a feminist and as an intellectual woman.[6]

THE TEXTUAL SIMONE DE BEAUVOIR

When I say that I am interested in Simone de Beauvoir as an intellectual woman, it may sound as if I am mostly concerned with biography. Yet my work is based on the assumption that there can be no *methodological* distinction between 'life' and 'text'. I have always been struck by the fact that Freud, in *The Interpretation of Dreams*, seems unable to distinguish between the psyche and the text: at the same time as he gives us a theory of interpretation, he also gives us a map of the human mind. To read the dream is at once to read the text and the person, not because the 'meaning' of the text is the person (that would be the reductive version of Freud's insights), but because for Freud, the person only reveals herself in the form of a text: to all practical purposes, the Freudian subject *is* a text. In the case of Simone de Beauvoir, whose autobiographies and letters alone run to well over a million words, Freud's discovery is particularly relevant. The intertextual network of fictional, philosophical, autobiographical and epistolary texts that she left us *is* our Simone de Beauvoir. In addition to this, we have all the texts about her: letters, diaries, newspaper interviews and reviews, scholarly studies, films, biographies, personal recollections by friends and enemies – all contribute to the production of the network of images and ideas we recognize as 'Simone de Beauvoir', and which certainly condition our perception of her texts 'in themselves'.

When it comes to biography and literary criticism, the life/text distinction normally carries an explicit or implicit value judgement: biographers often consider life more 'real' or more 'true' than the text; many literary critics have a tendency to think of the text as a pure aesthetic object that can only be defiled by the mess we usually call life. In the case of Simone de Beauvoir, however, it is particularly important to guard against such assumptions. In her first novel, *L'Invitée* (1943), she devotes a whole chapter to a seduction scene featuring her heroine Françoise and a young man named Gerbert.[7] One then discovers that in a late interview Beauvoir claims that this particular scene is a faithful rendering of a real-life event, her own seduction of the young Jacques-Laurent Bost. While her autobiography makes no reference at all to the occurrence, her posthumously published letters to Sartre describe the scene in a wealth of details; a few sentences first used in the letters even crop up verbatim in the published novel. It would be easy to conclude that, all in all, the letters must contain the 'real' version of events. The emotional impact described in the letters, however, turns out to be radically at odds with the one bestowed on the same events in the fiction. In the novel, moreover, the seduction scene entertains close intertextual relations with a flirtation scene described by Sartre in *Being and Nothingness* (1943). Seemingly 'general' theoretical passages in *The Second Sex* (1949) also turn out to contain scarcely veiled interpretations of the seduction scene in *L'Invitée*. It also has to be said that the novel displays a far more convincing – because far more complex – understanding of the events than any of the so-called non-fictional texts involved. Under such circumstances it would seem absurd simply to declare that the only 'text' in play here is that of the novel; or, on the other hand, to attribute superior biographical value to the 'documentary' texts (letters, diaries, interviews) as opposed to the 'literary' ones. Clearly the question of subjectivity (Beauvoir perceived as a speaking subject) and the question of textuality (Beauvoir perceived as a body of texts) here overlap completely.

If 'life' is treated as if it were composed of a number of different texts, it follows that literary or philosophical texts cannot be reduced to bio-graphical events. Rather all sorts of texts (conversations, philosophical treatises, gossip, novels, educational institutions) will be considered ele-ments participating in the same discursive network. The point is not to treat one text as the implicit meaning of another, but rather to read them all with and against each other in order to bring out their points of ten-sion, contradictions and similarities. Nothing has been more detrimental to our understanding of Simone de Beauvoir than the tedious – and often intensely hostile – efforts to reduce her achievements to mere effects of her personal circumstances. In the light of such attacks, I certainly appre-ciate the ethical integrity of the 'purely aesthetic' approaches to her work all the more. It nevertheless has to be said that most of these readings actually miss the real cultural significance of Simone de Beauvoir because they tend to treat her simply as a writer of *fictional* texts. While I am a great admirer of *L'Invitée* and *The Mandarins*, it is obvious to me that if Beauvoir had been nothing but a novelist, she would not have become a mytholo-gical figure, an imago that has made its presence felt in the thoughts and dreams of every intellectual woman in the Western world since the early 1950s. Her life as a pioneering intellectual woman in mid-century France as well as her famous relationship with Sartre are integral parts of the text we know as 'Simone de Beauvoir'.

This is why traditional biography actually has come closer than literary criticism to capturing something of the importance of Beauvoir for our century. Yet none of the three biographies published so far (by Claude Francis and Fernande Gonthier, Deirdre Bair, and Margaret Crosland) takes her writing seriously: dutifully pausing in their narrative of love affairs for a quick glance at individual works, her biographers fail to grasp the power and complexity of her greatest texts. Reading their work, one may be forgiven for concluding that the significance of Simone de Beauvoir derives largely from her relatively unorthodox relationship with Sartre and other lovers. But if she had not been one of the first female *agrégées* of philosophy in France, as well as the author of *The Second Sex* and a number of famous novels and memoirs, her private life would hardly have become the stuff that myths are made of. Only careful reading of the texts of the French *agrégation* of philosophy and *The Second Sex*, among others, can give us any understanding of why this would be so.

PERSONAL GENEALOGY

For a long time I hesitated to call this book *Simone de Beauvoir: The Making of an Intellectual Woman*. 'It sounds like a critical biography', my friends said. As it had never occurred to me to write the story of Beauvoir's life, their objections seemed conclusive: another title would clearly have to be found. The offending title nevertheless refused to go away: I could not help feeling that although I was not writing a biography, what I was writing about was precisely the *making* of Simone de Beauvoir as an intellectual woman, and in more ways than one. First of all, I write about the making of her as an intellectual in the most literal way: by studying her education, that is to say, the institutional structures that produced her as a philosopher and an intellectual in the first third of this century.

I also write about the making of Simone de Beauvoir as a major twentieth-century intellectual in the sense that I set out to study the works that 'made' her, as well as the works that tell us how she managed to make it. In my view, by the end of 1949, the year in which she published *The Second Sex*, Simone de Beauvoir had truly become Simone de Beauvoir: personally as well as professionally, she was 'made'. Her later life adds little to the repertoire of themes and obsessions established by this time: it is tempting to argue that *all* her major texts ceaselessly return to the period before 1950. Published in 1954, *The Mandarins*, for instance, represents her first attempt to return to the past, in this case to the political development in France from August 1944 (the Liberation) to the summer of 1947 (the beginning of the Cold War), and her own experience of passion and desire in the relationship with Nelson Algren which lasted from 1947 to 1950. Apart from the two relatively slight volumes of fiction from the 1960s, *Les Belles Images* and *The Woman Destroyed*, and her 1970 essay *Old Age*, after 1954 Beauvoir produced almost nothing but autobiography – that is to say, writing turned towards the past: by far the largest bulk of her memoirs dwell on the period before 1950. Although I range over the totality of Beauvoir's *oeuvre*, my textual attention is focused on *L'Invitée*, *The Second Sex* and her memoirs. I have of course felt free to deal with the time after 1950 – particularly in my reading of *Force of Circumstance* – whenever I thought that this would add depth to my understanding of a particular problem or theme.

Finally, I speak of the making of Simone de Beauvoir as an intellectual woman in a more general sense. By using the term *making* I want to emphasize the idea of production or construction, and thus to indicate that I see 'Simone de Beauvoir' as an extraordinarily complex effect of a whole network of different discourses or determinants. This is why this book cannot be confined to the traditional categories of biography or literary criticism. Although there is much biography and even more literary criticism in the pages that follow, this book also contains reception studies, sociology of culture, philosophical analysis, psychoanalytic inquiry and feminist theory. So what I am to call this thing I have written? Since no traditional terms will fit, I have decided to call this book a *personal genealogy*.[8]

Personal genealogy is not biography. I can best explain the difference by saying that personal genealogy is to biography as genealogy is to traditional history for Michel Foucault. Like traditional history, biography is narrative and linear, argues in terms of origins and finalities and seeks to disclose an original identity. Genealogy, on the other hand, seeks to achieve a sense of emergence or production and to understand the complex play of different kinds of power involved in social phenomena. Personal genealogy does not reject the notion of the 'self' or the subject but tries instead to subject that very self to genealogical investigation.

Personal genealogy assumes that every phenomenon may be read as a text, that is to say as a complex network of signifying structures. In this context, the concept of *overdetermination* becomes crucial. When Freud set out to explain, in *The Interpretation of Dreams*, that the human psyche is a split, contradictory and dynamic phenomenon, he used this term to account for its complexities. To cast textuality as an overdetermined process is to claim that signification emerges as an unstable compromise between the pressures exerted by a wide range of factors. Let us picture these factors ('determinants', 'discourses', 'voices', 'structures', etc.) as so many strands in the textual weave.[9] To read an overdetermined textual element, then, is to point to its potential plurality of meaning, to indicate that it takes its meanings from more than one textual strand. There is nothing reductive about this procedure. When I find that a particular logical blind spot in Beauvoir's philosophical writings seems to owe its existence to social or psychological factors, for instance, I do not mean to say that the particular textual element in question is no longer readable *as* philosophy, but rather that we must imagine this textual moment as a space in which the strand ('discourse', 'genre', etc.) of philosophy enters into collision with that of psychology and that of, say, the French intellectual field at the time. An example here might be my understanding of Beauvoir's idealization of men and masculinity in *The Second Sex*. For me, that idealization – which puts her argument about women's oppression in severe contradiction with itself – is the overdetermined effect of a certain metaphorical logic, of her relationship to Sartre, of her position as an *agrégée* in philosophy, and of her relationship to her mother. In this particular textual moment, I would argue, the power of the conflict generated by those different strands of her textual weave is such as to destroy the discourse of philosophy that Beauvoir takes such pride in mastering.

The personal genealogist, then, does not seek to deny the power or interest of any individual textual strand; but in so far as she considers texts overdetermined phenomena, she feels no obligation to preserve the illusion of generic purity, that is to say to register the effects of one and only one strand of the textual weave. Or to put it in more psychoanalytic terms: the personal genealogist is not surprised to discover that every discourse (including her own) is haunted by the ghosts of the individual and social unconscious.

Since there is no obvious end to the textual network explored by the genealogical project, that project can never lead to a final totalization of knowledge: a genealogist's work is never done. Genealogy, in fact, is very much like housework: like the housewife, the genealogist stops her work for fairly pragmatic reasons: the floor is clean enough; it is time to start cooking instead; it is too late and one is too tired to continue. The next day, there is always a need for more cooking, more dusting, more cleaning; occasionally, nothing short of complete redecoration will do. For this reason I have not written a conventional conclusion to this book: my 'Simone de Beauvoir' remains an unfinished text.

THREE TEXTUAL MOMENTS

This book is structured as a genealogical investigation of three textual moments in Beauvoir's work. Part I emerged out of my fascination with the scene in *Memoirs of a Dutiful Daughter* when Simone de Beauvoir and Jean-Paul Sartre sit down by the Medici fountain in the Luxembourg Gardens to discuss *her* philosophical ideas. At the end of three hours she was crushed: 'I am no longer sure what I think, nor whether I can be said to think at all', she noted in her diary (MDD344; MJF480). When I started to think about the implications of that conversation, it soon became clear that in order to understand it, I would have to investigate the difference between Beauvoir's and Sartre's education in painstaking detail. For their discussion takes place in July 1929, during the preparation for the oral part of the *agrégation* examination in philosophy. What does it mean for a woman in France in 1929 to prepare for that exam? Do Beauvoir and Sartre actually discuss as equals in this context? Does it matter that he was at the Ecole Normale Supérieure and she was not? That he was three years older? And how did others perceive the writings of a highly educated woman intellectual in mid-century France?

Chapter 1 takes as its starting point the crucial conversation in the Luxembourg Gardens. Reading it in the context of *Memoirs of a Dutiful Daughter*, I try to make sense of Beauvoir's representation of herself as an intellectual woman. Chapter 2 may be considered an attempt to investigate one important, but – to me – highly puzzling event: the fact that in 1929, Jean-Paul Sartre came first and Simone de Beauvoir came second in the competitive *agrégation* examination in philosophy. What does this mean? How does it affect Beauvoir's position as an intellectual woman? How does it affect her writing? And why does the writing she produces from that position get judged so harshly by the arbiters of taste in France? In chapter 3 I turn to the reception of Beauvoir's works, focusing on the ways in which her sex and her politics have affected her readers. In various ways, then, part I of this book explores Simone de Beauvoir's speaking position, as represented by herself and others.

In part II (chapters 4–7) I turn to the texts produced from that speaking position. The central textual moment that I seek to understand in my readings of *L'Invitée* and *The Second Sex* is Beauvoir's account of how, after a conversation with Sartre in 1946, she finally realized that to be born a woman is not the same thing as to be born a man. 'I was so interested in this discovery', she writes, 'that I abandoned my project for a personal confession in order to give all my attention to finding out about the condition of woman in its broadest terms' (FC103; FCa136; TA). In that moment, the idea of writing *The Second Sex* was conceived. The question that gives its energy to all the chapters in this section is very simple: what *did* it mean to Beauvoir to be a woman then? Or to put it in slightly more specific terms: how does Simone de Beauvoir represent the conflicts and contradictions of an intellectual woman in mid-century France?

In chapter 4 I read *L'Invitée* particularly in terms of its representation of love and the intellectual woman's sense of identity. In order to do so, it is of course necessary to take Beauvoir's own philosophical framework seriously: my reading seeks to explore both the philosophical and the psychological implications of her first novel. Chapter 5 raises the question of the ritual comparisons of Beauvoir and Sartre. Through close readings of the famous flirtation scene in *Being and Nothingness* and the seduction scene in *L'Invitée*, I try to explore the differences in their respective understanding of women's position. I also pay special attention to the complex relationship between personal and philosophical discourses in these texts. Turning to *The Second Sex*, I first (in chapter 6) read it as an essay in feminist philosophy, focusing particularly on its rhetorical strategies, its theory of female subjectivity under patriarchy and its problematic account of male and female sexuality. In chapter 7 I discuss the politics of Beauvoir's epochal essay by exploring the feminist responses to the text, the historical conditions that produced it, its representation of women's situation in France at the time, its analysis of the conditions of liberation, and its relationship to Sartre and Fanon's theories of black liberation which were published at roughly the same time.

Part III consists of only one chapter. Turning to Beauvoir's auto-

biographies, letters and diaries, chapter 8 explores the texts where Beauvoir
writes about herself as an intellectual woman and as a writer. The textual
moment that haunts me throughout this chapter is the end of *Force of
Circumstance*, where, at the age of 54, she pours out her feelings of sadness,
emptiness and disappointment: 'I have lost my old power to separate the
darkness from the light, to produce, at the price of a few thunderstorms, a
radiant sky. Death is no longer a brutal event in the far distance; it haunts
my sleep; in my waking hours I sense its shadow between the world and
me; it has already begun' (FC673; FCb507; TA). Why is Simone de
Beauvoir so depressed? In order to answer that question, I found myself
unravelling the psychological structures in Beauvoir's autobiographical
writings through close readings of her accounts of the famous pacts with
Sartre, her 'schizophrenia', and her relationships with other women. But I
also try to show how Beauvoir's melancholic moods affect the very texture
of her works, leading to quite remarkable oscillations in tone and style. This
chapter, then, represents an attempt to understand what it meant to Simone
de Beauvoir to be a writer. My brief afterword returns to the question of
love and the intellectual woman: why do so many people feel deeply hurt
by the discovery that Beauvoir did not, after all, lead a perfectly happy life
with Sartre?

SPEAKING ABOUT BEAUVOIR: THE EFFECTS OF GEOGRAPHY

Much of this book is concerned with Beauvoir's personal situation in one
way or the other. Sometimes I call that her speaking position and claim that
it affects her texts in important ways. 'What about *your* speaking position,
then?', my friends would ask. 'Aren't you going to say anything about
yourself?' My answer was always no. Like other intellectual women I
recognize myself in some, but by no means in all, of Beauvoir's experiences: there is nothing unusual in that. Unlike Simone de Beauvoir, I am
not the emblematic intellectual woman of the twentieth century. *Qua*
intellectual woman, I am therefore not of general interest.

In my personal trajectory there are nevertheless a few generalizable
factors that help to explain my interest in Beauvoir. There are, first, my
political affinities with the kind of materialist feminism she represents;
second, my need to reflect on my own identity as an intellectual woman;
third, the fact that I was never socialized to accept the high bourgeois
standards of taste that tend to make Beauvoir unpalatable to many; and,
fourth, the effects of geography: the fact that in the period since I first
thought about writing this book I have lived and worked in Norway,
Britain and the United States, but not in France. My relative cultural and

geographical marginality in relation to the French intellectual tradition has obviously made my work on Beauvoir more difficult, but it has also, paradoxically, given me the intellectual courage to undertake it in the first place. Lecturing in Scandinavia and many English-speaking countries, I have been encouraged to believe that my topic is truly intellectually challenging. In my parts of the world, then, it is quite possible to write on Simone de Beauvoir without feeling like an intellectual pariah.

To live and work in France, on the other hand, is to expose oneself to an intellectual milieu where most people take Simone de Beauvoir's lack of intellectual and literary distinction as a basic article of faith. The very same intellectuals who passionately defend every citizen's abstract right to speak are often only too eager to prevent anybody from speaking about Beauvoir. At one conference where I spoke about the cultural condescension evident in French responses to Beauvoir, the only comment of one of the more famous French intellectuals present was: 'You know, Simone de Beauvoir wasn't just stupid [bête], she was cruel [méchante] as well.' The brilliant smile he then produced revealed in a particularly fascinating way his own unshakeable conviction of legitimacy: to him, there could be no questioning of his right – and his power – to decide what is to count as interesting in intellectual life.

Several recent French books on intellectuals from the Dreyfus affair to our days manage not to mention a single woman. The patriarchal arrogance of such enterprises is compounded by the fact that the very same books often go to great lengths to include even extremely obscure males. According to Monique de Saint Martin, for instance, one study of French intellectuals in the period from 1880 to 1900 mentions no women at all. Her own cursory check of readily available material immediately located the names of 778 women writing in the same period.[10] In this context, it is also interesting to note that the prestigious Pléiade imprint has published editions of perfectly minor male writers such as Julien Gracq and Julien Green (let us not even mention Alexandre Dumas, or the truly awful Henry de Montherlant) and none at all of Simone de Beauvoir. When it comes to twentieth-century women writers, they can, apparently, stretch to Colette and Marguerite Yourcenar (there is also an edition of Nathalie Sarraute under way), but no further. To realize that the greatest feminist essay of this century is considered inferior to works such as Moïra, Les jeunes filles or The Three Musketeers is quite an eye-opener.

My point is not that Simone de Beauvoir ought at all cost to be in the Pléiade; I have little sympathy with the stuffiness of that particular institution. After all, André Breton and Aimé Césaire are not included either.[11] The Pléiade is just a symptom of a more general situation: the fact that in France young women (and men) are made to feel vaguely stupid – that is to say, unintellectual – if they show a conspicuous interest in Simone de

Beauvoir. Such cultural terrorism, moreover, does not only silence serious discussion of Beauvoir, it also prevents other marginalized voices from being heard. Given my own analysis of French cultural capital, I would surely have had a hard time writing this book on the Left Bank: the pine trees of North Carolina have been a blessing in more ways than one.

Part I

1

Second Only to Sartre

Simone de Beauvoir, woman of letters, Sartre's disciple . . .

(*Le petit Larousse*, 1974)

A CONVERSATION IN THE LUXEMBOURG GARDENS

For intellectual women today some of Simone de Beauvoir's choices are problematic, to say the least. Why, for instance, does she seize every opportunity to declare herself intellectually inferior to Sartre? Before meeting him, she writes, she had never felt intellectually dominated by anybody (see MDD342–4; MJF480). Yet this self-confident philosophy student only has to meet the star student of the Ecole Normale Supérieure (ENS) for her very sense of identity to be threatened. In one of the most brilliant passages of *Hipparchia's Choice*, Michèle Le Doeuff shows that all the essential elements of Beauvoir's 'erotico-theoretical' relationship to Sartre and to philosophy are to be found in one single passage in *Memoirs of a Dutiful Daughter*. This is the scene where Beauvoir describes a philosophical discussion between herself and Sartre. The crucial conversation takes place one summer morning in 1929, near the Medici fountain in the Luxembourg Gardens. Beauvoir is 21, Sartre has just turned 24. For the first time, she writes, she had decided to expose her own ideas to Sartre, as opposed to simply discussing relevant exam topics:

> One morning in the Luxembourg Gardens, near the Medici fountain, I outlined for him that pluralist ethics which I had cobbled together to vindicate the people I liked but whom I didn't want to resemble: he took it apart [*il la mit en pièces*]. I clung to my system, because it authorized me to

look upon my heart as the arbiter of good and evil; I struggled [*je me débattis*] for three hours. In the end I had to admit I was beaten: besides, I had realized, in the course of our discussion, that many of my opinions were based only on prejudice, dishonesty, or hastily formed concepts, that my reasoning was at fault and that my ideas were in a muddle. 'I'm no longer sure what I think, nor whether I can be said to think at all,' I noted, disconcerted. My vanity was not wounded: I was far more curious than domineering; I preferred learning to showing-off. But all the same, after so many years of arrogant solitude, it was something serious to discover that I wasn't the One and Only, but one among many, by no means first, and suddenly uncertain of my true capacity (MDD344; MJF480; TA).

The importance of this scene as emblematic of Simone de Beauvoir's persistent tendency to cast herself as Sartre's philosophical Other has been convincingly demonstrated by Le Doeuff, who asks herself why it is that Beauvoir, a brilliant student of philosophy, seems only too eager to aban- don philosophy to Sartre.[1] Presenting herself as struggling for three hours before being forced to give in to the undeniably more powerful man, Beauvoir surprisingly enough goes on to describe her undoing as an indispensable initiation into her new life as an independent woman. Her old ambition to 'tell all' was clearly too vague and emotional, she writes. Thanks to her necessary disillusionment, however, she now has more specific insights to communicate: 'But I didn't let myself be discouraged; the future suddenly seemed as if it would be much more difficult than I had realized but it had also become more real and more certain; instead of undefined possibilities I saw opening out before me a clearly-marked field of activity, with all its problems, its hard work, its materials, its instruments, and its inflexibility' (MDD345; MJF481).

Unfortunately, this upbeat account of her experience is not quite con- vincing. Appearing gaily to abandon the old project of 'telling it all' as at once too much and too little, and to extol the new 'clearly-marked field' which is opening up for her, she overlooks the fact that the new project remains peculiarly similar to the old: 'I no longer asked myself: what shall I do? There was everything to be done, everything I had formerly longed to do: to combat error, to find the truth, to tell it, to enlighten the world, perhaps even to help to change the world' (MDD345; MJF481; TA). The desire to 'tell all' (*tout dire*) has been transformed into a desire to 'do everything' (*tout faire*): the latter is hardly more specific than the former. The difference, if anything, is that the new project comes across as dis- tinctively philosophical in its ambition to seek truth and evangelically spread it to the world. But the fact is that, publishing her memoirs in 1958, Beauvoir is writing almost thirty years *après coup*. Best read as a vague outline of the Sartrean project of *littérature engagée*, produced well after the events which it is supposed to prefigure, Beauvoir's account here,

consciously or unconsciously, demonstrates the way in which the philosophical initiative now belongs to Sartre. In the course of three hours in the
Luxembourg Gardens Simone de Beauvoir has indeed been transformed: if
she arrived as a woman with a philosophical project of her own, the
elaboration of a new ethics, she leaves as a woman undone, or to put it
differently: as a *disciple*. 'Sartre trapped Simone de Beauvoir by insisting that
she follow him', Le Doeuff writes (*Hipparchia's Choice*, p. 138).

The violence of the debate ought not to come as a surprise to readers of
The Second Sex. If Sartre 'demolishes' or 'takes apart' (*mettre en pièces*) her
home-made ethics, it is not, as Beauvoir would have it, simply because he
is more intelligent but mainly because he has profited from a far better
education. In this way the primal scene in the Luxembourg Gardens
becomes a paradigmatic illustration of Beauvoir's own analysis of the role
of logic in male–female relationships. Women, she writes in *The Second
Sex*, often lose out in arguments with their husbands, since the husbands
profit from their greater experience in the real world, whereas women
often have not had the chance to acquire a thorough 'culture', or knowledge of the world:

> It is not through a mental defect that they [women] are unable to reason
> properly, it is rather that experience has not held them to strict reasoning; for
> them thought is an amusement rather than an instrument; even though
> intelligent, sensitive, sincere, they are unable to state their views and draw
> conclusions, for lack of intellectual technique. That is why their husbands,
> even when they are of much more mediocre ability, will easily dominate
> them and prove themselves to be right even when they are wrong. In
> masculine hands logic is often violence (SS482; DSb294–5; TA).

But if Beauvoir was capable of producing such a striking feminist analysis
of what one might call logical violence in 1949, why does she not allude
to it ten years later, when she is writing her memoirs?[2] Although it remains
true that such an analysis was not available to her in 1929, *Memoirs of a
Dutiful Daughter* in general is packed with the author's often highly sardonic
comments on her own youthful naivety and mistaken opinions. Here as in
so many other contexts it is as if Beauvoir's relationship to Sartre remains
the one sacrosanct area of her life, to be protected even against her own
critical attention. Thus Beauvoir does not draw our attention to the striking
similarity between the epistemological scene enacted in the Parisian park
and her own account in *The Second Sex* of the transformative violence at
work in the defloration of young girls:

> Formerly it was by a real or simulated rape [*rapt*] that a woman was torn from
> her childhood universe and hurled into wifehood; it remains an act of
> violence that changes a girl into a woman: we still speak of 'taking' a girl's

virginity, her flower, or 'breaking' her maidenhead. This defloration is not the gradually accomplished outcome of a continuous evolution, it is an abrupt rupture with the past, the beginning of a new cycle (SS394; DSb148).

There is nothing arbitrary about my juxtaposition here of the erotic and the theoretical: it is above all because Beauvoir *desires* Sartre that she feels the need to endow him with every phallic virtue. If she could not admire him, she could not love him. Michèle Le Doeuff is quite right to compare Simone and Jean-Paul to Héloïse and Abelard. In both cases the woman's desire turns the man into philosophy: his body comes to represent phallic knowledge to her. In her novels Beauvoir repeatedly returns to the theme of the intellectual woman's desire for and investment in precisely such erotico-theoretical relationships. Here one should simply note that Sartre's philosophical defloration of her thought leads Beauvoir to doubt every aspect of her former life. Her desire to develop an ethics based on the heart is rejected as lacking in logic, not retained as the starting point for new and more convincing elaboration. She even comes to doubt whether she is thinking at all: for a moment her faith in herself as a thinking being is nearly destroyed.

Her response is to insist, bravely, that she does not mind not shining in conversations, and that she is not averse to the role of disciple ('I preferred learning to showing-off'). But as Michèle Le Doeuff points out, Beauvoir *knows* that true thought, real philosophy, is not a matter of 'shining', but of pursuing truth (see *Hipparchia's Choice*, p. 139). So why does Beauvoir see Sartre's logical violence and conversational brilliance as necessarily revealing the dismal truth: that *she* is lacking in philosophy? Nor should it be forgotten that in 1929 Sartre was not yet Sartre: he was a 24-year-old student who somehow had managed to fail his *agrégation* the previous year. At this stage there would seem to be no need for anybody – least of all for Simone de Beauvoir – to construct him as her intellectual superior. Had she wanted to, Simone de Beauvoir, three years younger and without the privilege of attending the Ecole Normale Supérieure, could have made out a good case for her own intellectual parity with Sartre at the time. Instead of scrutinizing its causes, however, she chooses to cast Sartre's intellectual superiority as *natural*. As with all such ideological moves, the effect is to make explicit criticism (of his logical violence, for instance) extremely difficult.

In her memoirs, written in the late 1950s, she justifies her preference for a superior man as her partner in strikingly scholastic terms, arguing in effect that under patriarchy male superiority amounts to no more than equality: 'If in the absolute sense a man, who was a member of the privileged species and already had a flying start over me, did not count more than I did, I was forced to the conclusion that in a relative sense he counted less: in order for me to recognize him as my equal, he would have to prove himself my superior' (MDD145; MJF202; TA). Here Beauvoir tries to have it both ways: on the one hand she would seem to be saying that she cannot actually imagine *desiring* a man if he does not appear to be her superior; on the other she also implies that any superiority he might have would not really be credible, since it would be no more than a consequence of patriarchal injustice. In her encounter with Sartre, however, there is no such ambiguity: desire easily gains the upper hand; Sartre just *is* superior. 'I was convinced', she writes, 'that [Sartre] would one day write a philosophical work of the first importance' (MDD343; MJF479; TA). As for herself, as we have seen, she simply knows that she is no longer the 'One and Only [. . .] by no means first' (MDD344; MJF480).

THE IMPORTANCE OF BEING INTERESTING

Simone de Beauvoir's philosophical defeat in the Luxembourg Gardens leads to the painful loss of her belief in her own sovereign and exclusive status as a thinking being. For the rest of her life she continues to perceive herself as intellectually and philosophically second to Sartre. But *why* does she so eagerly embrace such a definition of herself as an intellectual woman? What disposes her to take up such a speaking position? In this chapter I intend to explore some of the subjective factors that may have influenced her choice. By 'subjective' I understand above all Beauvoir's own account of how she became an intellectual woman. I am also particularly interested in Beauvoir's choice of literature rather than philosophy as the field in which she sets out to make her mark. In chapter 2 I will discuss the objective – *public* – factors that contribute to her decision to define herself as second only to Sartre.[3] Emphasizing the idea of intellectual defeat, the reading of the scene in the Luxembourg Gardens outlined above represents my own initial reaction to Beauvoir's text. That reading helped me to formulate the problems outlined here. Exploring those problems, however, I ended up supplying two alternative constructions of the same scene. The three readings are not mutually exclusive: together they provide a sense of the contradictions inherent in the position of an intellectual woman in love with an intellectual man under patriarchy.

Finally, before returning to the epistemological primal scene by the Medici fountain, I would like to emphasize the ambiguity of Beauvoir's position. While many feminists rightly deplore her tendency to perceive herself as inferior to Sartre, it does not follow that she casts herself as inferior to any other man. My own view is that she sees herself as second *only* to Sartre, not to her other male university friends, such as Raymond

Aron, Maurice Merleau-Ponty, Paul Nizan and Claude Lévi-Strauss. Whatever else one might want to say about it, this is not exactly a position of utter subservience and self-abasement.

In the very first paragraph of her autobiography, Simone de Beauvoir describes herself at the age of two and a half, immediately after the birth of her sister, Hélène:

> I turn the page: here is a photograph of Mama holding in her arms a baby who isn't me; I am wearing a pleated skirt and a beret; I am two and a half, and my sister has just been born. I was, it appears, very jealous, but not for long. As far back as I can remember, I was always proud of being the elder: of being first. Disguised as Little Red Riding Hood and carrying a basket full of cakes and a pot of butter, I felt myself to be more interesting than an infant bundled up in a cradle. I had a little sister: that little baby did not have me (MDD5; MJF9; TA).

In this passage, jealousy, a key theme of Simone de Beauvoir's fiction, makes its first appearance in her memoirs. Dominant in her first novel, *L'Invitée* (1943), the theme of jealousy is also the major preoccupation of the title story of the collection of short stories *The Woman Destroyed* (1968), her last published fictional work. In Beauvoir's autobiographical writing, on the other hand, jealousy is given a modest place indeed.[4] Yet here, the very first time Beauvoir mentions the entry of another actor – her sister – on to her personal scene, it is as if the word slips out only to be denied and distanced in the next breath: 'I was, it appears, very jealous, but not for long.' This is reported speech: *other* people have told her that she was jealous, she herself cannot recollect anything of the kind. Yet, even assuming that the reports are correct – which nothing in the text guarantees – her purported jealousy would seem to have been superficial: an unimportant, trivial childhood incident. Reporting it here, Beauvoir manages to convey her taste for truth (even insignificant incidents will be recorded) as well as the trifling nature of the event in question.

To be the *first* is what matters to the little Simone. According to Beauvoir's 1958 account, the birth of her sister does nothing to threaten the little girl's superior position: she *is* after all the elder daughter, come what may. But closer scrutiny of the text reveals that she cannot assure her supremacy by her age alone: dressed as Little Red Riding Hood, she writes, she feels so much more *interesting* than her little baby sister. But where does this 'interesting' disguise come from? On the photograph, we are told, she was dressed in a skirt and a beret. Thinking back to the relevant period ('As far back as I can remember . . .'), Beauvoir conjures up an image of herself dressed as a character in a fairy-tale. Equipped with fictional prestige, she feels protected against jealousy. There is an elegant reference here to her future career as a writer: dressed in the garb of literature she will be so *interesting* that she will never have to yield her first place to anybody else. Yet the power of fascination is acquired at the price of a disguise: it is not enough just to be oneself, just to *be* the elder daughter. Love, the little Simone discovers, is never given for free; it is always necessary to please. Something must be added to mere being: if fiction makes one fascinating, it is because it is excess and, above all, masquerade.

The assertion that '*I* felt more interesting than my sister' is immediately followed by a proud declaration of possession: '*I* had a little sister, that little baby did not have me': Simone can only possess Hélène by dispossessing her. The privilege of feeling interesting would seem to require – or perhaps even produce – a sense of control over one's surroundings. Yet such control is always potentially threatened: to be first is by definition to risk being ousted by latecomers. As long as Simone is persuaded that she is more interesting than they are, however, such late arrivals will always remain mere also-rans. But interesting to whom? It is impossible to be *absolutely* interesting; one is always interesting *to* somebody. Who decides whether Simone is interesting or not? Even in the passage studied here her belief in her charm comes across as the effect of encouragement from some other source. Who, then, is Simone de Beauvoir trying to charm? If we are to take the allusion to Little Red Riding Hood seriously, it has to be the wolf. Or if not the wolf, then perhaps the brave huntsman who performs the lupine Caesarian section? Without evoking fantasies of rebirth from a monstrously male womb, Beauvoir's use of this fairy-tale contains at the very least a whiff of the desire – or obligation – to fascinate and please the male.

The next paragraph describes the physical surroundings of Simone de Beauvoir's earliest childhood. Her memories are confused, she writes, but she does remember something 'red, and black, and warm' (MDD5; MJF9). The red refers to the colour of the curtains and carpets of the flat of her parents, we are told. The rest of the paragraph describes her father's study (*le cabinet de papa*):

> The furniture in this awful sanctum [*antre sacré* – 'sacred cave'] was made of black pear wood; I used to curl up in the niche under the desk and envelop myself in its darkness; it was dark there and warm, and the red of the carpet jarred on my eyes. That is how I passed the early days of my childhood. Safely ensconced, I watched, I touched, I learnt about the world (MDD5; MJF10; TA).[5]

The womb-like qualities of this 'sacred cave' are unmistakable. Curled up in the warm, red and black security of the hollow niche under her father's desk, the little Simone discovers the world. If the first paragraph gives us a picture of the future writer as Little Red Riding Hood, this passage presents the future intellectual as a baby exploring the world from under her father's desk: a modern Athena sprung from the brains of Zeus. From her earliest childhood Simone de Beauvoir develops a belief in the existence of an unbreakable link between the idea of school, learning, reading – intellectual work, in other words – and the idea of interesting – pleasing, charming, fascinating, seducing – the father. As long as this equation holds, the young Simone is convinced of her supremacy and protected against rivals: she remains the First and the Unique.

The first blow to her sense of uniqueness and supremacy comes when, as a teenager, she realizes that her father resents her for her academic success, and instead transfers his affections to her younger sister Hélène, who is prettier and more conventionally feminine in her ways. The impact on Simone's self-esteem is crippling. Apparently, then, to be interesting is not enough. The father cannot be seduced by the spirit alone: women considered 'inferior' by Simone, precisely because they are 'uninteresting', may after all turn into redoubtable rivals for the father's attention. The mysterious lure of the elusive quality which under patriarchy is known as 'femininity' turns out to threaten her reign. Simone's first disappointment with intellectual work, then, comes when she discovers that a woman cannot seduce by her brains alone. Reacting with haughty pride and considerable rage to the narcissistic wound inflicted by her father, Simone de Beauvoir expels him from her affections altogether: from now on, in her writings, he will simply figure as an execrable, sexist, right-wing, egocentric mediocrity.

The second blow to her belief in the seductive powers of her intellect is the *débâcle* in the Luxembourg Gardens. But while shattering to her self-esteem, her reaction now is quite different. Instead of execrating Sartre, she turns him into the very figure of phallic perfection. It would seem to be precisely because she has an erotic relationship with him at the time that she manages to abdicate her intellectual supremacy without feeling threatened by the total loss of her powers to seduce. Again we are confronted with the intellectual woman's dilemma under patriarchy: from childhood she is used to seducing by being interesting, yet when she grows up, she discovers that she can never seduce *solely* by being interesting. While Simone de Beauvoir may well want Sartre to admire her intellect, she must have known – or at least obscurely felt – that under patriarchy her sexual needs and desires would have been badly served had she *won* the crucial discussion in the Luxembourg Gardens. Choosing the role as *helpmate* or assistant to Sartre's philosophical project, seeing herself as his right-hand woman, the principal defender of the new faith, as it were, Beauvoir arrogates to herself a far from insignificant role, perhaps the only one which at the time enabled her to seduce *both* as an intellectual and as a woman.

In this sense, then, her philosophical defeat by the Medici fountain by no means represents a total intellectual abdication. Nor does it represent a will simply to please by traditional 'feminine' wiles. As Michèle Le Doeuff has pointed out, Simone de Beauvoir does go on to become a formidable 'closet philosopher', a hidden thinker (see *Hipparchia's Choice*, p. 139). Instead – and this is my second reading of the scene – I think it should be seen as a compromise between the wish to fascinate as a woman and the wish to fascinate as an intellectual. Needless to say, it is the dominant patriarchal ideology of 'femininity' that produces such a dilemma for the intellectual woman in the first place. For Sartre there was never any moment in which his powers of seduction as a man came into conflict with his powers of seduction as an intellectual. On the contrary, in his case – as in that of so many other intellectual men – it would seem that the power of his intellect forcefully contributed to – even created – his charm as a man.

It is important to stress that the dilemma faced by Simone de Beauvoir here is to a great extent caused by her unique educational position as a pioneering woman within the university system in France. It is precisely because she is educationally equal or superior to her male friends and potential lovers that it becomes urgent for her as a desiring, heterosexual woman caught up in patriarchal ideology in 1929 not to be perceived as *more* masterful than her chosen lover if she is to conserve her powers of seduction.[6] This specific dilemma would not be so acute in the case of women lacking the educational or cultural capital of their male competitors.[7] It is therefore quite irrelevant to compare Beauvoir's behaviour here with that of, say, Colette, who never had much of a formal education, and who, in any case belonged to a different generation and a different social class, or, on the other hand, that of Simone Weil, who as an *agrégée* in philosophy educated at the Ecole Normale Supérieure accumulated at least as much educational capital as Beauvoir, but renounced her position as a desiring woman in order freely to develop her spiritual and intellectual concerns.

It is nevertheless understandable that feminists in the 1990s are disappointed by Simone de Beauvoir's life-long reiteration of her secondary philosophical role in relation to Sartre. But one has to remember that her assessment of her own position is not necessarily incorrect. While it is true that her destiny as a philosopher was in no way determined *before* the fateful summer day in 1929, the choice she made then was of the kind that tends to become a self-fulfilling prophecy. Having at the age of 21 cast herself as a second-rate philosopher in relation to Sartre, she will have neither the ambition nor the desire to undertake the hard work required to position herself as an independent philosopher: fifteen years later, Sartre will be the author of *Being and Nothingness*, Beauvoir of *Pyrrhus et Cinéas*. Only in *The*

Second Sex does she show her formidable capacity for original philosophical thought, but even there, as Michèle Le Doeuff points out, she goes out of her way not to *appear* to be a philosopher (see *Hipparchia's Choice*, p. 138). While Simone de Beauvoir's understanding of the meaning of the debate by the Medici fountain may not provide much satisfaction for feminists in the 1990s, her account can – and should – provide ample grounds for reflection on the difficulty of becoming an intellectual woman under patriarchy. And in this context, an 'intellectual woman' means a woman who refuses to accept the traditional patriarchal division between mind and body, sense and seduction.

TO KNOW AND TO WRITE

My freedom [. . .] was the carrying through of an initial project [*projet originel*], continually resumed and strengthened: the project of knowing and of expressing (ASD21; TCF25).

Yet there are some very old bonds in my life that have never been broken. Its essential unity is provided by two factors: the place that Sartre always had in it, and my faithfulness to my original design [*projet originel*] – that of knowing and writing (ASD39; TCF45).

In the last volume of her memoirs, *All Said and Done*, Simone de Beauvoir represents her life as united by two factors, Sartre and her 'fundamental project' [*projet originel*]: to know and to write, to learn about the world and to express the insights achieved. This fundamental project is also the leitmotif of *Memoirs of a Dutiful Daughter*. As a small child, Simone de Beauvoir did not at first associate knowledge with formal learning and paternal discipline, rather she perceived knowledge as eating. Eating the world, she conquered it, made it hers. Even as an adult, she writes, she continued to link the idea of ingesting the world with the experience of power and pleasure in knowledge:

If only the universe we inhabit were completely edible, I used to think, what power we would have over it! When I was grown up I wanted to crunch flowering almond trees, and take bites out of the rainbow nougats of the sunset. Against the night sky of New York, the neon signs appeared to me like giant sweetmeats and made me feel frustrated (MDD7; MJF12).

It is more than likely that as a little girl Simone de Beauvoir did in fact experience knowledge as an oral relationship to the world. At the same time, however, the pages evoking her appetite for the brightly coloured world around her read uncannily like a textual echo of Sartre's *theory* of knowledge as eating. In *Being and Nothingness*, Sartre claims that: 'Curiosity in an animal is always either sexual or alimentary. To know is to devour with the eyes.' A footnote to the last sentence adds that: 'For the child, knowing involves actually eating. He wants to *taste* what he sees' (BN739; EN639).[8] Like Beauvoir, Sartre insists that the desire to incorporate the object of knowledge reveals a desire for mastery and control:

> In knowing, consciousness attracts the object to itself and incorporates it in itself. Knowledge is assimilation. The writings of French epistemology swarm with alimentary metaphors (absorption, digestion, assimilation). There is a movement of dissolution which passes from the object to the knowing subject. The known is transformed into *me*; it becomes my thought and thereby consents to receive its existence from me alone (BN 739; EN639).

The object of knowledge nevertheless remains other: it is 'indigestible as a stone', and reminds Sartre of the legend of Jonah in the belly of the whale (BN739; EN639).[9] This symbol, Sartre writes, reveals our dream of 'non-destructive assimilation'. Unfortunately, according to Sartre, this is an impossible dream, since all desire in fact destroys its object.[10] For Sartre, then, knowledge is a form of destructive possession: it is a one-way relationship between an active subject of knowledge and a passive object of knowledge. Michèle Le Doeuff has brilliantly demonstrated the silliness of this argument (see *Hipparchia's Choice*, pp. 79–82). But where the adult Sartre's theories on this point may strike us as somewhat immature, Beauvoir's use of the same *topos* to describe her perception of the world *as a baby* is both pertinent and convincing.

If she insists on the delights of oral possession of the world, Beauvoir also stresses the double-edged nature of the process. For eating makes her grow: by swallowing the food given to her by her mother and her maid Louise, she is condemning herself to becoming too big to sit on her mother's knees: eating brings knowledge, but also exile, solitude and death:

> I had grown two or three centimeters; they would congratulate me, and I would swell with pride. But sometimes I felt frightened. [. . .] I would look at Mama's armchair and think: 'I won't be able to sit on her knee anymore.' Suddenly the future existed; it would turn me into somebody else who would say I and would no longer be me. I had forebodings of all the separations, the refusals, the desertions to come, and of the long succession of my various deaths (MDD7; MJF13; TA).

There may be an allusion here to the story of the Fall: by eating the fruit of the tree of knowledge she will be cast out of Paradise. However that may be, in her own representation of her early childhood there is a tension between the oral pleasure of dominating the world by assimilating it to oneself, and the fear of having to leave the maternal paradise in which such pleasure is possible. There are compensations for the loss of maternal protection, however: the little Simone is also capable of enjoying the seductive pleasures of fascinating the father or any other adult male. Describing her desire to please her parents' male visitors, she emphasizes the power of the men's *words*: 'I was particularly anxious to arouse the interests of the men: I tried to attract their attention by fidgeting and playing the ingénue, waiting for the word that would snatch me out of my childhood limbo and really make me exist in their world' (MDD8; MJF14; TA).

The tragedy is that the imaginary (in the Lacanian sense) knowledge achieved by digesting the world is incompatible with the command of language. 'To know and to express': for the little girl evoked by Beauvoir's memoirs, there is a deep and uncomfortable conflict between the two aspects of her own 'fundamental project', that is to say, the project which, according to existentialist philosophy, expresses the deepest needs and desires of her being. Somehow or other, language distorts the physical insights of the little girl. Her violent crises of rage would seem to have something to do with the pain of having to enter into the universe of words: 'Nevertheless, there must have been something wrong somewhere: I had fits of rage during which my face turned purple and I would fall to the ground in convulsions' (MDD11; MJF17). The arbitrary orders and refusals that surround the little girl become the objects of her rage. The young Simone is a veritable textbook illustration of the pain of having to submit to the Law: 'But I refused to submit to that intangible force: words. [. . .] At the heart of the law that weighed me down with the implacable severity of stones I glimpsed a giddying void: this was the pit I used to plunge into [*je m'engloutissais*], my mouth torn apart by screams of rage' (MDD12; MJF19; TA). The images of the 'abyss' or 'void' (*le gouffre*), vertigo, the idea of being swallowed up (*engloutir*) by a terrible power outside one's own control are recurrent in Beauvoir's works.[11] Often linked to depression or anxiety, such crises would seem to be the product of a conflict related to the difficulty of leaving the maternal universe of oral satisfaction and narcissistic omnipotence and entering into the paternal realm of the Law, language and sexuality. According to Beauvoir, the tension between the maternal and the paternal worlds, between her mother's Catholic moralism and her father's atheism, is also responsible for her choice of becoming an intellectual.

The same conflict also surfaces in relation to language. Although language is represented as belonging to the father's sphere of influence, both parents come across as bearers of a rigidly essentialist discourse, which the young Beauvoir immediately experiences as false: 'From my very first stuttering words, all my experience belied this essentialism' (MDD17; MJF26; TA). Her family represents everything in terms of black or white, good or bad, whereas she can only perceive nuances of grey. When, as a little girl, she tries to express her true perceptions, she has to abandon the effort as hopeless:

> I had to use words, and I found myself in a world of bony-structured concepts [des concepts aux dures arêtes]. Whatever I beheld with my own eyes and every real experience had to be fitted somehow or other into a rigid category: the myths and the stereotyped ideas prevailed over the truth: unable to pin it down, I allowed truth to dwindle into insignificance (MDD17; MJF26).

As a teenager, her conflictual relationship to her parents intensifies. Crushed by the difficulty of communicating with them, feeling exiled in the universe of false values from which she had for so long tried to escape, she claims that she 'had always fought against the tyranny of language' (MDD192; MJF266). Describing her attitude towards the language of her parents at the age of 17 or 18, Beauvoir produces a passage strikingly similar to the one describing her difficulties at the age of 4 or 5:

> Once more I would be shut up in that world which I had spent years trying to get away from, in which everything, without any possibility of mistake, has its own name, its set place and its agreed function, in which hate and love, good and evil are as crudely differentiated as black and white, in which from the start everything is classified, catalogued, fixed and formulated, and irrevocably judged; that world with the sharp edges [aux arêtes coupantes], its bare outlines starkly illuminated by an implacable flat light that is never once touched by the shadow of a doubt (MDD192–3; MJF266–7).

In fact, the relevant passages match each other so closely (through the reference to arêtes coupantes, for instance) as to arouse the reader's suspicions. Could Beauvoir really have had the very same perceptions of the false values of familial discourse at the age of 4 and the age of 17? In both cases one might see in these 'rigid' or 'bony' concepts an allusion to the oppressively phallic nature of the Law of the Father. Yet such a reading would overlook the philosophical underpinnings of Beauvoir's rhetoric here. For if Beauvoir in both passages criticizes her family in much the same terms, it is because the whole of her text is written from the same existentialist perspective. Referring to her parents' oppressive language as a form of 'essentialism' (MDD17; MJF26), for instance, she wants to convey the idea that this is a world in which values are perceived as always already given, not as always to be constructed. This is a faithful echo of Sartre's definition of bad faith. The bourgeois world evoked by Beauvoir corresponds precisely to Sartre's descriptions of the *lâches* (cowards) and *salauds* (swine) in *L'existentialisme est un humanisme*. The *lâches* seek to hide their freedom, and the *salauds* to see themselves as necessary. The rigidity of their concepts reflects their conviction that they do not have the power to change the world surrounding them. According to Beauvoir, then, at the age of 4 or 5 she already experienced the language of the bourgeois world in Sartrean terms.

In *Memoirs of a Dutiful Daughter*, Beauvoir thus goes to great lengths unobtrusively, yet quite unmistakably, to represent the bourgeois world against which she is to rebel in consistently existentialist terms. The problem is that she never states that this in fact is what she is doing. The existentialist – philosophical – underpinnings of her narrative are present from the very first page of her book, yet remain unthematized. Or to put it differently: by 1958 existentialism has long since become Simone de Beauvoir's spontaneous outlook on herself and the world. This is why her narrative manages to convey the idea that her *projet originel* – to find the truth and to express it – is nothing but a straightforward reaction against the stifling ideology of her childhood. But we also learn that, to be successful, the search for truth ought *not* to lead to the *univers aux concepts aux dures arêtes*. There is a desire here to find some other form of language, one which would be more malleable than the arid world of abstract signifiers to which she was exposed. In its nostalgia for a compromise solution, this wish is reminiscent of the desire to develop an ethics which would allow her to love the people with whom she disagreed, the very idea that is 'torn apart' by Sartre in the Luxembourg Gardens.

Yet *this* dream of a happy transcendence of the conflict between maternal and paternal values is not destroyed. As we have seen, after her defeat by the Medici fountain, Beauvoir eagerly goes on to espouse the Sartrean theory of freedom and action through philosophy. Her rationale for such apparent submission to his views is to proclaim his ideas as the answer to her prayers for liberation from the stifling universe of her family. Here, finally, is a philosophy which promises her truth, the language with which to express it and the encouragement to push ahead with her own projects. Rejecting mother and father alike, Beauvoir perceives Sartre as holding out a promise of true freedom. From now on, as the source of the dominant discourse in Simone de Beauvoir's life, he takes her mother's as well as her father's place. At one stroke the conflict between the maternal and the paternal discourses would seem to be resolved: Sartre comes across as the provider of the dialectical synthesis of the moral perspectives of her mother and the atheism of her father; here, at last, is a truthful language without the *arêtes coupantes*. If Beauvoir capitulates to Sartre in the Luxembourg Gardens, then, it is because he represents the fulfillment of her most utopian wishes. This claim is reiterated in *All Said and Done*, where Beauvoir writes that she 'adopted Sartre's friendships and [. . .] moved into his world, not as some people said because I am a woman, but because it was the world I had longed for for many years' (ASD29; TCF24).

Yet this rather pat version of events glosses over certain problems. We have already seen that Beauvoir's account of the scene in the Luxembourg Gardens in 1929 presupposes knowledge that could only have been developed much later, once Sartre had truly *become* Sartre (which I persist in thinking he was not at the time). This observation raises the problem of the point of view of *Memoirs of a Dutiful Daughter* in general. Briefly, it may be argued that Beauvoir elegantly posits her writing *persona* as a rather ironic, amused observer of her religiously devout childhood, and as a more sympathetic chronicler of the stifled and rebellious teenager. While she does not seek to conceal her distance from the young Simone, she nevertheless does her utmost to represent the development of her consciousness as the phenomenological unfolding of a relatively simple plot: first the young Simone feels stifled and oppressed by her family, then she rebels, and finally she meets Sartre. But as Sartre himself would have been the first to argue, the end gives meaning to what precedes it. The very philosophical terms in which Beauvoir's representation of herself are couched reveal all too clearly that *Memoirs of a Dutiful Daughter* is constructed so as to make the final meeting with Sartre look *necessary*: the perfect crowning of her own project of independence. In this way Beauvoir's representation of her own intellectual defeat at the hands of Sartre can be read as it surely was intended, as yet another piece of evidence that Sartre was indeed the man who exactly corresponded to her dreams at the age of 15.

A rhetorical *tour de force*, the structure and writing of *Memoirs of a Dutiful Daughter* manage to convey that Beauvoir's defeat at the hands of Sartre is not really a defeat at all. Rather than a *débâcle*, Beauvoir implies – and this, then, is my third reading of the passage – the scene in the Luxembourg Gardens represents a moment of truth, the moment in which the young Simone de Beauvoir finally comes face to face with *her own* fundamental project: to know and to write, or in other words: 'To combat error, to find the truth, to tell it, to enlighten the world, perhaps even to help to change the world' (MDD345; MJF481). On this reading Sartre *is* Beauvoir's own freely chosen project: the question of subordination and oppression does not apply. The two constant factors in her life, Sartre and her *projet originel*, turn out to be one and the same. This is, in effect, Beauvoir's own understanding of her meeting with Sartre: 'Sartre corresponded exactly to the dream-companion I had longed for since I was fifteen: he was the double in whom I found all my burning aspiration [*toutes mes manies*] raised to the pitch of incandescence. When I left him at the beginning of August, I knew that he would never disappear from my life again' (MDD345;

MJF482). Or in other words: Sartre is herself, only more so. The moment of defeat in the Parisian park, then, becomes the moment of construction of the problematic maxim of *On ne fait qu'un* ('We are one'): this unity is the hidden centre, the very *telos* of *Memoirs of a Dutiful Daughter*.

By showing how Simone de Beauvoir rhetorically constructs her philosophical defeat at the hands of Sartre as a necessary ingredient in her own freely chosen project, I am not at all implying that hers is a *false* account. On the contrary, I am convinced that this reading is the one that corresponds most closely to Simone de Beauvoir's own experience of her meeting with Sartre, and that she could not have given a more honest account of his importance to her. What I am arguing, however, is that even on Beauvoir's own philosophical terms, there is a touch of bad faith in her representation of the *necessity* of Sartre in her life. A heroic effort to reconcile a traditionally Romantic belief in the twin souls of the two lovers destined for each other from all eternity and the existentialist belief in freedom and contingency, Beauvoir's account of the meaning of Sartre in her life is psychologically impressive, but philosophically unconvincing.

Unlike Simone de Beauvoir, I do not believe that it is possible to lead a life of unfailingly lucid authenticity. Moreover, I suspect that our blind spots are to be found precisely in the areas which matter the most to us. What Beauvoir's representation of Sartre in *Memoirs of a Dutiful Daughter* reveals, then, is the way in which, by 1958, the myth of the unity between herself and Sartre functions as one of the most fundamental elements in her own sense of identity. However much she struggles to free herself from some of the more negative aspects of this myth, it remains the one untouchable dogma of her life. The source of much pride and much joy, it also becomes the cause of profound pain: the real blind spot of Simone de Beauvoir's memoirs is her inability to recognize that distress.

LITERATURE OR PHILOSOPHY?

Poised on the dividing line between literature and philosophy, Beauvoir's fundamental project – to know and to write – might have led to a life of philosophy rather than to a life of literature. Yet, as we have seen, after the scene in the Luxembourg Gardens, she firmly decides to cast herself as a second-rate philosopher compared to Sartre. All philosophers, however, cannot be Sartre. Beauvoir, like Merleau-Ponty, might still have found satisfaction in philosophical work, and gone on to establish herself as a formidable philosopher in her own right. It would seem that her very conception of philosophy, as well as her own desire for total epistemological mastery, made such an option unattractive to her. Deciding to become a novelist, Beauvoir chose not to pursue the discipline she preferred above every other as a young girl:

> The thing that attracted me about philosophy was that it went straight to essentials. I had never liked fiddling detail; I perceived the general signifi- cance of things rather than their singularities, and I preferred understanding to seeing; I had always wanted to know *everything*; philosophy would allow me to appease this desire, for it aimed at total reality; philosophy went right to the heart of truth and revealed to me, instead of an illusory whirlwind of facts or empirical laws, an order, a reason, a necessity in everything. The sciences, literature, and all the other disciplines seemed to me to be very poor relations to philosophy (MDD158; MJF220).

Casting philosophical truth as an indivisible totality, Beauvoir effectively implies that such truth must be the product of a single master discourse. Or as Descartes himself puts it: 'There is seldom so much perfection in works composed of many separate parts, upon which different hands have been employed, as in those completed by a single master' (*A Discourse on Method*, p. 17).

In many ways Beauvoir's account of her philosophical relationship to Sartre reads as a determined effort to back up the judgement of the examiners at the *agrégation* in philosophy in 1929. They classed her as second only to Sartre; she is doing her utmost to prove them right. But what exactly did the examiners say? Sartre's biographer, Annie Cohen-Solal, informs us that in 1929, sixty-six candidates sat the exam, twenty-seven were allowed to present themselves at the oral examinations, and in the end, thirteen candidates passed (p. 115). Cohen-Solal also talked to a philosopher, Maurice de Gandillac, who knew some of the members of the examining board, about the philosophical difference between the two star students:

> Rigorous, demanding, precise and technically stringent, Gandillac says, she was the youngest of the year: she was only twenty-one, and therefore three years younger than Sartre. [. . .] In any case two of the teachers on the board of examiners, Davy and Wahl, told me later that they had hesitated for a long time between her and Sartre for the first place. For if Sartre showed obvious qualities, such as a strongly asserted, albeit sometimes slightly imprecise intelligence and culture, everybody agreed that she *was* Philosophy [*LA philosophie, c'était elle*] (p. 116).

One might wonder exactly why she came second if she *was* philosophy, and he was not. Perhaps the examiners thought that the point was not to *be* but to *master* philosophy?

Beauvoir's representation of her philosophical inferiority to Sartre is not without contradictions. Emphasizing her own lack of originality, she nevertheless describes in great detail how Sartre would read new philosophers with some difficulty, whereas she would assimilate their ideas faster and more accurately than he did: '[Sartre] found great difficulty in jettisoning his own viewpoint and unreservedly adopting anyone else's', she writes in *The Prime of Life*, in a passage referring to the early autumn of 1935. Her quickness, however, turns out to be entirely due to her malleability: 'In my case,' Beauvoir continues, 'there was no such resistance to break down: my own thought immediately took on the shape of the thought I was trying to grasp' (PL220; FA254; TA). Her emphasis on his stubborn independence as against her own easy submission to the other's perspective is uncomfortably reminiscent of traditional patriarchal prejudices against women's intellectual capacities. Yet she also insists that she had a real talent for philosophy, and in no sense could be said to be passive or lacking in critical sense: 'In short, I possessed both considerable powers of assimilation and a well-developed critical sense; and philosophy was for me a living reality, which gave me never-failing satisfaction' (PL221; FA254).

To love philosophy is not necessarily all it takes to *become* a philosopher: Beauvoir persists in presenting herself as a relative philosophical failure. If I quote the two paragraphs in which she gives her reasons for the decision to become a writer, not a philosopher, at some length, it is because they are unusually slippery and contradictory:

> Yet I did not regard myself as a philosopher: I was well aware that the ease with which I penetrated to the heart of a text stemmed, precisely, from my lack of originality. In this field a genuinely creative talent is so rare that queries as to why I did not attempt to join the elite are surely otiose: it would be more useful to explain how certain individuals are capable of succeeding in that conscious venture into lunacy known as a 'philosophical system', and from *where* they get the stubbornness which gives their ideas universal applicability. As I have remarked before, the female condition does not facilitate the development of this kind of stubbornness.
>
> I might at least have undertaken a well-documented critical study – perhaps even aspiring to a degree of ingenuity – on some limited problem, involving an unknown or little-known author and a debatable point of logic. This did not attract me at all. When I talked philosophy with Sartre, and took the full measure of his patience and audacity, the idea of a philosophical career seemed wildly exciting – but only if one was bitten by a theory of one's own. Expounding other people's beliefs, developing, judging, collating, and criticizing them – no, I failed to see the attraction of this. When reading a work of Fink's, I asked myself: 'But how can one resign oneself to being the disciple of anybody?' Later I did, intermittently, consent to play such a role myself. But to begin with I possessed far too much intellectual ambition to let this satisfy me. I wanted to communicate the element of originality in my own experience. In order to do this successfully

I knew it was literature towards which I must orientate myself (PL220–1; FA254–5; TA).

On the one hand, then, Beauvoir's problem seems to be one of excessive ambition: if she cannot produce an original philosophical system of her own, become the master philosopher *par excellence*, she would rather not do philosophy at all. It is as if philosophy were an enterprise where there is only space for one at a time. If one cannot be a master builder one must either become a bricklayer or leave the site altogether. Her distaste for discipleship is curiously half-hearted: here she also alludes to her role as eager promoter of Sartre's thought in the 1940s. While she stresses that this was a project freely 'consented' to, there is nevertheless a certain poignancy about her presentation of this aspect of her career: it is as if the author of *Pyrrhus et Cinéas* and *The Ethics of Ambiguity* somehow feels the need to exhibit a certain resignation, to enforce the idea that nothing short of a dramatic loss of intellectual ambition could have made her write such derivative works. These passages, however, also serve to pre-empt the criticism she knows is due: by recognizing her own flaws she hopes to avoid having them pointed out by others. For a woman, however, it is all too easy to acquire the reputation of being the simple disciple of a great man; it is very much harder to lose it again. It is to no little extent due to Beauvoir's own representation of her intellectual status that throughout the 1970s her entry in the *Petit Larousse* presented her first and foremost as 'Sartre's disciple'. By 1987, the entry had changed a little, although not necessarily for the better, presenting her not simply as Sartre's disciple but as 'Sartre's disciple and companion, and an ardent feminist'.[12]

In the passage quoted, Beauvoir's unease with the question of her relationship to philosophy also surfaces in her attempt to close off any further inquiry into the matter. To raise the question of *why* she does not want to become a philosopher – as I am doing here – is futile, she writes, since only a handful of geniuses can expect to make a success of it in any case. That she is not such a genius, then, ought not to surprise us in the least. But the fact remains that historically speaking *all* these philosophical geniuses have been male: Beauvoir here neatly represses the question of sexual difference, only to return to it in the very next sentence. To construct an original philosophical system, she writes, takes an immense amount of obsessional energy, rarely found in women given the patriarchal conditioning that shapes their lives. It is as if Beauvoir simultaneously believes that patriarchy deprived her of the obsessional willpower required to produce philosophy, and that at the same time it endowed her with excessive philosophical ambitions, not to mention the stubborn willpower necessary to achieve original *literary* work, which here somehow comes across as distinctly less demanding than philosophy.

It is as if she both knows and does not want to know that the fact of being a woman in the philosophical institution inexorably groomed her for discipleship, rather than for original work. At one level, then, this passage provides an interesting example of the contradictions generated by Beauvoir's existentialist feminism: while thoroughly aware of the social conditioning of women's lives, Beauvoir's philosophy obliges her to argue for the individual's free choices. She must, then, at once present her vocation as the consequence of her own independent desire to write novels, *and* indicate that women under patriarchy, however brilliant they are, are unlikely to become great philosophers in the traditional mould. Yet her identification with the philosophical institution is such that she never once questions the tradition: for her, 'great' philosophers are universal geniuses who never bother with collective efforts. Even in her own account literature is marked as an 'easier' – more 'feminine' – option: somehow Beauvoir's free choice comes to coincide with dominant social ideas of what would make a suitable profession for an intellectual woman. This ought not to surprise us: as a highly educated intellectual woman in France at the time, Beauvoir's professional choices are conditioned by the social and educational institutions in which she found herself. Her account of her choice between literature and philosophy demonstrates with unusual clarity her unconscious internalization of objective social structures, or what Pierre Bourdieu would call her *habitus*.

In reality, however, the writing of fiction did not come easily to Simone de Beauvoir. She wrote almost every day for fourteen years (from 1929 to 1943) before she succeeded in getting her first novel, *L'Invitée* (*She Came to Stay*), published. By 1935 she had already accumulated two voluminous unpublished manuscripts.[13] Once she had managed to establish herself as a novelist, she lifted the embargo on philosophy, producing a series of short philosophical essays where she modestly signals her dependence on Sartre. In the 1940s and 1950s she also wrote a number of political and polemical essays (*L'existentialisme et la sagesse des nations*, *Privilèges*) explicitly intended to defend Sartrean existentialism against its political opponents. In this context, I would argue, *The Second Sex* (1949) represents both the culmination and the subversion of her philosophical and essayistic subservience to Sartre. But if most of her essays present themselves as singularly dependent efforts, their style and tone belie any such impression. In fact, her essayistic style tends to be peremptory, condescending, even arrogant. This is not the tone of a hesitant speaker acutely conscious of her own subordinate status, nor can it be written off simply as overcompensation for some hidden inner insecurity. It is as if her essays exhibit all the hallmarks of intellectual arrogance in the very act of announcing their own derivative and submissive status.

It would be foolish indeed to argue that Simone de Beauvoir somehow ought to have chosen a career as a professional philosopher rather than as a writer, or to imply, as she herself sometimes tends to do, that to produce original philosophy is intrinsically superior to the writing of fiction or autobiography. Her desire to become a writer cannot be reduced to a simple decision to leave philosophy to Sartre, but neither can it be presented as an unconditioned free choice. In her specific case, it is also, among other things, the result of her father's influence. Already at the age of 15 she declared that she wanted to become a famous writer when she grew up: 'I had set my heart on that profession, to the exclusion of everything else', she writes (MDD141; MJF196). The reason for her choice was the 'admiration I felt for writers: my father rated them far higher than scientists, scholars and professors. I, too, was convinced of their supremacy' (MDD141; MJF197; TA).

After the Dreyfus affair the French intellectual field was widely perceived as split into two warring factions, *professeurs* and *créateurs* (teachers and creators).[14] In this respect Beauvoir's father, who despised the *professeurs* as uncreative, lower-middle-class upstarts, and venerated writers as prophets and visionaries, exemplified the views of the anti-Dreyfusard right. Until some time after the end of World War I, French authors ('creators') of Georges de Beauvoir's own generation (he was born in 1878), such as Proust or Gide, tended to move in socially refined and intellectually influential *salons*. Already anachronistic by the 1930s, the image of the elegant, well-heeled and well-connected author who writes for pleasure, while spending most of his time moving gracefully through the *salons* of high society, corresponds exactly to what Georges de Beauvoir himself would have liked to be. In spite of his great respect for the writers of his own time, however, he knew very well that when it came to his daughter growing up in the harsher economic climate of the 1920s, such visions could be no more than mere fantasies.[15]

If Georges de Beauvoir hated his daughter's choice of teaching as a profession, it was precisely because it objectively placed her in a social group whose values he loathed: 'He thought all teachers were ill-mannered pedants. [. . .] He made more serious charges against schoolteachers; they belonged to the dangerous sect that had stood in defence of Dreyfus: the intellectuals' (MDD177–8; MJF246; TA). One of the reasons why he came to prefer Simone's younger sister, Hélène, was not only that she was prettier, but also that she decided to become a painter – a highly *artistic* or *creative* career, and one which might make people believe that her father was rich enough to keep her in paints and studios. 'He couldn't bear to think that he was driving both his daughters into the enemy camp', Beauvoir comments (MDD178; MJF247).

Hesitating between literature and philosophy, Beauvoir is caught between Sartre's demolition of her philosophical self-confidence in the

Luxembourg Gardens, and the unpalatable thought of having to please her father by becoming a writer. In fact, her father never lived to see his daughter's first novel published. In the late 1930s he seems to have given up his hope that she might go on to become a 'creator'. At the time family and friends saw her as sterile: 'In the family and among my childhood friends the whisper went around that I was a *fruit sec*; my father remarked irritably that if I had something inside me [*dans le ventre*], why couldn't I hurry up and get it out?' (PL365; FA416). Georges de Beauvoir died on 8 July 1941: later that summer his daughter finally finished what was to become her first published novel.

2

The Making of an Intellectual Woman

I had never had any feeling of inferiority, no one had ever said to me: 'You think that way because you are a woman'; my femaleness had never been irksome to me in any way. 'For me,' I said to Sartre, '[. . .] it just hasn't counted.'

(Force of Circumstance)

In 1929, Simone de Beauvoir came second to Jean-Paul Sartre in the *agrégation* examinations in philosophy at the Sorbonne. What does it mean for a woman to pass this examination at that time? What does it mean for her to study philosophy at all? And why does she so willingly accept the intellectual superiority of the candidate who came first? Does the fact that she was only 21 when she passed this exam matter? Or the fact that she was only the ninth woman in France ever to become an *agrégée* in philosophy? In short: how did her exceptional position within the French educational field shape her self-image as an intellectual?

In order to answer these questions it is necessary to grasp the impact on Beauvoir of those strange and archetypally French institutions known as the *agrégation* of philosophy and the Ecole Normale Supérieure. It is also, obviously, crucial to raise the question of sexual difference, that is to say, to ask what it meant to be a woman in the French educational field at the time. Gender alone, however, cannot explain everything: Simone de Beauvoir was also an impoverished Catholic *bourgeoise*, and she was born and raised in Paris. To understand the social process that contributed to the making of Simone de Beauvoir as an intellectual woman, I have found it helpful to imagine these factors (class, gender, religion, location) as so many different social discourses, and to consider 'Simone de Beauvoir' as a site where the various strands of the social text intersect.

Simone de Beauvoir herself would most certainly have objected to my project. In her account of the conversation in the Luxembourg Gardens – which took place between the written and the oral part of the *agrégation* exam – she represents the struggle between herself and Sartre as a contest of pure intellects; if she lost, it was because she was less intelligent. Judging from her version of events, Beauvoir never fully realized how different men's and women's positions actually were in French higher education at the time, nor does she acknowledge the concrete educational differences between herself and Sartre. In this chapter I want to show that Beauvoir's account is unsatisfactory, and that her conclusion about her own intellectual ability in fact was the overdetermined outcome of a great number of social factors.[1]

EDUCATING SIMONE

Simone de Beauvoir belonged to the very first generation of European women to receive a formal education on a par with their male contemporaries. Self-taught or educated at home, women intellectuals before her, such as Madame de Staël, George Sand, George Eliot or Virginia Woolf, never found themselves competing with men in the educational sphere. Depriving them of intellectual self-confidence, women's lack of access to institutionalized higher education undoubtedly made them feel inferior to their brothers. At the same time, their position as educational exiles may well have freed them from some of the constraints weighing on their male colleagues. The inevitable price paid for the relative freedom of the autodidact, however, is lack of prestige: as long as women remained marginal in relation to established intellectual institutions, only a few highly exceptional women could expect to gain positions of some intellectual influence.[2]

By the time Simone de Beauvoir reached school age, however, women's relation to education had been radically transformed. She was part of a new and confident generation of women who took their right to the highest education in France for granted. For the first time, large numbers of women came through the French educational system in much the same way as their male contemporaries. The number of female university students in France increased from 288 or 1.7 per cent of the total student population in 1890 to over 16,000 or almost 24 per cent in 1929, the year in which Simone de Beauvoir passed her *agrégation* in philosophy.[3] Yet hers was still a generation of pioneers, often the first to break through old barriers. Women's access to all areas of higher education in France was won through a slow and contradictory process of enterprising exploitation of loopholes in the system, half-hearted reforms imposed from above and genuine feminist struggle. Frenchwomen had to wait until after World War I, when a harsh economic climate forced an increasing number of middle-class women into the labour force, before obtaining near-equal access to higher education.

Born in 1908 as the eldest daughter of a Catholic family, Beauvoir entered the French educational scene at a time when traditional Catholic attitudes towards the education of women were undergoing profound changes. In the late nineteenth century, French Catholics were generally hostile to secondary and higher education for women. They educated their daughters in convent schools, and kept them in the family in the interim period between school and marriage. In 1931, Edmée Charrier concluded her magnificent study of women's higher education in France by declaring her satisfaction at the disappearance of this way of life: 'The time when the young girl just out of convent school spent her days sitting by the window with a dull and mournful embroidery is almost gone. Today woman is steadily increasing her share of learning' (p. 531). Roughly speaking, the transformation she describes started in 1880, but gathered real pace in the period from 1900 to 1930. It is a pleasant coincidence that 1908, the year of Simone de Beauvoir's birth, was also the year in which French state schools (as opposed to Catholic and other so-called 'free' schools) were finally allowed to prepare girls for the *baccalauréat*, the only exam to assure access to French universities.

Beauvoir's own family background can best be characterized as down-wardly mobile upper-middle-class, with social and cultural aspirations well beyond the family's financial means.[4] Her father, Georges de Beauvoir (1878–1941), was the younger son of a relatively wealthy civil servant, Ernest-Narcisse de Beauvoir, who had inherited from his father considerable properties in the Limousin region, and who could well have afforded, had he wished, to live off his private income alone. After the death of Ernest-Narcisse's wife Léontine in 1892, Georges was encouraged to practise the life-style of a scion of the aristocracy: desultory studies, a passion for amateur acting, no professional ambitions, aristocratic disdain for the idea of the 'self-made man'. 'My father was a true *boulevardier*', Hélène de Beauvoir, Simone's sister, once remarked in a television interview.[5] At the time of his marriage to Françoise Brasseur, Georges de Beauvoir, educated at the Catholic elite school for boys in Paris, the Collège Stanislas, had been admitted to the bar, and was working in the office of a reasonably well-known conservative Parisian lawyer.

Simone de Beauvoir's mother, Françoise (1886–1963), was the daughter of a dynamic banker in the Alsace-Lorraine region, Gustave Brasseur. Educated at a branch of the fashionable Couvent des Oiseaux, she was given the classical Catholic education of a girl from the French aristocracy or high bourgeoisie. Her father's successful financial undertakings enabled the Brasseur family, who lived in Verdun, to lead an opulent life of balls, hunting parties, summer seasons at well-known beach resorts and so on. When she married Georges de Beauvoir in 1907, she would seem to have been precisely what he was looking for: a woman of considerable private means. Unfortunately for Georges de Beauvoir, however, his father-in-law's financial ventures started to fail around the time of the wedding. In July 1909, his bank, the Bank of the Meuse, was ordered into liquidation. Even the personal possessions of the Brasseur family were sold by auction: Françoise Brasseur's dowry was never paid. There were suspicions of fraud: Gustave Brasseur was arrested and kept in provisional detention for thirteen months, and in 1910 he was sentenced to fifteen months in prison for fraudulent misuse of funds. On his release from prison he and his wife moved to Paris, where they settled in the Montparnasse district, not far from their daughter's flat over the well-known café La Rotonde on the corner of the boulevard Montparnasse and the boulevard Raspail.

After World War I, Georges de Beauvoir's finances went from bad to worse. Some unfortunate business ventures left him penniless: from then on the Beauvoir family had to live on whatever income he could earn. Having given up his position in the law firm, he eked out a living like another Leopold Bloom, selling advertising for the newspaper *Le Gaulois*. The family had to leave the flat over La Rotonde where Simone de Beauvoir was born, and moved to a smaller and less comfortable flat at 71, rue de Rennes. Francis and Gonthier comment:

> The refined man-about-town, who had once placed good manners above all else, demonstrated in outbursts his rage at being déclassé. His profession was always given as 'lawyer' in the *Bottin mondain*, the official directory of professions; he bore an elegant-sounding name; his father and brother 'owned property.' He would not stand for being mixed in with a class he considered inferior, and he made this clear with his loud and aggressive behavior. [. . .] He gave Simone the impression of having 'deliberately neglected' prosperity and success (p. 35).[6]

Simone de Beauvoir, then, grew up in an atmosphere marked by her father's desire to escape from his dreary social position, and her mother's feelings of shame and guilt at her own father's disgrace and her own subsequent lack of dowry. Intellectually and ideologically, the young Simone's parents were poles apart: if Georges de Beauvoir had a conventional respect for the Catholic faith, he considered religion a matter for women and children: his own views were staunchly secular. He was also ferociously right-wing, harbouring deep suspicions against foreigners, Jews and left-wing intellectuals alike. Françoise de Beauvoir, by contrast, was determined to practise everything she had learnt at the Couvent des Oiseaux, to become a model Catholic mother and wife. Given Georges de Beauvoir's philandering habits, she certainly needed the fortitude her strong religious convictions would seem to have lent her. As we have seen in chapter 1, Simone de Beauvoir herself insisted that the ideological split between her parents was the key to her own desire to become an intellectual.

The discrepancy between the high bourgeois culture and manners the Beauvoirs sought to inculcate in their daughters, and the rather straitened financial circumstances in which they actually found themselves, probably did as much as if not more than such ideological contradictions to propel their two daughters towards artistic or intellectual careers. Awkwardly posed as outcasts or *déclassées* in relation to the original social milieu of their parents, the Beauvoir daughters could neither identify with their origins nor cast themselves as petty bourgeois, which is all Georges de Beauvoir's position amounted to by the early 1920s.[7] In this sense, the role of the artist or writer, which requires much intellectual but rather less economic capital, represents an obvious escape: while artists and intellectuals may not have greater financial resources than the petty bourgeoisie, their life-styles are vastly different.

The fact that Simone de Beauvoir was a girl meant that her education, and particularly her early education, was almost exclusively determined by her mother. Traditionally, Catholic mothers would have the major say in their daughter's upbringing, whereas it was understood that once he had reached the age of reason, a boy's education could not remain a matter for women alone. It was also assumed that girls were easier to influence than boys, and that they therefore had to be more completely protected against secular impulses than their brothers. It was thus out of the question for the Beauvoir daughters to attend French state schools.

Ever since the major educational reforms of Jules Ferry in 1880 in which the state undertook to provide free, non-religious primary education for all, the schism between state and church schools in France had been total. Beauvoir's *bien-pensant* mother would under no circumstances have allowed her daughters to attend what she considered a godless institution: as a matter of course Simone and Hélène were inscribed at a Catholic school for girls, the somewhat ironically named Cours Désir (or, more correctly, the Institut Adéline Désir). As such schools were fee-paying whereas state schools were free, the clientele of Catholic schools was predominantly bourgeois. Although Catholic secondary schools for girls were expanding rapidly in Paris after 1902, there was little provision for such education in the provinces. As the daughter of a somewhat impoverished middle-class family living in Paris, Simone de Beauvoir was born into the very social group in which even a woman would have a real chance – and, as we shall see, real incentives – to complete a career in higher education. However stifling she found her family, her specific social and geographical background in all likelihood was the *sine qua non* for her future career as an intellectual.

The struggle between church and state over women's education did not date from the 1880s: already in 1863 Victor Duruy, then minister of education, was encouraging the creation of municipal 'cours supérieurs' for young girls. Although it only affected about 2,000 girls at the time, his reform was greeted with outrage by the Catholic right. According to Françoise Mayeur in her indispensable study of secondary education for young girls during the Third Republic, Duruy's fall in 1869 was to no small extent due to the effects of a clerical campaign 'without precedent' waged against his timid initiative (see Mayeur, p. 3).

If such secondary courses were vociferously opposed, it was partly because they were perceived as attempts to establish a lay alternative to the pension or the convent school. As such they were cast as a diabolical scheme to remove girls approaching the age of puberty from their mothers without safely enclosing them behind the grilles of a convent or the walls of a boarding school instead (Mayeur, p. 4). In Catholic day schools the mothers would sit at the back of the classroom listening to the teaching of the *bonnes soeurs* and supervising their daughters' behaviour. At the Cours Désir, for example, mothers had the right to be present until their daughters had reached the age of 10. According to Hélène de Beauvoir, Françoise de Beauvoir was particularly assiduous in her attendance at classes and other school functions: 'Mama never missed a single one of my classes. She would bring her needlework and make large tapestries in petit point [. . .]' ('Entretien', p. 23). When Simone was 18, Hélène tells us, her mother still opened and read all her letters – and, moreover, simply threw away the ones she felt were unsuitable for her daughter (see 'Entretien', p. 18). By thus enacting the contemporary Catholic ideal of total motherhood, Françoise de Beauvoir completely deprived her daughters of privacy and the right to a personal space of their own, and only succeeded in fuelling their anger, resentment and desire for escape. For Simone de Beauvoir, the way to escape went through the *baccalauréat*, studies at the Sorbonne, and, finally, the *agrégation* in philosophy.

That particular trajectory had not long been available to women. The law known as the Loi Camille Sée, named after its proposer, was passed on 21 December 1880. Paradoxically this law, which was to transform French women's access to secondary education, was neither particularly radical nor particularly feminist. Its main aim was to produce secular-minded wives for the male Republican elite which had come into power in 1870. The idea was to avoid the unfortunate tensions often observed between a devout Catholic wife, educated in a convent school, and a free-thinking or atheist

Republican husband. Another fundamental motivation behind the law was the wish to segregate the sexes in secondary education. Camille Sée himself emphasized the need to develop the 'specific female character as well as disinterested learning' (Mayeur, p. 394). In practice this amounted to keeping the new secondary education for girls isolated from the traditional mainstream of the French educational system. For although it provided for a full course of education for girls from the age of 12 to that of 17, the new law also prevented state schools from letting them sit for the *baccalauréat*. The girls' course lasted one year less than that required for the *bac*, did not comprise Greek or Latin, and led to a quite unique qualification, the so-called *diplôme* ('diploma of secondary education'), which, strictly speaking, qualified them for nothing at all. Girls from lower social classes who needed to earn their living had no use for the new diploma and preferred to sit the less advanced exams for the primary school teacher's certificate (the *brevet supérieur*). The vocationally meaningless 'diploma' remained the preserve of the better-off who could afford to stay on at school in order to take an exam which led nowhere.

The effects of the law were nevertheless wide-ranging. In so far as the principle of separate education for boys and girls was based on the belief that the specifically feminine virtues required a mode of teaching which differed from the coarser masculine approach, it led logically to the conclusion that young girls had to be taught by members of their own sex. At a stroke a whole new profession was opened to women: that of secondary schoolteaching. The need for female teachers, however, created a series of new problems for the government. At the time the only way a woman could qualify as a secondary schoolteacher in France was to pass the *bac*, go on to study at university and gain a *licence* (roughly similar to a BA degree), followed by a secondary teachers' training diploma, also awarded by the universities. The rarer and more coveted *agrégation* was a competitive exam (*concours*), which normally required attendance at university courses for two or more years after passing the *licence*. The number of passes at the *agrégation* each year was determined by the number of jobs available in the state schools at that particular moment. Holders of the *agrégation* became civil servants guaranteed a job for life. In return for such job security, they had to accept a rather military system of postings in which the ministry of education alone decided where they were to work and for how many years. An *agrégé* taught less and earned more money than a *licencié*. This system was not only still in place in the 1920s, when Beauvoir was a student: with some modifications (holders of the *agrégation* now tend to go on to teach in higher, not secondary education) it is still operative in France. Until well after World War II, to be an *agrégé* teacher of philosophy at a *lycée* in Paris was a highly respectable, even prestigious position for a French intellectual.[8]

Since it barred women in the state system from passing the *bac*, the Loi Camille Sée also excluded them from French universities. So how were they to become secondary schoolteachers? The solution chosen was to set up a new Ecole Normale Supérieure for women in 1881, at Sèvres (close to Paris, but not close enough to expose its female students to the sinful distractions of the capital).[9] The students at Sèvres were known as 'Sévriennes', as opposed to their male counterparts, the *normaliens* or *Ulmiens* from the 'real' ENS in the rue d'Ulm, in the very heart of the Latin Quarter. Access to Sèvres, as to the rue d'Ulm, was regulated by a competitive entrance exam. At Sèvres, the female students were expected first to prepare a *Certificat d'aptitude à l'enseignement secondaire dans les lycées et collèges de jeunes filles*, often known as the *licence de Sèvres*, and then to go on to prepare a specific *agrégation*, known as the *agrégation féminine*. The latter was a far broader and more general exam than its male counterparts. In 1885, the male professors who were grading these female *agrégations* expressed their satisfaction with the standards achieved by the Sévriennes: they were good, but well below those required for men, and thus entirely suitable for women (see Mayeur, p. 139).

At first the women at Sèvres could only choose between two *agrégations* (letters or sciences), but soon two more were added: mathematics, and history and geography.[10] Philosophy, classics and modern languages were not taught as specific disciplines. As philosophy and classics were not part of the syllabus for the girls' secondary-school diploma, the exclusion of these subjects is not so surprising. Modern languages, however, were required for the diploma. The curious exclusion of modern languages from the syllabus at Sèvres forced female language teachers to pass the same university *licence* or *agrégation* as their male colleagues. It is interesting to note that they do not seem to have derived any special prestige from their success in a masculine sphere: Françoise Mayeur points out that these women rarely became headmistresses, or achieved any other kind of career distinction. Their lack of professional success may be due, at least in part, to the low status of modern languages in general in the French academic hierarchy.[11]

In effect, then, women who wanted to teach subjects not provided for at Sèvres had to go to university, and thus had to acquire the *bac*. Before 1908, this could only be done through private tuition, or in schools outside the state sector. Unlike the Sévriennes, however, university-trained women were not guaranteed a teaching job in the state sector. Even when they did pass the *agrégation masculine*, they did so as supernumerary candidates, that is to say that there were no teaching positions earmarked for them. In practical terms, this meant that if one year there were twenty vacant positions for German teachers in the state sector, and five women made it into the top twenty at the *agrégation*, another five men would automatically be passed as well, taking the total of *agrégés* in German for that year to twenty-five. Even in 1929 successful women candidates did not compete with men for jobs – a fact which, according to Beauvoir, produced exceptionally friendly relations between male and female students: '[The male students] treated me without condescension, and even with a special kindness, for they didn't look upon me as a rival; girls were judged in the examination by the same standards as the boys, but they were accepted as supernumeraries, they did not compete for their places' (MDD295; MJF412; TA). By 1929, however, girls' secondary education had in effect become identical to that of boys, and female *agrégées* could expect to obtain permanent positions in girls' *lycées*.[12]

From a patriarchal perspective, the strategy of passing women as 'supernumerary candidates' had its flaws. While it kept women from competing with men for jobs, it did not protect the men from intellectual competition. Simone de Beauvoir underestimates the degree to which men managed to feel threatened by the very presence of females on the lists of exam results. In France such results were – and still are – publicly announced in the same way as the outcome of a sports competition, the candidate achieving the highest number of points being ranked as number one and so on. Although their jobs were protected, men therefore still had to suffer the indignity of being classed *after* women in a highly official context. According to Edmée Charrier, the blow to male pride was sometimes severe. In 1887, for example, in the exams for the secondary schoolteachers' diploma in English, nineteen out of the thirty-six candidates who passed were women, and eight women made it into the top ten, the top men being ranked fourth and tenth respectively. Would-be male German teachers fared little better: in that subject four women made it into the top five, with only a token male presence in third place. After that experience, the ministry of education suddenly decided to reform the system: from 1891 onwards women and men, still sitting the same exams, were to be ranked on separate lists. 'It is easy to guess the reasons for this little alteration', Charrier comments (p. 133). The same thing happened in all the *agrégations* in modern languages: from the early 1890s, women and men were ranked separately on the lists of exam results; joint rankings were not reintroduced until 1924.

From 1880 to 1908, paradoxically, one effect of the introduction of secondary state education for girls was to give the independent sector – and by far the largest part of that was made up of Catholic schools – exclusive rights to preparing girls for the *baccalauréat*. At first the church did not favour such endeavours, and Catholic girls' school did not fully exploit their prerogative. As economic and social circumstances changed, however, so did Catholic attitudes. In 1920, when Simone de Beauvoir was 12 and her parents were thinking about her secondary education, a Catholic educationalist, Fénelon Gibon, neatly summarized the attitudes prevalent among Parisian middle-class Catholics at the time. Given the slaughter of a whole generation of young men in the Great War, he insists, one must face the fact that many women will never get married: they need an education which will enable them to earn their own living. The secondary-school diploma 'is nothing but a luxury', he writes (p. 52); women who need to make money need the *baccalauréat* and nothing else.

Gibon here is simply spelling out a trend which had been growing in importance since the late nineteenth century, when the French bourgeoisie began to realize that many women would not have the necessary marriage portion (*dot*) to establish their own families, and that they would therefore need earned income if they were to maintain a reasonable life-style. After World War I, inflation destroyed the value of dowries and private incomes. Pure economic necessity pushed many middle-class and upper-class women on to the labour market. But bourgeois women both wanted and were expected to earn their living in a bourgeois fashion, and the way to the more 'acceptable' careers (as opposed to working-class jobs) went through the *bac*. Few middle-class women, for instance, passed the *brevet supérieur* to become primary schoolteachers.[13] In this respect, Simone de Beauvoir's choice of a career in secondary schoolteaching was a highly representative solution to the new dilemmas facing a growing number of upper-middle-class Parisian women. If her schoolfriend Zaza's intellectual ambitions and interests were more firmly repressed than Simone's, this was almost entirely due to the different economic standing of their two families. Zaza's wealthy background allowed her – or rather her mother – to hope for a conventionally suitable marriage, whereas Simone's impecunious circumstances forced her parents to abandon all such plans for her and her sister.

In 1902 a new type of *baccalauréat* was introduced, known as 'Latin and languages'. Unlike the traditional philosophical *bac*, this one required no Greek, and was said to be 'easy'. Women immediately flocked to take it. From 1902 onwards a whole series of independent institutions were set up to prepare them for this *baccalauréat*.[14] The Cours Désir was typical of the great majority of Catholic girls' schools in that it only prepared its students for the 'Latin and languages' *bac*, leaving the two other branches, philosophy and mathematics, to the boys. Simone de Beauvoir writes:

> At the Cours Désir we [Simone and Zaza] separated from the others. The school only prepared for the Latin-modern languages examinations. Monsieur Mabille wanted his daughter to have a good grounding in science; I myself liked things I could get my teeth into, like mathematics. An extra teacher was appointed who taught algebra, trigonometry, and physics (MDD150; MJF209; TA).

Zaza and Simone demonstrated their superiority by doing both *bacs* at once: Latin and languages as well as mathematics. The only way they could take the mathematics exams, however, was by paying for extra tuition from outside the school. Sciences were still not considered quite *comme il faut* for young girls, and one might well wonder why Zaza's father was so keen on the idea.

If Catholic schools in Paris from 1903 to about 1910 took the lead in providing teaching for the *baccalauréat* for women, the state sector soon caught up with them. Officially allowed to prepare women for the *baccalauréat* from 1908, many *lycées* had in fact already been offering the necessary teaching for several years. By the outbreak of World War I, all Parisian *lycées* offered the *bac* for girls as well as boys (Mayeur, p. 398). Certainly in the early 1920s Simone's free-thinking father seriously considered the *lycée* as an option for his daughters. In 1920 Fénelon Gibon warned that Catholic schools were losing out to the competition from the state schools, and that Catholics would have to come up with even better teachers than those of the *lycées* if they were to hold on to their clientele (pp. 72–3).

Beauvoir's own account of her teachers at the Cours Désir makes for rather distressing reading: 'They were richer in Christian virtues than in degrees and diplomas', she comments (MDD122; MJF170; TA). Her father did not hide his low opinion of their capacities either: 'He went as far as to suggest to my mother that my sister and I should attend the *lycée*; there we would enjoy a better education and at much less cost' (MDD122; MJF170; TA). This time, Simone's heart's desire coincided with her mother's religious objections: Simone did not want to be separated from Zaza, and it was out of the question for the Catholic Lacoin family ('Mabille' in the memoirs) to send *their* daughter to a lay institution. So Simone remained with her *bien-pensant* teachers: 'With Zaza and a few other fellow-pupils I used to make fun of [. . .] our teachers' foibles' (MDD122; MJF171). When passing her *bac* in 1925 she did badly in philosophy, scoring only eleven points out of twenty (ten points were required to pass) because of the abysmal teaching she had received from the philosophy teacher at the Cours Désir, *l'abbé* Trécourt (see MDD160; MJF223). According to her memoirs, 'All he did was to [. . .] make us recite the chapter we had been asked to learn in the textbook. Whatever the problem was, the author, the Révérend Père Lahr, made a rapid summary of human errors and instructed us in the truth according to Saint Thomas Aquinas' (MDD157; MJF219).

'A NEW LIFE, A DIFFERENT LIFE': THE SORBONNE

The autumn of 1925 marked a new epoch in Simone de Beauvoir's life.[15] At the age of 17 and a half she had finally seen the last of the Cours Désir;

at long last she was to become a real student. But what exactly was she to study? In her memoirs she makes it clear that her first thought was to go to Sèvres: she had read in a magazine a lyrical description of the pleasures of that school by a former student who 'described the gardens in which beautiful young women, athirst for knowledge, went walking by moon-light, the sound of their voices mingling with the murmur of fountains' (MDD159; MJF221). Prefiguring and reversing the traumatic scene by the Medici fountain, the blissful harmony of a protected moonlit enclosure imagined here is the exact opposite of the pain, confusion and defeat suffered in the Luxembourg gardens. Both scenes are set in a garden complete with fountains: the difference is the sex of the interlocutors. In Beauvoir's memoirs, a somewhat clichéd dream (the Romantic moonlight says it all) of all-female harmony gives way to the harsh daytime reality of intellectual power struggles between men and women.[16]

Beauvoir nevertheless decided against Sèvres: 'But my mother mis-trusted Sèvres,' she writes, 'and when I came to think about it, I hardly wanted to shut myself up with a lot of women away from Paris' (MDD159; MJF221–2). There were good reasons why her mother would not want her to go to Sèvres. Gibon points out that students from the independent sector (the *enseignement libre*), that is to say Catholic students, had to agree to go on to teach in state schools after graduating (pp. 189–90).[17] Françoise de Beauvoir, who had made considerable financial sacrifices to keep her daughters out of lay institutions, could hardly be expected to accept such a project with equanimity.

But the other reason why Beauvoir would not have wanted to attend Sèvres was her interest in philosophy. As we have seen, the women at Sèvres were neither allowed nor able to sit the so-called masculine philoso-phy *agrégation*. Initially, however, her parents refused to let her study philosophy at all. Whatever she was to study, her father insisted on financial security for his daughter: she was not to be allowed to end up giving private lessons. If she were to become a teacher, he wanted her to get her *agrégation* and teach in the state sector, which, as we have seen, would make her a prestigious civil servant with job security and a state pension on retirement. The financial argument was decisive: Françoise de Beauvoir gave in, and it was announced to the nuns and other teachers at the Cours Désir that Simone was to become a *lycée* teacher. Simone was delighted: her teachers' disapproval could only elate her: 'How scandalous! [. . .] It was with complete unconcern that I read in my teachers' eyes their opinion of my ingratitude, my unworthiness, my treachery: I had fallen into the hands of Satan' (MDD160; MJF223).

But if Beauvoir decided to stay out of Sèvres, why did she not consider going to the Ecole Normale Supérieure in the rue d'Ulm? Many critics, misled by the fact that they sat the same examinations in 1929, apparently believe that that is where she met Jean-Paul Sartre. According to her memoirs, however, the idea of applying to that school did not even occur to her. There were excellent reasons for this, not least that in 1925 the ENS did not officially accept women students at all. When one woman, Mlle Rivière, passed the entrance exams for the science section in 1910 (she had signed the relevant forms using only her initials), she was accepted as *élève de l'école* and was given full student status, including the small monthly allowance paid by the state, although she was denied board and lodging. The very next year, Edmée Charrier tells us, the board of the ENS decided to exclude women from the rue d'Ulm. From 1912 to 1926 four women nevertheless passed the entrance exams (all of them in sciences); all were refused status as *élève de l'école*, and instead offered something called a 'university fellowship' (*bourse de l'Université*). The last of these women, Mlle Jacotin, who passed the entrance exam in 1926, decided to protest against this unfair treatment; the press took up her cause, and in 1927 she was granted full student status at the school, thereby opening the way for the thirty-six women admitted from 1927 to 1939.[18] Only one year younger than Beauvoir, Simone Weil entered the school in 1928, that is to say in Sartre's last year, at a time when Beauvoir, in her eagerness to become financially independent, was already hard at work preparing her *agrégation*.[19]

In 1940 the school was again closed to women, officially on the grounds that Sèvres now offered exactly the same opportunities as the rue d'Ulm. Even in the 1930s, however, women students were not given exactly the same privileges as the men. One ex-Ulmienne, Mme Martinet, who entered the school in 1937, vividly recalls that women were not allowed to go into the refectory: they were to be protected against the foul language used by their male colleagues.[20] As women were allowed neither to live nor to eat at the school, they were *de facto* excluded from a large part of the more informal intellectual and social pursuits at the ENS.

In 1925, then, the ENS in the rue d'Ulm was not an option for Simone de Beauvoir. She would have to do a *licence* at the Sorbonne, followed by the teaching diploma and finally the *agrégation*. What she wanted was to study philosophy. Her mother discussed it with Simone's teachers: 'They told my mother that the study of philosophy mortally corrupts the soul: after one year at the Sorbonne, I would lose both my faith and my good character' (MDD160; MJF223). Simone agreed to study classics (*lettres*) and mathematics instead. Nor was she going to be allowed to see a lot of the sinful Sorbonne: she was to study mathematics at the Institut catholique and classics at the Institut Sainte-Marie at Neuilly, a single-sex institution founded and directed by the formidable Mme Danielou, a powerful advocate for the education of Catholic girls.[21] The Institut catholique was mixed: in 1928–9, Edmée Charrier informs us, 31 per cent or 461 of the 1,480 students there were women (Charrier, p. 235). This, incidentally, is about the same percentage of women students as that boasted by many an Oxbridge college in the 1980s. Both institutions were set up to prepare Catholic students for the Sorbonne exams, in order to spare them from exposure to the worldly ways of Sorbonne students and professors alike. 'In this way our connexions with the Sorbonne would be reduced to the minimum', Beauvoir comments (MDD168; MJF233).

During her first year of study (1925/6) Simone de Beauvoir took three *certificats*: one in literature, one in mathematics and one in Latin. In addition she was learning Greek from scratch. One appreciates these efforts more fully if one knows that at the time a *licence* would normally be composed of four *certificats*: the average student would aim to earn one a year, whereas an exceptionally gifted and hard-working student might manage to get two in a year. But she did not feel happy with her work: nothing really inspired her. Supported by Mlle Mercier at the Institut Sainte-Marie ('Mlle Lambert' in the memoirs), who must have been one of the first six female *agrégées* in philosophy in France, and a close collaborator of Mme Danielou, she decided to return to her first love, philosophy. This time, her parents agreed.

Not that it was usual for women to choose this particular subject. Beauvoir knew that philosophical women were rare indeed: 'I wanted to be one of those pioneers', she writes (MDD160; MJF222). She presents her own philosophical vocation as deeply inspired by the pioneering example of the first woman *docteur d'Etat* in philosophy in France, Léontine Zanta:

> I had read in an illustrated magazine an article about a woman philosopher who was called Mademoiselle Zanta: she had taken her doctorate; she had been photographed, in a grave and thoughtful posture, sitting at her desk; she lived with a young niece whom she had adopted: she had thus succeeded in reconciling her intellectual life with the demands of female sensibility. How I should love to have such flattering things written one day about *me*! (MDD160; MJF222; TA).[22]

Forgotten today, Léontine Zanta defended her doctorate in philosophy on the renaissance of Stoicism in the French sixteenth century at the Sorbonne in May 1914. The newspaper reports of the event are respectful, full of chivalrous admiration. One did not expect, one reporter marvels, that one of the two first women *doctoresses* in France should have decided to do a doctorate of philosophy, generally considered 'the most difficult and most formidable of doctorates, the one which requires such strength of mind and such experience in handling ideas that it is considered a male prerogative'.[23] The same journalist dwells on Mlle Zanta's wonderful defence of her thesis, which combined the 'ease of a woman of the world and the versatile frankness of a resourceful mind', and takes the opportunity to claim that no other country in the world has produced so many learned *and* feminine women as France.[24]

Born in Mâcon in the 1870s as the fifth child of an Alsacian *lycée* teacher, Léontine Zanta was an intellectual celebrity in her day, active in journalism and in the feminist movement of the 1920s. She was never given a position in higher education, and earned her living by private tutoring, journalism and writing. The author of several novels about intellectual women and of essays on feminism, she received the Légion d'honneur in the late 1920s.[25]

Simone de Beauvoir's wish to become one of the select handful of philosophical women in France might easily have run up against a series of institutional obstacles. In fact, had she been only a few years older she might not have been able to join them at all. Léontine Zanta, for instance, was never an *agrégée* in philosophy. Women in France were not allowed freely to sit all *agrégations* and other exams previously reserved for men until 1924. From the same date joint rankings were to be the rule for every exam: male feelings were no longer to be spared. As for the *agrégation* in philosophy, the most prestigious and therefore the most 'masculine' of all the male *agrégations*, the ministry of education decided in 1918 to exclude women from it altogether, with effect from 1919. Given the fact that by 1918 only one woman in France had ever succeeded in passing the philosophy *agrégation* at all (and that was back in 1905),[26] one might wonder why the men in power suddenly felt the need to prevent them even from trying. According to Edmée Charrier, the philosophy professors at the Sorbonne (all male) protested furiously, arguing that it would do serious injustice to their female students, and a year later the measure was recalled (pp. 135–6). From 1920 to 1928 seven women succeeded in getting the *agrégation* in philosophy, and in 1929 four out of thirteen successful candidates were women.[27] Or in other words: only five years earlier the famous *agrégation* result of 1929 – and therefore also the fateful philosophical conversation in the Luxembourg Gardens – would not have been possible. Simone de Beauvoir's perception of herself as second only to Sartre was certainly given a decisive boost by the fact that she came second at the *agrégation* where he came first. One wonders how she would have categorized herself had she been deprived of such powerful institutional sanctioning of her stance.

When Beauvoir writes in *The Second Sex* that her own generation of women no longer need to struggle for their basic rights since 'by and large we have won the game' (SS27; DSa29), this is a generalization based almost entirely on her own experiences as a student and young teacher of philosophy in the late 1920s and early 1930s, when she was fortunate enough never to encounter a single instance of crudely explicit institutional gender segregation. It is instructive to realize, however, how little it would have taken for her to have had quite a different experience of her educational career. Philosophy rankings, for instance, were joint in 1929, but split into gender-segregated lists again in the late 1930s. Women had only been allowed to sit all university exams on a par with men since 1924. By that time, the *lycée* syllabuses for girls and boys had become more or less identical: women as well as men were now expected to teach the *bac* programmes, and the female diploma fell into quasi-oblivion. In 1924, however, female *agrégées* were still earning less than their male counterparts. Now that they were expected to sit the same exams and teach the same syllabuses, they successfully argued for their right to equal salary as well, and in August 1927 male and female *lycée* teachers were granted equal salary.[28] When Simone de Beauvoir took up her first teaching position in Marseilles in 1931, she could expect to earn the same salary as Sartre in Le Havre, but that right had only been conquered four years earlier.

We have seen already that it was not until 1926 that Beauvoir was allowed to start studying philosophy. Under these conditions, the fact that she passed the *agrégation* with flying colours as early as 1929 is nothing short of astonishing. It may certainly be considered a more impressive feat than Sartre's achievement in coming first at the same exam. By 1929 Sartre had been studying philosophy at a tertiary level for no less than *seven years* (he passed his *bac* in 1922 and never deviated from his philosophical vocation). By contrast, due to her late start, Beauvoir had already lost out on one year's study of philosophy. In March 1927 she passed her *certificat* in the history of philosophy and in June the one in 'general philosophy' where, incidentally, she came second to Simone Weil. The third on the list was Maurice Merleau-Ponty ('Jean Pradelle' in the memoirs), who was already settled in the rue d'Ulm. She also got her *certificat* in Greek: in two years of study, she had already done the equivalent of one and a half *licences* (see MDD245; MJF339).

In 1927/8 Beauvoir was planning to do three more *certificats*, so as to get her two *licences* – classics and philosophy – finished that year. In March 1928 she got the two she needed for philosophy (ethics and psychology), but the last remaining *certificat* required for classics was philology. She decided that she could not face the aridity of the subject, and renounced the idea of getting a double *licence*. Her father, who would have liked to have a prodigy for a daughter if he could not have a marriageable one, was disappointed. 'But I wasn't sixteen any more: I stood my ground', Beauvoir drily comments (MDD266; MJF368). Instead, finding herself with a free summer term on her hands, she decided to prepare for the teaching diploma required for secondary schoolteaching at the same time as the *agrégation* – a quite unusual project, to say the least. This diploma required the presentation of a dissertation on some philosophical topic. On the advice of Léon Brunschvicg, professor at the Sorbonne, she decided to write on the 'concept in Leibniz' (MJF369).

Beauvoir's final year of study was perhaps the most arduous of all. But she worked with intensity: for her, the *agrégation* represented above all freedom – freedom to earn her own money, to move away from home and be accountable to nobody for her behaviour. For such a prize no effort could be considered too taxing. In January 1929 she did the period of practical teaching required for the teachers' diploma at the *lycée* Janson-de-Sailly, along with Claude Lévi-Strauss, who like herself was preparing for the *agrégation* in philosophy at the Sorbonne, and the *normalien* Merleau-Ponty, whom she knew well. In fact by this time she had already met most of the final year students at the ENS, except for the little clan consisting of Sartre, Paul Nizan and René Maheu.

Then as now, the *agrégation* examinations were based on a list of topics, perhaps as many as nine or ten. Only one of them would be set in the written examinations. This system explains how Sartre could fail at his first attempt in 1928: he may simply have been ill prepared for the topic that came up. With miraculous convenience, however, the topic of the written exam in 1929 was 'Freedom and contingency', and his triumph was total. There are two possible readings of this fact: either Sartre did so well at the exams because the topic was ideally suited to his preoccupations, or, as Michèle Le Doeuff once remarked, he spent the next fifteen years assiduously revising his exam scripts.

An important part of the oral examinations is the exercise known as the *discours*, a kind of mini-lecture where the candidate has a few hours in which to draft a talk on a previously unprepared topic. For this kind of test it is necessary to have both a smooth tongue and a substantial amount of technique. This is precisely where the specific education of the ENS students comes into its own: more intensely drilled in the requisite techniques than anybody else, in 1929 they certainly were considered better equipped for this kind of performance than candidates from the Sorbonne. In *Tristes tropiques*, Claude Lévi-Strauss gives a scathing critique of the inevitable tripartite pattern of thought favoured by the *agrégation* examiners:

> I started to learn that every problem, whether serious or trivial, can be settled once and for all by always applying the same method, which consists in opposing two traditional views of the question, to introduce the first by appealing to common sense, then to destroy it by means of the second, and finally to pack them both off, thanks to a third view which reveals the equally partial nature of the two others. By a trick of vocabulary both of these have now been reduced to complementary aspects of the same thing: form and contents, container and contained, being and appearance, continuity and discontinuity, essence and existence and so on. Such exercises quickly become purely verbal, based on the art of the pun which replaces thought. [. . .] Five years at the Sorbonne amounted to no more than learning this kind of gymnastics. [. . .] I prided myself on being able to

construct in ten minutes a solidly dialectical framework for an hour's lecture on the respective merits of buses and trams (pp. 52–3).

This system has not changed much since the 1920s. Apparently, students from the ENS can still be observed dividing their exam sheets into tripartite divisions and subdivisions before they know which topic they will have to lecture on. Indeed, some students feel they are being adventurous in the extreme by dividing their *discours* into two parts instead of three.[29] In his biography of Sartre, Ronald Hayman points out how the ENS did little to discourage Sartre's tendency to rely rather too heavily on brilliant improvisation:

> The Ecole Normale was no good at inculcating the habit of painstaking research into original sources; Sartre was not deflected from his tendency to depend on insufficient facts, insufficiently mastered. But he was already a virtuoso with words, and with his attractive voice he would have the lifelong ability to spellbind an audience of one person, five people or five hundred by speaking as if he were thinking out loud, while the verbal virtuosity already made it dangerously easy for him to write as if he were speaking impromptu (p. 54).

In the spring of 1929, Simone de Beauvoir became a close friend of René Maheu ('Herbaud' in the memoirs), and finally, after sitting the written part of the *agrégation*, she was officially invited to prepare the oral examinations together with Sartre, Maheu and Nizan. There can be little doubt that this probably helped her to do better at the oral exams than she might otherwise have done: after all, the experience of working intensively over several weeks with the elite of the ENS amounted to nothing less than a crash course in ENS exam techniques. The first time she met Sartre other than simply seeing him at lectures was one Monday morning in his room at the Cité universitaire, where he, Nizan and Maheu were expecting her to help them revise Leibniz. She must have felt as if she were sitting yet another exam: 'I was feeling a bit scared when I entered Sartre's room', Beauvoir writes. 'All day long, petrified with fear, I commented on the "metaphysical treatise" and in the evening Herbaud took me home' (MDD334; MJF467; TA). While this may sound a little like intellectual torture, it was in fact the opening gambit in an erotico-theoretical seduction game: only a few days later the two protagonists would be discussing philosophy in the Luxembourg Gardens.

THE SPIRIT OF THE ECOLE NORMALE SUPÉRIEURE

Before examining the impact of the Ecole Normale Supérieure on Simone de Beauvoir, it is necessary to consider for a moment Sartre's route towards the rue d'Ulm. His own background – born in 1905, he was brought up in Paris in the household of a teacher and intellectual – is typical of successful applicants to the ENS. The only atypical point in his school career is the fact that he spent three years (1917–20) at a *lycée* in La Rochelle (the dreaded provinces) before returning to Paris to prepare his *baccalauréat*. Unlike Beauvoir, then, Sartre benefited from the very best Parisian education of his time. From 1920 to 1922 he attended the *lycée* Henri IV, where one of France's most famous philosophers, Emile-Auguste Chartier (1868–1951), known as Alain, taught the special classes for students preparing for the entrance exams for the 'letters' section of the ENS. (Alain was later to teach Simone Weil.) Known to students in France as 'hypokhâgne' (first year) and 'khâgne' (second year) respectively, these preparatory classes in fact constitute a two-year course of intensive cramming for the competitive entrance exams. They are generally considered to be much harder work than the actual 'Grande Ecole'. Having passed their *bac*, students in Parisian 'khâgnes' normally also sit exams at the Sorbonne, with the result that many of them arrive at the ENS with an almost completed *licence* in hand. The four years at the school itself are spent finishing off the *licence* and preparing for the *agrégation* in a relatively leisurely, intellectually wide-ranging fashion.[30]

After passing the *baccalauréat* in 1922, Sartre and his friend Paul Nizan moved from Henri IV to the other prestige Parisian *lycée* at the time, Louis-le-Grand, to do their two years of preparatory courses for the ENS.[31] In August 1924 their efforts were crowned with success: they both entered the ENS that autumn, at a time when Beauvoir was still languishing at the Cours Désir. Sartre now had no less than five years (one more than usual, given his failure in 1928) in which to prepare himself for his destiny, that of being classed as number one in the *agrégation* of philosophy. Discussing Sartre's views of equality with him in 1974, Beauvoir confronts him with his own arrogance as a student:

> Simone de Beauvoir: At the Sorbonne you, Nizan and Maheu had the reputation of being extremely contemptuous of the world in general and of the Sorbonne students in particular.
>
> Jean-Paul Sartre: That was because the Sorbonne students represented beings who were not quite human [*des hommes*] (AF245; CA315; TA).

Gently upbraided by Beauvoir, Sartre declares that he got rid of such shockingly inegalitarian ideas later on. It might be argued that in so far as he did shed his obsession with classifications and hierarchies, turning down prizes and honours in later life, it was to no little extent because he had already managed to come out on top where it mattered. As Pierre Bourdieu has commented, nothing is more distinguished than disinterestedness – or in other words: only the rich can afford to appear poor (*Distinction*, pp. 53–6). That the young *normalien*, convinced of his own genius, considered the students at the Sorbonne as somewhat less than human is hardly surprising: in the educational field in France the ENS was considered the very incarnation of the highest intellectual virtues. At the time, the position of the ENS in France was far more dominant than, say, that of Oxford in Britain or Harvard in the USA today: every would-be intellectual in the country was under the sway of its prestige.

Simone de Beauvoir, herself a lowly Sorbonnarde, was no exception. She felt privileged to be allowed finally to join the self-important little clique around Sartre, and in her memoirs adorns the *normaliens* with the very intellectual qualities to which she herself aspired: 'I had prepared for the competitive examination at the double: their culture had a much more solid grounding than mine, they were familiar with hosts of new things of which I was ignorant and they were used to discussion', she writes (MDD344; MJF480–1). This, I would argue, is at once a realistic estimate of the differences between them, and one which thoroughly represses her own considerable claims to distinction. As we have seen, Beauvoir was only the ninth woman in France to become an *agrégée* of philosophy. 'So rare was this honor', her biographers tell us, 'that the pioneering recipients had their portraits in the photo weekly *Illustration*, often accompanied by a second photo of the distinguished laureate surrounded by her proud family' (Francis and Gonthier, p. 51). Beauvoir herself, however, does not allude to the uniqueness of her achievement. Nor does she tell us that at the age of 21 she was one of the youngest *agrégés* in France regardless of sex. Instead, she chooses to emphasize the superiority of her new friends from the Ecole Normale Supérieure – Sartre, Nizan, Aron, Politzer.[32]

Her low-key representation of herself signals her own identification with the intellectual values promoted by the ENS. Given the prestige of that institution, this is scarcely surprising. But we should not forget that she had another option: she might, like a Nizan or a Lévi-Strauss, have chosen to emphasize her own marginality, her relative distance and difference in relation to the young men at the ENS. Significantly enough, even at the time of writing her memoirs in the late 1950s, this idea does not seem to have occurred to the author of *The Second Sex*: throughout her life Beauvoir's criteria for intellectual excellence remained largely identical to those of the ENS. To this extent, her insistence that the star students of the ENS were the most promising intellectuals around tends towards the tautologous.

There is nothing exceptional in this: it is hardly imaginable that a successful candidate at the *agrégation* could escape the influence of the very ethos of the intellectual institution in which she worked. Moreover, through her relationship with Sartre she probably came to identify more closely with the *esprit normalien* than she might otherwise have done. Sartre – unlike Nizan – certainly thought he was having the time of his life at the school, describing his time there as 'four years [*sic!*] of happiness' (Preface to Nizan's *Aden-Arabie*, p. 22).[33] Sartre and Beauvoir's incessant emphasis on their *unity*, the refrain of 'we are one' (*on ne fait qu'un*) reiterated throughout the *Lettres au Castor* as well as in Beauvoir's memoirs, would in any case have made it difficult for her to establish any kind of distance between herself and the institution which produced Sartre. Yet for Beauvoir to subscribe to the intellectual ideology surrounding the ENS, an institution she never attended, was not at all the same thing as for Sartre to do so. Objectively and emotionally this move placed her in a position where it became both necessary and desirable to repress her own marginality.

The ideology of superiority surrounding the ENS in the 1920s and 1930s was similar to that surrounding philosophy at the time. Philosophy was seen as the queen of disciplines, the undisputed champion in the pecking order of academic subjects. It was assumed that only the most intelligent students could cope with the intellectual demands of this regal pursuit. To a certain extent, the prestige of the ENS and that of philosophy overlapped and intertwined. The philosopher supposedly had access to the highest of human realms, that of the spirit, and as such could properly consider himself an elite being. But so could the students at the ENS. Logically and in practice, the philosophy students at the school, such as Sartre, Nizan and Merleau-Ponty, represented the *crème de la crème* of French student life. In his essay of 1927, *La république des professeurs*, Albert Thibaudet, himself a literary critic and a simple *agrégé* of history and geography, casts teachers of philosophy as blossoms and teachers of more lowly subjects as mere foliage on the tree of knowledge: 'Our philosophy teachers remain the flower of our secondary education. But while listening to the flower, let us maintain a place for the leaves, such as the teacher of history for example' (pp. 245–6). Thibaudet – without a trace of irony, one presumes – goes on to endow philosophy with the power to purify even the shadiest of bankers and politicians:

> The philosophical vocation is in principle analogous to the vocation for the priesthood. Anybody who has ever prepared for the *agrégation* in philosophy, even if he has gone on to become a parliamentary horse-trader or the director of a dubious bank, has at a certain moment, like a student in a seminary, been touched by the idea that the highest human greatness is a life consecrated to the service of the spirit, and that it is possible to compete at the university for the positions which make this service possible. More than to the Roman Catholic clergy, this semi-clergy might be compared to the Protestant pastorate (p. 139).

At some point during the preparation of the *agrégation*, then, would-be teachers of philosophy are illuminated by the philosophical Spirit and elevated to a higher plane beyond the sordid realities of everyday life. This spiritual imprint, like that of priestly ordinations, lasts for the rest of the student's life, regardless of his later occupations. Thibaudet does not appear to find the imposition of rigorously competitive state exams on the candidates for such selfless philosophical service at all incongruous. As one might expect in 1927, the imagery of priests and pastors makes it abundantly clear that the lofty sphere of philosophy is no place for women. Although it is not essential actually to *pass* the philosophy *agrégation* – merely to prepare for it is sufficient – the stain of femininity is presumably such that not even philosophy can purify it. But women too shared the belief in philosophy as a sacred calling. In her novel *La science et l'amour*, published in 1921, the pioneering female philosopher Léontine Zanta has her mouthpiece, an unmarried female teacher of philosophy, admonish her students in well-worn clichés:

> To teach philosophy is not at all the same thing as to teach literature, mathematics or English. In order to be worthy of this task it is not enough simply to know and explain systems of thought, and to have a curious mind sharpened by incisive criticism, one must also have an elevated soul, galvanized by struggle and constant self-mastery. Do you know that such teaching is a kind of priesthood (p. 3)?

In general, the discipline of philosophy was represented as female, a subject to be handled with respect, violence or dominance by the elite males who were equal to it. This *topos* surfaces in the texts of writers as different as Julien Benda and Paul Nizan. In *Les chiens de garde* (1932) Nizan describes intelligence as 'this passive female ready to couple with anybody' (p. 16), and despairs at the bloodlessness of academic philosophy at the time: 'Will Philosophy remain *un ouvrage de dames*, the embroidery of a sterile old maid for a long time still?', he asks (p. 35). Responding to Julien Benda's claim that philosophy ought to remain a 'patrician virgin who would honour the gods' (*La trahison des clercs*, p. 152), Nizan accuses Benda and his ilk of being virgins themselves – that is to say, presumably, unable to ravish the frustrated virgin of philosophy (p. 67). What Nizan wants is virile, vigorous, activist philosophy – thought rooted in reality, eager to dirty its hands in the real world (p. 67). Taking its cue from Nizan's equation of activity with virility, Sartre's own philosophical rhetoric is notorious for its recourse to sexualized metaphors which cast the philosopher as virile, potent and above all male in his efforts to penetrate the unblemished virginity of the world.[34] The prevalent representation of philosophy (and truth) as female has wide-ranging implications which cannot be discussed here. But in relation to such a discourse an aspiring female philosopher is not positioned in the same way as her male comrades: for her to cast herself as the rigorous master of the female truth is not at all the same thing as for him to do it. Whether the woman, consciously or unconsciously, chooses to identify with the discourse of the philosophical institution in which she finds herself, or rather seeks somehow to marginalize herself in relation to it, she finds herself caught in an intellectual dilemma from which her male colleagues are absolved.

The *topos* of the indelible imprint surfaces in relation to the ENS as well; in fact, even its enemies contribute copiously to the belief in the mysteriously transformative powers of the Ecole Normale. In his celebrated diatribe against the boring, unmanly and somehow faintly perverse *professeurs* of the ENS, Emile Zola drives this particular point home. It is not a coincidence that his otherwise sour critique of the *normaliens* is reprinted in Alain Peyrefitte's self-indulgent collection of essays and reminiscences of student life in the rue d'Ulm:

> Whoever has ever been steeped in the air of the Ecole Normale is impregnated for life. Their brains have an insipid and musty smell of teacherdom, and it is always the same prickly attitudes, the need for the cane, the dull and impotent envy of old bachelors who lost out on women. [. . .] If you sow teachers, you will never reap creators ('Tous des pions,' p. 368).

If Zola's invectives may be said to represent one extremist approach to the Ecole Normale, the convoluted prose of Jean Giraudoux highlights its polar opposite. In 1935, in his capacity as a former *normalien*, Giraudoux (who was having an extremely secret affair with Simone de Beauvoir's sister, Hélène, at the time)[35] contributed a fulsome preface to J. Reignup's *L'esprit de Normale*. All students of the ENS, he writes, are 'servants of the spirit' (p. 7). In fact, one does not even need to have attended the actual school to partake in its spirit. Simply to have prepared for the entrance exams is enough:

> The *normalien* is of a spiritual race. [. . .] The spirit of the Ecole Normale is not reserved for those whom the luck of the entrance exams bring to the rue d'Ulm. A race is not decided by examinations. This spirit moves all those who have prepared for the School. [. . .] Preparing for the Ecole Normale is a choice and a liberation. It is the total and unrestricted opening of a young mind. It is the real academy, Plato's academy, the one that belongs to the beginning of life, and not the one that belongs to the end.[36] From this very moment, the future *normalien* is promoted to the rank of intimate friend of the great writers and the great ethical systems. He may very well remain small and mediocre, but he belongs to their race. He may speak and write their language pretty badly, but theirs is the only language he uses. [. . .] The

relationship between the great writers and the *normaliens* is like the relationship between famous fathers and their sons or nephews: such young men
keep their freedom and their right to criticize their forebears, who in any
case can only be charmed [*séduire*] by such outspokenness (p. 8).

In this masterpiece of mystification, Giraudoux would have us believe that
what an ex-candidate for the ENS actually *does* is of no significance:
however petty-minded, mediocre and incapable of writing decent French
he may be, he intrinsically belongs to the family of the great. In fact,
Giraudoux implies, the very shadow of the ENS magically resolves any
lingering Oedipal blockages in relation to the great predecessors (note the
significant slippage from 'sons' to 'nephews', and the dream of *seducing* the
father by clever criticism).

The *normaliens* own view of themselves was far from modest. According
to Reignup's ridiculously panegyrical view, the 'spirit' of the place would
transform the dullest mediocrity into a genius. On the one hand the
normalien hates the dull, the staid and the commonplace, easily demonstrating his own brilliance, daring and *panache* at every turn: on the other hand
such independence stops safely short of the revolutionary, since the
normalien has a natural respect for the only superiority that counts, the
hierarchy of intelligence. So it is that the anarchic individualists at Normale
readily buckle down to the tedious work of preparing exams, which they
then pass with their usual cavalier elegance. When a *normalien* takes up
some kind of intellectual or political position, it would be quite mistaken
to believe that he is *submitting* to some ready-made doctrine; on the
contrary, even when he turns socialist, he simply chooses to *impose* a
Marxist perspective on problems which interested him in any case (see
p. 48). *Normaliens'* judgements are always lucid, objective and *right*. In a fit
of Cartesian ardour, Reignup even singles out for praise what sounds
suspiciously like a propensity for combining wild generalizations with
tendentious reductionism:

> To know how to judge impartially and firmly in this way is the sign of an
> intelligence which sees things clearly and correctly, and which shows itself to
> be doing so. There is no walk of life in which such an asset is insignificant.
> [. . .] A *normalien* knows how to develop general ideas, and how to reduce
> the infinite number of particular cases to their essence or the exemplary case,
> classifying them by formulating a law referring them back to the general idea.
> In real life this capacity often translates itself in a real talent for compiling and
> analysing dossiers and extracting what useful information they may contain
> (p. 53).

Reignup's case is clear: the 'spirit of Normale' is independent yet disciplined, individualist yet suited to teamwork, original yet respectful of the
authentic values of French culture. In short, the *normaliens* are life's natural
aristocrats, and ought by right to rule us all. Given their endless capacity for

paperwork, moreover, they are sure to make excellent bureaucrats. Like Giraudoux, he emphasizes that one does not need actually to have attended the ENS to acquire such superior qualities: it is enough to have tried to get into it: 'It is in *khâgne* one finds the true educational impact of Normale', he exclaims (p. 15). If the world would only let itself be guided by the values represented by the ENS, Reignup insists (in 1935), it might yet be saved:

> For, whether one likes it or not, the Ecole Normale is one of the last sanctuaries of cultural freedom, respect for intellectual values and the belief in their rightful supremacy and beneficial effects. It is perhaps less in evidence at the present time, but destined, one must hope, to get its revenge for the sake of the temporal salvation of the modern world in danger (pp. 77–8).

By the 1970s the belief in the intellectual superiority of the ENS and its preparatory classes had changed suprisingly little. In his fascinating study of the various preparatory classes for the so-called 'Great Schools', 'Epreuve scolaire et consécration sociale: les classes préparatoires aux grandes écoles', Pierre Bourdieu, himself a *normalien*, caustically describes the 'jeunes maîtres' of the ENS as smug self-proclaimed geniuses:

> [They are] educated, as Durkheim once put it, to 'produce prematurely and thoughtlessly'. Their excessive confidence in books or their own genius leads them to develop the intellectual smugness of naive schoolboys [*grands écoliers*] who have seen it all. They are self-confident enough to oppose their knowing smiles to everything that does not carry the inimitable mark of the School, and to expose their inherited convictions in a *lycée* in the provinces, a professorial chair, an 'obscure' textbook or a 'brilliant' essay (p. 59).[37]

It may be salutary to remember that even in the 1920s and 1930s there were dissident voices. In *Aden-Arabie* (1932), Paul Nizan, for instance, rages against this school 'which pretends to be normal, and is said to be superior'.[38] Far from freeing the spirit or anything else, fulminates Nizan, the school in fact encourages arrogant uniformity:

> It [the ENS] is dominated by the *esprit de corps* of seminaries and regiments: one easily succeeds in making young men whose private weaknesses incline them towards collective pride believe that the Ecole Normale is a real being which has a soul – and a bmeautiful soul at that – a moral personality more charming than truth, justice and human beings [*hommes*]. [. . .] Most *normaliens* only judge themselves in terms which affirm their right to belong to the Elite (*Aden-Arabie*, p. 57).

In *Tristes tropiques*, as we have seen, Claude Lévi-Strauss, who never even prepared for the entrance exams to the ENS, caustically attacks the facile and superficial approach to philosophy inculcated in students preparing for the *agrégation*, a game for which the *normaliens* were presumed to be better equipped than anybody else. Far from allowing real thought to take place, he argues, the exam system encourages students to think in the most simplistic and reductive terms, inciting them to 'see in the variety of subjects for thought nothing but one single and invariable form, to be found simply by adding a few elementary corrections. [. . .] From this perspective,' Lévi-Strauss continues, 'the teaching of philosophy trained our intelligence while simultaneously withering our minds' (p. 53).

The arrogance of the all-male Ecole Normale inevitably produced a considerable amount of sexist prose. From 1950 to 1977, successive editions of Alain Peyrefitte's *Rue d'Ulm* reprinted unchanged an outrageously sexist attack on the *normaliennes* at Sèvres, no doubt in the belief that it was frighfully funny. Sartre's conviction that the Sorbonnards were somewhat less than human also re-emerges in this piece, apparently written some time in the 1940s:

> [The Sévrienne] offers a striking example of defective development for she displays characteristics typical of both males and females. She resembles the male, and particularly the inferior species which goes under the name of Sorbonnard, above all in the technical character of her conversation. [. . .] With women she shares the strange habit of uttering small, uninterpretable cries or a clucking or shrill laughter at the most unexpected moments (René Peyrefitte, pp. 334–5).

In order to supplement their meagre state salary, the *normaliens* often gave private lessons to *lycée* students, known in the school jargon as *tapirs*. The *Petit Robert* claims that this is a 'humourous metaphor', the 'tapir being a sedentary, edible and domesticable animal'. One assumes that the young men at the ENS saw themselves as rather more predatory beasts. When the private pupil is female, the male *normalien* surpasses himself in his disdain for her intellectual capacities: 'The young tapiress attends a Catholic school where one only goes to class once a week, and where the chorus of mothers and governesses at the back of the class whispers the right reply to the dear child.'[39] It is not unreasonable, I think, to suggest that this passage gives us nothing less than a fairly exact representation of Simone de Beauvoir and the Cours Désir as seen from the Olympian heights of the ENS.

THE CONFLICTUAL MARGINALITY OF SIMONE DE BEAUVOIR

Objectively, then, Beauvoir was right to describe herself as intellectually inferior to Sartre: by 1929 she had clearly amassed much less educational capital than he.[40] Whereas Sartre's trajectory from Henri IV to Louis-le-

Grand to the ENS and the coveted first place at the *agrégation* represents the accumulation of the maximum possible amount of educational capital in France at the time, Beauvoir's Cours Désir, Institut Sainte-Marie and Sorbonne have a decidedly inferior value, partly, but by no means entirely, compensated for by her brilliant ranking as number two at the *agrégation*. The fact that she was much younger than her fellow students further increases her educational prestige, as it was (and still is) considered a sure sign of brilliance (see Bourdieu, 'Epreuve scolaire', and Bourdieu and Saint Martin). Sartre nevertheless easily emerges from his education as the most *legitimate* of heirs to French culture, well placed to make his bid for cultural supremacy in the French intellectual field.[41] If Beauvoir does not fare quite as well, I would argue, it is due to the fact that she is a woman. Had she been a man, she would most certainly have attended the ENS or the equally prestigious Ecole Polytechnique. 'What a pity Simone wasn't a boy: she could have gone to the Polytechnique!', Beauvoir's father used to moan (MDD177; MJF246). In other words, if Beauvoir does not amass as much educational capital as Sartre, and moreover has more difficulty converting her educational capital into intellectual capital, it can only be explained by the fact that in the 1920s and 1930s the unspoken rules – the habitus – of both fields marginalized women.

For if one disregards gender, Simone de Beauvoir would seem not to belong to any obvious 'minority' group. Born into a somewhat *déclassé* professional middle-class family in Paris, she comes from exactly the kind of family background most likely to make her succeed in higher education in France. In terms of the intellectual field (as opposed to the educational field), however, her specific class background is not irrelevant: her cultural anxiety, for instance (discussed below), may well, among other things, be seen as an effect of the contradictions produced by the declining class status of her family. But her class status is not necessarily more uncertain than that of Sartre, for instance, whose widowed mother, Anne-Marie Sartre, *née* Schweitzer, possessed little economic or social status in her own right. Sartre's grandfather's position as a successful *agrégé* teacher of German in Alsace is itself no more than petty-bourgeois, although it carries far more intellectual capital than the uncertain business dealings of Georges de Beauvoir. The main social difference between the two families is that whereas the Beauvoirs suffered a marked loss of prestige, the Schweitzers did not. Such slight differences in social class between the two writers, I would argue, are not readily detectable in their texts. This is not, of course, to claim that Beauvoir's work cannot be read in class terms, but it is to argue that it is not class that distinguishes her from the majority of her male colleagues and friends in France at the time. The *only* obvious social stigma from which she suffered in the educational and intellectual fields of her day is that of femaleness.

Consecrated as crown prince by the institution, Sartre not only internalizes the belief that he is indeed a genius: by the very fact of doing so, he objectively becomes more likely to produce the evidence of being one. Bourdieu has admirably described this process – in which the socially sanctioned *belief* in one's own distinction is precisely what produces the objective conditions in which one is more likely to become distinguished, as a form of *social magic*:

> One must be noble in order to behave nobly; but one would cease being noble if one did not behave as a noble. In other words, social magic has very real effects. To assign somebody to a group with a superior essence (nobles as opposed to commoners, men as opposed to women, cultured people as opposed to uneducated people and so on) operates a subjective transformation determining a learning process which in its turn facilitates a real transformation apt to bring that person closer to the definition that has been bestowed on him. [. . .] Nothing reveals this anxiety to hoist oneself up to the heights of one's own high idea of oneself better than the somewhat pedantic efforts of the most ambitious students of the Ecole Normale (and particularly those who, due to their particular consecration, have chosen the most ambitious disciplines, such as philosophy) to impose on themselves the heroic poses or the complex roles of the intellectual nobility, or, if you like, their efforts to 'learn the difficult profession of being a genius' ('Epreuve scolaire', p. 53).

To gain admission to the highly selective preparatory classes for the ENS, to be accepted at the ENS itself, to succeed at the *agrégation*: all this may be read as so many *rites de passage*. If entry into the ENS signals rarity and therefore distinction, success at the most distinguished of exams, the *agrégation* in philosophy, adds lustre to the already successful *normalien* and legitimizes the otherwise less prestigious Sorbonne student. Beauvoir cannot expect to experience a conviction of genius equal to Sartre, but given the combination of her success at this exam, and her Parisian middle-class background, she would nevertheless seem to be objectively justified in perceiving herself to be as well placed for a distinguished intellectual career as any man except Sartre. In the 1920s and 1930s this was in fact Beauvoir's position. The blind spot is obvious: entirely overlooking the effects of gender, Beauvoir remains blithely unaware of the actual rules of the intellectual field she is in, she does not – and does not want to – see that the odds are stacked against her simply because she is a woman.

This is not to claim that Simone de Beauvoir is unaware of gender differences on a more general level. When discussing Sartre's depression, disappointment and boredom in 1935, at a time when he was still merely an unknown teacher of philosophy in Le Havre, Beauvoir, writing in 1960, comments that she was not well placed to understand him, since their situations were not as similar as they might appear:

> To pass the *agrégation* and have a profession was something he took for granted. But when I stood at the top of that flight of steps in Marseille [in 1931, when she had just arrived to take up her very first teaching position], I had turned dizzy with sheer delight: it seemed to me that, far from enduring my destiny, I had deliberately chosen it. The career in which Sartre saw his freedom foundering still meant liberation to me (PL212; FA244; TA).

Their common life as unrecognized talent languishing in the provinces must have suited Beauvoir's self-image much better than Sartre's, in so far as it enabled her to continue to minimize her own difference, and so feel *no more marginal* than Sartre or any other male *agrégé* of her generation. At the same time, she cannot help noticing the different social position and the different social expectations of men and women. Here, for instance, she clearly recognizes the different social significance of the same career. Faced with this kind of contradiction, Beauvoir tends to seek refuge in more personal explanations. In the paragraph quoted here, for instance, she immediately goes on to reinforce her representation of herself as inferior to Sartre. Another reason why she did not really understand Sartre's depression, she writes, was that her existence was no consolation to him, whereas his existence made all the difference to her: 'For me his mere existence justified the world that nothing could justify for him' (PL212; FA244; TA).

My point, then, is that there is an important tension in Beauvoir's social position from the late 1920s to the late 1940s. Internalizing and identifying with the habitus of the French intellectual field, she fails to recognize the extent to which that habitus favours men. Through her personal relationship to Sartre she gains an additional emotional stake in identifying with his aspirations to positions of cultural dominance. Yet the very fact of her femaleness places her in a far more marginal relationship to cultural legitimacy than her educational trajectory prepares her to believe. Beauvoir's specific position at once enables and disables her: if her access to higher education is what enables her to become an independent intellectual woman in the first place, it also makes her structurally incapable of perceiving the way in which she is marginalized as a woman by the intellectual field with which she identifies. Her position is doubly contradictory in that she ignores not only her own relative marginalization, but also the mechanisms of power and exclusion working in her favour. In order to understand the tensions in Beauvoir's texts, one must grasp the complexity of her situation: as an *agrégée* of philosophy she wields considerable symbolic power herself, yet as a woman she is victimized by the very same symbolic power and, moreover, enslaved to the mechanisms of the field by being unaware of both aspects of her position.

Simone de Beauvoir may thus be seen as at once victim and perpetrator of symbolic violence: perpetrator of violence in so far as she tends rhetorically to enact the very arrogance and snobbery cultivated by the ENS, or to reproduce highly condescending rhetorical structures typical of French elite teachers in their relations to their students;[42] victim of violence in her own position as a woman, whose destiny is always to be cast as no more than 'Sartre's double'.[43] Her own self-image as 'second only to Sartre' reflects this tension: submissive to Sartre; superior to everybody else, just as the examiners at the *agrégation* had said.

Given the relative absence of female predecessors, Beauvoir has to forge a space for herself in a patriarchal system, surrounded by male colleagues, friends and teachers. While repressing her own marginality, her belief in her own legitimacy also enables her to write as if she were a legitimate heir to French intellectual prestige. The result is particularly noticeable in her essays, the genre which comes closest to the kind of writing practised at school and university. It is not a coincidence that many feminists have accused Beauvoir of 'writing like a man', particularly in the early essays. The fact is that she does: not like any man (whatever that would mean), but like a highly specific group of men, the French *normaliens*. When she comes to write *The Second Sex*, she carries the polemical forcefulness of this style with her to great effect. Yet, I would argue, part of the power of *The Second Sex* is that it also undermines and transforms this rhetorical pattern. One of the most important reasons why it does so is that *The Second Sex*, unlike her previous essays, is the direct result of what one might call her auto-biographical impulse. In June 1946, she starts to think about writing her memoirs. At this point, for the first time in her life, the question of what it means to be a woman occurs to her:

> I realized that the first question to come up was: What has it meant to me to be a woman? At first I thought I could dispose of that pretty quickly. I had never had any feeling of inferiority, no one had ever said to me: "You think that way because you're a woman;' my femaleness had never been irksome to me in any way. 'For me,' I said to Sartre, 'you might almost say it just hasn't counted." 'All the same, you weren't brought up in the same way as a boy would have been; you should look into it further." I looked, and it was a revelation: this world was a masculine world, my childhood had been nourished by myths forged by men, and I hadn't reacted to them in at all the same way I should have done if I had been a boy. I was so interested in this discovery that I abandoned my project for a personal confession in order to give all my attention to finding out about the condition of woman in its

broadest terms. I went to the Bibliothèque Nationale to do some reading, and what I studied were the myths of femininity (FC103; FCa136; TA).

But if the desire for personal confession now spurs her to self-discovery, it does not seem to make her reflect on her own marginality: the movement in this passage is from 'what it means to *me* to be a woman' to 'the female condition *in general*'. The personal confession is turned into a generalizing essay, born out of deep personal investment, to be sure, but nevertheless presented as yet another masterful essay in the mould one might expect from a brilliant *agrégée*. Facing her femaleness, Beauvoir finds a powerful voice of her own and an intellectual terrain not blocked by father figures of one kind or another. Yet her approach is complex and contradictory, allowing her as it were at once to accept and deny the implications of being born a woman. If *The Second Sex* conclusively proves that women under patriarchy are oppressed and shunted into positions of marginality, nothing in Beauvoir's tone or style reveals that she has experienced this to be true in her own case. Instead we find all the resources of her excellent education deployed to the full: rapidly establishing the necessary index cards, digesting and generalizing her notes according to the rules of reason as taught in French academic philosophy at the time, Beauvoir in fact generalizes her own condition, apparently without any recognition that it is *herself* who provides the paradigm case.

In *The Second Sex* this strategy is carried to extreme lengths: blithely universalizing her own and her female friends' experiences, Beauvoir presents her findings as typical of *the* female condition everywhere. The British anthropologist Judith Okely has shrewdly pointed out that this in fact turns *The Second Sex* into concealed ethnography, 'an anthropological village study on specific women'. Beauvoir's village, Okely adds, is 'largely mid-century Paris and the women studied, including herself, are mainly middle class. [. . .] A paradoxical strength is the hidden use of herself as a case study' (pp. 71–2). Severely chastizing Sartre for *his* use of this specific intellectual strategy, Bourdieu sees it as a rejection of any specific social determination of the intellectual, that is to say, as the very antithesis of Bourdieu's own project: 'By the universalising of the particular case that occurs whenever an analysis of essence is applied to a lived experience of unspecified social particularity, Sartre converts the experience of the intellectual into an ontological structure, constitutive of human experience as a whole' ('Sartre', p. 12.).

At first glance, Beauvoir's use of this technique might seem to be counterproductive. If feminism in some sense or other has to assert the specificity of women against any generalizing discourse of 'man', one may question how it can profit from rhetorical strategies which inevitably tend to erase difference in the name of universal essences. One of the many paradoxes of *The Second Sex*, however, is the way in which Beauvoir's universalizing rhetorical strategy surprisingly often works in favour of her feminist project, rather than against it. For as Monique Wittig has brilliantly shown in her essay 'The Mark of Gender', to try to universalize the *feminine* under patriarchy is not at all the same thing as to concur in the universalization of the *masculine*. Rather, it must be seen as an effort to reverse the dominant structures of language and ideology. As such, it is one among a series of necessary strategies to be mobilized in what Wittig sees as the feminist guerilla struggle for liberation. To give the particular experience of some women the philosophical dignity of universal structures may in some contexts be a highly effective countermove to the patriarchal wish to consider women as insignificant, idiosyncratic and deviant from some male norm. This is not to say, however, that *The Second Sex* may be compared to *Les guérillères*. Deeply unaware of the nature of her own rhetoric in *The Second Sex*, Beauvoir does not control it: sometimes it works for her and sometimes it does not.

Unlike Wittig, however, Beauvoir is not producing her text from a position of conscious marginality: the tensions in her discourse can only be explained if, in some curious sense, one sees her as *investigating her own marginality from a position of centrality*. This is indeed the logical outcome of Beauvoir's speaking position, with its uneasy mixture of an assured belief in her own legitimacy juxtaposed with an intermittent awareness of her own secondary status in a patriarchal field. Her most powerful work – texts such as *L'Invitée*, *The Second Sex*, *Memoirs of a Dutiful Daughter* and *The Prime of Life* – is produced not from the repression of this contradiction, but from the painful conflict arising between these two opposing moments of identification.

BEAUVOIR AND DISTINCTION

Beauvoir's situation – one in which she is investigating her own marginality from a position of centrality – has far-reaching implications. Here I shall simply indicate how her specific position as an intellectual woman can account for much of the hostile reception of her work, and – more importantly – how it may help us to understand why her place in the current canon of modern French literature is decidedly precarious. More than anything, the striking lack of recent French research on Beauvoir bears witness to the current distrust of her work in France. Beauvoir, it would seem, is not *distinguished* enough to provide a promising terrain from which to launch an intellectual career. Given the influence of certain French intellectual trends in the English-speaking world, such feelings are not entirely absent outside France either.

There is, then, in Beauvoir's texts a conflict between her own desire to *minimize* her difference, to cast herself as a consecrated intellectual just like Sartre, and the fact of her relative marginalization as a woman. The tendency to minimize her difference surfaces even in small and relatively trivial details. When discussing the intellectual superiority of Sartre in *Memoirs of a Dutiful Daughter*, for instance, she claims that he was only two years older than she: 'Two years older than myself – two years which he had turned to good account – and having got off to a better start much earlier than I had, he had a deeper and wider knowledge of everything', she writes (MDD340; MJF475). But the fact is that he was born in June 1905 and she in January 1908. Given the French educational system, this means that in terms of *school attendance* the difference between them was *three* years: he sat his *bac* in 1922, she in 1925. Clearly dictated by rhetorical needs – after all, a sentence reading 'he was two and a half years older than me' would have seemed somewhat odd in its overexactness – Beauvoir's writing 'two years' rather than 'three years' serves to reinforce the impression that Sartre's intellectual superiority had little to do with his educational advantages over her. The tension between her own belief in her equality and her objective marginality often reveals itself as cultural *anxiety* or *insecurity*, as well as in a tendency to overdo things in order to reassure herself as to her competence. What her detractors label her 'school-marmish' manner, for example, is precisely the moments in which her own lack of assurance betrays itself. Ideally suited to brandishing Beauvoir as 'undistinguished', the *topos* of the schoolmarm signals above all that she is not *high-class* enough in her tastes, life-style and writings. In his preface to the English-language edition of *Distinction*, Bourdieu points out that intellectual life in France is organized according to an 'aristocratic model of "court society"' (p. xi). In the twentieth century, he claims, this tradition has been 'personified by a Parisian *haute bourgeoisie* which, combining all forms of prestige and all the titles of economic and cultural nobility, has no counterpart elsewhere, at least for the arrogance of its cultural judgements' (p. xi). There is then, in France, a continuous struggle to impose the values of this specific set on to the cultural field as a whole. If one specific trend turns out to become too 'popular', new ones are invented. In general, Bourdieu argues, high bourgeois taste in France is above all characterized by its high levels of aestheticization, stylization and distance from any conceivable utility and necessity. 'Economic power is first and foremost a power to keep economic necessity at arm's length', Bourdieu writes:

> Material and symbolic consumption of works of art constitutes one of the supreme manifestations of *ease*, in the sense both of objective leisure and subjective facility. The detachment of the pure gaze cannot be separated from a general disposition towards the 'gratuitous' and the 'disinterested,' the

paradoxical product of a negative economic conditioning which, through facility and freedom, engenders distance vis-à-vis necessity. [. . .] This affirmation of power over a dominated necessity always implies a claim to a legitimate superiority over those who, because they cannot assert the same contempt for contingencies in gratuitous luxury and conspicuous consumption, remain dominated by ordinary interests and agencies. The tastes of freedom can only assert themselves as such in relation to the tastes of necessity, which are thereby brought to the level of the aesthetic and so defined as vulgar (*Distinction*, pp. 55–6).

Presented as a simple schoolteacher, Beauvoir comes across as petty-bourgeois, not up to the standards of sensitivity, refinement, elegance and aesthetic sophistication expected by the true *noblesse*.

The next step is to turn her presumed lack of taste into an indictment of her politics. Beauvoir's autobiographical project is doomed at the outset: unless it rises to the aesthetic heights of a Leiris in *L'âge d'homme* or a Sartre in *Les mots*, the very genre of autobiography must be suspect in the eyes of the true aesthete. The saving grace of the autobiographies that do pass the test of distinction, it would seem, is that it is quite impossible to tell what actually happened to the author. Not so in the case of Simone de Beauvoir: methodically setting out to provide an earnest account of her life, dates and all, she proves herself to be entirely lacking in the necessary sense of 'serious playfulness' required by high French distinction. There is almost always in her texts a touch of anxious eagerness to be taken seriously, an interest in ethical and moral issues relevant to real life, fatal to anybody laying claim to true distinction in the French cultural field.

Her specific blend of ethical seriousness, literary realism and objective intellectual capital is precisely what makes her such a widely read novelist: Beauvoir's *appeal* is clearly petty-bourgeois, perfectly suited to readers who desire a certain intellectual *cachet*, but who are not 'advanced' enough to appreciate the purer pleasures of formal play.[44] In the eyes of the arbiters of taste in France, nothing can be more despicable than to be petty-bourgeois: if the truly popular, peasant or working-class object may be perceived as possessing a certain charming naivety or 'authenticity' of its own, the petty bourgeoisie is distinguished above all by its desperate cultural *anxiety*, its incessant striving to be *à la hauteur*. But this is the very antithesis of true distinction, which seeks to present itself as easy, relaxed and above all *natural*. Beauvoir's account in *The Prime of Life* of how she spent two years in wartime Paris systematically extending her knowledge of music, for instance, is enough to make any 'truly distinguished' *connoisseur* cringe:

In order to fill my all too ample leisure hours, I took to listening to music and, true to form, set about the business with obsessional intensity. I profited vastly from it, too: as in the most formative moments of my childhood, pleasure and knowledge coincided. [. . .] I played my records ten times in succession, analysing every phrase, trying to grasp it in its unity. I read a number of works on musical history and studies of various individual composers. I became a regular visitor at Chanteclerc's on boulevard Saint-Michel [. . .] and I filled numerous gaps in my musical knowledge (PL422; FA484; TA).

Beauvoir here makes the fatal mistake of presenting herself not only as an autodidact (that is to say, as lacking in educational capital), but as belonging to that coarse class of people deprived of a 'natural' sense of music. Turning music into an object of diligent self-improvement, Beauvoir only succeeds in revealing her inability to be distinguished. Or as Bourdieu, discussing so-called classical music, caustically puts it in *Distinction*:

As regards its social definition, 'musical culture' is something other than a quantity of knowledge and experiences combined with the capacity to talk about them. Music is the most 'spiritual' of the arts of the spirit and a love of music is a guarantee of 'spirituality.' [. . .] For a bourgeois world which conceives its relation to the populace in terms of the relationship of the soul to the body, 'insensitivity to music' doubtless represents a particularly unavowable form of materialist coarseness. But this is not all. Music is the 'pure' art par excellence. It says nothing and has *nothing to say*. [. . .] Music represents the most radical and most absolute form of the negation of the world, and especially the social world, which the bourgeois ethos tends to demand of all forms of art (p. 19).

In the same way, Beauvoir's account of her scholarly successes singularly fails to display the distance and disinterestedness typical of true – playful, elegant, aestheticizing – *bourgeois* distinction. It is as if Beauvoir in her memoirs at once *underestimates* her own intellectual achievements and *over-estimates* the importance of her *certificats* and diplomas by mentioning every one of them at some length. As far as I know Sartre never bothered to list his own *certificats de licence* anywhere: a consecrated genius does not need to justify himself in such petty ways. Given her objective marginalization in patriarchal society, a woman, on the other hand, *always* needs to justify her presence in male company: the catch is that 'true' distinction is entirely incompatible with anything but the most radical *insouciance*. To betray even the slightest sense of anxiety, vulnerability or displacement is fatal. In a patriarchal intellectual field, the female intellectual will never be able perfectly to display the cavalier disdain of the dandy: she is doomed to lose out in the game of distinction. On current standards of distinction in

French cultural life, Beauvoir stands no chance at all of becoming the Baudelaire – or even the Lord Byron – of our century.

3

Politics and the Intellectual Woman: Clichés and Commonplaces in the Reception of Simone de Beauvoir

In France, if you are a writer, to be a woman is simply to provide sticks to be beaten with.

(Force of Circumstance)

Her works, written with undeniable talent, are haughty, cold and dry. In this highly talented writer, the female intellectual has killed the generous resources of the heart (Chaigne, 1954).

Her passion-based politics turned Beauvoir into a ferocious enemy of France years ago (Chrestien, 1963, p. 229).

She never ceased being a docile pupil (Senart, 1963, p. 232).

One should not go too easy on the simplistic manicheism of this female philosopher overcome by political passion as others are overcome by debauchery (Domaize, 1964, p. 233).

Simone de Beauvoir's naiveté has its source in a supreme and limiting egoism (Marks, 1973, p. 19).

For over sixty years, without a hitch and without a surprise, she played on her little instrument the same old tune, so suitable for a board of examiners (Bourdoiseau, 1986).

To say that Beauvoir is perceived as an undistinguished writer is to make a fairly general claim. There is, after all, a whole variety of ways of falling short of the standards of distinction dominant in French literature. How does the question of gender surface in the responses to Beauvoir's works? And how do her outspoken political positions affect her readers? At first glance, the answer is obvious: together these two factors – her sex and her politics – are fatal to her reputation as a writer. Before examining this phenomenon more closely, however, one should remember that from the very beginning of her career, Simone de Beauvoir was an immensely popular writer. All her major works reached mass audiences. Challenging established hierarchies and conventions, they often provoked intensely engaged responses ranging from profound admiration to violent hostility. By producing a highly public persona for their author, her autobiographies added fuel to the controversies. The outright hostility of some of the French obituaries of Beauvoir indicate that by the time of her death in 1986 her name had lost none of its power to displease. To approach Simone de Beauvoir is to find oneself enmeshed in a web of hotly disputed opinions and entrenched public myths, and in this situation 'Simone de Beauvoir' is not simply the name of a person who wrote novels, essays and memoirs, but a site of ideological and aesthetic conflict. It is impossible to pretend to be 'neutral' in relation to Simone de Beauvoir: to write on Beauvoir is truly to become, in Sartre's sense, a committed writer. My own work is no exception: reading Beauvoir's critics, I realized just how difficult it is for a woman to be taken seriously as an intellectual, even in the late twentieth century. The indignation I felt – and still feel – at that discovery provided much of the energy required to write this book.[1]

I do not intend to survey the whole mass of existing literature on Simone de Beauvoir. So far, over forty full-length studies have appeared, hundreds of scholarly essays have been published, and there has been massive newspaper and magazine coverage. Instead I intend to explore the striking hostility of Beauvoir criticism: the fact that there is a surprisingly high number of condescending, sarcastic, sardonic or dismissive accounts.[2] The unusual acrimony of the reception of Beauvoir's works has also been noticed by Elaine Marks, in the introduction to her excellent anthology *Critical Essays on Simone de Beauvoir*:

> At least half of the critical essays I have included in this volume are, whether discreetly or obtrusively, sarcastic. They present Simone de Beauvoir as a slightly ridiculous figure, naive in her passions, sloppy in her scholarship, inaccurate in her documentation, generally out of her depth and inferior as a writer. Indeed the tone of superiority that many critics, of both sexes, adopt when writing about Simone de Beauvoir deserves special attention (p. 2).

In her meticulous study of Beauvoir's political commitment, Anne Whitmarsh makes a somewhat similar point: 'Partisan judgments on the work of Simone de Beauvoir are the norm,' she writes, 'tending to the extremes of either virulent attack or uncritical admiration' (p. 2). My own view is that there is far more denigration and far less adulation than one might expect, and that a surprising number of critics must have invested considerable time and energy in a writer they plainly detest. Equally striking is the way in which well-intentioned or ostensibly 'neutral' writers, while willingly declaring their admiration for Beauvoir's work, almost imperceptibly and in spite of themselves move into a position of critical superiority. In a whole range of different contexts, then, Simone de Beauvoir's qualities as a person and as a writer are critically judged and found wanting.

Comparable French women writers are not treated in this way: nothing in the criticism of, say, Simone Weil, Marguerite Yourcenar, Marguerite Duras or Nathalie Sarraute matches the frequency and intensity of virulence displayed by so many of Simone de Beauvoir's critics.[3] It is not easy for a feminist to deal with such an overwhelmingly hostile reception of a woman writer. There is an almost spontaneous desire to leap immediately to the wronged woman's defence, to assume that such critics *must* be patriarchal henchmen. But what if they could be shown to be right? Perhaps Simone de Beauvoir simply *is* an inferior writer? There can be no reason, not even for feminists, to object to discussion of problematic elements in a writer's work. But this is not what is going on in Beauvoir criticism. As I will go on to show, the hostile critics' favourite strategy is to personalize the issues, to reduce the book to the woman: their aim is clearly to discredit her as a speaker, not to enter into debate with her. These critics are out to cast doubts on Beauvoir's right to produce any kind of public discourse. By discrediting her status as a speaker, they intend to preclude any further discussion of what she actually says. In this situation, to defend Beauvoir is to do no more than to insist on her – and every other woman's – elementary democratic right to participate in the political, intellectual and literary debates of her time. It is only when this right has been firmly established that we can get on with the far more interesting task of analysing and criticizing Beauvoir's positions and views. My defence of Beauvoir's right to intervene in the intellectual and political fields – *and to be taken seriously* – is absolute. To insist on this point is precisely to clear the ground for *real* discussion of her own highly complex and sometimes more than dubious positions.

To have to insist on women's right to speak in the 1990s, more than forty years after the publication of *The Second Sex*, is disappointing, to say the least. Such was my naive belief in progress, at least on this point, that I originally intended to organize this chapter chronologically. The intention would have been to demonstrate how the reception of Beauvoir's works changed in different political contexts. Much to my chagrin I soon discovered that, on the whole, the very same sexist clichés surface unchanged from the 1950s to the 1990s: feminism has clearly not made that much of a difference, at least not in the French cultural climate.

Not even Beauvoir criticism, however, is wholly dominated by hostility. The first study ever published, Geneviève Gennari's warm and admiring *Simone de Beauvoir*, appeared in 1958, the year in which Beauvoir published the first volume of her autobiography. The publication of *Memoirs of a Dutiful Daughter* spurred several committed Catholics to write about her as the great lost daughter of the Catholic Church. Out to oppose Beauvoir's philosophical views, these sexist (and, it must be said, male) authors (Henry, Hourdin and Gagnebin) nevertheless emphasize their respect and admiration for Beauvoir's *oeuvre* and certainly take her seriously as an intellectual. There are also two sympathetic existentialist and/or socialist studies from the 1960s (Jeanson and Julienne-Caffié) and, as might be expected, a fair number of reasonably open-minded studies of a more or less scholarly kind. Beauvoir has also inspired a series of popular (and sometimes sensationalist) works intended for a non-academic market, ranging from the appalling *Hearts and Minds* by Axel Madsen to the somewhat sugary and glamorizing but still readable biography by Claude Francis and Fernande Gonthier, and the serviceable presentation of her life and work by Lisa Appignanesi. In 1990, Deirdre Bair's massive *Simone de Beauvoir: A Biography* finally appeared, aimed as much at a popular as at a scholarly market.[4]

In the 1980s, Beauvoir studies shifted decisively away from France as well as from so-called mainstream preoccupations with political and philosophical themes. Before 1980, Beauvoir critics were predominantly French: only five out of an estimated twenty-one full-length studies were published in English. The first English-language study, Elaine Marks's *Simone de Beauvoir: Encounters with Death*, did not appear until 1973. From 1980 to 1992, however, of twenty-one books devoted to Beauvoir, seventeen appeared in English. Of the remaining four, one was published in Sweden (Lundgren-Gothlin), two were written by French academics working in the United States (Zéphir, Francis and Gonthier's biography), and the fourth is not a study, but a personal memoir written by a friend of Beauvoir's, Françoise d'Eaubonne. Never strong (a few short theses, a couple of books intended for *lycée* students), intellectual interest in Simone de Beauvoir in France now seems almost non-existent. The one remarkable exception to this rule is the French feminist philosopher Michèle Le Doeuff and her incisive essays on Beauvoir's difficult relationship to philosophy, as well as her brilliant study *Hipparchia's Choice*, where Beauvoir is discussed in the context of women's relationship to philosophy in general.[5]

There are some obvious reasons for this well-nigh total desertion of Beauvoir by the French: in the 1970s and 1980s French intellectual fashions (structuralism, poststructuralism, Lacanian psychoanalysis, postmodernism) left no space at all for an unreconstructed existentialist humanist of Beauvoir's type. Poststructuralist feminist theory in France, as represented by Hélène Cixous, Luce Irigaray and Julia Kristeva for instance, has had very little to say about the author of *The Second Sex*.[6] Indeed, the group around *Psych et Po* always considered her a phallic woman, complicit with the dominant forms of masculine power. Interviewed by the left-wing newspaper *Libération* the day after Beauvoir's death in April 1986, Antoinette Fouque, the leading light of *Psych et Po*, expressed her hostility towards the author of *The Second Sex*: 'Only one month ago,' Fouque says, 'she was giving interviews in order to assert her universalist, egalitarian, assimilatory and normalizing feminist positions, roundly attacking anybody who did not fall into line' (p. 5). The gist of Fouque's argument is that now that Beauvoir is dead, feminism is finally free to move into the twenty-first century.

In Beauvoir studies, then, 1980 signals the start of a decade of Anglo-American feminism. But Beauvoir proves controversial for British and American feminists as well. Some feminists take up a hostile or disappointed position (Leighton, Mary Evans), some verge on the adulatory (Ascher, Patterson), whereas others produce some of the most judicious readings of her work to be found anywhere (Okely, Fallaize, Lundgren-Gothlin). Only one writer, Jane Heath, has tried to rescue Beauvoir for poststructuralist feminism. When men write on Beauvoir in the 1980s, it tends to be because they too are interested in feminism (Zéphir, Hatcher).[7] Although it is difficult to overestimate the importance of Beauvoir's feminist work, it may look as if critics writing after 1980 have neglected other aspects of her *oeuvre*. Whatever the importance of *The Second Sex*, it ought not to be forgotten that until she was well over 60, Beauvoir did not think of herself as a feminist at all.[8]

In general, however, the reception of Beauvoir's work remains far more hostile than might reasonably be expected. What is it about Beauvoir that produces this effect? Why do so many readers find themselves stirred to the point of irritation or even rage? While some of the answers to these questions must be sought in Beauvoir's own texts, it also remains true that the critics' own preconceptions or prejudices shape their perceptions of Beauvoir. By focusing on certain recurring themes in hostile responses to Beauvoir, I hope to detect the critics' own *parti pris* and subject their critical and ideological strategies to debate.[9]

REDUCING THE BOOK TO THE WOMAN

It is impossible to read much hostile Beauvoir criticism without noticing the recurrence of certain *topoi*, or commonplaces. 'Books by women are treated as though they themselves were women, and criticism embarks, at

its happiest, upon an intellectual measuring of busts and hips', Mary
Ellmann notes (*Thinking About Women*, p. 29). In the case of Simone de
Beauvoir, her political and philosophical positions are treated in this way as
well. It is as if the very fact of her femaleness blocks any further discussion
of the issues at stake, be they literary, theoretical or political. Instead the
critic obsessively returns to the question of femininity, or more specifically
to what one might call the *personality topos*, passionately discussing
Beauvoir's looks, character, private life or morality. The implication is that
whatever a woman says, or writes, or thinks is less important and less
interesting than what she *is*.

It is in this context that the figure of the *midinette*, or shop-girl, makes
her appearance. In France, the *midinette* has inescapable connotations of
naivety, shallow superficiality and sentimentality. The *Petit Robert* defines
the term as 'simple and frivolous city-girl'.[10] The *midinette topos* reaches its
most dignified expression in Claude Lévi-Strauss's *Tristes tropiques*, where in
splendidly patriarchal manner he accuses existentialism in general of being
nothing more than a kind of 'shop-girl metaphysics', since its so-called
thought is simply the 'promotion of personal preoccupations to the dignity
of philosophical problems' (p. 61). 'When she travels, she's a shop-girl
sending postcards to her family: "wonderful views!"', Eric Neuhoff writes
about *Adieux: A Farewell to Sartre*. The same reporter, in what is surely the
most distasteful reference to Beauvoir to be found anywhere,[11] does not
shrink from comparing Beauvoir to Milou, the dog belonging to the well-
known cartoon figure Tintin: 'Today, evidence in hand, one may be
allowed to think that Simone de Beauvoir was Milou. A Milou who a year
after Tintin's death would pee on his golf-trousers.' Etienne Lalou, review-
ing *Les Belles Images* in *L'Express*, insists on reading the text in the light of
the 'two opposing poles of Simone de Beauvoir's personality: the austere
philosopher and the sentimental shop-girl' (p. 108). Bernard Pivot sounds
the same note when he labels Simone de Beauvoir 'a true woman of letters
(for the agony column)'. The right-wing extremist Robert Poulet goes
even further and declares that *all* literary ladies including Beauvoir are
midinettes en diable (p. 174).

Many critics first reduce every text by Beauvoir to her own *persona*, and
then go on to declare that such autobiographical effusions cannot be
considered art at all. Such involvement with one's own life, they argue, is
no more than a kind of pedestrian labour of documentation, more akin to
history than to literature. Brian T. Fitch claims that *L'Invitée* (*She Came to
Stay*) is so autobiographical that it cannot be considered a 'work of art
existing in itself'; its interest is more a matter for literary history than for
literary criticism, he adds (p. 13). Not surprisingly, he proceeds to conclude
that Simone de Beauvoir lacks imagination (p. 149). Robert Poulet sees
The Mandarins as a typically female novel, that is to say as desperately

confessional and extremely uninteresting (see pp. 173–4). 'In fact,' he continues:

> Almost all these amazons of science, of thought or of politics pay for their spiritual independence with a kind of secret infantilism. [. . .] The female temper is not made for freedom: in order to make the most of its exquisiteness, it needs limits and constraints. Every time one hoists a daughter of Eve on to a summit, she behaves badly and says silly things. [. . .] To put it frankly, [Simone de Beauvoir] is not at all a strong woman, but a timid, hesitant and nostalgic being who forces herself to march with a determined step under the helmet of her artificially hardened cerebrality (pp. 174–5).

One critic demonstrates an unusually intense urge to reduce everything Beauvoir wrote to a distasteful expression of her personality. In this sense Jean-Raymond Audet comes across as a particularly extreme example of a widespread trend in Beauvoir-criticism. Insisting that *all* of Beauvoir's fictional characters (but particularly the female ones) 'are' Beauvoir herself, Audet – and the plethora of other critics who have recourse to the same strategy – proceeds to attribute every possible vice to the hapless author, including that of perversely attributing her own psychology to her characters. Needless to say, the circularity of this 'argument' is no deterrent. Heavily reliant on Elaine Marks's much more thoughtful work on the topic, Audet's study of Beauvoir and death is quite fanatical in its efforts to demonstrate that Beauvoir herself is narcissistic, egoistic and naive: 'What naivety! What narcissism! And what an obsessional desire [*manie*] to endow her characters with all the vicissitudes of her own psychological, sociological and political development!' (p. 91).

According to Audet, Beauvoir is not only Françoise of *L'Invitée* (p. 49), but the neurotic actress Régine of *All Men are Mortal* – 'an eminently faithful portrait of our author', he comments (p. 102) – in fact, she *is* every single character she ever invented, including the protagonists of the 1960s fiction, such as Monique in 'The Woman Destroyed', a housewife who has never had an independent career and who has a nervous breakdown when her husband of twenty years leaves her; and Murielle in 'The Monologue', a woman who drove her teenage daughter to suicide, and now is verging on the psychotic in her self-indulgent torrent of imprecations and denunciation of her family, ex-friends and ex-lovers. The anorexic advertising executive, Laurence, in *Les Belles Images* is another faithful representation of Beauvoir's own personality, Audet claims. In *All Said and Done*, Beauvoir comments on the way in which many readers strenuously seek to equate her with these characters:

> Yet many readers claim that they see me in all my female characters. Laurence in *Les Belles Images*, disgusted with life to the point of anorexia, is

supposed to be me. The angry university-woman in 'The Age of Discretion' is also supposed to be me. [. . .] And of course 'The Woman Destroyed' could not be anyone but myself. [. . .] One woman wrote to ask whether the chairwoman of her literary club was right in saying that Sartre had broken with me. Replying to questioners, my friend Stépha pointed out that I was no longer forty, that I had no daughters, and that my life was unlike Monique's in every way. They allowed themselves to be convinced. 'But,' said one of them crossly, 'Why does she fix it so that all her novels seem to be autobiographical?' 'She's only trying to make them ring true,' replied Stépha (ASD144; TCF180–1).

It is amusing to see how a critic of Audet's calibre tries to get round this statement, not to mention the texts themselves. Having quoted the passage reproduced here, his only comment is a smug and self-satisfied: 'What naive candour!' (p. 122). In fact, he says, he totally agrees with the 'chairwoman of the literary club', because what else but a break with Sartre could have produced the filthy language of 'The Monologue'? As for *Les Belles Images* he is even more inventive: 'This time we will not try to show that Laurence is Simone de Beauvoir', he triumphantly exclaims: 'For who else can she be?' (p. 125).

A traditional Romantic critic might have tried to turn Beauvoir's apparently endless capacity for projecting herself into a wide range of fictional characters into grounds for praise, comparing her to Shakespeare ('myriad-minded Beauvoir!') or at the very least to Walt Whitman ('I am large . . . I contain multitudes'). This never happens in Beauvoir criticism. Whenever the *topos* of the author's projection of herself into her fiction crops up, it is always in order to demonstrate her regrettable *limitations*. In particular it is invoked to 'prove' that Beauvoir as a person and as a writer is narcissistic, egocentric and arrogant: she is only interested in herself. Such extraordinary claims assume first, that Beauvoir in fact always writes about herself; second, that she always approves of all her characters as perfect incarnations of her own virtues (it should hardly be necessary to say that both assumptions are demonstrably false); and third – by far the most important point – that to show any sign of self-satisfaction is a bad thing in a woman.

The very fact of writing a multi-volume autobiography, for example, is presented as evidence of her relentless narcissism. It may be necessary to point out that this is not generally the reaction to male autobiography. While not hesitating to call Elias Canetti egoistic, a review of the third volume of his autobiography first signals Canetti's self-involvement: 'Canetti is interested in his fellows only for the discoveries they might lead him to; what compassion there is in his work is mostly reserved for himself. [. . .] His descriptions of others are rarely sweetened by generosity', only to turn such egocentricity into a virtue:

But although Canetti is one of the great egoists of literature, to dwell on his vanity would blind us to his true purpose, which is to convey the reality of the inner life in all its aspects. Flitting among many genres, he remakes each in his own image; he is constantly surprised by his perception, and the record is of a man charting new ways of experiencing himself (Campbell, p. 926).

Spanning many genres and comprising both travel writing and auto-biography, Beauvoir's *oeuvre* is in some ways similar to Canetti's. In her case, however, not only is the fact that she often writes in autobiographical genres used as evidence of her debilitating egocentricity; her discussions of traditional 'non-personal' topics, such as politics and philosophy, tend to be disparaged as mere displacements of the personal.[12] A favourite variation on this theme is the tendency to perceive Beauvoir's writings as the simple effect of her personal relationship to Sartre. Her emotional ties to him explain her texts, it is claimed; there is thus no need to assume that she possesses much creativity or insight of her own. When she received an important Austrian literary prize in 1979, *Figaro magazine* came up with the following headlines: 'A perfect bourgeoise: Simone de Beauvoir. Simone de Beauvoir, the first woman to receive the Austrian Prize for European Literature, owes everything to a man' (Cheverny, p. 57). On her death, *Le Monde* ran an article entitled 'Her works: popularization rather than creation' (Jannoud).

USING THE PERSONAL TO DISCREDIT THE POLITICAL

As might be expected, a politically outspoken woman such as Beauvoir attracts much hostility from her opponents on the left as well as on the right. Paradoxically, however, politically motivated critiques of Beauvoir contain surprisingly little discussion of politics and much apparently point-less dwelling on her personality and private life. In fact such dwelling on her personality is best described as the politicized use of the sexist person-ality *topos*. The intended effect is to depoliticize her by presenting her political choices not as the outcome of careful reflection on the issues at stake, but as the inexplicable *élans* of an overemotional or even hysterical woman. Having reduced their opponent to a neurotic woman, such hostile critics avoids having to reveal – and defend – their own politics, let alone their own personal problems.

The dividing line between sexist and other kinds of political use of this rhetorical strategy can never be clear: in many cases – whether intentionally or not – an ambiguous double effect is produced. Particularly efficient in this respect is the use of the patriarchal cliché of the 'unfeminine woman'.

Beauvoir is regularly represented as cold, selfish, egocentric and uncaring, and above all as *non-maternal*. 'She is totally devoid of the triple instinct with which woman is endowed', a female Catholic comments in 1984; 'the maternal instinct, the nurturing instinct, and the nest-building instinct' (Levaux, p. 17). Mobilized in political contexts, this *topos* is used to imply that her political commitment is devoid of normal concern for the well-being of the human race. However much Beauvoir herself emphasizes her opposition to exploitation, oppression and suffering, she is suspected of not 'really' caring for the suffering of every victim of every conflict in the world.

Hardly ever used against male politicians, this specific rhetorical strategy is deeply dishonest. It tends to be assumed that men take difficult political decisions with reluctance, weighed down by the burden of their heavy responsibilities. Churchill, Roosevelt or De Gaulle were never suspected of lacking ordinary human feelings every time they imposed costly sacrifices on their men. Even Sartre rarely gets attacked for his lack of humanity.[13] If Simone de Beauvoir tends to be accused of callousness by her political opponents, it would seem primarily to be because she is a woman who refuses to remain confined to the private sphere. Beauvoir, then, is regularly put in a classic double bind: if she writes about politics, she is told that she is cold, unfeeling and unfeminine, but also that her political ideas are simple displacements of her own emotional problems. If she actually writes about her own emotions, however, she is immediately accused of being selfish or unartistic. Like Virginia Woolf, Beauvoir pays dearly indeed for the sin of not being the incarnation of the ultimate non-writing woman, the Angel in the House.

An illuminating example of right-wing efforts to mobilize the personal in order to discredit the political can be found in Renée Winegarten's 1988 study with the somewhat understated title *Simone de Beauvoir: A Critical View*. Steeped in Reaganism, Winegarten's essay usefully demonstrates that Beauvoir has lost none of her power to threaten the *bien-pensants* of this world. Winegarten's primary concern is to present Beauvoir's political positions as utterly irrational, and therefore as further evidence of her extraordinary naivety, self-deception and lack of ordinary human qualities such as care and compassion for others. Her principal strategy is not openly to oppose her views, to meet Beauvoir head-on in the political arena, but to present her political decisions as the result of male influence and deep self-deception, and in any case as defying logic, common sense and so-called 'human values'. In Winegarten's text, the *topos* of the hysteric – the irrational, overemotional female – is skilfully blended with that of the harridan or shrew. Beauvoir's socialism, for instance, is reduced to a symptom of personal conflicts: 'If she remained unceasing in her opposition to the bourgeoisie,' Winegarten writes, 'it was doubtless because she heard in it her father's voice' (p. 15). If it is not Sartre or her father who is responsible for her political commitment, it is some other man, usually a lover. Her rejection of US politics in the McCarthy era is blamed on Nelson Algren, the Chicago novelist:

> He was among those oversimplifiers who were convinced of the decay of capitalism, and whose sympathies lay with the cause of revolution. [. . .] What he did was to show her the worst and darkest side of American life, confirm her prejudices, and inculcate an extreme view of the country as one of exploiters and exploited, a view from which she would never depart, and which would harden with the years (pp. 68–9).

Summarizing the whole experience as Beauvoir's 'slumming with Algren' (p. 69), Winegarten clearly thinks that only a woman blinded by erotic passion could believe that American society was made up of exploiters and exploited.

To Winegarten, Beauvoir's strong anti-imperialist stance comes across as utterly incomprehensible. How could she exult at her own country's defeat in Indochina and Algeria? Clearly utterly baffled by the whole question, the critic tries to make Beauvoir look like an overemotional hypocrite:

> Throughout the autobiography, there runs an account of her reactions to political affairs in which others were actively engaged: her anxiety, her indignation, her anger, her tears, her pain and horror at the suffering of the victims, her diasaffection, even her 'satisfaction' at the humiliating French defeat at Dien Bien Phu which ended the war in Indochina. [. . .] Such intellectual hatred of her culture and civilisation while at the same time serving it through her literary efforts is difficult to appreciate. It is a type of alienation that has grown more common (pp. 119–20).

For Winegarten, then, even to think that France, the colonial power, might not represent *democracy* to the vast majority of Vietnamese or Algerians is evidence of abject surrender to irrational and selfish egoism. Winegarten is particularly fond of the stereotype of the cold, unfeeling, inhuman, political woman. To her, Beauvoir's awareness, in *A Very Easy Death*, of the social aspects of her mother's final illness, for instance, is chilling evidence that the daughter sacrificed every normal human feeling on the altar of her embittered and misunderstood socialism.

Readings such as Winegarten's do not come across as entirely disinterested exercises. Winegarten herself, however, insists that she is out to correct Beauvoir's false views, to *demystify* the ideological aberrations of her subject in the name of truth: 'This study offers [. . .] an attempt to probe the mystifications of an all-too-common modern form of rationalism which leads its adherents to see only what they wish to see, where change and revolution are at stake – whether in personal or public relations' (p. 6). The rhetorical move here is obvious: the cumbersome periphrasis 'an all-too-common modern form of rationalism' is deployed as a trope destined to mask Winegarten's real target: any form of socialism or Marxism. Against the impaired eyesight of modern Marxists, she sets her own superior insights into the *true* nature of things. It goes without saying that where Beauvoir is blinkered and ideological, Winegarten is impartial and *right*. In this she remains faithful to the everyday definition of ideology, as summarized by Terry Eagleton:

> To claim in ordinary conversation that someone is speaking ideologically is surely to hold that they are judging a particular issue through some rigid framework of preconceived ideas which distorts their understanding. I view things as they really are; you squint at them through a tunnel vision imposed by some extraneous body of doctrine. There is usually a suggestion that this involves an oversimplifying view of the world – that to judge or speak 'ideologically' is to do so schematically, stereotypically, and perhaps with the faintest hint of fanaticism (p. 3).

Whatever else Winegarten's thinly veiled defence of imperialism, capitalism and exploitative individualism may be, it surely is not impartial: it ought not to be necessary to point out that she cannot possibly claim to have objective truth where Beauvoir only has ideology. For me, Winegarten is never more ideological than when she tries to pass her own political prejudices off not simply as universal truths but, more insidiously, as *common sense*.

JUDICIOUS BALANCE: LIBERALISM AND HUMAN SYMPATHY

Liberal critics tend not to define themselves as political. For them too ideology is always something somebody else suffers from, never a constraint on their own discourse. Explicitly setting out to produce independent-minded scholarly studies free from political bias and other forms of prejudice, liberals do not necessarily come across as more friendly towards Simone de Beauvoir than right-wingers. This is partly because they too draw heavily on the personality *topos*, and partly because these mild-mannered critics find Beauvoir's explicitly political and conflictual worldview particularly infuriating. Beauvoir's passionate refusal of humanist essentialism, as well as her tendency to hold even moderate beliefs extremely, only serves to alienate these critics further. Not surprisingly, then, their favourite invectives against her are 'dogmatic' and 'extremist'.

On the whole liberal critics tend to express their disapproval of Beauvoir not as a general critique of her basic positions, but in a relatively fragmented, point-by-point way. In many cases there is nothing wrong with this: if a critic has gone to the trouble of presenting a painstakingly detailed reading of a text, it is only to be expected that she will comment on contradictions, inconsistencies and flaws wherever she finds them. Not infrequently, however, there is a puzzling contradiction between the critic's explicit stance of well-intentioned judiciousness and the overwhelming amount of potentially damning critique she actually produces. The rhetorical effect of such a double stance is to give the impression that the true picture of Beauvoir has finally emerged: if even an impartial critic's conclusions are damning it must be because they are right. In this way, like Winegarten, these critics too come to reproduce what Eagleton calls the ordinary definition of ideology.

Terry Keefe, for instance, laments the fact that too much emphasis on Beauvoir's feminism and her relationship with Sartre 'has often resulted in a distorted picture of Beauvoir as a writer.' Explicitly setting out to provide a balanced study to rectify the distortions (p. 5), he is honest enough to own up to a certain unease about the nature of his own conclusions: 'Anyone approaching Beauvoir's writings with a reasonably open mind has a very great deal to gain,' he writes, 'and I hope that this emerges from the following pages, even where criticism of her ideas and literary achievements is severe' (p. 5). In fact his book is packed with grudging comments on the literary merits of Beauvoir's texts.[14] Keefe's final conclusion is that Beauvoir's essays are 'emphatic' and 'sweeping' (p. 228); that many of her novels 'do have such obvious aesthetic defects that one may be disinclined even to consider whether they are accomplished works of art' (p. 229); and that her autobiographical texts 'mostly leave us *such* strong impressions of contingency and facticity that we are easily drawn into reading them for the information of various kinds that they convey rather than for anything else' (p. 229). Grudgingly granting that there are exceptions to these rules, Beauvoir is then rated as a 'writer of some stature', albeit one whose work is marred by 'a distinctive kind of fragility or vulnerability' (p. 229).

In his *Histoire vivante de la littérature d'aujourd'hui, 1938–58*, a work which aims to present a reasonably objective panorama of contemporary French literature, Pierre de Boisdeffre allots far more space to Beauvoir than to any other French woman writer – indeed, far more than to the great majority of male writers discussed. Again there is a curious tension between the claim that Beauvoir is among the most important writers of her time and the rather uncharitable conclusions reached by the critic. On the one hand, *L'Invitée* is 'one of the best récits to have appeared in France in the wake of *Nausea*' (p. 111); on the other, Boisdeffre's praise is laced with disapproval: 'Who could deny the almost masculine strength and power of this novelist, the virility of an intelligence that obstinately refuses to let go, to yield to grace or even to the narcissism of her own nature?' (p. 269). If Beauvoir is not truly important as a writer after all, it would seem to be mostly because of her regrettable lack of femininity: 'It is not in intelligence or talent that Simone de Beauvoir is lacking, but perhaps in the humility required to receive the spontaneous gifts of life. [. . .] Marked by a wholly masculine ambition, her work gives rise to curiosity without exerting true influence' (p. 117).[15]

Elaine Marks's *Simone de Beauvoir: Encounters with Death*, an excellent example of liberal criticism, was published in 1973, well before feminism hit Beauvoir studies. It ought to be pointed out that Marks's later feminist work on Beauvoir is noticeable for its incisive and fair-minded approach (see for instance *Critical Essays* and 'Transgressing the (In)cont(in)ent Boundaries'). Serious and well researched, Marks's study also deploys an original and powerful methodological move – the juxtaposition of passages from different texts and often from different genres dealing with the same experience – which is strikingly successful in shedding new light on neglected connections between various aspects of Beauvoir's work. It cannot be denied, however, that her study also amounts to a scathing condemnation of Beauvoir herself. As her argument proceeds, consciously or unconsciously, Marks's tone becomes increasingly hostile: in the second half of her book, references to Beauvoir's 'pathological egotism' (p. 81), 'hysterical mode of reaction' (p. 95) and 'grotesque evasions' (p. 99) abound.

Marks's main argument is that Beauvoir's work constitutes one long meditation on death. Obsessed with death, Beauvoir nevertheless fails fully to confront it; her work in fact becomes one long series of 'evasions'. Marks's summary of her findings is bleak:

> The arguments and the flight are doomed. The body of her writings is a 'meditation on death'; all her themes and elaborations are pretexts for the endless wrestling with her own mortality, of which she is acutely aware but which she has no means, emotional or intellectual, of confronting without hysteria or ideology (p. 126).

In other words: Beauvoir is egocentric, emotionally and intellectually inadequate, and prone to hysterical and ideological distortions of reality as well.

It can be shown, I think, that Marks's distaste for Simone de Beauvoir is not simply idiosyncratic or coincidental, but a logical consequence of her unswerving loyalty to an unusually purified and abstract form of humanism. Marks sees Beauvoir's work as split by the tension between the sense of the absurd, defined as 'the feeling of emptiness at the heart of all things', on the one hand; and the 'desperate need to fill the emptiness, more commonly referred to as commitment', on the other (p. 3). This opposition, Marks argues, produces two different literary styles: the first, of which she whole-heartedly approves, focuses on the absurd, and seeks to describe 'things in the world as they are' (p. 3). The other is the rhetoric of commitment, which unfortunately also has its own deplorable aesthetics:

> The rhythm of commitment is busy and regulated. Its tone, concerned, humorless, optimistic is never ironic; its language, rhetorical and oracular, is solemn, full of confidence and conviction. The major theme is unity and the point of view is always moral, social, and political. Gratuity, the monarch in the universe of the absurd, is replaced by usefulness, play by total activity, analysis by synthesis, phenomenology by ideology. In the leap from the absurd to commitment, from death to history, a concrete problem is given abstract answers (pp. 3–4).

While the style of the absurd produces 'moments of heightened intensity, rigorous descriptions of sensations and sentiments; pitiless and poignant analyses of weaknesses' (p. 4), commitment, according to Marks, simply produces bad prose: 'an often mediocre, vulgar journalese in which endless explanations of the obvious and simpering moralistic clichés annoy and embarrass the reader' (p. 4). Marks's conclusion is not in the least intended as irony: 'Death and the absurd', she declares, 'are always more elegant and refined than history and commitment' (p. 4). True aesthetic refinement, in other words, is incompatible with political engagement, in Beauvoir's *oeuvre* as everywhere else. Art must have nothing to do with history: 'ideology' as opposed to the direct contemplation of 'things as they are' inevitably produces bad writing. Given this starting point, Marks's conclusions are predictable: since Beauvoir persists in juxtaposing existential anguish and social and political activity, she is 'annoyingly' and 'embarrassingly' sacrificing universal truths on the altar of history.[16]

Marks's strange insistence on the absolute *opposition* of death and history leads her to argue that contemplation of the metaphysical absurdity of death is *concrete*, whereas history, normally considered the arena where men and women live and die, is *abstract*. Her profound belief in the supreme reality of unchanging human essences could not emerge more clearly. It is this belief, radically opposed to Beauvoir's own philosophical concerns, which makes her reject any concern with politics, society or history, or indeed with *human community*, as ideological obscurantism.

Marks's peculiar definition of concreteness allows her to label every death described by Beauvoir as 'abstract'. In the end the reader must wonder whether any death, short of one's own, could possibly qualify as 'concrete' enough. In *Memoirs of a Dutiful Daughter*, for example, Beauvoir describes her despair when as a little girl she learnt of the death of their servant Louise's baby, a scene which for her is inextricably tied up with the poverty of Louise's surroundings (see MDD131; MJF182–3). To Marks, such a reaction is an evasion of the fact of death; it is, she argues, 'less an encounter with death than an encounter with "society," a human and therefore a remediable injustice' (p. 41). Such strategies deprive us of an 'uncluttered view of death' (p. 41), Marks complains. Nothing short of unswerving contemplation of absolute death will do. As long as Beauvoir refuses to comply with this demand, she is accused of being uncaring and unfeeling. Her disarray at the death of Louise's baby, Marks argues, is socially induced 'guilt', not pure anguish, and thus does not count as true sympathy. For Marks, to reach out to other people in a solidarity transcending strictly individualist concerns is to betray the dead.

On Marks's logic, it does not matter *who* dies, what matters is abstract and universal death. For Marks, Beauvoir's 'egoism' in fact consists in refusing to acknowledge this superior insight as truth. Nowhere, she argues, is Beauvoir's lack of common humanity more evident than in her distasteful condemnation of fascists and collaborators. It is true that Beauvoir was in favour of the death penalty, and in an essay first published in 1946, 'Oeil pour oeil' ('An Eye for an Eye'), she argues in favour of the execution of Robert Brasillach, the anti-semitic editor of the fascist review *Je suis partout*. During the Occupation, Brasillach used to publish the names and addresses of Jews in hiding from the police. In 'Oeil pour oeil', Beauvoir weighs the arguments for and against the death penalty for collaborators. One problem, she says, is that collaborators are brought to justice in a political situation radically different from that in which they committed their crimes. It is therefore difficult to see them as the hated power-figures they were; instead they tend to appear as lonely victims of a new order: 'We desired the death of the editor of *Je suis partout*', she writes, 'not the death of this man so eager to die well' ('Oeil', p. 149). Marks's commentary takes the liberal confidence in absolute and essential humanity to new heights:

> But the editor-in-chief of *Je suis partout* was and could only be a man, as Mussolini, Darnand, Hitler, Balue, and the assassins of Kharkov were men. The sense of a common humanity only seldom touches Simone de Beauvoir; when it does, she writhes in anguish. Her inability to relate to people with whom she is not intimate prevents her from feeling for them. She is prevented from exposure to reality by the words she has previously chosen to describe that reality (p. 69).

If Marks were simply trying to argue against the death penalty, I would certainly support her as against Beauvoir. True to her abstract humanist commitment, however, Marks does not raise such concrete political concerns. Her point is not only that we ought to *feel for* the death of Hitler and Mussolini, but that Beauvoir betrays her lack of humanity (the *topos* of the cold and uncaring political woman) in refusing to do so in 1946.

AN INTELLECTUAL IMPOSTOR: IRONY AS A RHETORIC OF HOSTILITY

Not surprisingly, the most important *topos* used to disparage Beauvoir, an outspoken woman and a highly qualified teacher of philosophy, is that of the bluestocking. Insisting on the cold, dry, desexualized nature of the intellectual woman, this figure tends to merge with that of the *unfeminine* or *non-maternal* woman studied above. Thus Konrad Bieber is astonished to discover that when Beauvoir found herself cooking meals for Sartre and their friends during the war, the food actually turned out to be edible: 'The idea of this reputed bluestocking cooking meals that found approval, in a hotel room, on make-shift ranges is not without its spice', he exclaims (p. 64).

One of the most fascinating exploitations of the *topos* is to be found in a lengthy article on Beauvoir published in the Rouen newspaper *Paris-Normandie* in 1954. Entitled 'Simone de Beauvoir – "popess" of existentialism', the report purports to reproduce some diary notes jotted down by one of Beauvoir's students at the *lycée* Jeanne d'Arc in Rouen in 1934. The student remains unidentified, and the authenticity of this 'diary' strikes me as extremely dubious. Whether fiction or fact, however, this piece of journalism provides an excellent illustration of the way a provincial French newspaper in 1954 saw fit to present an internationally known female intellectual. More than two-thirds of the purported diary excerpts are taken up with detailed descriptions of Beauvoir's physical attributes. The first impression is of a relatively plain being who lacks equilibrium: 'The teacher, Mlle de Beauvoir, walks with mincing steps, as if she might lose her balance at any moment. [. . .] I look at her: she is a small, very young and pleasant woman, but she is not pretty.' After some detailed descriptions of her face and head, the student concludes that there are two really remarkable things about this woman: 'Two things hold one's attention: the temples and the veins on the neck. When she talks, they swell up and throb, revealing an intense intellectual activity.' Having thus transferred the phallus to the thinking woman's head, the student logically enough goes on to declare it missing elsewhere: 'The rest of this childish body is not harmonious. When she stands up, she seems out of balance', she writes. 'One has the impression that something is lacking.'[17] The teacher's body, it would seem, is neither female nor male, but childish; lacking not only in phallic power, but in any kind of adult sexuality.

An interesting variation on the cliché of the bluestocking is the *topos* of the priggish schoolgirl or the stuffy schoolmarm. In the French context, the explicit reference to the school situation has a series of quite specific implications. This is not simply a general dismissal of women's pathetic efforts to appear as learned as men are. What really irks Beauvoir's critics, and particularly the French ones, is the fact that she is an intellectual woman whose formal training and qualifications more often than not outshine their own. In a review of *The Prime of Life* from 1961, René Girard uses the figure of the schoolgirl to great effect:

> Early in life, Mlle de Beauvoir was one of those little female prodigies who win all the prizes in school and get the *mentions très bien*, thus poisoning the lives of their more relaxed brothers and cousins. These female prodigies are one of the truly national institutions of France. Academic achievements of children are a major field of competition between families of the middle class. The girls are usually ahead of the boys because they are more eager to please their fathers. Immediately after the *baccalauréat*, however, they are expected to abandon all intellectual pursuits in order to become wives and mothers. Competition is suddenly shifted to other fields. Little geniuses with their heads full of trigonometry and Kantian philosophy are often seen never to open another book for the rest of their lives.
>
> Being a particularly brilliant subject, Mme de Beauvoir could not stand the thought of forsaking the *mention très bien*, and she simply refused to be reconverted to home life, thus manifesting for the first time that spirit of rebellion which made her famous and which is still alive in her. However much we admire this valorous feat, we must not exaggerate the scope of the revolution. [. . .] Mme de Beauvoir is the voice of all the other feminine first prize winners (p. 85).

Girard brilliantly conveys the meaning of the *topos*: schoolboys are relaxed and easygoing; schoolgirls are swots and killjoys, turning their brothers into mere also-rans, not because they are more intelligent, but because they overwork in order to please their fathers. Schoolgirls, moreover, are never true intellectuals: as soon as they come first in the all-female competition for the only important first prize in life – a man – they are only too happy never to touch a book again.

In France, journalists and reviewers in popular magazines and newspapers are particularly fond of this figure. In forms ranging from mere quips to spiteful obituaries, the *topos* is wheeled out whenever Beauvoir's ideas are to be dismissed.[18] 'Her memoirs are very neatly [*très sagement*] organized around certain themes,' Mathieu Galey writes in his review of *All Said and Done*, 'the dissertation is well constructed.' 'One has the impression [. . .] of listening to a lecture *ex cathedra*', *Le monde* complains after seeing Beauvoir on television (Sarraute, p. 11). Occasionally, the figure turns up in reverse:

how surprising that Beauvoir is *not* a ferocious bluestocking! In a well-intentioned review of *Memoirs of a Dutiful Daughter*, Geneviève Gennari exclaims: 'And we do not in fact meet a *monstre sacré*, a Minerva sprung fully armed from the brains of the god of philosophy, or perhaps emerged by spontaneous generation!'.

Schoolgirls and schoolmarms are desexualized (the dried-up spinster and old maid are not far away), rigid, predictable and *confined* in their knowledge; true intellectuals are virile, wide-ranging, supple and inventive. School suits women because it is the place for serious and disciplined submission to the *doxa*; real intellectual creativity, however, is playful, unpredictable and transgressive, and as such necessarily male. If Beauvoir quickly earned a reputation for 'courageous effort, prodigious research and straightforward habits of thought', as Mary Ellmann once put it ('The Dutiful', p. 94), this is not altogether as flattering as it may sound.

Much in evidence throughout Beauvoir criticism, the sarcasm and irony that Elaine Marks comments on are nowhere more apparent than in the frequent attacks on the pretensions of the intellectual woman. It should be remembered, however, that the generalized use of the personality *topos*, which seeks to displace interest away from the woman's thoughts and on to her body or character, also has deeply anti-intellectual effects. Among critics who are out to disparage Beauvoir as an intellectual, one of the most frequent terms of abuse is *naïvety* and its near-synonyms. If the figure of the *midinette* is used as often as it is, for instance, it is precisely because it efficiently and economically signals female ignorance and naivety. The combination of irony with the accusation of naivety, I would argue, is not a coincidence. Rhetorically, classical irony signals above all *distance* and *superiority*. As a highly successful intellectual woman Beauvoir is deeply threatening to insecure males with academic or journalistic pretensions: as René Girard shows, she simply refuses to leave the intellectual race to the men. Through the use of irony, the critic manages at once to situate himself at a safe distance from his female challenger, and to signal his own subtle superiority of insight.

Classical irony relies for its effect on the assumption of a clear-cut opposition between appearances and truth: the ironist is presumed to have true insight; his victim to be blinded by ignorance. It can be shown that such irony works by appealing to a set of values assumed to be shared by the ironist and her audience.[19] If this process fails, the irony disappears. This, incidentally, is why the patriarchal irony liberally bestowed on Beauvoir is so galling to feminists. By relying on the implicit assumption of common standards, such irony represses the need for explicit confrontation of opposing world-views. Deeply aggressive, however, classical irony reproduces the triangular structure of victimization which Freud finds at work in jokes and witticisms (see chapter 5 of *Jokes and their Relations to the*

Unconscious). For the irony to work there must be complicity between the ironist and the 'ironee', a complicity where both take their superiority over the 'ironized' for granted. As one of the aims of the irony is to produce maximal distance between the values and insights of the ironist and her victim, the 'ironized' victim tends to come across as the embodiment of whatever is taken to be the direct opposite of the ironist's own standards.

The opposite of irony is naivety: what could be more distant from the rhetorical elegance of irony than the artless and childish lack of discrimination of the naive? The figure of irony, then, is deeply epistemological: the distinction to be made is that between knowledge and ignorance, insight and blindness. This, I think, accounts for the frequency and prevalence of the use of sarcasm and irony in Beauvoir criticism. Nothing can be more *ironic* than to attack an intellectual, a teacher of philosophy, a writer of philosophical and political essays for her *ignorance*. By working the naivety *topos* to exhaustion, her critics want to convey a picture of a childlike creature, unconscious of the effects of her own discourse. As such this figure rejoins and reinforces that of the schoolgirl: both work together to produce the image of a *false intellectual*. That it is a woman who is denounced as an epistemological impostor in this way is precisely the point: women's right to intellectual activity – and particularly to philosophy – has always been hotly contested by patriarchal ideology. Simone de Beauvoir's fate at the hands of her critics shows that the struggle is by no means over today.

PART II

Part II

4

L'Invitée: An Existentialist Melodrama

Literature is born when something in life goes slightly adrift. [. . .] My strict work routines remained futile till the day came when [my] happiness was threatened, and I rediscovered a certain kind of solitude in anxiety. The unfortunate episode of the trio did much more than supply me with a subject for a novel; it enabled me to deal with it.

(The Prime of Life)

BEAUVOIR'S POINT OF VIEW

In *The Prime of Life* Simone de Beauvoir claims that the end of *L'Invitée* is an aesthetic disaster: 'I have often been criticized for this conclusion, and it is beyond any doubt the weakest aspect of the book,' she writes, 'to kill is not a commonplace action. Françoise, as I have depicted her, is just as incapable of murder as I am. [. . .] My error is all the more flagrant in that I failed to make daily life topple over into tragedy' (PL339–40; FA387–8; TA).[1] Incriminating herself even further in the eyes of the arbiters of taste, she goes on to cast doubts on the whole structure of her novel, confessing that this disastrous scene was not the result of a desperate last-ditch attempt to bring her text to an end, but the very *raison d'être* of the whole novel. Moreover, she writes, she even took pleasure in producing this piece of inferior writing: 'In so far as literature is a living activity, it was essential that I should end with this denouement, which possessed a cathartic quality for me personally' (PL340; FA388). In the writing of *L'Invitée*, Beauvoir experienced a conflict between her own aesthetic and intellectual values and her sense of psychological necessity:

Rereading the final pages, today so contrived and dead, I can hardly believe that when I wrote them my throat was as tight as though I had the burden of a real murder on my shoulders. Yet so it was; and sitting there, pen in hand, it was with a sort of terror that I experienced separation. Xavière's murder may look like the abrupt and clumsy conclusion of a drama I had no idea how to finish; but in fact it was the motive force and *raison d'être* behind the entire novel (PL340; FA389; TA).

It is as if Simone de Beauvoir here simultaneously seeks to excuse herself for having committed the literary crime of bad writing – producing an 'abrupt' and 'clumsy' end to her novel – and to affirm the utter necessity of that crime. That necessity, however, is neither literary nor philosophical, but physical and psychological: 'my throat was tight', 'it was with a sort of terror that I experienced separation.' On the same page she also insists on the fantasmatic and bodily nature of this writing experience: 'I must work my fantasy through to the bitter end, embody it [*lui donner corps*]' (PL340; FA389; TA). Writing the murder of the other woman, Beauvoir would seem spontaneously to have felt that she was, as Hélène Cixous might have put it, 'writing the body'.

After reading this extraordinary passage I find it difficult not to ask *why* Françoise's killing of Xavière represents such a moment of intense psychological investment for Beauvoir. Is it possible to read *L'Invitée* in a way that manages to seize the psychological significance of Françoise's final crime? Can one really construe the asphyxiation of Xavière not simply as an unfortunate literary mistake, but as the *raison d'être* of the whole text? To be sure, the author's own comments imply that one cannot. If we are to believe Beauvoir, the final murder breaks with the psychological and philosophical logic of her own text; it is as if she feels that to write the body is to fail as a writer. By the time she is writing *The Prime of Life*, at least, she seems to have resigned herself to the idea that the final scene of *L'Invitée* represents a moment of unfortunate literary excess. Her own account of how she *felt* when she wrote it comes across more as an attempt to explain how she came to perpetrate such an unpardonable offence against taste than as a vindication of her own act. What interests me in this context is the tension between Beauvoir's genuflexion to legitimate literary taste ('I *know* the end is bad') and her overwhelming psychosomatic investment in precisely that end ('I *had* to write it'). Is there another logic at work in *L'Invitée*, one in which the death of Xavière does not come to stand simply as a piece of 'clumsy' writing? A logic that operates in the interstices of Beauvoir's òwn reading? And what, if anything, might such a logic have to do with Beauvoir's uneasy feeling of having produced 'bad' literature?

AN EXCESSIVE MURDER: MELODRAMA AND THE DETECTIVE STORY

It is impossible simply to deny Beauvoir's feelings of unease about the end of *L'Invitée*. There *is* something illogical, unrealistic – something excessive – about the murder of Xavière.[2] Even given Beauvoir's own philosophical premisses, Françoise – an aspiring writer deeply involved in her work – hardly needs to kill to escape the tyranny of the Other and achieve authentic, responsible freedom. She might just as well have settled down to write, a solution which worked well enough for Simone de Beauvoir herself:

> But above all, by releasing Françoise, through the agency of a crime, from the dependent position in which her love for Pierre kept her, I regained my own personal autonomy. The paradoxical thing is that to do so did not require any unpardonable action on my part, but merely the description of such an action in a book. However attentive the encouragement and advice one receives, writing remains an act for which the responsibility cannot be shared with any other person (PL340; FA388–9).

When it comes to claiming one's unique and exclusive responsibility for an irrevocable act, writing can clearly be as satisfying as murder: the killing of Xavière cannot be explained by philosophy alone.

In *L'Invitée* excessive or exaggerated writing is not confined to the final scenes. As the narrative develops, Françoise's language becomes increasingly marked by a kind of luridly gothic imagination. In general, such moments of slightly surreal exaggeration surface in relation to Xavière, who is endowed with everything from tentacles with which to swallow Françoise alive (see SC295; I367) to the power to engulf (*engloutir*) the whole universe (SC292; I364). As Françoise's involvement with Xavière grows more extreme, so does her language. The killing of Xavière thus provokes passages of stunning intensity, but also of a curious simplicity. Consider, for instance, the language in this scene, which occurs just before the cathartic denouement. Xavière has just accused Françoise of stealing her boyfriend, Gerbert, in a plot motivated by pure jealousy:

> She crossed the passage, staggering as though blind, and tears burned her eyes. 'I was jealous of her. I took Gerbert from her.' The tears, the words, scorched like a hot iron. She sat down on the edge of the couch, dazed, and repeated, 'I did that. That was I.' In the shadows, a black fire flickered round Gerbert's face, and the letters scattered on the carpet were as black as an infernal pact. She put her handkerchief to her lips. A black torrid lava was coursing in her veins. She wanted to die (SC406; I499).

Françoise's consciousness of guilt and shame, and her feeling of being *condemned* – or rather *damned* – by Xavière is conveyed by the repetitive insistence on blackness and burning, associated with hellfire and torment. Like another Faust, Françoise sees her letters as the visible sign of an 'infernal' pact with the Devil himself. Poised to kill, Françoise is in the grip of a fantasy of a Manichean struggle between good and evil. In the passage quoted here, she almost succumbs to Xavière's judgement: for an instant she sees herself as evil. In *L'Invitée*, however, this time-honoured struggle is situated on epistemological terrain; at stake is the power to *define* the world, to decide what is to count as truth, to become the unchallenged possessor of true knowledge.

Pondering the implications of these observations, it occurs to me that the word I need to describe this kind of style is *melodramatic*. Perhaps, in spite of its intellectual profile, literary ambitions and philosophical scope, *L'Invitée* still carries the stigma of the melodramatic? Nothing could contribute more to its perception as slightly excessive – slightly *illegitimate* – in the eyes of the consecrated wielders of power in the French literary field. And as we have seen, there is every reason to believe that Simone de Beauvoir herself shared the values of the dominant powers in that field. At the same time, though, her own position in relation to intellectual and literary prestige in France was highly ambiguous: as a woman she internalized and identified with a set of values which contributed to her own marginalization. Perhaps the tensions produced by this particular position can explain why the melodramatic creeps into a narrative that tries very hard to be the quintessential intellectual novel? Perhaps, even, it is easier to be perceived as melodramatic – and indeed to perceive oneself as melodramatic – if one ends up describing a struggle to the death between two *women* rather than two *men*?

Without a more detailed understanding of the nature of the melodramatic impulse in literature, it is hard to move beyond idle speculation. According to Peter Brooks, in his influential study *The Melodramatic Imagination*, melodrama is above all a mode of *excess*. Driven by the impulse to 'express all' (p. 4), Brooks writes, pure theatrical melodrama stages an 'intense emotional and ethical drama based on the manichaeistic struggle of good and evil [. . .] Their conflict suggests the need to recognize and confront evil, to combat and expel it, to purge the social order' (p. 13). But traditional theatrical melodrama is not the only way in which the melodramatic imagination expresses itself: according to Brooks, the melodramatic mode is also central to modern sensibility. Insisting that 'behind reality, hidden by it yet indicated within it, there is a realm where large moral forces are operative, where large choices of ways of being must be made' (p. 21), the melodramatic imagination seeks transcendence, significance and meaning in the apparently ordinary details of everyday life. In so far as it takes every sign to refer to some other transcendent truth hidden behind the veneer of contingent phenomena, melodrama turns everything into a potential metaphor.

But melodrama also has a psychological or psychoanalytic dimension. The deepest source of the appeal of melodrama, Brooks claims, is the fact that its rhetoric represents a 'victory over repression' (p. 41). Its drive to 'say all', to defy censorship and repression, may be precisely the reason why melodrama tends to embarrass critics, and thus to be cast as 'bad' literature: it voices 'identifications judged too extravagant, too stark, too unmediated to be allowed utterance' (p. 42). In this sense, one might add, it may be that if melodrama embarrasses us, it is because it comes across as too close to the crudely narcissistic daydreams or fantasies we usually seek to repress. As a rule, other people's fantasies are repulsive to us, Freud writes in his 1908 essay on 'Creative Writers and Day-dreaming'. If the fantasies of the creative writer please us, it is only because they are wrapped in the seductions of style, or what Freud calls the *fore-pleasure* of the 'purely formal' or 'aesthetic' (p. 153). If *L'Invitée* produces a faint feeling of displeasure or unease in its reader, it may be precisely because it austerely refuses to display the slinkily seductive 'technique' extolled by Freud, the *art* which would at once entice and authorize us truly to enjoy the unaesthetic and undistinguished fantasies we all secretly harbour.

On my reading of the genre, melodrama, or more precisely the melodramatic mode, has a distinctly epistemological aspect to it: it is about the need for insight or clarification, the need to spell out the opposing factions engaged in moral or ethical battle. Moreover, I take it that in so far as melodrama always attempts to express – to lift the repression of – basic psychological conflicts, its struggle for moral insight always masks, but never entirely hides, a deeper psychological conflict between its pro-tagonists.[3] I am obviously about to claim that *L'Invitée* can be read precisely as a modern melodrama. But this is not all. I also believe that the *reason* why *L'Invitée* becomes a melodramatic text is highly overdetermined, and there-fore to be sought not exclusively in the quirks of Beauvoir's imagination, or in her ambiguous position in the French literary field, but also in the main philosophical intertext to her novel, Sartre's *Being and Nothingness*. Or in other words: if *L'Invitée* is a melodramatic novel, it is above all because existentialism is a melodramatic philosophy.

If one could show that *Being and Nothingness* has more than a touch of the melodramatic about it, it would not be surprising to discover that a series of elements in *L'Invitée* also come across as influenced by the mode of melodrama. But existentialism is not the only melodramatic element in *L'Invitée*. Beauvoir herself draws our attention to a rather more obviously melodramatic influence on her first novel. Her main literary sources of inspiration for *L'Invitée*, she tells us, were Dostoyevsky, Hemingway,

Dashiell Hammett and Agatha Christie (see PL344: FA392-3). Specifically invoking the thriller and the detective story, generally considered prime examples of modern melodramatic genres, Beauvoir particularly insists on the parallels between her novel and Agatha Christie's detective stories:

> Because of each character's limited knowledge, the plot development is often as enigmatic as that of a good Agatha Christie thriller, and the reader does not at once grasp its implications [. . .] no character is the repository of absolute truth. In the novel's more successful sequences I achieved a situational ambivalence corresponding to the kind of thing one meets in real life (PL344; FA392–3).

Here Beauvoir would seem to encourage a comparison between *L'Invitée* and the traditional detective story only in order to undermine her own point: if the detective story requires anything, it is surely the revelation of an unambiguous truth. On the one hand the reader of *L'Invitée* is invited to cast herself in the role of the detective, as the instance who has to piece together disparate clues in order to track down the elusive truth. On the other hand Beauvoir would seem firmly to deny that *L'Invitée* offers the reader any final truth at all. On first approach, then, the reader would seem to be doomed to frustration, endlessly groping around for a closure which is never to be had. But Beauvoir's denial of closure is not in fact entirely convincing: for Françoise, at the very least, the death of Xavière does constitute a moment of truth in which the flux of interpretation finally comes to a halt.

L'Invitée opens not with a murder but, as the title indicates, with an invitation (Françoise asking Xavière to stay in Paris with Pierre and herself), which triggers the same process of anxious overreading as the murder does in a detective novel. Losing her self-confidence, Françoise soon comes to doubt her own motivations, even her own innermost feelings; soon her previous sense of easy epistemological mastery breaks down. The struggle over the meaning of Françoise's seduction of Gerbert, Xavière's young lover, is only the most acute case of the various conflicts of interpretation enacted in this novel. At the time of the seduction, Françoise perceived it as a light, loving, delightful thing to do. But when Xavière finally discovers the truth, she accuses Françoise of the blackest treason, of being a frustrated and embittered woman who 'stole' Gerbert simply because she was jealous of Xavière's relationship with Pierre. 'How had that innocent love become this sordid betrayal?', moans the shock-stricken Françoise (SC406; I500). On this level of the plot, then, Françoise kills Xavière above all to enforce *her* version of the truth, to refute and repress Xavière's image of her, to stop the endless spiral of interpretation and to establish the innocence of her relationship with Gerbert one and for all: ' "No," she repeated, "I am not that woman" ' (SC406; I500).

L'Invitée shares with the detective story a deep investment in knowledge as the signifier of authority and power. The dominant image of knowledge in this text is the physical and visual act of *reading*: the final conflict is triggered by a quite literal struggle over the right to read the letters sent to Françoise by Pierre and Gerbert. These letters do not only reveal the truth of Françoise's erotic relations with Gerbert, they also make it abundantly clear that Xavière is the only one of the four protagonists to be kept deliberately in ignorance by the three others. Perceived as unworthy of knowledge by all her friends and lovers, she has been betrayed not only by Françoise, but by Pierre and Gerbert too. In this way, the overall plot structure of L'Invitée tends to corroborate Françoise's image of Xavière as shifty and unreliable.

One may argue, then, that in so far as it starts with a transgressive act (the invitation) that disrupts the order of Françoise's life and triggers a process of quasi-paranoid epistemological search for a safe and stable truth, L'Invitée resembles the detective story. But in so far as it is the *crime* which re-establishes innocence and thereby reconstructs the lost order, the structure of the detective story is reversed. An effort to solve the question of Françoise's identity, the final murder closes rather than opens the inquiry: in her very consciousness of crime, Françoise is claiming her identity and independence. Much like Sartre's *The Flies*, then, L'Invitée is a narrative of how to become a murderer and thereby get rid of anguish.

A MELODRAMATIC PHILOSOPHY

In *The Prime of Life* Simone de Beauvoir tells the story of how, one day in 1932, Raymond Aron, by pointing to an apricot cocktail,[4] first persuaded Sartre to take a serious interest in phenomenology:

> We spent an evening together at the Bec de Gaz in the Rue Montparnasse. We ordered the speciality of the house, apricot cocktails; Aron said, pointing to his glass: 'You see, my dear fellow [*mon petit camarade*], if you are a phenomenologist, you can talk about this cocktail and make philosophy out of it!' Sartre turned pale with emotion, or almost did. Here was just the thing he had been longing to achieve for years – to describe objects just as he saw and touched them, and to make philosophy out of it (PL135; FA156; TA).

In *Being and Nothingness* Sartre packs his texts with examples from Parisian everyday life in the late 1930s and early 1940s. Readers of Sartre's philosophical treatise will thus not only learn something about his views of the for-itself and the in-itself, but also about the *mores* of mid-century French intellectuals. This is not simply an effort to turn philosophy into literature, to demonstrate his effortless mastery of *writing* as well as of *thinking*, but a logical consequence of the wish to make philosophy out of *everything*: nothing can be too low, too mundane, too quotidian to be philosophically significant.

For Sartre, existence is to be theorized as a totality. The totality of our being inhabits every one of our acts. It therefore follows that our slightest gestures or most harmless habits are potentially as revealing of the whole as our most grandiose or dramatic projects. If I have a penchant for apricot cocktails, in other words, it *must* be possible to figure out, not only its existential meaning for me, but what it says about my existential project in general. In order fully to understand the implication of my tastes, however, it is necessary to understand the nature of the *object* of my disgust or predilection. This is the task of 'existential psychoanalysis', which Sartre defines as a 'psychoanalysis of *things*' (BN765; EN661).

In the chapter of *Being and Nothingness* entitled 'On quality as a revelation of being', Sartre sets out to illustrate this idea. The 'slimy' or 'sticky' (*le visqueux*)[5] may attract or repel us, but in both cases it is the recognizable – objective – qualities of the sticky which exercise their effects on us. While we are certainly dealing with the *human meaning* of qualities, this meaning is as *real* as the world. For Sartre, there can be no question of assuming that the things in the world (which is always the world-for-humans) can be filled with just any signification. While the meaning of stickiness in my existence is not given (I may be repelled or fascinated by it), what I react to is the objective qualities of stickiness, that which differentiates it from, say, wetness. According to Sartre, stickiness, unlike wetness or dryness, represents the attempt of the in-itself to swallow up, engulf or immobilize the for-itself. The sticky, he writes, represents the 'sugary death of the For-itself' (BN777; EN671). My *relationship* to this danger is not given; what is given is the fact that stickiness symbolizes and expresses it. The fact that Sartre also describes *le visqueux* as 'a soft, yielding action, a moist and feminine sucking' (BN776; EN671), and as the 'sickly-sweet, feminine revenge' of the in-itself (BN777; EN671), only reveals the way in which sexist prejudice tends to insinuate itself into the most unexpected philosophical contexts.[6]

Whether I love or loathe stickiness, then, my disgust or pleasure reveals my fundamental relationship to being. Let us assume that I, unlike Sartre, happen to *like* stickiness:

> To what fundamental project of myself am I referred, if I want to explain this love of an ambiguous, sucking in-itself? In this way *tastes* do not remain irreducible givens; if one knows how to question them, they reveal to us the fundamental projects of the person.[7] Down to even our alimentary preferences they all have a meaning (BN783; EN676).

Or in other words: there *are* no irreducible tastes or predilections, since 'they all represent a certain appropriative choice of being' (BN784; EN677).

Sartre's own novels are full of meaningful acts and significant tastes. In *The Age of Reason*, Daniel's failure to drown his cats is as significant as his tendency constantly to stare at himself in the mirror, and Boris's disgust at the mere thought of having sex is no more and no less revealing of his existential project than the thrill he gets from difficult shop-lifting projects. If *L'Invitée* is a novel in which the characters spend an extraordinary amount of time talking in cafés, it is not only because it is written by a French intellectual, but also because the main subject of conversation between Pierre and Françoise is the effort to decipher the existential meaning of Xavière's slightest *moue*. Has she brushed her hair? Will she turn up on time? Does she have a headache? Is she sulking? And what does it all *mean*?

If anything is truly excessive in *L'Invitée*, it is the sheer mass of apparently futile conversation in which the reader is expected to take as delighted an interest as the protagonists themselves: neither Françoise nor Beauvoir seem able to imagine that such a maniacal search for significance may appear pointless to others. In this sense, at least, *L'Invitée* moves entirely within the framework of existentialist thought. The existentialist passion for meaning, juxtaposed with the existentialist awareness that meaning is not given but constructed, is precisely what gives *L'Invitée* its atmosphere of epistemological insecurity and its counterbalancing desire to locate knowledge beneath the ambiguous surface of phenomena. Whatever the individual reader's reactions may be (and I must confess that I am paranoid – or melodramatic – enough to take pleasure in the minutest details of such games of interpretation), there can be no doubt that *L'Invitée* is an excellent example of the melodramatic impulse to search for meaning beneath the seemingly ordinary surface of everyday life.

The fundamental project of Sartrean philosophy, then, is the attempt to understand *everything*, and to express this total understanding in philosophical terms. 'Every project can be understood by everybody [*tout homme*]', Sartre writes in *L'existentialisme est un humanisme* (p. 70). In order to enable the philosopher to sustain his claim to total knowledge, however, it becomes vital to refute the psychoanalytic theory of the unconscious. Large sections of *Being and Nothingness* – particularly those concerning bad faith – constitute deliberate attempts to invade terrain occupied by psychoanalysis. Referring to the early 1930s, Simone de Beauvoir explains that '[Sartre's] notion of bad faith [*mauvaise foi*] [. . .] embraced all those phenomena which other people attribute to the unconscious' (PL128; FA148). For existentialism, in other words, the world is a complex system of potentially meaningful phenomena, a system in which the philosopher –

and certainly not the psychoanalyst – becomes the privileged reader of signs.

Enacted in the relationship between Françoise and Pierre, Sartre's and Beauvoir's ideal of total transparency in human relations is also linked to their belief in the absolute *readability* of every action and every feeling. In *The Prime of Life* Beauvoir explains that Sartre and his small group of friends at the Ecole Normale Supérieure (*les petits camarades*) developed the habit of 'telling everything' while they were still students:

> What is known as *la vie intérieure* aroused the greatest disgust among his group of friends at the ENS; the gardens where sensitive, refined souls cultivated their delicate secrets they regarded as stinking swamps, a place for constant discreet trafficking in bad faith and the secret enjoyment of the foul pleasures of narcissism. In order to dissipate these gloomy miasmas, they themselves had acquired the habit of exposing their lives, thoughts, and feelings in broad daylight (PL23–4; FA29–30; TA).[8]

On my reading of this passage, I get the impression that the young Sartre first develops a habit of rough, uncouth, 'masculine' honesty as a reaction against what he perceives as the ethereal and somewhat feminized gushing of 'beautiful souls'. Beauvoir's language here plunges deep into the existentialist horror chamber of swamps, gloom, stench and muddied waters, often associated with femininity in Sartre's and Beauvoir's texts; only the Sartrean crabs and lobsters are missing. Later on, Sartre proceeds not only to incorporate his thirst for daylight and insight into his relationship with Simone de Beauvoir, but also to turn it into a basic tenet of his philosophy. The Sartre of *Being and Nothingness* not only assumes that everything *can* be expressed, but that it is morally inferior (a case of 'bad faith') *not* to do so. The fact that some people (many men and most women, if we are to believe the examples of bad faith given in *Being and Nothingness* and *Vérité et existence*) cannot tolerate the 'truth' illustrates only *their* weakness, not that of the theory.

Beauvoir's early wish to 'say all' (*tout dire*) may have been influenced by Rousseau. In the company of Sartre, however, it is given a new twist: it is a matter no longer simply of total sincerity and the utmost effort to express one's feelings and experiences, but also of maximal insight into the meaning of the world. If the melodramatic impulse seeks to read the messages lurking beneath the surface of ordinary and everyday life, to lift repressions and 'say all', it is certainly present in Sartre's philosophy. The difference is, perhaps, that in his denial of the unconscious, Sartre attempts to repress the very notion of repression, only to resurrect it with a vengeance in the concept of bad faith.

The melodramatic imagination, Brooks claims, always acts out starkly dualistic moral scenarios: good versus evil, the powers of light versus the powers of darkness. Existentialism, on the other hand, explicitly denies the existence of given moral values. Our acts define us. Since God is dead, we are free to act as we please. Action – our projects or transcendence – is in fact what distinguishes us as human beings. Human consciousness *is* project – a throwing forward, a transcendence. Whatever we do, we cannot escape the responsibility for our own acts: to try to do so is a prime strategy of bad faith. To pretend to have no choice is to deny freedom, and that, precisely, is the very definition of bad faith. In fact, we are responsible even for our passions, Sartre says in *L'existentialisme est un humanisme* (see p. 38).[9] The total freedom inherent in our very condition as human beings provokes anguish (*angoisse*). There is no way to avoid anguish: to pretend not to choose is as much of a choice as any other. Inauthentic behaviour is behaviour which in some way or other seeks to avoid the anguish that comes with freedom. While there is no given set of ethical standards for existentialists, then, there can be no doubt that this is in fact a deeply dualistic moral system, structured over the split between the positive values of freedom, authenticity, transcendence and good faith and the negative ones of denial of freedom, inauthenticity, immanence and bad faith. This is indeed a melodramatic universe in which I can damn or save myself through stark moral choices.[10]

Finally, I think it is quite possible to locate a recurrent underlying fantasy at work in the rhetoric of *Being in Nothingness*. Unfortunately, this is not the place to undertake a full-scale psychoanalytic reading of *Being and Nothingness*. My initial working hypothesis, however, would be to try out the idea that the primary structuring fantasy of Sartre's philosophical tome is the wish to perceive the world as it appears to the pre-Oedipal baby at the height of primary narcissism, the omnipotent creature Freud refers to as 'His Majesty the Baby' ('On Narcissism', p. 91). In order to make the case for this idea, one would have to investigate the curiously imaginary (in the Lacanian sense) relationship between the 'I' and the 'Other' in Sartre's text, the extreme confidence in the omnipotence of thought, the tendency to perceive knowledge as all-powerful and to exemplify thought processes by sensuous images of eating and devouring, as well as his penchant for equating sexual images (rape, defloration) with eating and swallowing. There is also an explicitly declared preference for non-genital sexual relations, combined with a marked hostility towards women, perceived as lacking in lucidity and good faith on the one hand, and as endowed with castrating and devouring vaginas on the other. The point of such an investigation would be to examine how far such a ruling fantasy interferes with the philosophical logic of Sartre's work, forcing him to contradict himself or to take up bizarre or untenable positions.[11]

Considering *L'Invitée*, however, I find few traces of this specific version of primary narcissism. By choosing an epigraph from Hegel: 'Each consciousness seeks the death of the other', Beauvoir draws our attention to the implacable hostility between consciousness and the other in existentialist philosophy.[12] More than the relationship between consciousness and the world, between the for-itself and the in-itself, it is the relationship between two consciousnesses that fires Beauvoir's imagination. In the case of *L'Invitée*, the mortal struggle between consciousnesses is enacted primarily in the relationship between Xavière and Françoise. Its counterpart is the seemingly all-too-harmonious relationship between Pierre and Françoise. It is by studying these two relationships in some detail that I hope to discover the specific psychological scenario – the psychoanalytic family romance – enacted by *L'Invitée*. Locating this fantasy will enable us to understand not only to what extent *L'Invitée* is a melodramatic novel, but also, perhaps, why Simone de Beauvoir felt that she *had* to produce such a lurid end to her very first novel.

On Ne Fait Qu'un: We Are One

The opening scenes of *L'Invitée* are set in Paris at the *rentrée*, the return to school and university in early October 1938; that is to say soon after the Munich accords. The happy and somewhat unconventional couple Françoise Miquel and Pierre Labrousse are working hard to prepare Pierre's adaptation of Shakespeare's *Julius Caesar* for the opening night. Pierre is a successful theatre director and actor, and, we are told, also working on a play of his own expected to become the major event of the following year's season.

Françoise's professional role is more uncertain. Translating plays, finding props and overseeing the smooth working of the theatrical machinery, she would seem to be employed as Pierre's assistant, or possibly as a kind of dramaturge. She also reads all the new plays sent to Pierre, only passing on the ones she judges worthy of his attention. In addition to her work at the theatre, she is a struggling writer, desperately trying to find the time to work on her own novel. We hear very little about this book during the course of *L'Invitée*, mostly because it would seem never to be a subject of discussion between Pierre and Françoise.[13] We must assume that Françoise receives a regular salary for her work at Pierre's theatre, although this is left unclear. Her own perception is that her collaboration with Pierre is not only the cornerstone of her happiness, but more satisfying and important than sex:

> Of all her lucky breaks, the one she valued the most was that which gave her
> the opportunity of collaborating with Pierre. The weariness they shared and

their efforts united them more surely than an embrace [*une étreinte*]. There was not one moment of all these harassing rehearsals that was not an act of love (SC39; I55).

For a present-day feminist Françoise appears, at least initially, as the typical *helpmate*, a woman who achieves fulfillment of her own erotic and professional ambitions through being the indispensable assistant of a powerful, much loved and much respected man. Her sincere devotion to her work nevertheless sets her apart from every other female character in the novel: Xavière is described as being incapable of any kind of sustained work, and Elisabeth only paints in order to produce an *image* of herself as a successful young artist.

At the start of the novel, Françoise is not only entirely unconcerned with what others might think of her; she can hardly imagine that other people exist:

> 'It's almost impossible to believe that other people are conscious beings, aware of their own inner feelings, as we ourselves are aware of our own,' said Françoise. 'To me, it's terrifying when we grasp that. We get the impression of no longer being anything but a figment of someone else's mind. But that hardly ever happens, and never completely' (SC6–7; I18).

One might assume that Pierre, at least, would be perceived as truly other by Françoise. But this is not the case. Instead of perceiving him as a separate, autonomous human being, she sees him as an extension of herself.[14] Watching Pierre on stage from her seat in the dark theatre, she is overcome by a feeling of utter unity with him:

> 'It's true that we are really one,' she thought with a burst of love. Pierre was speaking, his hand was raised, but his gestures, his tones, were as much a part of Françoise's life as of his. Or rather, there was but one life and at its core but one entity, which could be termed neither he nor I, but we (SC44; I61).

The two are one: Pierre can never threaten Françoise's sense of uniqueness. Thus Françoise never calls Pierre by his name when they are alone, and also realizes that for a very long time she has never said 'I', only 'we'.

When the narrative starts, then, for Françoise there is no distance between Pierre and herself. Although he himself comes across as entirely self-contained, Pierre does not seem in the least disturbed by this situation, and in fact goes out of his way to ensure that it continues. In the following exchange the two protagonists have just been discussing the concept of fidelity. Pierre regularly has affairs with other women, whereas Françoise has remained monogamous during the eight years they have been together, even resisting a brief temptation to seduce the young and attractive Gerbert on the grounds that she feels perfectly happy with Pierre:

> 'No,' she said. 'It's something stronger than myself. I'm the faithful sort.'
> 'It's impossible to talk about faithfulness and unfaithfulness where we are concerned,' said Pierre. He drew Françoise to him. 'You and I are simply one. That's the truth, you know. Neither of us can be described without the other.'
> 'That's thanks to you,' said Françoise. [. . .] 'We are simply one,' she murmured (SC17; I29–30).

According to Pierre, the unity between the two makes traditional semantic differences meaningless. His elegant deconstruction of terms is nevertheless profitable only to himself: on this logic Françoise gets no credit for her behaviour, whereas he escapes all potential blame for his. Knowing her place, Françoise not only acquiesces in this arrangement, but proceeds to credit him with the success of their harmonious union. What Françoise initially may have experienced as a union between equals is in fact represented as a symbiotic relationship between a dominant man and a dominated woman. The two of them may well be one, but *he* is the one they are.

At this stage, psychoanalytically inclined readers may well want to argue that Françoise's relationship with Pierre exemplifies an imaginary fantasy of unity with the Other, and that the novel as a whole attempts to chronicle her difficult separation from this imaginary matrix and her painful entry into the symbolic order. Such a reading would certainly make sense of Françoise's attacks of extreme anxiety and depression. Nor can there be any doubt that the final murder represents Françoise's supreme effort to become a separate individual in relation to Pierre. However that may be, here I simply want to stress that the very idea of unity between two lovers runs counter to Sartre's – and Beauvoir's – view that every consciousness is pitted in deadly battle against every other consciousness.[15]

As Simone de Beauvoir was working on *L'Invitée* (1938–41), Sartre was working on *Being and Nothingness* (1939–42). At this time, then, both were apparently busy demonstrating to each other and the world that it is impossible to be *one* with one's beloved. In the letters he wrote to Beauvoir from September 1939 to June 1940, Sartre nevertheless frequently uses the phrase *on ne fait qu'un* – 'we are one' – which in *L'Invitée* soon becomes the very symbol of Françoise's delusions and disappointment. As with Pierre in *L'Invitée*, Sartre's epistolary *on ne fait qu'un* serves above all to placate and pacify the woman in situations where she might well become 'difficult'. By affirming, quite against his own philosophical principles, the unbreakable unity of their couple, a unity which somehow soars above vulgar material details such as actual behaviour, Sartre apparently feels free to continue his various other affairs precisely as he pleases.[16] At the time, among other things, this involved proposing marriage to Wanda Kosackiewicz, Olga's sister and, according to Deirdre Bair, the model for some of the more unpleasant aspects of Xavière (see Bair, p. 231).[17]

As Pierre's relationship with Xavière develops, Françoise realizes that by alienating herself in him, she has lost all sense of her own identity. Pierre, on the other hand, has not in the least lost his individual freedom: 'For many years now she had ceased to be an individual; she no longer even possessed a face. [. . .] Our past, our future, our ideas, our love . . . never did she say: "I." And yet, Pierre determined his own future and his own heart: he disengaged himself, he retreated to the boundaries of his own life' (SC173; I216). Françoise's development in *L'Invitée* is parallel to that of Simone de Beauvoir in *The Prime of Life*, where she stresses the lessons she learned from the painful experience of the so-called 'trio' with Sartre and Olga Kosakiewicz. She had been mistaken, she writes, to believe in the idea of a given, unbreakable harmony between herself and Sartre: 'When I said "We are one person," I was dodging the issue [*je trichais*]. Harmony between two individuals is never a *donnée*; it must be worked for continually' (PL260; FA299). Accordingly, in *L'Invitée*, Françoise's illusions of communion and unity are subjected to nuanced but critical scrutiny, whereas absolutely nothing is allowed to taint the figure of Pierre.

Reading *L'Invitée* it is, for instance, extremely difficult to understand why Françoise does not simply ask Pierre to give up his relationship with Xavière. Several times he offers to do so, and every time she refuses to say the word. While there is some truth in Françoise's own explanation (that she wants Pierre to prefer her freely and spontaneously, and not out of duty), a closer reading of the text reveals that she hesitates to tell him what she feels because it is impossible for her to do so without appearing in some way or other to be *blaming* him for his behaviour. On the one hand she flatly refuses to admit that Pierre is anything but 'perfect': 'It was unfair to be angry with him, he behaved so perfectly with her' (SC157; I198); on the other she knows perfectly well that he cannot stand being criticized: 'He was on the defensive; he had a horror of being in the wrong' (SC158; I199). As long as Pierre keeps assuring Françoise that he loves her as much ever, *she* feels guilty about pointing out that his behaviour does not quite correspond to his words. Perceiving the contradiction between Pierre's words and deeds, Françoise chooses to question the truth value of *all* discourse, rather than express the slightest doubt concerning her lover's integrity. At one point she nevertheless breaks down and reveals that she really has come to doubt Pierre's love in spite of his protestations. Her lover then tells her to stop crying, proves to her that her logic is far from consistent, and finishes by reaffirming his love for her:

> He looked at her. 'You don't believe me?'
> 'I believe you,' said Françoise.
> She believed him; but that was not precisely the point. She did not really
> know any longer just what was the point at issue.
> 'That's sensible [*tu es sage*],' said Pierre, 'but don't start all over again'
> (SC163; I204).

Françoise's attempt to explain her feelings to Pierre is well and truly
defeated: at the end she no longer knows what it was she was trying to say.
Structurally reminiscent of the discussion in the Luxembourg Gardens
which led to the philosophical defeat of the young Simone de Beauvoir,
this scene enacts the emotional defeat of Françoise. In both cases the male
protagonist is represented as blameless. Superior, innocent, unlucky to have
to deal with the tantrums of an overemotional woman, Pierre ends up
talking to Françoise as if she were a naughty child (*tu es sage*).

While the first half of *L'Invitée* takes Françoise to the depths of despair
through an illness in which she is tempted to give up the struggle for
identity, to abandon her projects and even her life, the second half presents
her in a new position. She now realizes that others exist, that her relationship to Pierre is unsound, that the fault is all her own, and that what she
needs to do is to affirm her own identity and independence. Pierre, of
course, needs to do nothing at all. In this scenario Xavière alone incarnates
the Other whose projects and perspectives threaten the very existence of
Françoise's own shaky identity.

Strangely enough, *L'Invitée* takes it for granted that the way to independence from Pierre goes through independence from Xavière. The
murder of Xavière comes across as somehow indispensable if Françoise is
to be freed from her unhealthy dependence on Pierre. This is also the
implication of Simone de Beauvoir's own account of the end, where, as we
have seen, she insists that Françoise needed to kill in order to experience
separation and freedom: '[I released] Françoise, through the agency of
a crime, from the dependent position in which her love for Pierre kept
her' (PL340; FA388). This is, to say the least, a puzzling statement. It is as
if, through a curious process of substitution (projection or transference,
perhaps), the body of Xavière becomes the only ground on which
Françoise can erect an independent relationship to Pierre. What, then, does
Xavière represent in this scenario?

XAVIÈRE'S TENTACLES

If Françoise alienates herself entirely in Pierre, it is to no small extent due
to the fact that they tell each other everything: for her, her experiences are

not real until they have been heard by him. Total transparency is in fact the very definition of love for Françoise. When Françoise believes that Xavière is about to tell her the truth about the loss of her virginity, she immediately conjures up a vision of a perfect union between them:

> 'Tell me what is upsetting you so much,' [Françoise] said in an urgent tone. 'Tell me.'
> In Xavière's face something wavered. Françoise was waiting, hanging on her lips. In one sentence, Xavière was on the verge of bringing about what Françoise had so long desired: the complete union, which would encompass their joys, their worries, their torments (SC321; I398–9).

Xavière's refusal to confess brings about an attack of spiteful rage, the desire to penetrate Xavière by force: 'Françoise longed to crush that obstinate little head between her hands until it split open' (SC322; I399). But Françoise's constant practice of confession also saves her from something she vaguely calls the *grouillements confus* of her mind:[18]

> When, in the past, she had been shy with Pierre, there were a number of things that she had brushed aside in this way: uncomfortable thoughts and ill-considered gestures. If they were not mentioned, it was almost as if they had not existed at all, and this allowed a shameful subterranean vegetation to grow up under the surface of true existence where she felt utterly alone and in danger of suffocation. Little by little she had told him everything: she no longer knew aloneness, but she had rid herself of those chaotic subterranean tendrils [*grouillements confus*]. Every moment of her life that she entrusted to him, Pierre gave back to her clear, polished, completed, and they became moments of their shared life (SC17; I30; TA).

In order to establish a sharp contrast between the polished, purified, stone(*pierre*)-like discourse elaborated through interaction with Pierre, and the shameful, confused, organic, subterranean abyss which threatens to asphyxiate or suffocate (*étouffer*) its lonely victim, Françoise deploys an imagery reminiscent of that of Roquentin confronted with the roots of the chestnut tree in *Nausea*, an imagery which in its turn recalls the 'miasmic swamps' of the *vie intérieure* denounced by Sartre and his fellow students at the ENS. To cast Françoise's images in terms of the opposition between the for-itself (consciousness) and the in-itself ('things in the world') is nevertheless not convincing: unlike Roquentin's tree-roots, these humiliating organic growths represent parts of Françoise's own mind. Rather, this passage reads as an image of the opposition between free and transparent consciousness and the subterranean threat of the unconscious.

Sharing her slightest thought with Pierre, Françoise feels protected against the threat of the return of the repressed, or to put it more precisely:

she feels, much like Sartre in *Being and Nothingness*, that repression is no longer a relevant term. What is feared, what threatens to choke her (and it is impossible not to remember here that Françoise kills Xavière by asphyxiation), is not only the vague, truly repressed *grouillements confus*, but also the very thought of *having* such a shameful part of herself, an aspect of her mind which *by definition* escapes her. Thanks to Pierre, in other words, Françoise can pretend that everything is under control; that she has no unconscious.

The price she pays for such massive repression of the idea of the unconscious is high. Not only does she suffer from unmotivated anxiety crises; when her defences do start to fail, she experiences a violent and profoundly painful regression to the most archaic layers of her psyche. Many of Françoise's fits of depression are represented as the humiliating dissolution of the clear, organized, shining, polished stone that *is* the Françoise constructed by Pierre. Thus, when she falls ill with despair and pulmonary congestion, she first registers that she is 'nobody', and then collapses to the point where she thinks of herself as nothing but 'an inert mass, she was not even a coherent body [*un corps organisé*]' (SC177; I222; TA).

In the second half of *L'Invitée*, Xavière increasingly becomes cast as the character around which the threat of the *grouillements confus* crystallizes. Once Françoise has realized that Xavière is no longer simply a sweet but trying child, but a grown-up who feels herself to be a sexual agent in her own right, she also starts seeing her as deeply menacing, perceiving Xavière's hotel room, for instance, as frighteningly hostile:

> Since she had watched the growth of jealousy and hatred in Xavière's heart, this place of refuge frightened her. It was not only a sanctuary where Xavière celebrated her own worship; it was a hothouse in which flourished a luxuriant and poisonous vegetation; it was the cell of a bedlamite [*un cachot d'hallucinée*], in which the dank atmosphere adhered to the body (SC274; I342).

Moving from hostile vegetation to the idea of mad hallucinations, Françoise perceives the tropical growths as clearly female and clearly poisonous, associating them at once with madness or hysteria and the idea of 'stickiness', which Sartre in *Being and Nothingness* labels 'a poisonous possession' (BN776; EN671). The reference to Xavière's worship of herself alludes to her stubborn narcissism, her desire to be inviolable, never vanquished, never defeated. 'Strictly speaking,' Freud writes in his essay 'On Narcissism' (1914), 'it is only themselves that such women love with an intensity comparable to that of the man's love for them' (p. 89). The narcissistic woman, Freud adds, is self-contained, inaccessible and appears to be enigmatic because she succeeds in maintaining an 'unassailable libidinal position' (p. 89). It is precisely Xavière's ferocious desire to keep herself *pure*, unsullied by others, that makes her such an opaque figure for Françoise and Pierre. For them, she truly is an X, the unknown factor symbolized by her initial. In this context, their ceaseless efforts to interpret her come across as an attempt to penetrate her narcissistic defences, to violate her virginal integrity. Given Sartre's theory of knowledge as visual rape ('The scientist is the hunter who surprises a white nudity and who rapes it [*la viole*] by looking at it' – BN738; EN639; TA), this is not, I believe, a particularly fanciful interpretation.[19]

During a night spent at a Spanish night-club with Xavière and Pierre, Françoise watches Xavière as she slowly and methodically burns herself with a cigarette. At the sight of Xavière's smile, Françoise is seized with horror and fear: 'It was an intimate, solitary smile, like the smile of a half-wit; the voluptuous tortured smile of a woman possessed by pleasure. The sight of it was almost unbearable, it concealed something horrible' (SC284; I354; TA). Xavière's self-mutilation is invested with the sexual pleasure of a madwoman, but there is also more than a hint that *every* woman 'possessed by pleasure' may be equally terrifying, mad and tormented. For Françoise, 'what was going on was intolerable' (SC284; I354). Underneath this unbearable sight lurks an unspeakable, monstrous horror (*quelque chose d'horrible*): this is a spectacle of truly melodramatic terror.[20]

Watching Xavière blow away the ashes covering her sore in order deliberately to burn herself again, Françoise describes the spectacle in transparently sexual terms: 'She once more pressed the glowing end of her cigarette against the open wound [*contre la plaie mise à nu*]' (SC284; I354). There is here a deliberate *undressing* or *unveiling* of the wound, a desire to transform it into an exposed, naked opening, ready to meet the burning end of the cigarette. In *The Second Sex*, published six years after *L'Invitée*, Simone de Beauvoir furnishes a striking commentary on this scene. According to the later text, young virgins often indulge in sado-masochistic rituals of self-mutilation: 'The young girl may gash her thigh with a razor-blade, burn herself with a cigarette, cut herself, peel off skin' (SS377; DSb124; TA). Such practices signify at once the desire for and the revolt against defloration; as such they are above all a challenge to the future lover: ' "You will never inflict on me anything more hateful than I inflict on myself" ' (SS377; DSb124). Protest as well as capitulation, such self-inflicted pain is always of a sexual nature: 'These are proud and sullen gestures of initiation to the sexual adventure. [. . .] When she cuts or burns herself, she is protesting against the impalement of her defloration: she protests by annulling [it]' (SS377; DSb124).

In terms of the plot of *L'Invitée*, Xavière's act spells out the fact that she is on the verge of becoming a sexually active woman; thus we learn that she has just spent the preceding night dancing with Gerbert; the very next night she loses her virginity to him. One may well wonder why it is that although Beauvoir's novel bestows massive ontological and psychological importance on the episode of the cigarette burn, and although her essay stresses its sexual implications, her autobiography reduces it to tedious insignificance:

> Olga had momentary fits of aberration: during the Easter holidays in Paris, when we were visiting Camille, she burned her hand with a lighted ciga-rette, pressing it into the flesh with positively maniacal concentration. I brought this episode into *She Came to Stay*: it was a kind of self-defence against the confusion which so complex an adventure had brought about in her (PL258; FA297).

Watching Xavière push the cigarette into her open wound, Françoise feels sick: her body literally refuses to stomach the spectacle of a sexually desiring Xavière. A few pages later, the message is spelt out: 'She hated to look upon Xavière as a woman with the desires [*des appetits*] of a woman' (SC300; I373). During the scene in the night-club, however, Françoise's disgust turns out to mask a deeper horror:

> Behind that maniacal grin, was the threat of a danger more positive than any she had ever imagined. Something was there that hungrily hugged itself, that unquestionably existed on its own account. Approach to it was impossible even in thought. Just as she seemed to be getting near it the thought dissolved. This was no tangible object, but an incessant flow, a never-ending escape [*fuite*], transparent only to itself, and for ever impenetrable (SC285; I354-5; TA).

There is an obvious philosophical – existentialist – gloss on this passage. That reading is readily furnished by Françoise herself: 'It had happened to her before, as now it was happening tonight, that she had felt her being dissolve to the advantage of inaccessible other beings; but never had she been aware of her own annihilation with such perfect lucidity' (SC293; I365). Or, in another version of the same idea, Françoise's horror is said to be caused by her fear of death, a fear brought about by the discovery that '[Xavière] has a consciousness like mine' (SC296; I369; TA). In *Being and Nothingness*, Sartre declares that 'The Other is first the permanent flight [*fuite*] of things' (BN343; EN301), and argues that the presence of the Other represents a 'pure *disintegration* of the relations which I apprehend between the objects of my universe' (BN342; EN301). Françoise's case represents an extreme version of this notion, in which the Other (Xavière) succeeds in annihilating Françoise's sense of subject-being entirely: Françoise has become nothing but an object for Xavière, that is to say that she no longer exists *as* Françoise, she is annihilated, erased, exiled, dead. The horror is that she is not quite dead enough; that she still exists just sufficiently to *register* her own destruction.[21]

While clearly pertinent, the philosophical reading so eagerly preferred by Françoise herself (and, one must add, by Beauvoir in her memoirs) is nevertheless not entirely satisfactory. It can say nothing about the sexual allusions in Françoise's experience of objectification. Nor can it explain why it is in the presence of a sexually menacing *woman* that Françoise feels sick. And, finally, it has nothing to say about the intensity of Françoise's language or the nature of her metaphors. To explore these questions further, it is useful to take a closer look at Françoise's reactions in the night-club. When Xavière tries to burn herself for the second time, Françoise's reaction is even more vehement: 'She seemed to be in the grip of hysterical ecstasy', observes Françoise, who herself is sweating, almost suffocating with emotion, and experiences her own thoughts as 'burning like a torch' (SC292; I363):

> This hostile presence, which earlier had betrayed itself in a lunatic's smile, was approaching closer and closer: there was now no way of avoiding its terrifying disclosure. Day after day, minute after minute, Françoise had fled the danger; but the worst had happened, and she had at last come face to face with this insurmountable obstacle which she had sensed, behind a shadowy outline, since her earliest childhood. At the back of Xavière's maniacal pleasure, at the back of her hatred and jealousy, the abomination [*le scandale*] loomed, as monstrous and definite as death. Before Françoise's very eyes, and yet apart from her, something existed like a sentence without appeal: detached, absolute, unalterable, an alien consciousness was taking up its position (SC292; I363–4; TA).

In French, this passage is constructed as one single sentence, structured as a mounting crescendo exploding on the punchline of the 'alien consciousness', a horrifying vision which comes complete with its own philosophical gloss. But this should not make us overlook the references to the 'insurmountable obstacle' which has pursued her since her 'earliest childhood'. This ever-present danger, Françoise continues, is like death, it is total negation and eternal absence, it is an 'abyss of nothingness' in which 'the entire universe was engulfed' (SC292; I364). A monstrous abyss, an emptiness ceaselessly engulfing reality, producing annihilation, death, destruction, the 'hostile presence' is a redoubtable monster indeed. By the end of the night, Françoise is ready to flee to the ends of the earth to escape Xavière and her 'avid tentacles which wanted to swallow [*dévorer*] her alive' (SC295; I367; TA).

Surrounding Xavière, then, is an imagery of sexual menace, suffocation, claustrophobia and death, and a morbid insistence on the idea of being swallowed, engulfed, poisoned, held down, choked or strangulated. Her *mouth* is also repeatedly emphasized, not only through the metonymical cigarette, but also through references to her crazy and voluptuous smile ('the smile of a half-wit', 'that maniacal grin', 'the voluptuous, tortured smile of a woman possessed by pleasure'), or by an emphatic insistence on her lips, as in the following passage describing Xavière's jealous face: 'A wave of violent hatred and suffering swelled her face. Her mouth was partly open in a smile [*rictus*], like a cut on an over-ripe fruit; and this open wound exposed to the sun a secret, venomous pulp' (SC328–9; I407). This gaping wound giving birth to a secret poison recalls the wound made by the burning cigarette: in both cases Xavière is described as impudently baring that which ought to have remained hidden.

Xavière is also represented as being intensely jealous of Françoise, much more so than Françoise is of her. While not attempting to deny her anguish, Françoise does try to convince herself as well as the reader that she has overcome her own slight jealousy by the time she recovers from her illness. From then on, she tends to minimize and finally to deny her own jealousy. When Françoise finally allows herself to *hate* Xavière, this is presented as a long-delayed response to the undisguised jealousy of the young woman (see SC358–60; I442–5). It is in this frame of mind that Françoise goes off on a walking holiday with Gerbert and ends up seducing him.[22]

The last few chapters of the novel constitute a veritable character assassination of the younger woman: first Françoise is present at a scene in which Pierre, in order to vent his own jealousy, proceeds to tear Xavière's character and motivations apart; later Pierre decides not to pursue a relationship with her after all, precisely because she has shown herself to be too jealous of Françoise. Exposing Xavière's perfidy for all to see, these scenes allow Françoise to behave with apparently impeccable altruism, for instance by trying to persuade Pierre to go back to Xavière in spite of everything. The actual murder of Xavière is represented as committed out of pure hatred, not out of jealousy. In fact Françoise does not decide to kill until Xavière accuses her of having been jealous of *her*. There is more than a whiff of projection in her outrage: it is hard not to wonder whether Xavière here is not made to embody Françoise's own rivalrous feelings. It is as if the very thought of being labelled 'jealous' is the worst vilification imaginable for Françoise. Staging a circular exchange of the despised label of jealousy between the two women, the novel excludes the men from the game: Pierre never hides his jealousy of Gerbert, and thus does not need to transfer it on to anybody else, and Gerbert, apparently, does not even know the meaning of the word.

When Françoise realizes that Xavière's version of events is that Pierre still loves her desperately, but that she nobly renounced his love because of Françoise's unreasonable jealousy, she immediately pictures her as an evil, death-dealing creature: 'There, in the sepulchral [*mortuaire*] light of her room, Xavière was sitting wrapped in her brown dressing-gown, sullen and maleficent' (SC398; I490). While deeply tempted to show Xavière the letters from Pierre and Gerbert, to teach her a lesson and finally '[annihilate] this insolent pride' (SC400; I493), she restrains herself by remembering that Xavière is nothing but a 'poor, hunted victim, from whom no vengeance could be extracted' (SC402; I495). Thus Xavière does not have the truth thrown at her by a Françoise driven to paroxysms of rage; instead, Beauvoir makes her steal the key to the desk containing the revealing letters.[23]

In the final scene between the two women, Françoise feels none of the satisfaction she had hoped to derive from telling Xavière the truth. For even after reading the letters, the young woman persists in thinking that *she* is in the possession of the *real* story: 'You were jealous of me because Labrousse was in love with me. You made him loathe me, and to get better revenge, you took Gerbert from me' (SC405; I498–9). Surprisingly enough, Françoise's reaction is to feel tricked or *trapped*: 'And now, she had fallen into the trap, she was at the mercy of this voracious consciousness that had been waiting in the shadow for the moment to swallow her up' (SC406; I500; TA). Condensing the images of a voracious mouth (Xavière is about to *swallow* or *engulf* [*engloutir*] Françoise) and the idea of choking, suffocation or claustration (the tentacles, the closed room, the trap), this image sets the tone for the actual killing of Xavière:

> Face to face with her aloneness, beyond space, beyond time, stood this hostile presence that had for so long overwhelmed her [*écrasait*] by its blind shadow: Xavière was there, existing only for herself, entirely self-centred, reducing to nothingness everything for which she had no use: she encompassed the whole world within her own triumphant aloneness, boundlessly extending her influence, infinite and unique, everything that she was, she drew from within herself, she barred all dominance over her, she was absolute separateness (SC408; I502–3; TA).

Killing Xavière, Françoise attempts to kill a devouring and destructive monster, one that has weighed upon her from the earliest times, a monster that exists outside time and space, dimensionless, endless, omnipresent and forever resting in itself. In the presence of such a ghoulish creature, there is no possible place for Françoise. The universe itself is not big enough for the two of them: with a determined twist of her hand, Françoise turns on the gas in Xavière's room.

My Monster/My Mother/My Man/Myself

Who or what, then, is Françoise killing? What *is* the repressed fantasy or family romance of this existentialist melodrama?[24] On the surface of it, the triangle established by Pierre–Françoise–Xavière *looks* like an obviously Oedipal father–mother–daughter structure in which Gerbert figures as a supplementary, consolatory Oedipal son for the mother. In this scenario, Françoise has to be the mother who kills the rivalrous daughter. But such a reading takes no account at all of the imagery surrounding Xavière. Looking carefully at Françoise's metaphors, it is hard to escape the conclusion that the timeless, suffocating monster that leaves no space in the world for Françoise is the very image of the omnipotent and malevolent archaic mother threatening to devour her daughter. Under the Oedipal scenario, then, lurks another fantasmatic configuration in which Françoise is the daughter killing the cruel, invasive and rivalrous mother. Appearing in the interstices of the more obvious triangular structure, this second fantasy does not in the least cancel out the Oedipal scenario. The fantasy of a dual struggle between the two women, which is responsible for the melodramatic language in *L'Invitée*, must also be the compelling force that drives Beauvoir to produce her melodramatic end. Insisting that *this* specific end was the very *raison d'être* for the whole novel, Beauvoir is implicitly saying that, for her, the way to publication, the way into the public sphere went through the cathartic and enabling murder of a fantasmatic mother figure. While it may not at all be what Hélène Cixous has in mind when she extols the virtues of 'writing the body', I believe that this is why Beauvoir's throat is dry and her body tense as she is writing the crucial scenes: to kill the mother surely requires participation by every cell of the woman writer's body.

There is considerable intertextual evidence for the theory that Xavière represents a mother figure for Françoise. In *A Very Easy Death* the mother's death comes as a shock to Simone de Beauvoir, precisely because it forces her to situate her mother in time and space. She had, she writes, always thought of her mother as belonging to a timeless, mythical space: 'For me, my mother had always existed and I had never seriously thought that some day, that soon I should see her go. Her death, like her birth had its place in some legendary [*mythique*] time' (VE18; UM27; TA). Just as the murder of Xavière enables Françoise literally to liquidate her monstrous fantasies, and become an autonomous agent, the death of her mother forces Simone de Beauvoir to abandon the fantasy of her eternal existence.

The fact that the final conflict in *L'Invitée* is caused by Xavière's unauthorized reading of Françoise's *letters* must remind readers of *Memoirs of a Dutiful Daughter* and *A Very Easy Death* that both Simone de Beauvoir and her sister Hélène felt deeply threatened by their mother's jealous and intrusive spying on their every move. She censored her daughters' letters, for instance, until they were 18 years old. In *A Very Easy Death*, Beauvoir writes that her mother 'embittered [*a empoisonné*] several years of my life' (VE90; UM148), and uses terms such as tyranny and excessive jealousy to describe her mother's constant efforts to invade her daughters' privacy: 'At home we had to leave all the doors open, and I had to work under her eye, in the room where she was sitting. When, at night, my sister and I chattered from one bed to the other, she pressed her ear against the wall, eaten up with curiosity, and called out, ' "Be quiet!" [. . .] She could not bear to feel left out' (VE34; UM54–5). One scene in which Simone de Beauvoir's mother opens a letter sent to Hélène from Simone is described in some detail: 'Maman opened my letter and read it aloud in front of Poupette, shrieking with laughter at its confidences' (VE36; UM57). In Deirdre Bair's biography, the ageing Beauvoir is still bitter about her mother's intrusive manners: 'She said she wanted to be my friend, but she treated me like a specimen under a microscope. She probed into everything I did, from reading my books to reading my letters' (Bair, p. 95). As we have seen, Françoise is both fascinated and repelled by Xavière's mouth. In *A Very Easy Death* the repressed relationship between mother and daughter returns to haunt the daughter precisely in the form of the mother's *mouth*: 'I talked to Sartre about my mother's mouth as I had seen it that morning and about everything that I had interpreted in it [. . .]. And he told me that my own mouth was not obeying me any more: I had put Maman's mouth on my own face and in spite of myself, I copied its movements' (VE28; UM44).

I do not quote such autobiographical passages to prove that Françoise 'really' is Simone de Beauvoir. Rather I want to show that certain themes raised in the novel also occur in other texts by Simone de Beauvoir, and that when they do, they tend to cluster around the image of a mother figure. It is particularly important to guard against the idea that Beauvoir's autobiographical texts somehow are 'truer' – closer to 'real life' – than the essays and the fiction. What are we to make, for instance, of the intense fictional elaboration of the scene of Xavière's cigarette burn, as opposed to the laconic account in the autobiography? And are we to assume that the sexual meaning attributed to it in *The Second Sex* is relevant to the fiction but not to the autobiography? Or vice versa?

And what are we to think when we discover that Simone de Beauvoir's mother's name was Françoise? In relation to my own reading, it may not be particularly significant: I am after all trying to show that Françoise is *not* the principal mother figure in *L'Invitée*. One may nevertheless choose to see a nice irony here: in naming her character after her, Beauvoir turns her own mother into a murderess. What *is* significant, however, is that

Simone de Beauvoir chooses to give this name to the heroine of her *first* novel, a heroine, moreover, who is an aspiring writer and who ends up killing an intrusive mother figure. By naming her heroine Françoise, Beauvoir is defiantly marking her entry into the literary field in France as an absolute *triumph* over and *liberation* from the realm of the mother.[25]

In her essay 'Feminine Guilt and the Oedipus Complex' the French psychoanalyst Janine Chasseguet-Smirgel writes at some length about women's complex relationship to creativity. According to Chasseguet-Smirgel, the daughter poised on the brink of separation from the mother goes through a period in which she idealizes the phallus (represented by the father) and loathes and detests the mother, perceived as the one who blocks her access to the idealized father, and, more importantly, as the powerful, all-encompassing figure from which the daughter must escape if she is to become an independent individual. In this process, the idealized phallus becomes an indispensable ally in the girl's struggle for individuation, or entry into the symbolic order. In fact, she argues, the idealization of the father is more correctly seen as the result of the splitting of the mother imago into a good and a bad part, where the image of the 'good mother' is projected on to the father, and the mother is cast as the repository for all that is evil. While necessary and important for the girl's development, such a phase of phallus worship is not destined to last. Once the little girl has achieved the necessary independence, Chasseguet-Smirgel claims, she may develop a more classical Oedipal position: one in which she can identify with a more realistic mother-imago and desire the father. If the mother, for one reason or another, is perceived as too frustrating, however, the road to such an identification will remain blocked.

In my view, then, *L'Invitée* explores a psychic situation in which the protagonist has remained in such a phallus-idealizing phase. As I understand it, this is a curiously ambivalent position, one in which the daughter casts her mother as her evil enemy precisely because she has *not* completed the process of separation from her. Fantasizing the mother as destructive, the daughter paradoxically signals her persisting unity with her. In the same way, her intense fear of *becoming like* her mother expresses her experience of *not* being sufficiently different as it is. Experiencing the mother as castrating and sadistic *vis-à-vis* the father, Chasseguet-Smirgel argues, the daughter represses her own aggression towards the phallus, fantasizing that, unlike her mother, *she* will protect and nourish the father. Instead, she directs all her aggression on to the mother. In this position the daughter may suffer various inhibitions in relation to heterosexual activity. Given the fact that heterosexual intercourse implies the incorporation of the penis into the woman's vagina, the daughter-figure may unconsciously equate such an act with the bad mother's castrating of the father, and, as a result, develop profound guilt feelings. One defence against such guilt,

Chasseguet-Smirgel argues, may be a wish for homosexual relations with women, precisely because such sexual relations do not involve the possibility of symbolically castrating the father's penis. Perhaps this is the reason why Françoise, at least intermittently, feels the attraction of the physical charms of Xavière, and why there is little or no sexual activity between Françoise and Pierre.[26]

To understand Françoise as caught up in such an ambivalent position, at once separated and not separated from the mother, helps us to understand why the monstrous enemy feared by Françoise contains at once highly regressive, pre-Oedipal features (the oral imagery of mouths, eating and suffocation, the image of an omnipotent, formless creature outside time) and the much more Oedipal trait of a highly threatening sexuality aimed at the father-figure. These two aspects of the mother-figure in *L'Invitée* are condensed in the image of the sexually grotesque and disgusting mouth of Xavière. Chasseguet-Smirgel's account of the phallus-idealizing daughter also allows us to understand Françoise's curiously symbiotic professional relationship with Pierre. For this is a position in which the daughter equates intellectual work with phallic values, and therefore fears that she will castrate the father (steal or destroy his penis) if she displays an aggressive creativity of her own. Françoise's position as a highly efficient collaborator of Pierre's at the theatre, but as a frustrated writer of her own novel, is typical in this respect. Such a woman is not autonomous in regard to her love object, Chasseguet-Smirgel writes; on the contrary, 'she is closely dependent on it and is also its *complement*. She is the *right hand*, the assistant, the colleague, the secretary, the auxiliary, the inspiration for an employer, a lover, a husband, a father' (p. 124). On this theory, Simone de Beauvoir's own understanding of the meaning of the final murder turns out to be highly convincing. Killing Xavière, Beauvoir claims, Françoise establishes her own autonomy from Pierre. According to Chasseguet-Smirgel, the daughter who manages to break out of her negative symbiosis with the mother will be able to give up the defence of idealizing the paternal phallus, and as a consequence she will no longer experience her own creativity as castrating. *This* is why the road to Françoise's independence from Pierre goes through the violent death of Xavière. On this level, then, the very existence of *L'Invitée* as a text *enacts* or *embodies* the fantasmatic resolution of Françoise's problems.[27]

This complex scenario is crucial to my understanding of *L'Invitée*. It may nevertheless be necessary to stress the deeply dualistic – untriangulated or non-Oedipal – nature of the struggle between the two women. On the philosophical level, Sartre's theory of the Other is partly responsible for this dualism: it is not difficult to show that for Sartre, the relationship between the 'I' and the 'Other' is similar to Lacan's notion of alienation in the mirror stage. Yet if Beauvoir makes this specific notion the cornerstone of

her novel it can only be because it enables her to work through fundamental fantasies of her own: my psychoanalytic reading is not intended to
displace Beauvoir's philosophical gloss, but rather to point to the overdetermined nature of her own philosophical investments.

It is important not to pull the reading outlined here too far in an Oedipal
direction. I perceive Françoise as *suspended* or *in transition* between an
archaic symbiosis with the mother and a fully developed Oedipal position.
This ambiguity produces the complexity of the relations between the
maternal and the paternal in the text. In my view, Françoise's melodrama
takes place on what Gregorio Kohon has called the *hysterical stage*, a stage
positioned *between* the pre-Oedipal period in which the mother is still the
primary libidinal object for the little girl, and that of the Oedipal phase, in
which the father has become the primary object for the daughter. Stressing
the instability of this 'stage', Kohon explicates the pun of his term: 'I am
referring to it as a *stage*', he writes, 'not in a developmental sense, but more
as a place where something happens, on which a performance takes place,
a drama is developed, and at the same time, as a distance between two
stopping places' (p. 378).[28]

My own reading also seeks to emphasize the ambiguity of Françoise's
position. Affecting the text as a whole, the very same 'hysterical' ambiguity
is evident in what one might want to call the text's relative inability to
distribute sexual difference: the idealized 'masculine' phallus attributed to
Pierre represents at once Françoise's way into the symbolic order, and her
identification with the imaginary phallus of the mother. In this respect,
Françoise's dilemma is not unlike that of Freud's Dora. Interestingly
enough, for instance, both *L'Invitée* and *Dora* play out a complex scenario
of sexualized and gendered struggle for the authority of knowledge: in both
texts the *right to interpret* is finally what is at stake.[29]

A straightforwardly Oedipal reading of *L'Invitée* overlooks the ambiguous staging of the daughter's drama of separation. Distinguishing too readily
between the paternal and the maternal, such a reading would have to
repress the fact that Françoise kills Xavière in order to free herself *from*
Pierre, not simply in order to get him for herself. Wishing to escape from
her painfully hierarchical symbiosis with Pierre, Françoise wants to create
a healthy, united relationship between two free, responsible individuals.
Struggling to present this as the solution actually achieved by Françoise, the
narrative weakens its case by its persistent idealization of Pierre. While this
can readily be explained as a case of daughterly phallus worship, this is not
all there is to it. For Pierre is represented as the antidote to Xavière's
poison: *he* becomes the imaginary good mother, the narcissistic refuge that
Xavière cannot provide. If Pierre is an idealized father-figure in this novel,
it is because he is bearer of all the positive values of the good mother. His
considerable phallic prestige – conquests of other women, social and artistic

success and so on – helps to mask the relatively asexual relationship between the two protagonists. Theirs is above all a union based on the fantasy of total openness: this is a conjunction of minds, not of bodies. On the fantasmatic level, then, Pierre comes across as a vaguely incestuous maternal wolf in heavily idealized phallic clothing. Conveniently projected on to the hapless Xavière, every negative aspect of Françoise's symbiotic union with Pierre is obliterated from view, leaving Pierre as phallic perfection incarnate.[30] During her adult life Simone de Beauvoir rarely dreamt of her father, but often of her mother: 'She often played the most important part,' Beauvoir writes in *A Very Easy Death*, 'she blended with Sartre, and we were happy [*heureuses*] together' (VE89; UM147; TA). While grammatically it is Sartre who merges with the mother here (the feminine plural of *heureuses* tells us that the dream perceives Sartre *as* a mother), the dreamtext enacts the opposite movement ('*she* blended with Sartre'): a more or less unconscious belief that if only her mother were more like Sartre, mother and daughter could finally be happy together.[31]

At the end of the book, Françoise proclaims her independence. But her declaration of autonomy is not quite convincing. While the persistent imagery of symbiosis and union is repeatedly questioned in the text, Françoise nevertheless intends to continue her practice of telling Pierre everything: 'Alone. She had acted alone: as alone as in death. One day Pierre would know. But even his cognizance of this deed would be merely external' (SC408–9; I503). The last sentence here is particularly striking. What else than an 'external cognizance' can even the minutest narrative of one's own actions ever be to anybody else? Are we to assume that *other* events can still be understood by Pierre from the *inside*, as it were? And why does she need to have recourse to the comfort that sooner or later Pierre will indeed share the knowledge of her crime after all?

There is another twist to this tale. For, as we have seen, Xavière does not simply represent a negative mother-figure: she is also closely associated with the *grouillements confus* of Françoise's own mind. As the repressed unconscious, the mysterious X that always escapes a final, controlling interpretation, Xavière comes across as a traditional patriarchal representation of femininity in modernist garb: Xavière's closest fictional sister is surely André Breton's Nadja. Her power to stir and unsettle all fixed representations, to incarnate a certain revolutionary hysteria, may also awake associations from Freud's Dora to Marguerite Duras's Lol V. Stein.[32] But where Breton and Duras – in widely different ways, to be sure – *valorize* the transgressive, disordering power of their heroines, Beauvoir feels deeply threatened by it: not for her the delights of unconscious femininity or the *jouissance* of the disruptive sliding of the signifier. Cast as Xavière's positive counterpart, Pierre is kept *outside* – untainted by – the slippery economy of the unconscious. Together Françoise and Pierre are polished stones, protected against the terrors of the voracious maternal monster lurking in the depths of the unconscious. For Françoise, to kill Xavière is symbolically to murder her own unconscious, to expel the bad mother from her psyche and to claim total control over body and mind. If successful, such an action will put an end to anxiety crises and psycho-somatic breakdowns alike: to kill Xavière is to deny that the repressed ever returns.

For Beauvoir to finish *L'Invitée* was as liberating as for Françoise to kill Xavière. 'Why was it that from this point on I always had ' "something to say"?', Beauvoir asks at the end of *The Prime of Life*: 'Before writing *She Came to Stay* I spent years fumbling around for a subject. From the moment I began that book I never stopped writing' (PL606; FA694). Her own answer is political: the outbreak of World War II made her see that unhappiness existed in the world: 'After the declaration of war things finally ceased to be a matter of course. Misfortune and misery [*le malheur*] had erupted into the world, and literature had become as essential to me as the very air I breathed' (PL606; FA694). But it was not only historical un-happiness that triggered the writing of *L'Invitée*: Beauvoir started her novel in the autumn of 1938, well before the outbreak of war, but only a year after the crisis provoked by Sartre's infatuation with Olga Kosakiewicz in 1936–7.

For Beauvoir, unhappiness stems from lack: she writes to plug the gap of absence and loss, what she calls 'the scandal of loneliness and separation' (PL607; FA695; TA). Such a strikingly fetishistic notion of writing enables Beauvoir to see her writing as at once a consolation against the pain of solitude and lack, and a weapon against the power of the Other. No wonder she never let it go again. Having killed the fantasmatic bad mother in the very act of writing, an act over which *she* has total control, she can now let herself represent her: 'From now on, I always had something to say.'[33]

5

Freedom and Flirtation: The Personal and the Philosophical in Sartre and Beauvoir

'I have never been able to follow the rules of flirting,' she was saying. 'I can't bear being touched: it's morbid.'

In another corner, a young woman with green and blue feathers in her hair was looking uncertainly at a man's huge hand that had just pounced on hers. [. . .] She had decided to leave her bare arm on the table and as it lay there, forgotten, ignored, the man's hand was stroking a piece of flesh that no longer belonged to anyone.

(L'Invitée)

SEXUAL COMPARISONS

Some philosophers take Beauvoir to task for deviating from Sartre's philosophical premises, for instance in *The Second Sex*. Others claim that since her philosophical perspective exactly matches his, there is no point in devoting a separate chapter (or section, or paragraph) to *her* work. The result is, Margaret Simons writes, that 'few surveys of contemporary continental philosophy, even those focusing on issues in socio-political philosophy [. . .] include discussions of her work' ('Beauvoir and Sartre', p. 165). Accusing Beauvoir of being too dependent on Sartre, feminists have also rejected her as unoriginal, or 'male-identified'. Rightly incensed by the patriarchal harping on the theme of *midinettes* and schoolmarms, other feminists, notably Margaret Simons, have tried to counter the charge of philosophical epigoney by showing that Beauvoir was the first of the two to take an interest in the social constraints on freedom.[1] Focusing on the Hegelian and Marxist elements in *The Second Sex*, Eva Lundgren-Gothlin also stresses Beauvoir's difference from Sartre.

Unfortunately, the reasonable feminist wish to explore Beauvoir's works on her own terms is often taken by patriarchs to indicate a fanatical desire once and for all to 'prove' her superiority to Sartre: as if being interested in Beauvoir means slighting Sartre. Such attitudes lead to futile debates indeed. It is certainly true, for instance, that Beauvoir took an early interest in the social determinants of individual freedom. But it is also true that it was Sartre and not Beauvoir who went on to write *Critique of Dialectical Reason*. Yet, given the fact that he defined himself as a philosopher and she did not, that should hardly surprise us. There is clearly no end – because there is no clear point – to this particular debate, and personally I find the endless preoccupation with the question of intellectual superiority between the two writers quite tedious. If patriarchal critics did not blithely assume that an intellectual woman's work *must* be judged in relation to that of her male lover(s), the comparison game would never have become a standard *topos* of critical and journalistic debate on Beauvoir. While most critics insist on Sartre's leading role, some do not shrink from attributing Beauvoir's opinions to Nelson Algren, or to Claude Lanzmann. The reverse, of course, never applies: according to patriarchal critical opinion no male intellectual ever learnt anything from a female lover. This is surely why nobody bothers to judge Sartre's – or Lanzmann's – work in relation to that of Beauvoir. And why is nobody comparing Beauvoir to Julien Green or Mauriac, or – with far greater relevance – to Fanon? Could it be because she never had sexual relations with any of them?

In spite of my own impatience with the subject, I have to recognize its persistence and dominance in Beauvoir criticism. I also have to take account of Beauvoir's own representation of herself as second only to Sartre: in the 1990s it is still not possible to escape the issue. In spite of my misgivings, I shall therefore compare the two writers through a detailed reading of two central and thematically very similar passages, written roughly at the same time. In this chapter, then, I want to explore the question of women's freedom in heterosexual relations as discussed by Sartre in *Being and Nothingness* and by Beauvoir in *L'Invitée*, both published in 1943. My juxtaposition of a philosophical and a fictional text is quite deliberate. I have already argued that because she defines herself as philosophically inferior to Sartre, Beauvoir chooses to give priority to literature. On this logic, however, it follows that Beauvoir's deepest and most thoughtful engagement with the question of freedom is more likely to be found in *L'Invitée*, on which she worked for almost five years, than in *Pyrrhus et Cinéas* (1944), which she wrote in three months. My subject, then, is the discussion in *Being and Nothingness* of the woman who has gone off to a first rendezvous in a Parisian café, and the scene in *L'Invitée* where Françoise seduces Gerbert.

A RENDEZVOUS IN A PARISIAN CAFÉ

Sartre's discussion of bad faith in a woman can be found in the chapter of *Being and Nothingness* entitled 'Patterns of Bad Faith', where he is trying to show that it is possible to lie *to oneself*.[2] 'What must be the being of man', Sartre asks at the end of one paragraph, 'if he is to be capable of bad faith?' 'Take the example of a woman', he continues at the beginning of the next, 'who has consented to go out with a particular man for the first time' (BN96; EN91). The awkward transition from 'man' to 'woman' is striking, to say the least: signalling Sartre's commitment to producing a philosophy valid for all, this turn of phrase also reveals that he radically underestimates the difficulties involved in such a project.

According to Sartre, this café scene is to be considered a pheno-menological description. Philosophically speaking, such descriptions only work if they are perceived as accurate by their readers: no wonder *Being and Nothingness* provides so much insight into the everyday life of Parisian intellectuals in the early 1940s. Yet what may have been perceived as unproblematic in 1943 does not necessarily remain so fifty years later: to me, at least, many aspects of Sartre's analysis come across as rather puzzling.

Sitting at the café table, the woman involved in a first rendezvous knows perfectly well, according to Sartre, what the man's intentions are. 'She knows also that it will be necessary sooner or later for her to make a decision. But she does not want to realize [*sentir*] the urgency,' Sartre continues, 'she concerns herself only with what is respectful and discreet in the attitude of her companion' (BN96; EN91). Refusing to see his conversation as an attempt to carry out 'what we call [*ce qu'on nomme*] "the first approach"' (BN 96; EN91), she refuses to acknowledge the possible temporal developments of his behaviour, Sartre complains. When the man declares 'I admire you so much',[3] he continues, the woman more or less perversely persists in taking it literally: she actually pretends to *believe* him. Depriving the sentence of its 'sexual background', Sartre writes, she takes his discourse at face value. Or in other words: it does not even occur to Sartre that the woman may genuinely be taken in by the man's declarations of esteem and admiration. According to Sartre, every one of these aspects of her behaviour demonstrates the woman's bad faith. In the end, he argues, her problem is that 'she does not quite know what she wants. She is profoundly aware of the desire which she inspires, but crude and naked desire would humiliate and horrify her' (BN97; EN91; TA).[4] It is hard to judge from this sentence whether Sartre believes that the woman's bad faith consists in not knowing what she wants, or whether, on the contrary, it consists in most certainly knowing that the expression of *le désir cru et nu* –

crude and naked desire – would be humiliating. Summarizing her initial behaviour, Sartre sees it as a refusal to 'apprehend the desire for what it is; she does not even give it a name; she recognizes it only to the extent that it transcends itself towards admiration, esteem, respect' (BN97; EN91).

This, then, is Sartre's analysis of the initial stages of the rendezvous. Trying to make sense of his account, I come up against a series of difficulties. First there is the fact that Sartre relies entirely on his readers' tacit recognition of the man's motives. But is he really implying that we all know that when a man meets a woman in a café he consciously and deliberately perceives it as nothing but a prelude to sexual intercourse? Contemplating this problem, I am struck by the casual reference to 'what we call "the first approach"'. The rhetorical move here is obvious: gesturing towards a real world of shared conventions, Sartre attempts to establish a tacit community of values between himself and the reader. Masquerading as a general dictionary definition – we all call this the 'first approach', do we not? – the phrase in fact reveals that Sartre imagines himself to be addressing men, not women. In French, *approches* in the plural (*les premières approches*) carries certain military connotations, referring to the efforts of an assailant to penetrate a fortress, or to covert underground attempts to undermine the enemy. According to *Le petit Robert*, this rather ancient military connotation has carried over in its more general and figural sense, which is 'self-interested advances, manoeuvres to achieve a goal'. Carrying an unmistakable flavour of male camaraderie, the phrase may well have been – and have remained – current in conversations between men. I cannot believe that most women at the time would use the phrase about their own attempts at flirtation. Unless they found him wickedly cynical, I also doubt that most women would use it about a man's attempt to flirt with them. But the fact that she would not dream of saying such a thing is precisely Sartre's point: refusing to take the different social conventions applying to the two protagonists into account, Sartre can only see her refusal as a sign of her will to self-deception. The full implications of his casual turn of phrase now become evident: *as long as the woman refuses to speak as if she were a man, she is in bad faith.*

This unfortunate conclusion emerges in spite of the fact that Sartre's basic philosophical premiss is supposed to be sexually neutral. To his mind, sexual difference has nothing to do with bad faith; every thinking subject has the same capacity for good or bad faith. Yet here he argues as if every thinking subject were a man: he has, in other words, overlooked the social and sexual differences which radically shape the discourse and behaviour of the agents involved in this scene. The result is patriarchal philosophy, not the truly universal analysis he sets out to produce.

Sartre does not stop, either, to consider the problem involved in defining the activity engaged in in this scene. Using the word 'flirt' to describe the café scene (BN97; EN91), he nevertheless insists on its goal-oriented nature: the man knows what he wants, the woman is to blame at once for pretending not to know what *he* wants, and for truly not knowing what *she* wants. But if this is supposed to be a case of flirtation, his assumption runs counter to my own experience of social reality: surely, not every flirtation posits a clear sexual goal as the necessary outcome of the activity? Perhaps Sartre is not talking about flirtation at all? Perhaps this scene ought rather to be read as a seduction scene? But what difference would it make?

According to *Le petit Robert*, a flirtation designates 'more or less chaste amorous relations [*relations amoureuses*], generally devoid of deep feelings'.[5] The word has no specific epistemological dimension: while perfectly superficial, a flirtation does not necessarily involve deceit. Given its rather open-ended, playful character, it is not supposed to be an authentic expression of deep feelings either. One may very well flirt without 'meaning' it: my point is that if one 'meant' it, flirtation would no longer be the appropriate word. Flirtation, then, is based on ambiguity: it is a game in which one does not declare one's hand. To have to 'come clean', to confess what is 'really' the case, is to destroy the very possibility of flirtation. In this sense, flirtation is not a goal-oriented activity. Because it does not promise anything, it does not commit its participants to anything either: flirtation is a game from which one can always escape without damage. The point of the game is on the one hand to make all participants feel good: you make me feel attractive, I make you feel desirable; I brighten your day, you brighten mine. On the other hand, this agreeable game can, if desired, also be considered a pleasant space in which to figure out whether flirtation is *all* one wants to engage in.[6] A structurally ambiguous, playful activity with no clearly defined sexual aim, flirtation is eminently useful for women subjected to strict patriarchal control of their sexuality, since it provides them with an opportunity to play with the thought of involvement without actually getting involved, and thus without risking the loss of their virginity, honour, reputation, or entire future at a stroke.[7]

In French, to be *séduisant* is not necessarily to concoct Machiavellian schemes of depravation: it is simply to be exceptionally charming and attractive. In this sense, a certain measure of *séduction* would seem to be an eminently useful ingredient in any flirtation. In its restricted and strong meaning, however, to seduce is etymologically to 'lead astray' (*seducere*), to make somebody take a wrong turn. According to *Le petit Robert*, to seduce is to 'turn away from good, to make somebody misbehave'; its synonyms are verbs like *corrupt, dishonour, debauch, misuse, mislead, deceive* and so on. Always projecting a clear sexual goal as the end result of its activities, seduction also involves false appearances, lies and pretexts of one kind or another. According to the dictionary, men and women flirt in equal measure, but when it comes to seduction, women are its victims, and men its perpetrators: 'A cynical seducer taking an unfortunate foreign woman away from her husband' is the quote helpfully supplied by *Le petit Robert* to explain the nature of such a relationship.[8] In seduction one person is taken to manipulate the other cynically, as for instance in the case of Valmont and Cécile de Volanges in *Les liaisons dangereuses*. The person who is seduced is seduced precisely because she is *ignorant* of the real circumstances. According to Sartre, one may add, a liar is not in bad faith (see BN87–8; EN83–4); neither, one must assume, is the victim of the lie.[9]

Sartre and his male protagonist would seem to be firmly convinced that what is going on is a scene of seduction. According to Sartre, the man is not in bad faith: knowing what he wants, *he* would presumably not find it difficult to talk about the 'first approach', or to acknowledge that all his talk about his admiration and respect for the young woman amounts to not much more than a means to an end. He is, in other words, a seducer. But Sartre does not say this. On the contrary, according to him, the woman is a coquette (BN99; EN93) precisely because she pretends not to know that the man is a seducer. But given that at this stage nothing but pleasant conversation has transpired between the protagonists, it is hard to see how she could tell. After all, even men flirt. The real problem in this passage is not the woman's interpretation, but Sartre's bland assumption that he knows more than the woman.[10] The solidarity between Sartre and his male protagonist recalls that between Freud and Herr K, whereas the *jeune coquette*, like Dora, finds herself defined as epistemologically inferior, or to put it in more Sartrean terms, as sunk in immanence and facticity.

If, according to Sartre, the young woman is already in bad faith in these initial stages of the proceedings, it is because she refuses to cast herself as transcendent and posit a desiring project of her own. But what is a project? In this scene, the notion takes on a strong psychological flavour: it is the man's conscious wish to get the woman into bed. In this context, bad faith consists in denying that one is free to choose one's projects: 'Since it conceals the total freedom of engagement, bad faith is obviously a lie', Sartre bluntly states in *L'existentialisme est un humanisme* (p. 81). To pro-ject oneself into the future, then, is to transcend facticity, to realize one's freedom and thus to become fully human.[11]

Generally speaking, Sartre tends to describe the project in fairly phallic terms: it represents an active, transcendent and teleological 'throwing forward': the project hurls itself forward into time and space until it strikes home. In *What Is Literature?* (1948), he sees prose writing as a form of action, that is to say, as a transcendent project. Words are like loaded pistols (p. 38), he writes, or like a handy prolongation of 'our' body: they are 'a sixth finger, a third leg' (p. 35). Such body parts must not be used at random: if the writer speaks, he shoots: 'He may be silent, but since he has chosen to fire, he must do it like a man, by aiming at targets, and not like a child, at random, by shutting his eyes and firing merely for the pleasure of hearing the shot go off' (p. 38). The result of this ballistic performance is change: 'To speak is to act; anything which one names is already no longer quite the same; it has lost its innocence', Sartre claims (p. 36). Echoing and reversing his account in *The Second Sex*, Beauvoir sees in male sexuality the very incarnation of the existentialist project. Desiring erotic pleasure, the man's body behaves in perfect keeping with his transcendent consciousness as the desiring male 'projects himself towards the other without losing his independence' (SS393; DSb147).[12] Metaphorically, both Sartre and Beauvoir cast the transcendent project as violent, penetrative and phallic. No wonder, then, that Sartre automatically takes seduction and not flirtation to be the paradigmatic example of authentic sexual behaviour.

But if one disengages oneself from the Sartrean equation of male seduction with transcendence, there is no reason not to think that the woman may be involved in a perfectly transcendent project of her own, and that that project is flirtation. In this sense, her aim may well be to produce a space in which she can take some pleasure without too much risk, a space in which she can observe the man at leisure and decide what kind of involvement she may or may not wish to have with him. Sartre, in fact, is perfectly aware of this: 'The point is', he writes, 'to postpone the moment of decision as long as possible' (BN97; EN91; TA). It is obvious that such a project may be extremely irritating to a male hell-bent on rapid seduction; it is equally obvious that it *is* a project and as such in no way inferior to the man's. At this point, it may be worth remembering that France in 1943 was a country in which a woman was sent to the guillotine for performing illegal abortions.[13] It was also a country in which contraception was outlawed, and where the main method of birth control was withdrawal or the bidet. Under such circumstances, the woman would have to trust the man considerably before deciding to have sex with him. No wonder she wanted to take her time. Based on the unargued assumption that she *has no project of her own*, Sartre's analysis casts the woman as an absence, a zero: she becomes at one and the same time the blank screen on which the man is expected to inscribe his project, and a mindless and opaque obstacle to his transparent transcendence.[14]

Against Sartre, then, I hold that the initial stage of this rendezvous may be read as a confrontation between two conflicting projects, the woman's flirtation and the man's seduction. The situation is strictly symmetrical, in so far as both parties believe that the other person's project coincides with or ought to coincide with their own. This stalemate is finally broken by the man: 'But then suppose he takes her hand', Sartre writes (BN97; EN91). Quite rightly stressing the difficult position in which the woman now suddenly finds herself, Sartre shrewdly analyses her dilemma: if she withdraws her hand, she breaks the 'charm' of the evening; if she does not, she

may be taken to express consent and engagement. While all this is true, this
account still presupposes that the woman has no project of her own. In
Sartre's view, her behaviour simply represents a desire not to engage
herself: she is cast as utterly passive. At the end of his phenomenological
description of the woman in bad faith, Sartre's prose is remarkably perceptive, but still fails to capture the logic of the woman's position:

> We know what happens next; the young woman leaves her hand there, but
> she *does not notice* that she is leaving it. She does not notice because it happens
> by chance that she is at this moment all intellect [*tout esprit*]. [. . .] She shows
> herself in her essential aspect – a personality, a consciousness. And during this
> time the divorce of the body from the soul is accomplished; the hand rests
> inert between the warm hands of her companion – neither consenting nor
> resisting – a thing.
> We shall say that this woman is in bad faith (BN97; EN91–2).

For Sartre, the man's grabbing of the woman's hand highlights the essential
logic of the whole scene. For me, it introduces a dramatic change in
relation to the initial situation. Acting from a position of social power, the
man is free to seize the woman's hand. Seizing the initiative, imposing his
hand on the woman, the man now defines the stakes: *he* is free to move his
hand any time, under any pretext, without necessarily breaking the mood
of the evening. Were *she* to withdraw her hand, however, she would most
certainly, as Sartre puts it, 'break the troubled and unstable harmony which
gives the hour its charm' (BN97; EN91), presumably because the man
would get angry or start to sulk. Yet, I would argue, the man, by making
his move, has already broken the ambiguous charm of the moment:
revealing his project of seduction, his act literally forces the woman's hand:
she is now *obliged* to choose her line of action on *his* terms, not on her
own.[15]

No wonder that Simone de Beauvoir, when describing the same scene
in *L'Invitée*, has the woman 'looking uncertainly at a man's huge hand that
had just pounced on hers' (SC52; I72). Her vocabulary here represents a
considerable shift in perspective: where Sartre has the man's 'warm' hand
'taking' the woman's, Beauvoir sees the 'fat' or 'huge' (*grosse*) hand of the
man 'pouncing on' (*s'abattre sur*) the woman's. Once one perceives the
violence of the man's move, the woman's abandonment of her hand
represents a desperate but doomed attempt to cling to her own original
project.[16] But on this point, of course, Sartre is right: once things have gone
this far, the woman can no longer maintain the ambiguous space of
flirtation: the man's grabbing of her hand most certainly forces her to take
his project into account. Whatever she decides to do now will be nothing
but a response to a situation defined by the man. But to define oneself
simply as the negation or affirmation of somebody else's project is pre-

cisely not to assume one's existential freedom. It is astonishing to discover that *this* precisely is the 'decision' Sartre apparently sees as the only course of authenticity for the woman in the café. But this is more than a little illogical: if each individual defines herself by freely recognizing responsibility for her own projects, the woman can only be defined by her own project, not by anybody else's.

On Sartre's own philosophical terms, then, there is *no* authentic mode of behaviour for a woman in this position. Abandoning her hand like a thing, she seeks refuge in facticity and the *en-soi*, and is obviously in bad faith. But were she to make a forceful decision there and then, she would still not be positing a project of her own. In this café scene, the 'freedom' to choose whatever project one likes is sorely circumscribed in one case and not in the other. Or to put it differently: here the man represents what existentialists would call the woman's *situation*, whereas she is not his. The lack of reciprocity in this situation flies in the face of the existentialist belief in the necessity of respecting the fundamental freedom of *every* consciousness: 'As soon as there is engagement,' Sartre writes in *L'existentialisme est un humanisme*, 'I am obliged to want the freedom of others along with my own; I cannot take my freedom as my aim unless I also take that of others as my aim' (p. 83). On this definition, the hand-grabbing man's understanding of freedom and good faith leaves rather a lot to be desired.[17] The fact that Sartre here displays such an unshakable rhetorical solidarity with his male protagonist makes me wonder about the autobiographical roots of his example. By now, this scene is starting to look suspiciously like another example of what Pierre Bourdieu calls Sartre's tendency to 'universalise the particular case' ('Sartre', p. 12).[18]

Two points remain to be made. First, I am not arguing that every time a man takes a woman's hand he is engaging in abusive sexual power play. If the man had been more aware of her project and less hell-bent on his own, his move might have been better timed and less troublesome. Secondly, one might of course imagine the woman taking the man's hand first. In the case of clear mutual sympathy between the two this might have been unproblematic, although in France in 1943, the power relations between the sexes would certainly work against the woman. For her, such a move would be perilous behaviour in a way it would not be for him: the man could always ridicule her act, make her feel stupid, greedy, aggressive, or out of place.

AN ENCOUNTER IN A MOUNTAIN BARN

Is there, then, any conceivable way in which women can successfully flirt or seduce and still remain in good faith? Towards the end of *L'Invitée*, in the chapter describing Françoise's seduction of Gerbert as seen from Françoise's point of view (part II, chapter 8), Simone de Beauvoir sets out to answer precisely that question.[19] Dwelling on a sexual encounter somewhere in the French mountains, it is the only chapter in *L'Invitée* in which there is not a single café. In terms of the plot of the novel, the chapter is intended to demonstrate Françoise's complete sexual victory over her rival Xavière. From a structural point of view, however, the 'seduction chapter' reads as a rather awkward interlude in the densely melodramatic closing stretches of *L'Invitée*: one may well wonder why Beauvoir feels the need to produce so many pages simply to send Gerbert into Françoise's arms. It is as if she decided that the thematic concerns of her only non-Parisian chapter – the questions of freedom, desire and discourse – were too important to be sacrificed in the name of structure or plot.

The *raison d'être* of this specific chapter is nevertheless not entirely philosophical. According to Beauvoir herself, Françoise's seduction of Gerbert is an accurate representation of her own seduction of the young Jacques-Laurent Bost: 'It all happened exactly as I tell it in *L'Invitée*', she says to Francis and Gonthier (p. 176). Providing documentary evidence for this claim, the publication of her *Letters to Sartre* enables us to compare the fictional and the epistolary versions of the seduction scene. In a letter from Albertville, dated 27 July 1938, Beauvoir writes: 'Something extremely agreeable has happened to me, which I didn't at all expect when I left – I slept with Little Bost three days ago. It was I who suggested it, of course' (LS21; LSa62; TA). This breezy account of the ease with which she ended up in a haystack at Tignes with Bost has little in common with the anguish of the desiring Françoise in *L'Invitée*. It is as if Beauvoir here is trying a little too hard to demonstrate her own relaxed and non-conflictual relationship to sex: 'I am very fond of him. We spend idyllic days, and nights of passion. But have no fear of finding me sullen or disoriented or ill at ease on Saturday; it's something precious to me, something intense, but also light and easy and properly in its place in my life, simply a happy blossoming of relations that I'd always found very agreeable' (LS21; LSa63). One would like to believe her. Unfortunately, however, a quick comparison of Sartre's *Lettres au Castor* and Beauvoir's *Letters to Sartre* casts her apparently spontaneous seduction of Bost in a rather different light.

Having left Paris on 13 or 14 July, Beauvoir meets up with Bost in Haute Savoie the very next day. Writing to Sartre on 27 July, she announces that she has started sleeping with Bost three days earlier, that is to say, on 23 or 24 July. By the time they ended up in bed together, in other words, the two of them had already been walking in the mountains for ten days. Why would their friendship suddenly take on a sexual dimension at this specific point? Did something happen to give it a decisive push in that direction? Looking at Sartre's letters to Beauvoir, one discovers that during the period from 14 to 17 July Sartre writes two voluminous letters describing every sordid sexual detail of his relationship with 'Martine Bourdin' (who in Beauvoir's replies is referred to by her real name, Colette Gibert).[20] On 22 July, Beauvoir thanks Sartre for his 'long letters', received on 21 July, and claims that she took great pleasure in reading them and is eagerly awaiting the rest of the story. In the meantime, however, she finds his tale 'elegant', and concludes that 'You're very sweet to have told me the whole story in such detail, my love' (LS19–20; LSa54). A day or two later she is in bed with 'Little Bost'.

As for the end of the story, Sartre duly obliges on 20 July with a blow-by-blow account of how he liberated 'Martine Bourdin' from her virginity, in spite of the fact that he had promised Beauvoir not to 'go all the way'. His final letter from this period, dated 24 July, informs Beauvoir of his sexual transactions with the still virginal Wanda Kosakiewicz in Rouen. On 30 July the two philosophers meet again, and we hear no more about 'Martine Bourdin' until she surfaces again in February 1940 as the victim of a singularly unpleasant ploy of Sartre's.[21] According to the epistolary version of events, then, Beauvoir's seduction of Bost is a rather obvious case of tit for tat. There is something pathetic about Beauvoir's role in all this: bravely struggling to copy Sartre's own cavalier disdain for the ordinary human emotions involved in sexual relationships, she comes across as a dutiful little daughter trying to please a father who is not worth it. It makes for sad reading indeed.

In the novel, the social relationship between the two protagonists appears to be strikingly unequal. Endowed with more social, intellectual and cultural capital than Gerbert, Françoise is in every way his social superior. She is 30, he is 20; she is the consort of the prestigious actor-director Pierre Labrousse, and a successful dramaturge and aspiring novelist in her own right, whereas he is just a young, unknown actor who idolizes Pierre. Initially, at least, the problem confronting Françoise as a character, and Beauvoir as a novelist, would seem to be that of finding a language in which to express female desire for a socially inferior man. Yet this is not quite the case, since we know that under patriarchy the mere fact of *being* a man carries symbolic capital: Gerbert's social inferiority is mitigated – but not entirely obliterated – by his maleness.

In literary terms, Beauvoir is exploring a relatively new field: before her, the sexual dilemmas of the professionally successful, independent woman desiring a younger and less powerful man had not received much literary attention in France.[22] It would be excessive to claim that this is the first scene of its kind in French women's writing, but it certainly ranks as an early example of the genre.[23] Labelling them bluestockings, viragos, spinsters and harridans, patriarchal ideology tends to represent women in positions of power as the antithesis of seduction. Given the absence of alternative discourses, in France in 1943 it would require unusual literary powers indeed to forge a language breaking with common clichés: Françoise as well as Beauvoir are up against formidable odds.

By the time Françoise and Gerbert arrive at a lonely mountain inn, the former is consumed by desire: 'The vague yearning that had been hanging over her all these days [. . .] had become choking desire' (SC362; I446). Sitting down by the fire at the inn, she dreams of touching Gerbert: 'If only she had been able to touch Gerbert's hand, to smile at him with affection' (SC363; I448), but such behaviour is clearly out of the question. Françoise is left feeling that the whole situation is meaningless. The idea of touching Gerbert nevertheless continues to haunt her: 'Was he really beyond reach? Or was it just that she had never dared to reach out her hand to him? Who was holding her back?' (SC364; I449). The palms of her non-touching hands are moist with desire and anxiety: 'Why did she not make up her mind to will what she hoped for?' (SC364; I449).

In the light of what is *not* being said in this scene, the inane dia-logue between the two becomes both witty and poignant. Unlike Sartre's Casanova, Gerbert *truly* respects Françoise: in this scene there will be no sudden pouncing on hands. If Françoise's social superiority makes the traditional discourse of female flirtation unavailable to her, Gerbert's in-feriority makes him incapable of making the first move: 'She was distressed [*angoissée*] now. He was there, facing her, alone, unattached, absolutely free. Owing to his youth and the respect he had always shown Pierre and herself, she could hardly expect him to take any initiative. If she wanted something to happen, Françoise could count only on herself' (SC366; I451). By the time the meal nears an end, Françoise would seem to be on the verge of a nervous breakdown. At this point Gerbert starts complaining about how difficult it is to be relaxed and easy with women, referred to in the third person plural, as if Françoise had nothing to do with the species: 'you always have to make a fuss of them or you always feel you're in the wrong' (SC366; I451). What he likes, he says, are relationships where one can be oneself, without the 'fuss' (*manières*):

'Don't stand on any ceremony with me,' said Françoise. Gerbert burst out laughing.
'Oh you! You're like a man! [*Vous êtes comme un type!*]' he said warmly.
'That's right, you've never regarded me as a woman,' said Françoise. She felt a queer smile on her lips. Gerbert looked at her inquisitively. She looked away and emptied her glass. She had made a bad start; she would be ashamed to treat Gerbert with clumsy flirtatiousness [*coquetterie maladroite*], she would have done better to proceed openly [*franchement*]: 'Would it surprise you if I were to suggest that you sleep with me?' or something of that sort. But her lips refused to form the words (SC366; I452).

Françoise's dilemma is here made graphically evident. Her exceptional position as a woman who can deal with men on an equal footing, that is to say without making them feel ill at ease, is confirmed when Gerbert compares her to one of the boys. Here at least, she is being acknowledged as an equal. Given her evident social superiority to Gerbert, however, there is more than a touch of irony in such an accolade. And the prize she pays is steep: she can only accede to a position of equality at the cost of her femininity. The sexism of Gerbert's description of the 'fuss' required by the women he knows is obvious, and remains unquestioned by the text: there is little doubt that the narrator concurs in the idea of Françoise's exceptional status.

On this point, L'Invitée is quite representative of Beauvoir's own position at the time. At least until the 1950s, and possibly until the 1970s when she joined the women's movement, she delighted in feeling unique among women. In Memoirs of a Dutiful Daughter she reports that 'Papa used to say with pride "Simone has a man's brain. Simone is a man"' (MDD121; MJF169; TA). According to Deirdre Bair, Beauvoir took her father's remarks as 'the highest compliment he could pay her' (p. 60). For Simone de Beauvoir, an exceptional woman is one who is a woman, but who also displays all the virtues normally associated with masculinity. In her own life, then, Beauvoir enjoyed all the advantages of being a token woman, as she herself candidly admits in Force of Circumstance:

> No; far from suffering from my femininity, I have, on the contrary, from the age of twenty on, accumulated the advantages of both sexes; after L'Invitée, those around me treated me both as a writer and as a woman; this was particularly noticeable in America: at the parties I went to, the wives all got together and talked to each other while I talked to the men, who nevertheless behaved towards me with greater courtesy than they did towards the members of their own sex. I was encouraged to write The Second Sex precisely because of this privileged position. It allowed me to express myself in all serenity (FC199–200; FCa264).

The paradox, of course, is that Beauvoir is right in insisting that it was precisely her unique speaking position that allowed her to write The Second Sex.

Françoise's riposte – an effort to reclaim her femininity through coquetry – misfires entirely. Spoken by the young woman at the Sartrean café table, these lines ('you've never regarded me as a woman') would produce an instantaneous rejoinder of the 'oh but to me you are very much a woman' kind. But Gerbert says nothing. Traditional female flirtation presupposes the subservient status of the woman: for the superior Françoise the discourse of flirtation simply does not work. Her alternative, she concludes, would be plain speech ('she would have done better to proceed openly'), but at this point she discovers, much to her dismay, that she cannot even bring herself to open her mouth: the literal expression of her desire is physically impossible. As Sartre puts it in *Being and Nothingness*, 'crude and naked desire would humiliate and horrify her' – or to be precise, the *expression* of brute desire would be humiliating to her even if *she* were the one to voice it.

Cued to take up a position as Gerbert's equal, Françoise automatically finds herself cast as an honorary male ('you're like a man'). Such a discursive position puts her in a double bind, preventing her at once from flirting like a female and from speaking (or grabbing hands) like a man. From her position as honorary male, she could hardly start telling Gerbert – one of the boys, after all – how much she admires and respects him, as Sartre suggests a would-be male seducer might. 'To say it straight', then, represents Françoise's dream of escaping from what she herself perceives as the bad faith or dishonesty of traditional female flirtation, without falling into the cynical stance of male seduction, and without foundering on the reef of *le désir cru et nu*.

For Beauvoir, what is at stake in this scene is Françoise's status as a free consciousness. Perceiving Gerbert as another freedom, Françoise wants to be perceived as a freedom by him. The existentialist ideal explored by Françoise here is that of *reciprocity*, where each freedom recognizes that of the other. Behaving like Sartre's male seducer, Françoise would simply negate Gerbert's freedom. So what is she to do? Desperately looking for an acceptable female model for her enterprise, the only thing that comes to her mind is the wholly negative example of Pierre's sister Elisabeth, who describes herself as a 'woman who takes'. The very thought of Elisabeth, however, makes Françoise blush: 'a woman who takes; [. . .] she loathed the thought' (SC368; I454).

Although Elisabeth's image of herself is that of an independent woman who takes her sexual pleasures where and when she wants to, *L'Invitée* in fact never shows her actively and deliberately seducing a man. On the contrary, she is portrayed as victimized by her married lover, and unhappy and humiliated in her various other sexual liaisons. In the context of the novel as a whole, Françoise's seduction of the young actor Gerbert is constructed as a rather pointed contrast to Elisabeth's casual affair with the young actor Guimiot. Finding his way into Elisabeth's bed even before she has considered whether she really wants him there, Guimiot makes love with professional competence and distanced irony. His body and movements are somewhat feminized – he is described as 'supple', 'smooth' and 'graceful' (SC82; I107); he has 'feminine hands' and a 'sinuous [*fluide*] and gentle' body (SC84; I110) – and Elisabeth does not fail to notice that in spite of his technical expertise, he is utterly self-centred in the sexual act itself: 'Guimiot's mouth was curved and his eyes were screwed up with pleasure. At this moment, he was thinking only of himself, with the greed of a profiteer. She closed her eyes again. A scorching humiliation swept over her. She was anxious for it to end' (SC84–5; I110). Revealed as pure sham, Elisabeth's self-proclaimed stance as 'a woman who takes' is bad faith incarnate. The cruelty of Beauvoir's treatment of Elisabeth contrasts with her indulgence for Françoise, represented as truly striving for authenticity in her every action.

In Françoise's vision of Elisabeth's sexuality we glimpse her horror of becoming a woman who is not truly desired by the men she sleeps with: Elisabeth's lovers screw her for convenience, not for passion. But Françoise's distaste for such relations is not simply an effect of social conventions; it expresses her deep-seated philosophical commitment to her own freedom. If she wants Gerbert freely to *choose* her, it is not only because this will make her feel desirable, but because it is only by appealing to his freedom that she can avoid being reduced to a simple object in his eyes. Or in other words: only by offering one's freedom to the freedom of the other can one hope to have one's own freedom respected in return. On this logic of reciprocity it follows that it is only by having Gerbert choose *her* in the same movement as she is choosing *him* that Françoise can hope to escape having their sexual relationship reduced to no more than a casual sexual encounter. As the scenes invoking Elisabeth show, the belief that a one-sided 'taking' of the other represents freedom is philosophically and psychologically self-defeating.[24]

No wonder, then, that Françoise finds that she cannot make herself utter the crucial words: deprived of discourse and caught in the double binds of sexual politics, she has not the slightest idea of what 'the words to say it with' might be. Her silence, however, is only a temporary retreat. Spurred on as much by self-respect as by desire, Françoise refuses to abandon her project: 'She did not want this trip to end in regrets that would soon turn into remorse and into self-hatred: she would speak' (SC368; I454; TA). Unlike Sartre's female flirt, then, Françoise knows exactly what she is doing. Moreover, unlike Sartre's male seducer, Françoise is suddenly seized by doubt about her own capacity to produce pleasure in Gerbert: 'But did she even know whether Gerbert would find pleasure in kissing her?' (SC368; I454). Hanging on to her self-respect, she decides that the only honest course is to go ahead, while making sure that he has every opportunity to make a 'frank refusal' (SC368; I454). By the time the two of them are getting into their sleeping bags in the barn, Françoise remains determined, but speechless: 'She had absolutely no idea how to approach the question' (SC369; I455; TA). After an increasingly desultory dialogue, Françoise reaches a stage of acute distress: 'Despite the cold draught coming through the broken pane, she was perspiring. She felt as if she had come to

a halt above an abyss, without being able to advance or withdraw. She was
without thought, without desire, and suddenly the situation seemed plainly
absurd. She smiled nervously' (SC371; I457).

Seeing her smile, Gerbert engages her in a tense exchange of the 'I know
what you are thinking, but I won't say' kind, until Françoise is on the verge
of tears: 'Suddenly, tears rose to her eyes. She was at her nerves' end: now
she had gone too far. It was Gerbert himself who would force her to speak,
and perhaps this delightful friendship between them would be ruined for
ever' (SC371; I458). Here Françoise does not worry simply about losing
the initiative of the conversation, but about losing her freedom: if she were
to speak just because Gerbert forced her to, she would lose her sense of
independence in relation to his projects. In that case, one may add, she
would be in exactly the same position as Sartre's *coquette* after the seizing of
her hand. Speaking out, Françoise risks it all: her metaphysical freedom, her
self-respect as an acting subject, her sense of her own femininity and
Gerbert's friendship:

> Françoise emptied herself of all thought [*fit le vide en elle*] and finally the
> words crossed her lips.
> 'I was smiling because I was wondering how you would look – you who
> loathe complications – if I suggested that you should sleep with me.' [*Je riais
> en me demandant quelle tête vous feriez, vous qui n'aimez pas les complications, si
> je vous proposais de coucher avec moi.*]
> 'I thought you were thinking that I wanted to kiss you and didn't dare,' said
> Gerbert (SC371–2; I458; TA).

It is interesting to note that these lines occur almost verbatim in Beauvoir's
letter to Sartre.[25] A masterpiece of syntactical and grammatical circumlocu-
tion, Françoise's attempt to 'tell it straight' would seem to imply that the
most direct expression possible of female desire takes place in the past
conditional tense. The principal effect of the quasi-vocative subclause
inserted in the middle of the phrase is to delay the final expression of desire
and to stress the distancing *vous* which now occurs no less than three times
in the crucial sentence. But the *vous* also emphasizes the mutual respect of
the two interlocutors: neither seeks to invade the other's intimacy by the
familiar *tu*. An attentive reader might nevertheless hesitate for a second at
Gerbert's euphemistic 'kissing' as opposed to Françoise's direct 'sleeping
with'. Does this term not mark him as slightly childish in relation to
Françoise?

After another page of hesitations, Gerbert at last expresses his desire.
Finally, then, we have arrived at the crucial moment in which the two
bodies are about to touch for the first time, the moment in which
Françoise's project is about to be crowned by success. At this point,

something strange would seem to happen to Beauvoir's – and Françoise's – style: 'I'd love to kiss you', Gerbert says. Françoise's reply is astonishing, to say the least: "Well, kiss me, you silly little Gerbert," she said offering him her mouth [*Eh bien, faites-le, stupide petit Gerbert, dit-elle en lui tendant sa bouche*]' (SC373; I460). Supposedly playful and inviting, Françoise's reply is in fact dismayingly condescending and clumsily unerotic. Producing the wholly unintended ideological effect of casting Françoise as a maternal figure in relation to the 'little' and 'stupid' Gerbert, this highly embarrassed and embarrassing textual moment drains Françoise's discourse of its sexuality and unwittingly castrates Gerbert in the process. Yet the whole point was to represent Françoise as a mature, autonomous, *sexual* woman: fleeing from the body in the very moment Françoise's erotic project succeeds, Beauvoir's own discourse loses its power.

From this point on, the chapter throws itself into an orgy of saccharine sweetness and ends up reading like pure Harlequin romance.[26] Suddenly the text goes out of its way to bestow every possible emotional reward on Françoise. After a few kisses, the two protagonists discover that they have in fact desired each other for a long time. When the two lovers' discourses finally coincide, their bodies meet in a chastely symbiotic embrace where skin sticks to skin:

> Françoise pressed her cheek against his.
> 'I'm so glad I didn't get discouraged,' she said.
> 'So am I,' said Gerbert.
> He put his warm lips to her mouth and she felt his body cleave tightly [*se colla étroitement*] to hers (SC374; I462).

By the end of the chapter Gerbert is declaring his passion for Françoise in no uncertain terms: ' "I've never loved any woman in the way I love you," said Gerbert. "I love you far, far beyond" ' (SC375; I463). It is as if the author of *L'Invitée* wants to make us believe that every woman who speaks her desire will be blessed with love, sex and friendship after all. The author of *The Second Sex*, however, knows better: the desiring woman, she writes, 'risks remaining a useless object if the male disdains her. This is why she is deeply humiliated if he rejects her advances' (SS698; DSb610; TA). By insisting on the emotional rewards reaped by Françoise, the text comes close to representing her desire as justified by love after all, thus turning the final pages of the chapter into a liberated, existentialist version of the 'ideal romance' described by Janice Radway.[27]

How are we to explain such a radical shift of discursive register? In my view, Beauvoir's sudden change of tone indicates the moment in which the discursive and the philosophical projects of the text suddenly and dramatically start to diverge. Françoise's autonomous exploit succeeds, but it is no longer carried forward by an equally autonomous discourse: instead of originality we get clichés. The fact that this *décalage* occurs exactly at the moment when the two lovers' bodies are about to meet for the first time reveals the anxiety produced by the appearance of the body in Beauvoir's works. The most physical passage in *L'Invitée* remains the description of Elisabeth's wholly negative sexual experience with Guimiot. As for Françoise and Pierre, they undress behind screens and turn the lights off before quietly sliding into bed.

Beauvoir's modesty may of course have much to do with the sexual repression of the Vichy regime, but this cannot fully explain the logic of this scene. Her sudden change of register represents a flight away from the body and into the romantic soul. Until the moment of sexual convergence, Beauvoir succeeds reasonably well in representing free consciousness in a desiring woman. It is when the very project of that free consciousness is on the point of materializing in a desiring female body that the trouble starts. 'Desire', Sartre writes, 'is defined as *trouble*' (BN503; EN437). Beauvoir's stylistic switch to romantic clichés at this point unconsciously signals the difficulty she experiences in writing about the desiring female body in general. What I have registered as an astonishing shift in tone and style, then, points to a fundamental philosophical problem in Beauvoir's works: the problem of how the body, and particularly the desiring female body, relates to the projects of consciousness. Neither a thing in the world, nor free consciousness, neither transcendence nor brute facticity, the body, as Sartre says, spells trouble. Because it represents such a large and complex topic in Beauvoir's work, I will not discuss it any further here: body trouble will be a central preoccupation of my next chapter.

FREE WOMEN OR GENDERLESS SUBJECTS?

Displaying the same preoccupation with consciousness, freedom, responsibility and transcendence as *Being and Nothingness*, Beauvoir's seduction scene would seem to be absolutely faithful to Sartre's original concepts. Yet her own brief café scenes already provide a gentle reminder of the violence that may be involved in a man's sudden pouncing on a woman's hand. In the seduction scene, the difference between her and Sartre emerges more starkly: having reversed the gender roles, Beauvoir is forced to display a much greater awareness of the social pressures on her protagonists than Sartre. Beauvoir poses the question of reciprocity and respect for the other's freedom; Sartre does not. She registers the impact of social roles; he does not. Furthermore, Françoise's physical inability to speak her desire vividly dramatizes the situation of women under patriarchy.

Precisely because of this swerve away from Sartre, Beauvoir's account is no longer a 'seduction scene' in the traditional sense. Nor is it an example of flirtation: Beauvoir's effort to represent free female desire in fact ends up questioning the very categories of flirtation and seduction. The remarkable shift in tone at the moment of the successful seduction suggests that in 1943 Simone de Beauvoir failed fully to grasp the implications of her own discourse. One reason for this failure is the fact that, in spite of the considerable differences between these two texts, Beauvoir's is not a conscious critique of Sartre. I have already claimed that Beauvoir must be understood as investigating her own marginality from a position of centrality. The consequence of this structural ambiguity is a noticeable uncertainty about whether her theme is 'women' or the 'free (genderless) subject'. By her own admission, by 1943 Beauvoir had given no thought at all to matters of sexual politics: she thinks of Françoise as a free consciousness, not as a free woman. Writing about Françoise, Beauvoir firmly believes that she is doing the same thing as Sartre writing about Mathieu. The paradox is that in the very act of imitating Sartre she ends up criticizing and transforming his categories.

This transformation, however, does not go far enough. Beauvoir's relative lack of awareness of the gender of her heroine, for instance, is to a large extent responsible for the desexualization of Françoise. In Beauvoir's fiction, women struggle with what they take to be universal philosophical problems as if it were their obvious duty and right. By contrast, Sartre's fiction does not portray a single thinking woman. In *The Age of Reason*, for instance, all the principal male characters – Mathieu, Brunet, Daniel, Boris – wrestle with the problems of freedom and responsibility and of how to define themselves in relation to others and the world. The female characters – Marcelle, Ivich, Lola – are strikingly unconcerned with such issues. Where the men are in good or bad faith, lucid or self-deluding, bourgeois or working-class, the women are voracious wombs or capricious virgins. Compared to Sartre, Beauvoir's absolute faith in women's moral and philosophical capacities is refreshingly non-sexist. This positive result is the direct consequence of the fact that it never occurs to her to label thought or philosophy 'male'. Yet the price she pays is high: in autobiography as well as essays and fiction, what one might call the problem of the incipient masculinization of the free woman returns to haunt her texts.

If the ostensibly genderless free subject of existentialism is in fact marked as masculine in Sartre's and Beauvoir's discourse, any attempt to cast women as free subjects must have the effect of marking them as somewhat masculine as well. This is clearly what happens to Françoise, caught up as she is in the contradictions created by her role as 'one of the boys'. In my view, this is a theoretical and not a psychological problem: it does not follow that Beauvoir 'wants' women to become like men. On this point, her own earnest protestations to the contrary should be taken at face value: Beauvoir does not expect women to take on any particular identity at all, she simply wants them to be *free*. This must not be taken to mean that Beauvoir is *against* identity. Unlike many present-day feminists, however, she sees identity as a consequence and not as a cause of freedom. For her, women do not have a secret, long-oppressed identity which must be liberated if the struggle for freedom is to be won. On the contrary, the struggle for freedom is what will enable women freely to forge their own identity unencumbered by patriarchal myths of femininity.

Beauvoir's blindness to the sexual politics of existentialism is rooted in her own personal and historical situation. Her later development amply confirms her capacity to transform her own analytic categories. Even *The Second Sex*, however, does not display the sophisticated understanding of rhetoric and ideology required to develop a sustained feminist critique of her own philosophical categories. In this sense, I would argue, the real cause of Beauvoir's problems is above all the fact that she relies on Sartre's disastrously simplistic theory of language as a transparent instrument for action (see *What Is Literature?*), and that her only approximation to a concept of ideology is the schematic and limited notion of 'mystification'. What she fails to see, then, is the way in which patriarchal power relations sometimes worm their way into the very core of philosophical concepts.[28] This blindness, I would argue, is largely responsible for the contradictions and difficulties of her attempt to represent Françoise as a free woman. Given the logic of her own problematics of freedom and domination, however, it does not follow that such power relations cannot be overthrown: on the contrary, for Beauvoir as for Sartre, the very fact of exposing them is already a first step towards change.

THE PERSONAL AND THE PHILOSOPHICAL

On my reading of the two seduction scenes, Beauvoir's analysis of heterosexual seduction is more powerful, more complex, and more alert to the contradictory interests at stake in such a situation than Sartre's discussion of flirtation in *Being and Nothingness*. Were I to argue with the acumen of the average patriarchal critic, I would now conclude that Beauvoir turns out to be superior to Sartre after all. Such a claim would of course be absurd: one cannot ground a claim for general superiority on one example alone. The fact that patriarchs regularly get away with the practice does not make it any better. What matters, clearly, is what one is reading *for*: in this chapter, my own deliberate strategy has been to shift the ground of the debate. Given that every other critic seeks to compare Beauvoir to Sartre on *his* terrain by raising questions belonging to the repertoire of classical philosophy, I think it is only fair for once to compare Sartre to Beauvoir on *her* terrain: the subject of women's – and particularly intellectual women's – position in patriarchal society. By reading one of her literary texts, I also decided to take seriously Beauvoir's claim to be a novelist rather than a philosopher. What I have shown is that when it comes to the question of women's freedom in general, and their sexual freedom in particular, Sartre – not surprisingly – does not have much to offer. My reading, then, does not prove that Beauvoir is 'superior' to Sartre: what it does demonstrate is that there is at least one significant field of inquiry – that concerning women's freedom – in which Beauvoir's analyses are more subtle than Sartre's. That fact alone ought to make it harder to return to further mindless rounds of the comparison game.

Before leaving the subject, however, I would like to look at some of the deeper reasons why Sartre's analysis of the woman in bad faith fails to convince. In general, I would argue that the basic flaw of his analysis is his tendency to universalize from the particular case, or to put it differently: to represent his own personal experience as universal.[29] On the theoretical level, Sartre in the 1940s refuses to admit to the existence of personal or 'subjective' determinants of philosophical discourse. For him, to accept the influence of passion – let alone the unconscious – on his theory or his actions is to deny freedom: 'Every man who hides behind the excuse of his passions, every man who invents a determinism is in bad faith', he proclaims in *L'existentialisme est un humanisme* (pp. 80–1). Sartre's fear of the 'determinism' of the unconscious is such that he even refuses to consider the idea that the writer may not be in total control of his work: 'However far [the reader] may go,' Sartre writes in *What Is Literature?* (1948), 'the author has gone further. Whatever connections [the reader] may establish among the different parts of the book [. . .] he has a guarantee, namely, that they have been expressly willed' (p. 61). The evidence, however, is not on Sartre's side: there is more than a trace of his own unconscious fantasies in his analysis in *Being and Nothingness* of desire, of holes and slime, or, say, his claim that scientific inquiry is like rape. Nor can I quite believe that Sartre actually *intended* his analysis of the woman in bad faith to be a case study of philosophical sexism. Adamantly refusing to see himself as a particular instance of the general, Sartre desires to write himself on to the world without ever admitting that the world also writes itself onto him.

It is precisely when it comes to the question of the presence of the personal that the rhetoric of *Being and Nothingness* differs sharply from that of *The Second Sex*. To begin with, Beauvoir herself explicitly recognizes that *The Second Sex* was the unexpected outcome of her wish to write an autobiographical *essai-martyr*, a text in which the protagonist exposes the innermost truth of her being, regardless of the consequences (see FC103;

FCa136). Yet as we have seen in chapter 2, her masterpiece is also a philosophical essay produced according to the rules of the French philosophical field. As a result, the conflict between the personal and the philosophical makes itself felt in the very structure of her rhetoric. Rarely using the phenomenological 'I', Beauvoir often indicates her own involvement in certain scenes and anecdotes: her 'I' is, on the whole, attractively unassuming. This does not prevent her from concealing her own subjectivity behind the third person singular 'woman'. In this way, for instance, we find her troubled relationship to the female body written into the very argument of *The Second Sex*, just as Sartre's penchant for compulsive seduction, convincingly displayed in the 'Martine Bourdin' affair, is erected into a philosophical monument in *Being and Nothingness*.

The effect of Beauvoir's use of 'woman', however, is quite subtle. On the one hand, a woman reader confronted by this relentlessly universal 'woman' at every turn may feel that 'she' blocks her from expressing experiences running counter to Beauvoir's claims. On the other hand, many women have also experienced the text as profoundly legitimizing, as evidence that their own experience was not unique, aberrant or illicit after all. This ambiguous effect is above all due to the fact that Beauvoir's 'woman' is not particularly well disguised, or in other words, to the fact that *The Second Sex* is far more transparently autobiographical than *Being and Nothingness*. It is precisely this ambiguous transparency in relation to the autobiographical, I would argue, which saves *The Second Sex* from reading just like another falsely universalizing master text. Exhibiting all the traces of an intense struggle between the discourse of the classical French philosophy essay and the more personal discourse required by a truly existentialist commitment to experience, Beauvoir's rhetoric in *The Second Sex* remains deeply ambivalent. While the struggle is not resolved, the very fact that it exists reveals a deeper understanding of the implications of existentialist thought than Sartre's more traditional respect for – and mastery of – the classical forms of philosophical rhetoric.

To feminists, illicit generalizations have always been particularly irksome: the prime example, after all, is the attempt to claim the experience of white, bourgeois males as universally human. Understandably disgusted with the strategy, some feminists have sought to avoid general discourses of every kind, for instance by seeking refuge in the confessional mode. The problem is that they often forget that if the expression of the personal is to be interesting to others, it must necessarily be general as well. To accept that one's own theoretical or scientific discourse carries the mark of the personal is not to reduce theory to nothing but an expression of the self: if feminists cannot produce tenable theoretical generalizations, feminism has no political future. Paradoxically enough, then, it is because of my commitment to theory that I argue for the necessity of *marking* the personal *as* personal wherever it occurs. The problem with Sartre's discourse, after all, is not that it is too general, but that it is not general enough. In order to avoid the pitfalls of illicit generalization, we need to develop a reasonably sophisticated awareness of our own discursive strategies: there is a world of difference between the tacit universalization of one's own case, and the explicit attempt to use oneself as a potentially significant case study. On this point, Freud's psychoanalytical and Bourdieu's sociological efforts converge: if we are to avoid being the mere playthings of our own passions, we need not only to be able to experience them, but to know that we are doing so as well.

Sartre, we may remember, wanted to make philosophy out of an apricot cocktail. For Simone de Beauvoir too existence *is* ideas in so far as one's every action reveals a whole philosophy of life: 'In truth, there is no divorce between philosophy and life', she writes in 1948, in the introduction to *L'existentialisme et la sagesse des nations* (p. 12). In my own view, one of the great strengths of existentialism is precisely its conviction that the personal, ultimately, *is* the philosophical. While Sartre's and Beauvoir's status as heirs to French philosophical legitimacy leaves its mark on their respective rhetorical strategies, Beauvoir's more marginal position enables her to push the rhetoric of the personal further than Sartre. For her, any easy distinction between the personal and the impersonal, between the autobiographical and the philosophical, is impossible: 'Nevertheless, this power you have to live an idea, body and soul, is unusual', Pierre says admiringly to Françoise in *L'Invitée*. 'But to me, an idea is not a question of theory,' Françoise replies, 'one experiences it [*ça s'éprouve*]; if it remains theoretical it has no value' (SC302; I376; TA). Whether one sees Françoise as experiencing her emotional suffering in philosophical terms or, alternatively, as experiencing philosophy emotionally, she is an excellent illustration of Simone de Beauvoir's life-long project: to break down the distinction between philosophy and life so as to endow life with the truth and necessity of philosophy and philosophy with the excitement and passion of life.[30]

6

Ambiguous Women:
Alienation and the Body in
The Second Sex

Divided, torn, disadvantaged: for women the stakes are higher; there are more victories and more defeats for them than for men.

(The Prime of Life)

THE AMBIGUITY OF EXISTENCE

In 1947 Simone de Beauvoir published a brief philosophical essay entitled *The Ethics of Ambiguity* (*Pour une morale de l'ambiguïté*). 'Of all my books, it is the one that irritates me the most today', she comments impatiently in *Force of Circumstance* (FC75; FCa99). *The Second Sex*, on the other hand, never faded in her mind: 'It is possibly the book that has brought me the greatest satisfaction of all those I have written', she exclaims: 'if I am asked what I think of it today, I have no hesitation in replying: I'm all for it' (FC202; FCa267). Where *The Second Sex* is a source of pride and satisfaction, *The Ethics of Ambiguity* apparently represents nothing but embarrassment to its author. Criticizing its empty idealism, lofty moralism and lack of realism, she sees the whole book as a failure: 'I was in error', she writes, 'when I thought I could define an ethics outside a social context' (FC76; FCa99; TA). In spite of her own objections, however, Beauvoir does not really question the basic idea of her essay, first voiced in a conversation at the Café de Flore, that it is possible to construct an ethics based on *Being and Nothingness*. In the introduction to *The Second Sex*, she has not changed her mind: 'Our perspective', she writes, 'is that of existentialist ethics' (SS28; DSa31). But Sartre never published the ethics promised at the end of *Being and Nothingness*;[1] in France in 1949 the only existentialist ethics in print was the one proposed by Simone de Beauvoir.[2]

Finishing *The Ethics of Ambiguity* in the late spring or early summer of 1946, Beauvoir found herself at a loose end: 'My essay was finished,' she writes, 'and I was asking myself: What now? I sat in the Deux Magots and gazed at the blank sheet of paper in front of me. I felt the need to write in my fingertips, and the taste of words in my throat, but I didn't know where to start, or what' (FC103; FCa135). Sitting in a café in Saint Germain-des-Prés in June 1946, Simone de Beauvoir realized that she wanted to write about herself, discussed the matter with Sartre, and discovered that she had to take into account the fact of being a woman. As we have seen in chapter 2, the result of their conversation was *The Second Sex*: 'I abandoned my project for a personal confession in order to give all my attention to the condition of woman in general' (FC103; FCa136; TA). Biographically as well as philosophically, then, the starting point for Beauvoir's own favourite text is to be found in the one essay she came to loathe.

This is not to say that Beauvoir was wrong to dislike *The Ethics of Ambiguity*: I find it repetitive, badly constructed and mostly unconvincing. Her initial analysis of the fundamental ambiguity of human existence nevertheless remains crucial to an understanding of *The Second Sex*. The 'tragic ambivalence' (EA7; MA9) of human existence, Beauvoir claims, is not only the fact that we are born to die, but that we know this to be true. Awareness of death implies awareness of our own material existence as bodies: the 'tragic ambiguity' of life consists precisely in the tension between our consciousness of death and the fact of death itself (EA7; MA10).

For Beauvoir, only Sartrean existentialism explores the fundamental ambiguity of existence. For the Sartre of *Being and Nothingness*, human beings are above all conscious beings. Spontaneously reaching out to the world, consciousness is nothing but consciousness of that which it is not: it is *for-itself* [*pour-soi*], consciousness itself, in other words, is *nothing* [*néant*]. The world, on the other hand, is *in-itself* [*en-soi*]: deprived of consciousness, it simply *is*. In so far as consciousness can only know the world as that which it is not, it is pure negativity. It follows that it is impossible for consciousness to *be* – to become a thing in the world (an in-itself) – without losing itself in the process. For Sartre, the desire to achieve a synthesis between being in-itself and being for-itself nevertheless remains the fundamental passion of consciousness. If such a state could be achieved, we would be God. 'But the idea of God is contradictory and we lose ourselves in vain', Sartre concludes: 'Man is a useless passion' (BN784; EN678).

According to Sartre, the relationship between the for-itself and the in-itself is not one of simple opposition. On the contrary, the two aspects of the world are linked by the for-itself itself: 'The For-itself, in fact,' Sartre writes, 'is nothing but the pure nihilation [*néantisation*] of the In-itself; it is like a hole in being at the heart of Being' (BN785–6; EN681). Through the nihilating activity of consciousness, through the very enactment of my failure to *be*, I paradoxically make myself *exist* as a human being. Human existence, in other words, is this constant failure of being.

Following Sartre, Beauvoir stresses that the effort to overcome the split between consciousness and facticity – between consciousness and death – is condemned to failure. The human being, she writes, is 'a being who is at a distance from himself and who has to be his being' (EA11; MA15).[3] It is precisely because our being is not given but always – and impossibly – to be achieved that we need an ethics: one does not, after all, propose a moral code to God, as Beauvoir succinctly puts it (see EA10; MA14). As consciousnesses we are 'lack of being' (*manque d'être*), yet it is only through the apprehending activity of our consciousness that the world acquires its meanings and values. 'Man', Beauvoir writes, quoting Sartre, '*makes himself a lack of being in order that there might be being*' (EA11; MA15). Or in other words: my lack produces your fullness, my failure brings the world to be.

There is no point in dwelling on the details of Beauvoir's rather tortuous efforts to explain how ethical action consists precisely in the lucid accept-ance of this paradox.[4] In general terms it is enough to insist on her basic idea, which is that we need to valorize the free transcendent activity of consciousness that makes the world *be*. Neither given by any instance outside consciousness (such as God), nor intrinsic to things and activities in themselves, values and meanings are the products of the transcendent activity of consciousness. This is why life is not absurd (in the sense of meaningless), but *ambiguous*: 'To say that [existence] is ambiguous is to assert that its meaning is never fixed, that it must be constantly won', Beauvoir writes (EA129; MA186). As we shall see, this sense of a funda-mental *openness* of meaning is central to Beauvoir's understanding of the female condition.

THE RHETORIC OF PHILOSOPHY IN *THE SECOND SEX*

'The style makes the value of the prose', Sartre writes. 'But it should pass unnoticed. Since words are transparent and since the gaze looks through them, it would be absurd to slip in among them some panes of rough glass' (*What Is Literature?*, p. 39). While Simone de Beauvoir herself may well have thought of *The Second Sex* as an exemplary case of transparently committed writing, to me her text reads quite differently. For me, Beauvoir's language calls attention to itself to such an extent that I cannot discuss her philosophy without also commenting on the effects of her style. I will give an example of what I mean by considering her general analysis of women's oppression.

'Every time transcendence falls back into immanence, there is a degradation of existence into the "in-itself," of freedom into facticity', Beauvoir
writes: 'This downfall is a moral fault if the subject consents to it; if it is
inflicted upon him, it takes the form of frustration and oppression. In both
cases it is an absolute evil' (SS29; DSa31; TA). Claiming that a subject may
have facticity or immanence *inflicted* upon herself, Beauvoir is here making
one of the most fundamental – and most productive – moves in *The Second
Sex*. Taking as her starting point the assumption that women's social,
political and historical circumstances are responsible for most – if not all –
of their shortcomings, Beauvoir here argues that women cannot automatically be accused of being in bad faith when they fail to behave as authentically free beings.[5] Without this shift from Sartrean ontology to sociology
and politics, *The Second Sex* could not have been written.[6]

There is no theoretical justification for Beauvoir's move to a sociological
perspective in *Being and Nothingness*. Strictly speaking, Sartre's ontology of
consciousness does not allow us to claim that one has to act in any special
way – or indeed to act at all – in order to prove one's ontological freedom;
in so far as consciousness *is* transcendent, we are 'condemned' to be free.
To claim that consciousness is transcendence, then, is not to claim that one
must do anything in particular. No value judgements – no moral hierarchies of behaviour – can be derived from this: in principle, any act may
be carried out in an authentic or inauthentic way. In *The Flies* (*Les mouches*,
1943), for instance, Oreste's murder of Egisthe and Clytemnestre is supposed to be a case of authentic action, but it only becomes so once Oreste
decides to shoulder his responsibility for it. Refusing to accept her own
responsibility for the very same murders, Electre, on the other hand, turns
herself into a quintessential example of bad faith. Similarly, Hugo's murder
of Hoederer in *Dirty Hands* (*Les mains sales*, 1948) is radically ambiguous:
only a perfectly arbitrary choice allows him to claim it as a political act
rather than a simple *crime passionnel*. And in *Men Without Shadows* (*Morts
sans sépulture*, 1946) it would seem that we remain free to assert our
transcendence even under torture. As we have already seen in chapter 5,
however, none of this prevents the ostensibly non-ethical Sartre from
producing a highly moralizing account of female flirtation: in spite of his
own claims to the contrary, *Being and Nothingness* itself is rather less of a
pure ontology than Sartre thinks. When Beauvoir leaps from ontology to
sociology and politics, she may well claim that Sartre's own text encourages
her to do so. Beauvoir is not, of course, 'worse' than Sartre (after all, he
cannot philosophically justify his excursions into moralizing any more than
she can justify her move into sociology); my point is rather that it is worth
examining the rhetorical effects of Beauvoir's strategy.

Beauvoir makes no attempt to bridge the gulf between ontological
freedom and concrete action in the world. Rhetorically speaking, as far as

I can see, her much praised shift away from Sartre's ontology to history and sociology proceeds by way of a massive metaphorical operation. In *The Second Sex* social and political freedom is represented not so much as being *derived from*, but as being *like* or *similar to* ontological freedom.[7] Occasionally, however, metaphor gives way to metonymy or synecdoche.[8] To define human beings as living creatures equipped with consciousness, for instance, is one thing; to take the part for the whole is quite another. As we shall see, this specific figural move – the substitution of consciousness for the whole of the human being – turns out to be the source of much of the 'body trouble' in *The Second Sex*.[9] To complicate matters further, in existentialist philosophy that initial metonymic substitution soon gives rise to a proliferation of metaphors. Since consciousness is defined as transcendence, for instance, human beings quickly become represented as essentially *similar* to the ceaseless activity of phenomenological consciousness. When people fail to live up to the metaphorical image of themselves (for instance by failing to behave in an active and energetic way), they are accused of being in bad faith. The same logic of metaphorical similarity is at work in the assumption that a concrete project in the world is 'inauthentic' unless it is *similar to* the constant projection of consciousness towards the world. The implications of such thought are rather odd: how can we be said to resemble our own consciousness? And if we do, why is it necessary to warn us against the moral dangers of somehow *failing* to do so?

In *The Ethics of Ambiguity* Beauvoir insists on the *movement, drive* and *upsurge* of freedom (see EA31; MA44). 'To exist is to *make oneself* a lack of being; it is to *throw* oneself into the world', she writes (EA42; MA61; TA). The effect of such metaphors of energetic exertion is to push her into proclaiming *vitality* as the highest virtue of human beings. People lacking in this 'living warmth' are perceived as retentive, ungenerous, unseductive; in short, as true *Untermenschen*: 'Those who occupy themselves in restraining this original movement can be considered as sub-men [*des sous-hommes*]', Beauvoir proclaims (EA42; MA61). As we shall see, her persistent representation of transcendence as movement also turns out to have the most curious consequences for her analysis of sexual intercourse.

The existentialist project too is represented as movement, but only as upward or forward movement, given that the basic image of the project remains male erection and ejaculation. If Sartre describes the project metaphorically as a 'throwing forward' or a 'lifting up', for Beauvoir the non-project becomes a 'fall' or a 'degradation'. To launch concrete projects in the world becomes a case of 'throwing oneself forward' into the future: on this logic only linear projects count. Repetitive, circular, cyclical, erratic or random modes of activity, ranging from flirtation to housework, can never hope to be classified as authentically transcendent. Sometimes different figures enter into conflict with each other: because human beings have been metonymized as consciousness, childbirth, for instance, regardless of its actual metaphorical similarities to the phallic projection of a thing into the world, would seem to be considered too biological, too bound up with facticity, to be valorized as transcendent.

By insisting on a rather repetitive set of phallic metaphors to illustrate their theory of freedom and transcendence, Sartre and Beauvoir manage to produce a substantial amount of deeply sexist prose, rightly criticized by feminists. Even more striking, however, is the fact that the fairly narrow range of metaphors deployed actually restricts the potential field of authentic action. In this way, Sartre's theory is put in contradiction with itself: where his theory claims that all action is potentially transcendent, his metaphors suggest that this is not so. But to claim that Sartre's and Beauvoir's metaphors suggest a radical *limitation* of their own original theory of freedom amounts to saying that these specific images represent neither the necessary consequence nor the intrinsic 'meaning' of their philosophy: they might always have chosen others. The reasons why they did not – as well as the reasons why they did not perceive the problem in the first place – are to be found in their own specific historical and intellectual circumstances.

Beauvoir and Sartre's obsessive sexualization of their central terms is neither necessary nor ideologically innocent. As readers of their prose today we are not obliged to repeat their obsessions: to suggest otherwise amounts to casting readers as nothing but defenceless victims of the text. Drawing on the existentialist notions of freedom and transcendence, *The Second Sex* offers us both a strong theory of human agency and a positive as well as a negative concept of freedom (freedom *to* act as well as freedom *from* oppression). Feminists do not need to reject these signal strengths of Beauvoir's theory simply because we feel that we cannot escape her metaphors: as I have tried to show, to gender freedom and transcendence as male or masculine in fact produces a contradiction within existentialist theory that a gender-neutral reading of the terms would avoid. Even for an existentialist, in other words, to claim that consciousness is free and transcendent is not *intrinsically* to claim that it is an erection. In Latin, *transscandere* means to climb up, to step over or cross something, or to surpass, excel or exceed. There is in this expression a whole range of potential references to difference, divergence and emergence, to mountain walks and to the pleasure of finally getting to the point with the most beautiful view; fortunately we are entirely free to put any or none of these or other images to productive use.[10]

If the imagery of the project is problematic for existentialism, so is the image of the absence of one. If it is necessary to carry out concrete projects in the world in order to exercise one's freedom, the non-project – often labelled 'immanence' by Beauvoir – becomes the very hallmark of bad faith. Occurring only twice in *Being and Nothingness* and entirely absent from *The Ethics of Ambiguity*, the term 'immanence' is in fact characteristic of *The Second Sex*.[11] Most precisely defined as *non-transcendence*, 'immanence' in *The Second Sex* would seem to include everything from the state of thing-like facticity sought by the for-itself to bad faith and various kinds of unfree situations. Running all the way through the thousand pages of Beauvoir's essay, metaphors of immanence leave an indelible mark on her analysis of women's condition. In general, she tends to make the metonymically induced mistake of considering anything that happens to the female body as utterly unrelated to consciousness; having assumed that such events (sexual desire, orgasm, pregnancy, childbirth and so on) never partake of transcendent consciousness, she inevitably represents them as figures of pure facticity. In this way, childbirth and breast-feeding, for instance, are cast as immanent: 'giving birth and suckling are not *activities*, they are natural functions; no project is involved', she writes in the chapter on women's history (SS94; DSa112). Given this somewhat flawed premiss, we should perhaps not be surprised to see Beauvoir draw the perfectly logical – and utterly absurd – conclusion that since childbirth is immanent and murder and warfare are transcendent, the latter are therefore more valuable to humanity: 'For it is not in giving life but in risking life that man is raised above the animal,' she argues, 'that is why superiority has been accorded in humanity not to the sex that brings forth but to that which kills' (SS95–6; DSa113). In such passages, there would seem to be a tension between transcendence as an ontological category and transcendence as a value we should pursue: sliding from fact to value and back again, as it were, Beauvoir lays herself open to blistering critique from feminists and patriarchs alike.

In *The Second Sex* the idea of immanence appears as an irresistible magnet for an astonishing range of obsessional images of darkness, night, passivity, stasis, abandonment, slavery, confinement, imprisonment, decomposition, degradation and destruction. There is no appreciation here of the positive aspects of passivity: rest, recollection and tranquillity are words that fail to emerge from Beauvoir's pen. We have already seen that the imagery of the project produces philosophical contradictions by *restricting* the potential field of its application. Beauvoir's representation of immanence, on the other hand, undermines its own logical coherence by *expanding* the concept beyond rational limits. It is hard to understand, for instance, how a desire for anything at all – even for the destruction or annihilation of oneself – can be anything other than transcendent. Philosophically speaking, Beauvoir's imagery of the dark night of immanence tends to leave the for-itself entirely out of sight. But short of death, we always retain a glimmer of consciousness, however alienated, misguided and sunk in bad faith we may be: if human beings suffer from it, one might say, immanence cannot possibly be the same thing as death. The very power of Beauvoir's obsessional imagery of womb-like darkness and destruction, I would argue, has less to do with the requirements of her argument than with the intensity of her own personal obsession with annihilation, emptiness and death.[12]

THE AMBIGUITY OF WOMEN

So far, everything Beauvoir has said is true for men as well as women. We are all split, all threatened by the 'fall' into immanence, and we are all mortal. In this sense, no human being ever coincides with herself: we are all lack of being. In order to escape from the tension and anguish (*angoisse*) of this ambiguity we may all be tempted to take refuge in bad faith. But this is where the generalities end:

> Now, what specifically defines the situation of woman is that she – a free and autonomous being like all human creatures – nevertheless discovers and chooses herself in a world where men compel her to assume the status of the Other.[13] They propose to turn her into an object and to doom her to immanence since her transcendence is for ever to be transcended by another consciousness which is essential and sovereign. The drama of woman lies in this conflict between the fundamental aspirations of every subject – which always posits itself as essential – and the demands of a situation which constitutes her as inessential (SS29; DSa31; TA).[14]

This is perhaps the single most important passage in *The Second Sex*, above all because Beauvoir here poses a radically new theory of sexual difference. While we are all split and ambiguous, she argues, women are *more* split and ambiguous than men. For Beauvoir, women are fundamentally characterized by a doubled (ontological and social) *ambiguity* and *conflict*. The specific contradiction of women's situation is caused by the conflict between their status as free and autonomous human beings and the fact that they are socialized in a world in which men consistently cast them as Other, as objects to their subject. Woman's transcendence is objectified by another transcendence. The effect is to produce women as subjects painfully torn between freedom and alienation, transcendence and immanence, subject being and object being. This fundamental contradiction is *specific to women under patriarchy*. For Beauvoir, at least initially, there is nothing ahistorical about this: when oppressive power relations cease to exist, women will be no more and no less split and contradictory than men. (As I will go on to show, however, her analysis actually implies that while the major contradictions of women's situation may disappear, women will always remain somewhat more torn by conflict than men.)

Again, Beauvoir's theory relies on a fundamental metaphor: the social oppression of women, she implies, *mirrors* or *repeats* the ontological ambiguity of existence.[15] Revealing the philosophical urgency and dignity of the question of women's oppression, Beauvoir's argumentation also runs the risk of naturalizing or, to be more precise, of 'ontologizing' it. Moving between the political and the ontological in this way, Beauvoir takes considerable philosophical risks. Paradoxically, however, her analysis also gains in potential strength from its metaphorical structure, since the absence of any logical link between the two levels of analysis leaves us free to reject the one without having to deny the other as well. In this way, Beauvoir's account of women torn between freedom and alienation under patriarchy may well be experienced as convincing even by readers radically at odds with Sartre's theory of consciousness.

Rich and varied, Beauvoir's own vocabulary of ambiguity and conflict ranges from ambivalence, distance, divorce and split to alienation, contradiction and mutilation. But every ambiguity is not negative: in *The Second Sex* the value of ambiguity is never given in advance. Every one of the descriptions of women's 'lived experience' in *The Second Sex* serves to reinforce Beauvoir's theory of the fundamental contradiction of women's situation. Unfortunately, the sheer mass of material makes it impossible to discuss the whole range of her analyses. I will therefore focus on her account of female subjectivity and female sexuality which remains the most important – and by far the most complex – example of contradictions and ambiguity in *The Second Sex*. By 'sexuality' I understand the psychosexual as well as the biological aspects of female sexual existence, or in other words, the interaction between desire and the body.

Male and Female Alienation

'One is not born a woman, one becomes one', Beauvoir writes (SS295; DSb13; TA). The question, of course, is how. How does the little girl become a woman? In her impressive history of psychoanalysis in France, Elisabeth Roudinesco credits Simone de Beauvoir with being the first French writer to link the question of sexuality to that of political emancipation.[16] Beauvoir's interest in the various psychoanalytic perspectives on femininity was so intense, Roudinesco tells us, that a year before finishing her book, she rang up Jacques Lacan in order to ask his advice on the issue: 'Flattered, Lacan announces that they would need five or six months of conversations in order to sort out the problem. Simone doesn't want to spend that much time listening to Lacan for a book which was already very well researched. She proposes four meetings. He refuses' (Roudinesco,

p. 517).[17] It is not surprising that Lacan was flattered by Beauvoir's request: in Paris in 1948, she possessed much more intellectual capital than he; or to put it more simply: she was famous, he was not. Given their highly Lacanian disagreement on timing, however, the tantalizingly transgressive fantasy of a Lacanian *Second Sex* must remain in the imaginary. While she never sat at Lacan's feet, Beauvoir nevertheless quotes his early work on *Les complexes familiaux dans la formation de l'individu*, and much of her account of early childhood and femininity reads as a kind of free elaboration on Lacan's notion of the alienation of the ego in the other in the mirror stage.[18]

The term alienation, in fact, turns up everywhere in *The Second Sex*. Mobilized to explain everything from female sexuality to narcissism and mysticism, the concept plays a key role in Beauvoir's theory of sexual difference. It is unfortunate indeed that this fact fails to come across in the English translation of *The Second Sex*. In Parshley's version, the word *aliénation* tends to get translated as 'projection', except in passages with a certain anthropological flavour, where it remains 'alienation'. But *aliénation* even shows up as 'identification', and on one occasion it masquerades as 'being beside herself'. As a result, English-language readers are prevented from hearing the particularly Hegelian and Lacanian overtones of Beauvoir's analysis. In my own text I amend all relevant quotations, and I also signal particularly aberrant translations in notes.[19]

According to Beauvoir, the little child reacts to the crisis of weaning by experiencing 'the original drama of every existent: that of his relation to the Other' (SS296; DSb14; TA). This drama is characterized by existential anguish caused by the experience of *délaissement*, or, in more Heideggerian terms, *Überlassenheit*, often translated as 'abandonment' in English. Already at this early stage the little child dreams of escaping her freedom either by merging with the cosmic whole, or by becoming a thing, an in-itself:

> In carnal form [the child] discovers finiteness, solitude, abandonment in a strange world. He endeavours to compensate for this catastrophe by alienating his existence in an image, the reality and value of which others will establish. It appears that he may begin to affirm his identity at the time when he recognizes his reflection in a mirror – a time which coincides with that of weaning.[20] His ego blends so completely into this reflected image that it is formed only through its own alienation [*il ne se forme qu'en s'aliénant*] [. . .] He is already an autonomous subject transcending himself towards the outer world, but he encounters himself only in an alienated form (SS296–7; DSb15; TA).

Initially, then, all children are equally alienated. This is not surprising, since the wish to alienate oneself in another person or thing, according to Beauvoir, is fundamental to all human beings: 'Primitive people are alienated in mana, in the totem; civilized people in their individual souls, in their egos, their names, their property, their work. Here is to be found the primary temptation to inauthenticity' (SS79; DSa90). But sexual difference soon transforms the situation. For little boys, Beauvoir argues, it is much easier to find an object in which to alienate themselves than for little girls: admirably suited to the role of idealized *alter ego*, the penis quickly becomes every little boy's very own totem-pole: 'The penis is singularly adapted for playing this role of "double" for the little boy – it is for him at once a foreign object and himself' (SS79; DSa90). Projecting themselves into the penis, little boys invest it with the whole charge of their transcendence (see SS79; DSa91).[21] For Beauvoir, then, phallic imagery represents transcendence, not sexuality.[22]

The little girl, however, has a more difficult time of it. Given that she has no penis, she has no tangible object in which to alienate herself: 'But the little girl cannot incarnate herself in any part of herself', Beauvoir writes (SS306; DSb27).[23] Because they are impossible to grab hold of (*empoigner*), it is as if the girl's sex organs do not exist: 'in a sense she has no sex organ', Beauvoir writes: 'She does not experience this absence as a lack; evidently her body is, for her, quite complete; but she finds herself situated in the world differently from the boy; and a constellation of factors can transform this difference, in her eyes, into an inferiority' (SS300; DSb19). Deprived of an obvious object of alienation, the little girl ends up alienating herself in herself:

> Not having that *alter ego*, the little girl does not alienate herself in a material thing and cannot retrieve her integrity [*ne se récupère pas*]. On this account she is led to make an object of her whole self, to set herself up as the Other. The question of whether she has or has not compared herself with boys is secondary; the important point is that, even if she is unaware of it, the absence of the penis prevents her from becoming conscious of herself as a sexual being. From this flow many consequences (SS80; DSa91; TA).

Regardless of whether they know of the penis's existence or not, little girls are already objects for themselves, irredeemably caught up in their own alienated self-image. But this is not all. On the evidence of this surprising passage, little girls are forced by their anatomy to alienate themselves in themselves. Furthermore, Beauvoir claims, they fail to 'recover' or 're-trieve' (*récupérer*) themselves. Offering a condensed version of the whole of Beauvoir's theory of alienation, these remarks have a series of wide-ranging and complex implications which I will now go on to explore.

Much like Lacan, Beauvoir casts the moment of alienation as constitutive of the subject; but unlike Lacan, she believes that the subject only comes into authentic being if it completes the dialectical movement and goes on to *recover* (*récupérer*) or reintegrate the alienated image of itself (the double, the *alter ego*) back into its own subjectivity. Drawing on this Hegelian logic, Beauvoir insists that little boys easily achieve the required synthesis, whereas little girls fail to 'recover' themselves. Why, then, do little boys easily 'recover' their own transcendence? For Beauvoir, the answer is to be found in the anatomical and physiological properties of the penis. Projecting his transcendence into the penis, the boy projects it into an object which is part of his body, yet which has a strange life of its own: 'The function of urination and later of erection are processes midway between the voluntary and involuntary', Beauvoir writes; the penis is 'a capricious and as it were foreign source of pleasure that is felt subjectively. [. . .] The penis is regarded by the subject as at once himself and other than himself' (SS79; DSa90).[24] Not so foreign and distant as to appear entirely without connections with the boy, yet not so close as to prevent a clear-cut distinction between the boy's subjectivity and his own projected transcendence, the penis, according to Beauvoir, enables the boy to *recognize* himself in his *alter ego*: 'Because he has an *alter ego* in whom he recognizes himself, the little boy can boldly assume his subjectivity,' she writes, 'the very object in which he alienates himself becomes a symbol of autonomy, of transcendence, of power' (SS306; DSb27; TA).

The idea of *recognition* here must be taken to allude to the Hegelian *Anerkennung*. By being relatively other (thus allowing the positing of a subject–other distinction), yet not quite other (thus making recognition of oneself in the other easier), the penis facilitates the recuperation of the boy's alienated transcendence back into his subjectivity. Recuperating his sense of transcendence for himself, the boy escapes his alienation: his penis–totem becomes the very instrument which in the end allows him to 'assume his subjectivity' and act authentically. To discern the Hegelian influences in Beauvoir's argument, however, is not to claim that she is being particularly orthodox. Freely developing the themes of recognition and the dialectical triad, Beauvoir entirely forgets that for Hegel, 'recognition' presupposes the reciprocal exchange between two *subjects*. The implication is that it is not only the little boy who must recognize himself in his penis, but the penis that must recognize itself in the boy. Fortunately, perhaps, Beauvoir does not fully realize this; at least she never pretends that the penis actually speaks back.[25]

As we have seen, Beauvoir holds that the girl's anatomy makes her alienate herself into her whole body, not just into a semi-detached object such as the penis. Even if she is given a doll to play with, the situation does not change. Dolls are passive objects representing the whole body, and as such they encourage the little girl to 'alienate herself in her whole person and to regard this as an inert given object' (SS306; DSb27; TA). In her alienated state the little girl apparently becomes 'passive' and 'inert'. But why is this the outcome of the girl's alienation? The 'alienated' penis, after all, was perceived by the boy as a proud image of transcendence. Why does this not happen to the girl's whole body? Where does *her* transcendence go?

On this point Beauvoir's text is not particularly easy to follow. I take her to argue that the girl's alienation sets up an ambiguous division between herself and her alienated image of herself. 'Woman, like man, *is* her body,' Beauvoir writes about the adult woman, 'but her body is something other than herself' (SS61; DSa67). The adult woman, then, has still not achieved the reintegration of her transcendence. The reason why she fails to do so is, paradoxically, that she was not alienated enough in the first place. Precisely because her body *is* herself, one might say, it is difficult for the girl to distinguish between the alienated body and her transcendent consciousness of that body. Or in other words: the difference between the whole body and the penis is that the body can never be considered simply an object in the world for its 'owner': the body, after all, *is* our mode of existing in the world: 'To be present in the world implies strictly that there exists a body which is at once a material thing in the world and a point of view towards this world' (SS39; DSa40).

Alienating herself in her body, the little girl alienates her transcendence in a 'thing' that remains ambiguously part of her own original transcendence. Her alienation, we might say, creates a murky mixture of transcendence, thingness, and the alienated *image* of a body–ego. The treacherous indeterminacy of this amalgam of the in-itself and the for-itself recalls Sartre's horrified vision of the 'sticky' or 'slimy' as that which is eternally undefined and always threatening to engulf the for-itself. Permitting no clear-cut positing of a subject and an other, this ambivalent mixture prevents the girl from achieving the reintegration of her alienated transcendence which, apparently, is so simple for the boy. In so far as what one 'recovers' is supposed to be something different from oneself, the absence of an unproblematic opposition between the two first moments of the dialectic makes it almost impossible for the girl to 'recover' her alienated transcendence in a new synthesis.

It does not follow from this, however, that the little girl has no sense of herself as transcendent at all. If that were the case, she would be *entirely* alienated, which is precisely what she is not. Instead, Beauvoir appears to suggest that there is an ever-present tension – or even struggle – between the little girl's transcendent subjectivity and her ambivalent alienation.[26] On this suggestion, the girl's psychological structures under patriarchy must be pictured as a complex and mobile *process*, rather than as a static and fixed *image*. There is in Beauvoir's theory a productive tension between her initial, highly reified concept of alienation, and the more mobile and fluid outcome of the process in the case of little girls. The result is that her theory of female subjectivity is far more interesting and original than her rather too neat and tidy account of male psychological structures.[27]

Towards the end of *The Second Sex*, Beauvoir argues that the process of alienation is constitutive of narcissism. (On this point, one may add, her position is entirely compatible with that of Lacan.) 'Narcissism is a well-defined process of alienation', Beauvoir writes, 'in which the ego is regarded as an absolute end and the subject takes refuge from itself in it' (SS641; DSb525; TA). For the narcissistic subject, her ego or self is nothing but an alienated and idealized *image* of herself, another *alter ego* or double in danger in the world. As far as I can see, the difference between the narcissistic and the non-narcissistic woman is that the latter conserves a sense of ambiguity or contradiction, whereas the former persuades herself that she *is* the image projected by her alienation. This is why narcissism, according to Beauvoir, represents a supreme effort to 'accomplish the impossible synthesis of the *en-soi* and the *pour-soi*': the 'successful' narcissist really believes that she is God (SS644; DSb529).

For Beauvoir and Sartre, when we alienate ourselves in another thing or person, we deprive ourselves of the power to act for or by ourselves. Deprived of agency, our alienated transcendence is defencelessly delivered up to the perils of the world. For Beauvoir, there is thus no need to mobilize a specific theory of castration anxiety to explain why little boys feel that their penis is constantly endangered. To worry about the safety of one's penis, however, is infinitely preferable to feeling obscurely threatened in one's whole person, as little girls do:

> The diffuse apprehension felt by the little girl in regard to her 'insides' [. . .] will often be retained for life. She is extremely concerned about everything that happens inside her, she is from the start much more opaque to her own eyes, more profoundly immersed in the obscure mystery of life, than is the male (SS305–6; DSb27).

In this passage, as everywhere else in *The Second Sex*, Beauvoir's subtle and incisive exploration of women's situation is juxtaposed with a far too sanguine view of masculinity. In the light of her own belief in the influence of social factors on the development of sexual difference, she also hugely overestimates the efficacy of the penis as a foolproof instrument of alienation and reintegration. Every little boy or every adult male does not, after all, come across as an authentically transcendent subject. Beauvoir's admiration of masculinity is such that she even assumes that girls brought up by men rather than by women 'very largely escape the defects of femininity' (SS308; DSb30). I take this to mean that such women somehow will be less alienated than others. Considering the fact that it is *patriarchy* that exacerbates women's particular form of alienation, this is, to say the least, a rather strange claim, one which seems plausible only if one assumes that men are always *less* likely than women to impose patriarchal ideology on little girls. Given Beauvoir's general analysis of patriarchy, however, such a position strikes me as more than a little contradictory.

There are strong biographical reasons for Beauvoir's misguided admiration of the male (unconscious idealization of the father, admiration for Sartre, and so on), yet the main rhetorical source of Beauvoir's touching confidence in the penis would seem to be metaphorical: since she can only conceive of the existential project as active, linear and phallic, she ends up finding the virtues of the free project mirrored in the movement of the penis. Littered with references to the powerful symbolic effects of urination from a standing rather than from a crouching position, her text repeatedly emphasizes the penis's capacity for quasi-independent motion as well as for the projection of liquids over a certain distance. What apparently fascinates her above all is the idea that the male organ moves, and, moreover, that it is *upwardly mobile*, particularly in its grandiose projection of urine: 'Every stream of water in the air seems like a miracle, a defiance of gravity: to direct, to govern it, is to win a small victory over the laws of nature', Beauvoir claims, quoting Sartre and Bachelard to substantiate her point (SS301–2; DSb22).[28]

By stressing the links between alienation and anatomy in Beauvoir's theory, I run the risk of making her sound as if she believes that the development of different forms of alienation depends entirely on the anatomical presence or absence of the penis. Yet Beauvoir herself insists that hers is a theory of the *social* construction of femininity and masculinity, and, moreover, categorically refuses the idea of a biological or anatomical 'destiny' of any kind. On the contrary, she argues, it is the social context that gives meaning to biological and psychological factors: 'True human privilege is based upon anatomical privilege only in virtue of the total situation [*la situation saisie dans sa totalité*]' (SS80; DSa91). It is only when the girl discovers that men have power in the world and women do not that she risks mistaking her difference for inferiority: 'She sees that it is not the women, but the men who control the world. It is this revelation – much more than the discovery of the penis – which irresistibly alters her conception of herself' (SS314; DSb38).

Given the proper social encouragement, Beauvoir argues, girls may still manage to recover their transcendence. While the penis is a privileged possession in early childhood, after the age of 8 or 9 it holds on to its prestige only because it is socially valorized. Social practices, not biology, encourage little girls to remain sunk in passivity and narcissism, and force little boys to become active subjects. It is because little boys are treated more harshly than girls, and not because they are intrinsically less self-indulgent, that they are better equipped to project themselves into the competitive world of concrete action (see SS306–7; DSb28–9). It would seem that Beauvoir's theory of alienation actually implies that social

factors have *greater* influence on girls than on boys: precisely because girls'
transcendence is precariously balanced between complete alienation and
authentic subjectivity, it does not take much to push the girl in either
direction. Less pronounced in boys, one might argue, this ambiguity makes
girls particularly susceptible to social pressure:

> Along with the authentic demand of the subject who wants sovereign
> freedom, there is in the existent an inauthentic longing for resignation and
> escape; the delights of passivity are made to seem desirable to the young girl
> by parents and teachers, books and myths, women and men; she is taught to
> enjoy them from earliest childhood; the temptation becomes more and more
> insidious; and she is the more fatally bound to yield to those delights as the
> flight of her transcendence is dashed against harsher obstacles (SS325;
> DSb53).

I take Beauvoir's constant appeal to social factors to be one of the
strongest points of her position. But when it comes to explaining exactly
how we are to understand the relationship between the anatomical and
the social, her discourse becomes curiously slippery. Not to have a penis,
for instance, is not necessarily a handicap: 'If woman should succeed in
establishing herself as subject, she would invent equivalents of the phallus;
in fact the doll, incarnating the promise of the baby that is to come in the
future, can become a possession more precious than the penis' (SS80;
DSa91).[29] Dolls, then, do not inevitably cause alienated passivity after all:
'the boy, too, can cherish a teddy bear, or a puppet into which he projects
himself [*se projette*]; it is within the totality of their lives that each factor –
penis or doll – takes on its importance' (SS307; DSb29).
   Beauvoir's contradictory feelings about the role of dolls reveals a deeper
theoretical difficulty: that of finding a way of linking an anatomical and
psychological argument with a sociological one. The fact that she makes no
attempt explicitly to raise this problem causes her to overlook an important
hiatus in her own account of alienation. Attentive readers may already have
noticed that her text moves directly from the Lacanian theory of the
alienation of the child in the gaze of the other to the rather different idea
that boys and girls alienate themselves in their bodies. Unfortunately,
Beauvoir makes no attempt to relate Lacan's view to her own. For her,
apparently, the two simply coexist. Failing to perceive this as a problem,
she also misses out on a crucial opportunity to bridge the gap in her own
theory, by suggesting, for instance, that it is the gaze of the other that
originally invests the child's alienated image of itself with the phallocentric
values it then goes on to repeat in its own work of alienation. The gaze of
the other, one might add, would necessarily see – and, in most cases,
instantly ideologize – anatomical differences, and therefore proceed to

invest girls and boys with different psychosexual values. By giving her own theory a slightly more Lacanian twist on this point, she might, in my view, have managed to produce a more satisfying account of the relationship between the biological and the psycho-social than she actually does.

It is unfortunate, to say the least, that Beauvoir makes her perceptive theory of femininity function as a foil to what amounts to little more than mindless admiration of masculinity. Persistently juxtaposing wholesome male alienation and complex female ambiguity, her rhetoric tends to devalorize the female position, regardless of her own arguments to the contrary. Yet, as I will go on to show, her idealization of the phallus flatly contradicts Sartre's account of masculine desire and transcendence. Paradoxically enough, then, it is in the very passages where Beauvoir unconsciously seeks to pay tribute to Sartre that she betrays his philosophy.

I want to emphasize that Beauvoir's overvaluation of masculinity does not prevent her from developing a strikingly original theory of female subjectivity under patriarchy. In her vision of women caught in an ambiguous contradiction between their own transcendent consciousness and their identification with an alienated and patriarchal image of themselves, I see a courageous attempt fully to grasp the contradictions of women's position. The strength of her theory of alienation as constitutive of sexual difference is not only that it manages to suggest – albeit somewhat imperfectly – that patriarchal power structures are at work in the very construction of female subjectivity, but also that it attempts to show exactly *how* this process works. There is an admirable effort here to develop a fully *social* understanding of subjectivity. The major flaw of her analysis remains the absence of any real discussion of the relationship between the anatomical and the social. As I have suggested, however, this difficulty might be resolved, perhaps through a less diffident use of Lacan. Providing the basis for a sophisticated analysis of women's difficulties in conceiving of themselves as social and sexual subjects under patriarchy, Beauvoir's account implies that it is both unjust and unrealistic to underestimate the difficulty involved in becoming a free woman. Bound up with the idea of the body, Beauvoir's theory of alienation can nevertheless not be fully assessed in isolation from her analysis of the female body in its sexual and reproductive aspects.

The Body in Trouble

'Woman, like man,' Beauvoir writes, '*is* her body, but her body is something other than herself' (DSa67; SS61). Woman both is and is not her body; the fact of having a female body is what makes her a woman, yet this very fact also alienates and separates her from herself. So what is a woman?

A free subject? Or a free subject struggling against her female body? Is the desire of the body compatible with freedom?[30] Crucial to Beauvoir's understanding of women's oppression and their eventual liberation, these questions require us to examine her understanding of desire and sexuality in general.

For Beauvoir, women are the slaves of the species. Every biological process in the female body is a 'crisis' or a 'trial', and the result is always alienation. Her list of the troubles and pains experienced during menstruation is impressive, to say the least, ranging from high blood pressure, impaired hearing and eyesight to unpleasant smells, destabilization of the central nervous system, abdominal pains, constipation and diarrhoea (see SS61; DSa66).[31] It is at this time, Beauvoir claims, that the woman 'feels her body most painfully as an obscure, alienated thing [*une chose opaque aliénée*]' (SS61; DSa67). But the discomfort of menstruation pales in comparison to the horrors of gestation: 'Woman experiences a more profound alienation when fertilization has occurred and the dividing egg passes down into the uterus and proceeds to develop there', she claims (SS62; DSa67). Pregnancy, childbirth and breast-feeding all undermine the woman's health and even put her life at risk: 'Childbirth itself is painful and dangerous. [. . .] Nursing is also an exhausting obligation [*servitude*]; [. . .] the nursing mother feeds the newborn at the expense of her own strength' (SS62–3; DSa68; TA).

Only the ageing woman escapes the servitude of reproduction, albeit at the cost of traversing the 'crisis' of menopause: 'Woman is now delivered from the servitude of the female species, but she is not to be likened to a eunuch, for her vitality is unimpaired. And what is more, she is no longer the prey of overwhelming forces; she coincides with herself' (SS63; DSa69; TA).[32] For Beauvoir, as we have seen, patriarchy produces a conflict between women's free subjectivity and the pressure to alienate and objectify that subjectivity. Given that women also suffer from a series of involuntary biological processes (menstruation, pregnancy, lactation, menopause), the same contradictory scenario is repeated, but never overcome, on the level of the body itself: the woman is condemned to suffer from her subordination to the species. The more the woman wants to assert herself as an individual, the harder it is for her to accept her biological destiny. Of all mammals, Beauvoir writes, the human female is 'the one who is the most profoundly alienated, and the one who most violently resists this alienation. [. . .] It would seem that her destiny weighs especially heavily on her because she rebels against it by asserting her individuality' (SS64; DSa70; TA).

The man, on the other hand, is 'infinitely favoured', Beauvoir declares, 'his sexual life is not in opposition to his existence as a person, and biologically it runs an even course, without crises and generally without mishap' (SS64; DSa70–1). Positioned at a distance from herself, the woman can never know the unproblematic physical integrity of the male. When describing sexual desire, Beauvoir reproduces this contrast between male simplicity and female complexity. Male sexual arousal, Beauvoir claims, is uncomplicated, authentic and transcendent; female arousal is exactly the opposite. First of all, women's sexual organs are neither neat nor clean:

> The sex organ of a man is simple and neat as a finger [. . .]; the feminine sex organ is mysterious even to the woman herself, concealed, mucous, and humid, as it is; it bleeds each month, it is often sullied with bodily fluids, it has a secret and perilous life of its own. Woman does not recognize herself in it, and this explains in large part why she does not recognize its desires as hers (SS406–7; DSb166).

Unlike the little boy, Beauvoir implies, the woman is unable to alienate her transcendence in her sexual organs, and so fails to 'recognize' herself in them. Or in other words: the woman has nowhere to 'place' her transcendence; her sexual desire is absorbed back into her whole, alienated body. But as we have already seen, for Beauvoir an alienated body is an abandoned object exposed to the perils of the world. Mercilessly delivering her up to the transcendent power of the male, female desire deprives the woman of control of her own body.

It follows that when the male penetrates the woman, her sexual subjectivity is objectified and possessed by him. For Beauvoir, the desiring woman is truly in trouble: 'Being more profoundly alienated than the man because she is desire and arousal [*trouble*] in her whole body, she only remains a subject through union with her partner',[33] Beauvoir writes about the woman engaged in heterosexual intercourse (SS417; DSb183; TA).[34] Fortunately for her feminist readers, such an astonishing conclusion does not in fact follow from her own theory of women's *incomplete* alienation ('woman *is* her body'). To claim, as she is doing here, that the woman is *entirely* alienated in the man is to shift her position considerably. Apparently, then, for Beauvoir the very experience of desire causes female consciousness to slip into complete alienation; or in other words: sexual desire swallows up whatever is left of the alienated woman's transcendence:

> She suffers from arousal [*trouble*] as from a shameful illness; it is not active: it is a state from which, even in imagination, she cannot find relief by any decision of her own. She does not dream of taking, shaping, violating: her part is to await, to want; she feels dependent; she feels in danger in her alienated flesh (SS345; DSb82; TA).

Describing actual sexual situations, Beauvoir tends to represent the female body as pure facticity. At the same time, however, she implies that there is enough transcendent subjectivity left in the desiring woman's body for that body to be at war with the woman's sexual projects: 'her anatomy compels her to remain clumsy and impotent like a eunuch', Beauvoir claims, 'the wish for possession is fruitless for want of an organ in which it is incarnated' (SS398–9; DSb155). What Beauvoir is describing here is a kind of ultimate frustration of the whole woman's body: it is as if the mere possession of a penis would magically resolve the situation, give female desire its necessary outlet and transform the body from facticity to transcendence. Implausible though it may be, this is precisely what Beauvoir believes. When the man desires, she writes, his body becomes an uncomplicated expression of his transcendent project:

> Erection is the expression of this need; with penis, hands, mouth, with his whole body, a man reaches out towards his partner, but he himself remains at the centre of this activity, being, on the whole, like the subject in relation to the objects he perceives and the instruments that he manipulates; he projects himself towards the other without losing his independence; the feminine flesh is for him a prey, and through it he gains access to the qualities his sensuality demands of every object (SS393; DSb147; TA).

When the woman desires, on the other hand, she has to struggle to transform her active desire into passivity. This effort produces a new conflict in the woman's experience of herself: 'To *make* oneself an object, to *make* oneself passive, is a very different thing from *being* a passive object', Beauvoir insists (SS400; DSb156); in the sexual act, the woman is obliged to perform the most delicate balancing act between 'ardour' and 'abandon' (SS400; DSb157). If the woman seeks to exercise too much control – or even simply to move – she destroys the passive spell (*envoûtement*) that alone can give her pleasure:

> All voluntary effort prevents the feminine flesh from being 'taken'; this is why woman spontaneously declines the forms of coition which demand effort and tension on her part; too sudden or too many changes of position, any call for consciously directed activities – whether words or behaviour – tend to break the spell (SS400; DSb157).

The imagery in these passages says it all: Beauvoir's representation of male and female desire is entirely ruled by her own metaphors. If transcendence is like an erection, erections must be transcendent. If the female body has no organ that moves upwards and outward, woman's desire must be immanent. If transcendence is movement, women having sex must necessarily be lying stock still. Having put her firmly in her place, Beauvoir then goes on to argue that the very position the woman now is in – flat on her back – symbolizes *defeat*, and therefore increases her feeling of being nothing but a mere prey for the male (see SS406; DSb165). The difficulty of squaring the circle, or in other words of explaining how any kind of desire, be it male or female, can conceivably be immanent, leads to convoluted attempts at establishing a difference between 'straightforward' activity and the active effort to turn oneself into passivity.

Always passive, the female sexual body also becomes an object of disgust: Sartre's descriptions of holes and slime are only thinly disguised in Beauvoir's account of female sexual arousal:

> Feminine sex desire is the soft throbbing of a mollusc. Whereas man is impetuous, woman is only impatient; her expectation can become ardent without ceasing to be passive; man dives upon his prey like the eagle and the hawk; woman lies in wait like the carnivorous plant, the bog in which insects and children are swallowed up. She is absorption, leech-like suction, inhalation [elle est succion, ventouse, humeuse], she is pitch and glue, a passive demand [appel], insinuating and viscous: thus, at least, she vaguely feels herself to be (SS407; DSb167; TA).

There is something delirious about this fantasy of the desiring woman as a gigantic, slimy, carnivorous hole in whose dirty, moist interiors death and destruction lie in wait. The rhetorical intensity of this passage signals the presence of strong unconscious obsessions. If sexual arousal is threatening, however, the moment of orgasm represents total obliteration: 'She bathes in a passive languor; with closed eyes anonymous, lost, she feels as if borne by waves, swept away in a storm, shrouded in darkness: darkness of the flesh, of the womb, of the grave. Annihilated, she becomes one with the Whole, her ego is abolished' (SS658; DSb555). During sexual intercourse women close their eyes, Beauvoir adds, because they want to lose themselves 'in a carnal night as shadowy as the maternal womb' (SS417; DSb183). The heavy imagery of darkness, oceanic depths, wombs and death speaks for itself: when the woman succumbs to the man – lets herself be carried away – she rejoins the still foetal waters of the archaic mother. There is a striking resemblance in tone and intensity between the passages describing Xavière or the subterranean tendrils of the unconscious in L'Invitée and the imagery of the sexual woman in The Second Sex. In both cases I suspect that the intensity, hostility and rawness of Beauvoir's prose spring from the same source: a deeply ambivalent relationship to the mother.[35]

The relationship between this theory and Sartre's account of desire in Being and Nothingness will not be discussed in detail here. When it comes to understanding male desire, however, Beauvoir's position is strikingly different from that of Sartre. 'Desire is defined as trouble', Sartre writes. 'If the desiring consciousness is troubled it is because it is analogous to the troubled

water' (BN503; EN437). Like muddy water, desire is experienced as something that deprives consciousness of its translucence and clarity, something that exists everywhere and nowhere in particular, but which manages
to leave its mark on everything else. Sexual desire is neither 'distinct' nor
'clear' (BN504; EN437); it 'has fallen wholly into complicity with the
body', Sartre writes (BN504; EN438), before appealing to 'our' common
experience of the matter:

> Let everyone consult his own experience: one knows that consciousness is
> clogged, so to speak, by sexual desire; it seems that one is invaded by
> facticity, that one ceases to flee it and that one slides towards a *passive* consent
> to the desire. At other moments it seems that facticity invades consciousness
> in its very flight and renders consciousness opaque to itself. It is like a yeasty
> tumescence of *fact* (BN504; EN438; TA).[36]

Without going into the details of his account, there can be no doubt that
for Sartre even male desire threatens to drag consciousness down into
facticity. Sartre's striking description of a man overcome by desire bears this
out: 'Everyone has been able to observe the appearance of desire in
another. Suddenly the man who desires becomes a heavy tranquillity which
is frightening, his eyes are fixed and appear half-closed, his movements are
stamped with a heavy and sticky sweetness; many seem to be falling asleep'
(BN504–5; EN438). I should perhaps say that, so far, my own research in
Parisian cafés has failed to confirm Sartre's confident observations of glazed
and drowsily desiring males. Whatever the reality of the matter, Beauvoir's
belief in the transcendence of male erections remains entirely absent from
Sartre's representation of sexual intercourse:

> We may in fact observe the organic passivity of the sex organ in coitus. It is
> the whole body which advances and withdraws, which *carries* the sex organ
> forward or withdraws it. Hands help to introduce the penis; the penis itself
> appears as an instrument which one manages, which one makes penetrate,
> which one withdraws, which one utilizes. And similarly the opening and the
> lubrication of the vagina cannot be obtained voluntarily (BN515; EN447;
> TA).

The contrast to Beauvoir's view of the erect penis as 'simple and neat as a
finger' (SS406; DSb166) could not be greater. For Sartre, the penis is
precisely *not* a finger, *not* a straightforward expression of consciousness.
Beauvoir compares vaginal lubrication to carnivorous plants and child-
eating swamps; he compares it to the penis; and where he downgrades
the penis to a mere instrument, she divinizes it as the very image of
transcendence.

In 1945, Beauvoir favourably reviewed Maurice Merleau-Ponty's essay on the *Phenomenology of Perception* for *Les temps modernes*. Praising his analysis of the body as our mode of being in the world, Beauvoir also stresses the 'richness' of his analysis of sexuality (p. 367). In her studiedly neutral account of Merleau-Ponty's philosophical difference from Sartre (unlike Sartre, Merleau-Ponty holds that since consciousness is always incarnated in a body, existence cannot be analysed as a pure for-itself), Beauvoir refrains from commenting on the disagreement. In *The Second Sex*, she also refers approvingly to Merleau-Ponty, yet her praise remains superficial, and she never really engages with his analyses.

What Beauvoir apparently fails to see is that Merleau-Ponty's understanding of sexuality is highly consonant with her own theory of the ambiguity of female alienation. For Merleau-Ponty, sexuality contains the key to the understanding of human life. 'The body expresses existence in every moment', he writes (*Phénoménologie*, p. 193); for him, there can be no question of considering the sexual body as *less* transcendent than the walking or running body. For Merleau-Ponty, sexuality *is* ambiguity, that which can never be fully grasped by consciousness, but which nevertheless is constitutive of our perception of ourselves and the world:

> Without being the object of a deliberate act of consciousness, sexuality can motivate the privileged forms of my experience. Understood in this way, sexuality is like an ambiguous atmosphere, and becomes coextensive with life. Or in other words: ambiguity [*l'équivoque*] is essential to human existence, and everything we experience and think always has several meanings (*Phénoménologie*, p. 197).

For Merleau-Ponty, the fundamental indeterminacy or ambiguity of sexuality makes it impossible to draw a clear dividing line between sexual and non-sexual acts. Sexuality is 'a principle of indeterminacy in human existence', he writes, and this indeterminacy is the fundamental structure of existence (*Phénoménologie*, p. 197). By stressing the presence of sexuality as a principle of ambiguity in every human action, Merleau-Ponty avoids postulating the radical opposition between mind and body or between consciousness and desire which prevents Sartre and Beauvoir from developing a more convincing and less phallocentric vision of sexuality. To my mind, his view offers far more fertile ground for the production of a non-sexist account of female sexuality than Sartre's evocation of a 'distinct' and 'clear' consciousness lapsing into the chaos of the body. To Simone de Beauvoir, who after all explicitly enjoins us to valorize the ambiguity of existence, the advantages of Merleau-Ponty's position ought to have been obvious. Yet her own texts place ambiguity and indeterminacy firmly under the control of the lucidity of transcendent consciousness. Nowhere is Beauvoir's fundamental allegiance to Sartre clearer – and more costly for her own philosophical project – than in her preference for *Being and Nothingness* over *The Phenomenology of Perception*.[37]

Drawing on Sartre's distinction between the active – acting – body and the passive 'flesh' (*la chair*) (see EN439–40), Beauvoir genders this opposition even more thoroughly than Sartre himself.[38] So far at least, she would seem to have no valid defence against feminist critiques of such an account of female sexuality. Before drawing our final conclusions, however, we have to consider the fact that, according to Beauvoir herself, what she is dealing with is patriarchal ideology. 'Woman is thoroughly indoctrinated with collective representations that endow male excitement [*rut*] with splendour and make a shameful abdication of female arousal [*trouble*]: woman's intimate experience confirms the fact of this asymmetry', she writes just before launching into her murderous account of female desire (SS406; DSb166; TA). The 'collective representations' alluded to here are the myths of femininity analysed with such brio in the first part of *The Second Sex*, where Beauvoir delivers a blistering attack on the very terms she herself uses to describe female orgasm:

> To say that Woman is flesh, to say that the flesh is Night and Death, or that it is the splendour of the Cosmos, is to abandon terrestrial truth and soar into an empty sky. For man also is flesh for woman; and woman is not merely a carnal object; and the flesh takes on specific meanings [*des significations singulières*] for each person and in each experience (SS285; DSa398; TA).

At the beginning of the second part of *The Second Sex*, that is to say, of the volume which contains her account of female sexuality, Beauvoir explicitly warns us that she is setting out to study the 'traditional destiny of woman', the 'burdensome past' of woman's condition, 'the common basis that underlies every individual female existence' (SS31; DSb9; TA). But does it follow that she herself does not actually *believe* that women's sexuality is passive, immanent, reminiscent of carnivorous plants and murderous swamps, and so on? There are *some* arguments to support such a view. First of all, Beauvoir is probably right in insisting on the sexual misery of women in France in the 1940s: women who find themselves systematically deprived of sexual information, contraception and the right to abortion, and subjected to the usual patriarchal double standard of morality, may indeed have trouble finding sex an uncomplicated source of pleasure.[39] In *The Second Sex*, there is, moreover, no implication that the deplorable situation Beauvoir is exposing cannot change. It ought not to surprise us to find Beauvoir firmly declaring that *all* the sexual problems she has described are due to patriarchal oppression:

> The asymmetry that exists between the erotism of the male and that of the female creates insoluble problems as long as there is struggle between the

sexes; they can easily be solved when woman finds in the male both desire and respect; if he lusts after her flesh while recognizing her freedom, she finds herself essential in the very moment she makes herself object; she remains free in the submission to which she consents (SS421–2; DSb189; TA).

In this reciprocal context, however, men are also objects for women: there is still a trace of Beauvoir's male-centred perspective in this passage. Her point nevertheless remains clear: under non-oppressive conditions, sexual intercourse may after all become a profound experience of reciprocity: 'Under a concrete and carnal form there is mutual recognition of the self and of the other with the keenest awareness both of the other and of the self' (SS422; DSb189; TA).[40]

While most of women's sexual problems may be ascribed to their social situation, the differences in anatomy obviously remain. For Beauvoir, it would seem that even a free woman *submits* to the man, albeit without alienating her freedom in the process. The anatomy of the female body, she argues, simply makes the active *possession* of the other impossible: for her, such a thought apparently has nothing to do with patriarchal ideology. Whether we accept or reject her Sartrean privileging of the category of possession,[41] it is hard to avoid the conclusion that on Beauvoir's logic it will *always* be harder for women than for men to experience themselves as sexual beings and free subjects at one and the same time: in some way or other, women will always be up against their anatomy. Even in a free society there will always be a subtle non-coincidence between women and their anatomy ('but her body is something other than herself'). Sexual difference, perceived as an aspect of the materiality of the body, proves to be fundamental to Beauvoir's analysis of women's fate under patriarchy: for her, women and men will never simply be the *same*. The point to be grasped, however, is that *nothing* in particular follows from the recognition of biological difference, since for Beauvoir, as for any existentialist, the *meaning* of that difference is never given, but always to be constructed anew.

While patriarchal ideology seeks to intensify and maximize the woman's alienation, not all women internalize oppressive structures to the same extent. Already in *The Blood of Others*, published in 1945, Beauvoir emphasizes the difference between passively submitting to desire and actively choosing it. The fact that the same woman experiences both situations demonstrates her belief in women's capacity to change, as well as in the power of existential choice. When Hélène is on the brink of being seduced by her fiancé Paul, about whom she feels more than a little ambivalent, Beauvoir mobilizes exactly the same negative vocabulary of plants, insects, softness, darkness and stickiness as in *L'Invitée* and in *The Second Sex*.

Closing her eyes, Hélène feels that Paul's caresses transform her into a plant or a tree:

> She felt her bones and muscles melt, her flesh became a humid and spongy moss, teeming with unknown life; a thousand buzzing insects stabbed her with their honeyed stings. [. . .] She could hardly draw breath, she was sinking into the heart of the night, she was out of her depth; her eyes closed, paralysed by that net of burning silk, it seemed to her that she would never rise again to the surface of the world, that she would remain for ever enclosed in that viscid darkness, for ever an obscure and flabby jellyfish lying on a bed of magic nettles (BO79–80; SA105–6; TA).

When, on the other hand, Hélène decides to go to bed with Jean, whom she loves, Jean is overcome by the experience of her freedom:

> In my arms, you were not a submissive [*abandonné*] body, but a living woman. You smiled straight at me, so that I might know that you were there, freely, that you were not lost in the tumultuous coursing of your blood. You did not feel that you were the prey of a shameful fate; in the midst of your most passionate impulses, something in your voice, in your smile, said: 'It's because I consent to it.' Through your constancy in affirming your freedom, you gave me inward peace (BO106; SA139).

However wide Hélène opens her eyes in order to emphasize her freedom, she and her lover still share Beauvoir's fundamental horror of *abandon*: above all one must never let oneself go. The fall into facticity is an ever-present threat: beneath every act of authentic freedom lurks the danger of immanence.

Beauvoir's representation of female desire, then, is more complex than it may seem. On the one hand, she chillingly demonstrates how even the most private and personal aspects of the lives of oppressed women are blighted by patriarchal oppression. In this sense, hers is above all an analysis of the way in which patriarchal ideology comes to be internalized by its victims. On the other hand, however, Beauvoir also tends to become thoroughly ensnared in the very patriarchal categories she sets out to describe, above all because of her own remarkably phallocentric understanding of transcendence. Finally, there can be no doubt that Beauvoir's visceral disgust at the female sexual organs reveals an unconscious horror of more than just patriarchy: here, surely, lurks the threatening image of the mother, so central to the melodramatic imagination of *L'Invitée*.

Philosophical discourse is always haunted by the ghosts of the unconscious: if Sartre's logic loses its stringency as soon as he thinks about women, it may look as if Beauvoir's arguments threaten to go awry as soon as she approaches, however indirectly, the subject of female sexuality.[42] On closer examination, however, I am inclined to think that this formulation fails to capture the dialectical dynamics of Beauvoir's lapses in argument. For, if anything, Beauvoir's logic fails rather more dramatically in relation to the phallus than in relation to the female body: nothing can be more absurd than her explicit claim that men (and post-menopausal women) actually *coincide with themselves*, since on Sartre's and Beauvoir's own logic, *no subject* ever coincides with him- or herself: condemned to be free, we are all involved in an utterly futile [*inutile*] quest for being.

Beauvoir's body trouble, then, is not exclusively related to women. Rather it would seem that the logic at work in *The Second Sex* is the same as in *L'Invitée*. Suspended between the mother and the father, striving to separate from the ever-present mother's body by abjecting the mother and idealizing the phallus, the author of *The Second Sex* moves on the same unstable and ambiguous 'hysterical stage' as the heroine of *L'Invitée*. But this is not all: as I will now go on to show, Beauvoir has still a surprise in store for us.

Embodying Humanity

In *The Second Sex*, women's condition under patriarchy is theorized as a series of conflicts situated on three different levels. On the ontological level, women and men are equally split, equally divided: we are all caught in the tension between the desire for being and the nothingness of existence; nobody ever coincides with herself. On this level, we are all tempted to fall into immanence and bad faith; in the heterosexual human couple both partners are in principle equally keen to project their own bad faith on to the other. 'Instead of living out the ambiguities of their situation [*de leur condition*],' Beauvoir writes at the end of *The Second Sex*, 'each tries to make the other bear the abjection and tries to reserve the honour for the self' (SS737; DSb658).

Human beings, however, also live in society. On the social level, patriarchal oppression consists in a series of unjust restrictions of women's freedom. Against such oppression, Beauvoir argues for equal participation in economic and political life, equal opportunities and freedom of choice. Such equality, moreover, cannot be realized without free access to contraception, full abortion rights and readily available childcare for all.[43] Social oppression, however, also consists of the production of myth and ideology. According to Beauvoir, the social representation of women forces facticity upon them: women are put in a position where they are torn between freedom and alienation, transcendence and immanence. The result is the production of a specific psychosexual subjectivity characterized above all by alienation, understood as an uneven rift between the woman's freedom and her own identification with the alienating image of femininity as objectified otherness. This particular split does not affect men. Although patriarchy also produces strait-jacketing images of masculinity, these images do not cast males as Other in relation to some other social group: however irksome, such images cannot produce the radical objectification of the subject that Beauvoir labels alienation. It does not follow, of course, that men are never alienated, only that if they are, it is not *patriarchy* that forces alienation upon them.

On the social and psychosexual levels, then, the oppression of women consists in the repetition and reinforcement of the general ontological split between transcendence and facticity. The third and final level on which women's oppression acts itself out is the level of the body. Drawing on the existentialist theory of the totality of meaning, Beauvoir assumes that anatomical sexual difference – above all the absence of the penis, but also the reproductive biology of women's bodies – may be considered a meaningful part of the totality of women's existence. Women's experience of their own bodies therefore necessarily inflects their subjectivity and their perception of the world.

For Beauvoir, ontological, social and biological factors all converge in human sexual activity; under patriarchy, sexuality therefore becomes the arena where the general conflicts of women's lives are most acutely felt. 'The erotic experience', Beauvoir writes, 'is one that most poignantly discloses to human beings the ambiguity of their condition; in it they are aware of themselves as flesh and as spirit, as the other and as subject' (SS423; DSb190). For Beauvoir, then, sexual experience reveals the ontological drama of our existence. Because of the objectification imposed upon them by patriarchy, the conflicts of women's existence become particularly acute:

> This conflict has a more dramatic shape for woman because at first she feels herself to be object and does not at once find in sexual pleasure a sure independence; she must regain her dignity as transcendent and free subject while assuming her carnal condition – an enterprise fraught with difficulty and danger, and one that often fails (SS423; DSb190).

Precisely because of the difficulty of their situation, Beauvoir claims, women are not duped by the mystifications accepted by men, who are taken in by the 'deceptive privileges accorded [them] by [their] aggressive role and by the lonely satisfaction of the orgasm' (SS423; DSb191). But if the human condition is characterized by ambiguity and conflict, and if, due to their anatomy, biology and social situation, women are even more exposed to ambiguity and conflict than men, it follows that *under patriarchy women incarnate the human condition more fully than men*. This, in fact, is precisely what Beauvoir argues: 'Woman', she writes, 'has a more authentic experience of herself' (SS423; DSb191; TA).[44]

Exposed to the duplicity and cowardice displayed by men in their sexual dealings with women, women often spontaneously '[come] upon the ambiguity of all principle, of all value, of everything that exists', Beauvoir writes (SS624; DSb503). To face the fundamental ambiguity of existence is to live authentically: on Beauvoir's analysis, women's lives offer greater scope for existential authenticity – and greater risks of existential failure. Existentially speaking, under patriarchy women risk more, fall deeper and rise higher than men; while the woman who fails in her struggle for authenticity is not to be condoned, she most certainly is to be understood.

In Beauvoir's account, sexuality becomes a powerful source of insight for women. The woman who rises to the challenge, who surmounts her difficulties and realizes herself as an authentic human being in and through her sexuality, will have had to face the truth of the human condition in a deeper and more complex way than an authentic man. Sacrificing her sexuality, a woman sacrifices the better part of her humanity: if *The Second Sex* created such an uproar on its publication, it was above all because it was perceived as scandalous in its injunction to women to integrate their freedom and sexuality.[45]

In *Force of Circumstance*, Beauvoir still seems somewhat puzzled by her own conclusions:

> I should have been surprised and even irritated if, when I was thirty, someone had told me that I would be concerning myself with women's problems and that my most serious public would be made up of women. I don't regret that it has been so. Divided, torn, disadvantaged: for women the stakes are higher; there are more victories and more defeats for them than for men (FC203; FCa268; TA).

Her surprise is understandable. As a successful product of French philosophical education, Beauvoir clearly expected, in the early stages of her career, to make her mark by dealing with the classical philosophical problems. Taking men to be representative, Western philosophers have always cast women as particular: before writing *The Second Sex*, Beauvoir was no exception. Yet, in *The Second Sex*, the strength of her analysis of women's condition is precisely the way in which it manages, against the odds, and with considerable difficulties, to interrupt in its own discourse the usual philosophical alliance between masculinity and universality: in the end, Beauvoir argues, the universal human condition is more fully incarnated by women. Her analysis, moreover, does not simply reverse traditional patriarchal paradigms: Beauvoir does not claim, after all, that women are universal and men particular. The strength of her argument is precisely its basic assumption of equality: unusually enough in the Western philosophical tradition, Beauvoir holds that men are just as human as women.

At this point, however, the enormous contradictions in Beauvoir's account of men become apparent. For as we have seen, the author of *The Second Sex* also glorifies and idealizes the phallus, firmly believes that men 'coincide with themselves', and takes men's freedom to be blissfully unconstricted by social and historical circumstances. Men, moreover, easily behave in transcendentally free and authentic ways, if not in their dealings with women, then at least in their dealings with each other. Even the specific conflict between the woman's body and 'herself' is unknown to men: 'Woman, like man, *is* her body: but her body is other than herself.' It is as if Beauvoir genuinely believes that men's bodies somehow are less *biological* than women's. The juxtaposition of idealized masculinity and Beauvoir's visceral disgust for the female sexual organs can only be disparaging to women. Yet it is precisely through her analysis of female sexuality that Beauvoir reaches the conclusion that women, after all, embody the human condition more fully than men. Mindlessly climaxing in their easy orgasms, men remain epistemological dupes: there is more than a trace of condescension in that particular observation.

Nowhere in *The Second Sex* are the tensions between the personal and philosophical stronger than in Beauvoir's representation of masculinity. As we have seen, the paradoxes of *The Second Sex* are the paradoxes of *L'Invitée*. If Beauvoir argues that women under patriarchy are torn by conflict and inner strife, the very texture of her book reveals this to be no less true for herself than for other women. *The Second Sex* enacts the very contradictions described by Beauvoir; confirming her analysis, her text also undoes it. The deepest paradox of all is that the most powerful anti-patriarchal text of the twentieth century reads as if it is written by a dutiful daughter only too eager to please the father.

Let us not try to resolve this paradox, to reduce *The Second Sex* to nothing but an anti-feminist attack on women, or, on the other hand, to transform it into a flawless monument of political correctness. In so far as this chapter focuses exclusively on Beauvoir's account of subjectivity and sexuality, it already seems to overstate the importance of these themes. There is also a touch of anachronism in my approach: to look to Beauvoir for an account of female sexuality, one might argue, is like turning to Hélène Cixous for an analysis of women in the French working class. Or in other words: to read Beauvoir for a theory of female subjectivity is to read her on premises drawn up by the feminist theorists of the 1970s who, for excellent historical reasons, decided that the time had come to celebrate women's difference from men.[46] Judging by the available evidence, however, the hundreds of thousands of women who found inspiration, comfort and the will to fight in *The Second Sex* in the 1950s and 1960s did not pay much attention to Beauvoir's account of sexuality: what they found was a scorching critique of bourgeois marriage, a blistering attack on repressive laws concerning contraception and abortion, and the best analysis of housework ever written. They also found a breathtaking vision of freedom that sustained them through their often difficult lives. It is to this vision that I now turn.

7

Beauvoir's Utopia:
The Politics of *The Second Sex*

The free woman is just being born.

(The Second Sex)

What woman essentially lacks today for doing great things is forgetfulness of herself; but to forget oneself it is first of all necessary to be firmly assured that now and for the future one has found oneself.

(The Second Sex)

IT CHANGED MY LIFE: FEMINIST RESPONSES TO *THE SECOND SEX*

Ever since its publication *The Second Sex* has produced a surprisingly contradictory range of responses from women. The liberating effects of Beauvoir's pioneering essay are nevertheless well documented. 'It changed my life', is the refrain one hears from women of all ages and many different nationalities.[1] Kate Millett conveys the sense of danger and excitement that surrounded the book during the first decade or so after its publication:

> It was a very disturbing book. In fact, early editions often had nude ladies on the cover and it almost had a sort of mischievous cachet. Apparently it was so subversive that it got mixed up with being a little sexy too. You were a real firebrand if you read that book [. . .]. People fought about that book all the time. [. . .] It was a siren call to a lot of other people, and a very dangerous book. It could make you not just want to be one of the good girls that went to college, but you wanted to kick the windows in too (Forster and Sutton, pp. 20–2).

The anger and outrage with which the French establishment received *The Second Sex* on publication fully confirms Millett's account. As soon as the first excerpts appeared in *Les temps modernes* in 1948/9, Beauvoir became the target of an unprecedented range of vicious and sexist attacks: 'What a festival of obscenity!', she exclaims in *Force of Circumstance*. 'Unsatisfied, cold, priapic, nymphomaniac, lesbian, a hundred times aborted, I was everything, even an unmarried mother. People offered to cure me of my frigidity or to satisfy my ghoulish appetites' (FC197; FCa260; TA).[2] While Camus upbraided her for making the French male look ridiculous, the Catholic bourgeoisie claimed to be shocked by her language: François Mauriac could not restrain himself from commenting that, after this, Beauvoir's vagina no longer held any secrets for him.

Encountering Beauvoir's essay well after the emergence of the new women's movement, younger women have also testified to its effects on them. In the late 1970s, Angie Pegg, a lonely and depressed housewife in Britain, read *The Second Sex* and literally changed her life:

> I saw Simone de Beauvoir's book one day in the bookshop and I just bought it because it was called *The Second Sex* and that was intriguing. I read the bit about housework. I bought it one day in 1979 and I started reading it about eight o'clock and I don't think I went to bed until four, it just turned me inside out. It was as if somebody had come into the room and talked to me for the first time, and said, 'It's all right to feel what you are feeling. It's all right.' [. . .] A few months after reading de Beauvoir, I realized I had to do something for myself. [. . .] I applied to university with quite a lot of resistance on the part of my husband (Forster and Sutton, pp. 55–7).

The move Angie Pegg made that day led her to a university degree in philosophy, but also to divorce, a new marriage and another child. Her experience testifies to the fact that women continued to be moved by Beauvoir's text even after the women's movement made scores of other feminist books available to them. In the 1950s and early 1960s, on the other hand, *The Second Sex* was the *only* book women could turn to for a non-conformist analysis of their situation. Paradoxically, the repressive social context in which *The Second Sex* first appeared helped to turn it into a symbol of hope for thousands of women. Crushed by the family-oriented ideology of the 1950s, many women found Beauvoir's insistence on the oppressive effects of marriage and motherhood liberating. Where patriarchy insisted that *they* were to blame if they did not feel marvellously fulfilled, Beauvoir's message was that it was only natural to suffer from the hypocrisy of patriarchal ideology and the social constraints placed on women's freedom.[3]

To some, this idea was clearly too painful to confront: 'When I first read *The Second Sex*, in the early fifities,' Betty Friedan writes, 'I was writing 'housewife" on the census blanks, still in the embrace of the feminine mystique. And the book's effect on me was so depressing that I felt like going back to bed – after I had made the children's breakfast – and pulling the covers up over my head' (*It Changed My Life*, pp. 304–5). At about the same time, a successful American intellectual such as Elizabeth Hardwick apparently felt neither inspired nor disturbed by *The Second Sex*. Taking Beauvoir to task for failing to realize that the patriarchal status quo is inevitable, Hardwick reveals a conservatism that can hardly have been in her own best interests:

> Housework, child rearing, cleaning, keeping, nourishing, looking after [. . .] must be done by someone, or worse by millions of someones day in and day out. In the home at least it would seem 'custom' has not been so much capricious as observant in finding that women are fairly well adapted to this necessary routine. And they must keep at it whether they like it or not (p. 53).

Liberating to Angie Pegg, Beauvoir's analysis of housework only irritates Elizabeth Hardwick: perhaps the difference has something to do with the amount of domestic drudgery each woman actually had to carry out.

A generation after the publication of *The Second Sex*, women's situation in the Western world has undergone considerable change. Many have been spared the painful experiences of a Betty Friedan or an Angie Pegg. A new generation of women take recently won opportunities for granted and often find 'established' feminist discourse tedious and irrelevant. In this situation, Jenny Turner, a young Scottish student, looks to Beauvoir for a sense of something new and fresh. Unlike Beauvoir, Turner complains, modern feminists lack courage and a real interest in history and the world around them. *The Second Sex*, on the other hand, 'took great courage to write. That's the sort of courage women need to find again, to look at everything afresh. We can't take anything for granted, everything is up for grabs' (Forster and Sutton, p. 42).

Paradoxically, it would seem that since the 1960s it is feminist intellectuals – women who write, teach and publish on feminist issues – who have produced the harshest critiques of Beauvoir. By the very act of becoming intellectuals, such women have made themselves the true daughters of Beauvoir: no wonder that many have felt the need to separate themselves from such a powerful mother imago. Denouncing their precursor for hating the female body, glorifying maleness, lacking any sympathy with or understanding of traditional female pursuits including marriage and motherhood, such feminists resent her for not being *positive* enough in her representation of women. The British sociologist Mary Evans, for instance, argues that Beauvoir 'reflects male standards and assumptions in her assessment of what constitutes virtues' (p. 98). According to Evans, Beauvoir's concept of freedom is not simply 'male', but representative of the sexist ethics of Western capitalism as a whole. Moreover, Evans argues, Beauvoir's dogmatic dependence on Sartre's individualist voluntarism renders her incapable of recognizing the social constraints on freedom. Finally, even Beauvoir's call for independence and autonomy for women is suspect because these are 'values derived from the capitalist ethic of ind- ividualist responsibility' (p. 128). This, Evans adds, explains why Beauvoir 'becomes the "free" woman for many feminists in the United States: she provides an explanation, and endorsement, of the economically self- sufficient heterosexual woman with liberal sympathies which is perfectly in accord with the values of North American liberalism' (p. 128).

When one actually turns to American feminism, however, there is scant evidence of hyperbolic capitalist admiration for Simone de Beauvoir. Like Evans, the great majority of American feminists criticize Beauvoir for being male-identified in some way or other, and for failing to appreciate the virtues of women. 'Simone de Beauvoir', Jean Leighton complains, 'paints the female condition as absolutely inferior in itself' (p. 34). The Second Sex, the same critic insists, is not only a 'long and dolorous lamentation about woman's woes, but also a diatribe against the female sex' (p. 118). 'Beauvoir's pervasive pragmatic, rational, and anti-sexual world-view', another critic writes, 'causes her to ignore or undervalue the positive side of many characteristics associated with women' (Greene, p. 206).

Perhaps the greatest paradox of all is the fact that feminists inspired by the so-called French feminist theory developed in the 1970s tend either to ignore Beauvoir, or to dismiss her as a theoretical dinosaur. In her epochal essay on *écriture féminine*, 'The Laugh of the Medusa', for instance, Hélène Cixous makes no reference at all to the author of *The Second Sex*. The absence of Beauvoir's name in Cixous's text is all the more startling since her essay first appeared in the special 1975 issue of *L'Arc* devoted precisely to Simone de Beauvoir.[4] When Beauvoir died in 1986, Antoinette Fouque, leader of *Psych et Po* and founder of the publishing house *des femmes*, with which Hélène Cixous used to be associated, took the opportunity to declare her own implacable hostility to the author of *The Second Sex*. Arrogating to herself the virtues of pluralism and openness, Fouque sang the praises of the 'fruitful differences that, as everybody knows, flow from, are informed by and find their origins in the difference between the sexes', and proceeded to see in Beauvoir a representative of an 'intolerant, assimi- lating, sterilizing universalism, full of hatred and reductive of otherness' (*Libération*, p. 5).

In her pioneering study of philosophy and femininity, *Speculum of the Other Woman* (1974), Luce Irigaray never alludes to the founding figure of feminist philosophy in France. When she finally declares, in 1990, that she too was once a reader of *The Second Sex*, it is only to represent Beauvoir as a disappointingly frustrating figure, an 'older sister' who inexplicably enough remained remote in relation to Irigaray: 'How can one understand this distance between two women who could have – indeed who ought to have – worked together?', Irigaray complains (*Je, tu, nous*, pp. 10–11). Perhaps it is such frustration that drives her to launch a vehement attack on every woman who – like Simone de Beauvoir – believes that the social equality of the sexes is a desirable aim for feminism. According to Irigaray, such feminists seek to eradicate sexual difference. It follows, apparently, that they are against procreation, and thus actively calling for a new Holocaust: 'To want to abolish sexual difference', Irigaray writes, 'is to call for a more complete genocide than every other destruction in history' (p. 13). Beauvoir, in other words, is not just an Eichmann, she is worse than one.

Before the publication of her 1990 novel *Les Samouraïs*, the name of Simone de Beauvoir is hard to find in Julia Kristeva's writings.[5] A deliberate allusion to Beauvoir's *The Mandarins*, the title of Kristeva's novel nevertheless signals a belated moment of acknowledgement of the woman Mary McCarthy once called the 'leading French *femme savante*' (McCarthy, p. 44). In an interview with *Le monde*, Kristeva admits to a certain identification with Beauvoir, 'even if it is a pretty vain ambition to risk a gesture similar to hers' (p. 19). Stressing precisely the ritual hostility which greets the works of intellectual women in France, in another context Kristeva compares the reception of *Les Samouraïs* to that of *The Mandarins*. Beauvoir – and by implication, Kristeva herself – is always represented as a 'doubly frustrated woman, both because of her sex, and because she belongs to the class of mandarins' (*Lettre ouverte à Harlem Désir*, p. 84). Apparently, then, it is only when Kristeva turns away from theory and towards fiction that she feels free to declare her admiration for her great intellectual precursor.

It would be wrong, however, to take such responses to be representative of all French feminists. In a strong symbolic gesture, the group around the feminist journal *Questions féministes* invited Simone de Beauvoir in 1977 to act as their director. Rejecting what they considered the cult of difference in, say, the *Psych et Po* collective, the women in this group, which at various times included Christine Delphy, Monique Plaza, Colette Guillaumin and Monique Wittig, argued for a materialist feminism, very much in the spirit of Simone de Beauvoir herself.[6] In French feminist philosophy the anti-Beauvoirean stance of Luce Irigaray is powerfully countered by the scrupulous analysis of Beauvoir's position as a philosopher developed by Michèle Le Doeuff, particularly in *Hipparchia's Choice*.

It should be clear, even from such a brief overview, that in spite of considerable disagreement on other issues, the great majority of feminist intellectuals – French and American alike – feel, above all, that Beauvoir fails to value women's difference. As we have seen in chapter 6, such criticisms are not without foundation. If many feminist critiques of Beauvoir strike me as fundamentally flawed, however, it is not so much because they misread Beauvoir's position on difference (although some do), as because they utterly fail to grasp that Beauvoir's political project is radically different from their own. Taking for granted the assumption that effective feminist politics presuppose a theory of female identity, such critics fail to consider alternative positions. And so, measured against such an alien standard, *The Second Sex* is bound to be found lacking; the premisses of such debates virtually assure the misrecognition of Beauvoir's project.

In order to avoid certain basic misunderstandings, then, I would ask readers of this chapter to bear in mind that the fundamental axiom of *The Second Sex* is that consciousness is *free*, not that it is or ought to be sexually differentiated or defined. For Beauvoir, the opposite of freedom is oppression: her problematics is one of *power*, not one of identity and/or difference. If she insists on the necessity of equal social, political and economic rights for women, it is because the absence of such rights provides *carte blanche* for male tyranny. For her, the scandal of human history is the fact that one group of free subjects have been coerced into defining themselves as objects, as *other* in relation to another group of free subjects. Such a domination of the other's freedom is always intolerable and never to be condoned. For Beauvoir as for Sartre, 'existence precedes essence'; it follows that questions of identity become secondary to questions of action and choice. For her, women forge their differential identities through their actions in the world. The identity that emerges from a woman's existential choices, moreover, is always open to change: only death puts an end to the potential reconstruction of our being.[7]

But if her critics fail fully to grasp the nature of Beauvoir's concerns, they also tend to miss the complexity of her theory of liberation. Mary Evans, for instance, claims that there is in *The Second Sex* a striking absence of 'any suggestion of the ambiguities in rewards and values of relationships between men and women' (p. 73). As we have seen in chapter 6, however, *The Second Sex* is nothing if not a theory of ambiguity. What does remain perfectly unambiguous in Beauvoir's essay is her representation of male sexuality as unfailingly phallic, and of men as absolutely free. But while Beauvoir certainly idealizes men, it does not follow that such idealization is intrinsic to her theory of women's liberation. Needless to say, it is impossible to reach an understanding of Beauvoir's feminism without taking into consideration her vision of freedom.

In this chapter, then, I intend to discuss the politics of *The Second Sex*. Given the amount of misconception generated by this text, much of my analysis may amount to little more than a fairly pedestrian attempt to set the record straight. My own account of Beauvoir's politics, moreover, only becomes meaningful in the context of my discussion, in chapter 6, of the rhetorical, philosophical and emotional implications of Beauvoir's discourse. In an intellectual field dominated by identity politics, *The Second Sex* represents a real challenge to established dogmas: if we are to escape from current political and theoretical dead ends, feminism in the 1990s cannot afford to ignore Beauvoir's pioneering insights.

UTOPIA AND HISTORY: THE MOMENT OF *THE SECOND SEX*

Writing *The Second Sex*, Simone de Beauvoir often claimed, turned her into a feminist.[8] In the film about her life, Sartre insists on the same theme: 'Writing the book, you became a feminist, you realized who your enemies were, you attacked them, and then you made it clear what it meant to be a woman' (Dayan, p. 67). Here Sartre rightly assumes that simply to discuss women's social situation, their sexuality or their identity is not in itself a feminist enterprise. To be a feminist is to take up a political position: it requires the capacity to posit certain goals and to define one's enemies, and the will and ability to attack them. Feminism, one might say, requires us not simply to describe the status quo, but to define it as unjust and oppressive as well. It also requires a vision of an alternative: a utopian perspective which inspires and informs the struggle against current oppression.[9]

There is, in *The Second Sex*, an extraordinarily consistent vision of freedom. In every chapter, Beauvoir's implacable dissection of women's destiny under patriarchy derives its energy and panache from her absolute conviction that slavery and oppression can be brought to an end; every account of women's misery is followed by Beauvoir's insistence on the possibility of freedom. Polemical through and through, *The Second Sex* is also — and above all — a ferocious assault on patriarchal power structures. At once agonistic and oppositional, the politics of Beauvoir's essay may well be understood as *resistance* to power: 'Where there is power, there is resistance,' Foucault writes in *The History of Sexuality*, 'and yet, or rather consequently, this resistance is never in a position of exteriority in relation to power' (p. 95). What Foucault does not say is that every act of resistance is inspired by a vision of something better. That vision, however, is not at all external to the situation being opposed. Presupposing a critique of their own historical moment, utopian visions are derived from the negative aspects of the present. Utopia, one might say, is the negation of the negation of the status quo. Every political strategy, however 'negative', is informed by a dream of a desirable life: if *The Second Sex* is such a unique document in the history of feminist theory, it is above all because it makes the relationship between utopia and critique unusually explicit.

Emerging from her critique of oppression, Beauvoir's vision of liberation, then, is as constrained by its own historical moment as any other utopia. Simone de Beauvoir started writing *The Second Sex* in June 1946, and finished it exactly three years later, in June 1949.[10] In this period she also visited the United States for the first time (January–May 1947), and took time off to write a full-length account of her travels, entitled *America Day By Day* (1948). What political issues dominated French debate at this time? Which ones did Beauvoir herself feel involved in? What was her position in French intellectual life? And what was the situation of French women in general? A full treatment of these issues could easily fill a book of its own: I can only hope that a brief account of relevant material is better than none at all.

The best source of information on many of these questions is the first volume of Beauvoir's *Force of Circumstance*, which covers the post-war years from the Liberation of France in August 1944 to the summer of 1952. In this period Beauvoir's public image was transformed: from being a relatively unknown writer, at the end of the war she was catapulted to fame as Sartre's companion and the leading lady of existentialism. Already by 1945 existentialism had become a fashionable phenomenon, inspiring everything from films and night-clubs to hair-styles and clothes (long hair and black sweaters). Sartre and Beauvoir quickly became household names, not only in France but all over the Western world. In 1945 they launched *Les temps modernes*, an intellectual journal which immediately became the focus of literary and political attention on the Left Bank. Publishing essays (*Pyrrhus et Cinéas*, 1944; *The Ethics of Ambiguity*, 1947; *L'existentialisme et la sagesse des nations*, 1948), novels (*The Blood of Others*, 1945; *All Men are Mortal*, 1946), and even a play (*Who Shall Die?*, 1945) in rapid succession, Beauvoir's productivity in this period was astonishing. The scandal produced by *The Second Sex* hardly detracted from its impact. The Vatican even placed it on the Index. By the time she turned 42 in January 1950, Simone de Beauvoir's reputation as the – highly controversial – leading intellectual woman in France was firmly established. For a woman to forge a brilliant intellectual career in France at the time was extremely unusual, and the resentment bred by her success can be measured by the French critics' increasingly hostile reactions. Beauvoir, then, clearly writes as what Bourdieu would call a *miraculée* – a miraculous exception to the statistical rule.[11]

Beauvoir's position as a highly successful writer protected her against many of the injustices of the French patriarchal system. This is not to say that she was unaware of them: *The Second Sex* would hardly have been written had that been the case. In 1944 French women were given the right to vote, as a reward for their participation in the Resistance. By her own account, by 1949 Beauvoir had not yet exercised her new privilege. The Vichy regime had been brutally misogynistic: during Pétain's time in office women were refused the right to work, except in traditionally female occupations, abortion became a crime against the state, and contraception remained illegal. The result was that female unemployment increased steadily throughout the period from 1940 to 1944; on 30 July 1943, Marie-Jeanne Latour was guillotined for performing abortions; and women and men were sentenced to long prison terms simply for providing contraceptive advice.[12]

While such outrageously patriarchal laws were abolished by the Fourth Republic, many glaring injustices remained. Before 1970, married women in France did not have formal parental rights over their children: in his capacity as *chef de famille*, the father alone had the right to sign necessary medical and juridical forms concerning his children. Married women had to wait until 1965 before gaining the right to open a personal bank account, or to exercise a profession without the permission of their husbands. Before 1965, moreover, the husband alone had the right to decide where the couple should live. Married and single women alike suffered from a deeply restrictive legislation concerning contraception and abortion: contraception was only legalized in France in 1967, and abortion remained outlawed until 1974.[13]

In the late 1940s, Communists as well as right-wingers remained committed to pro-natalist and family-oriented policies. The result was an atmosphere intensely hostile to women's sexual freedom, but also a strong legislation guaranteeing maternity leave, free state nurseries and state schools of excellent standards, economic incentives to families with many children and so on. For these reasons, more than most other countries, France today makes it relatively easy for women of all social classes to combine motherhood and work outside the home. In 1949, however, the development of the French welfare state was still largely to come: Beauvoir's assessment, in *The Second Sex*, that most women could hardly expect to be able to combine the care of children with a demanding work schedule remained true.

On a different political level, the period from 1944 to 1952 saw the jubilant hopes of the Liberation turn to ashes: the dream of a new, united and socialist France, undivided by pre-war class politics, shared by the overwhelming majority of French intellectuals in 1944, was in ruins by 1947. Instead of forming a broad united front, French political life quickly split into three warring blocs, ranging from the Gaullists on the right, through the various Christian democrat, liberal or self-styled 'radical' parties at the centre, to the socialists and the communists on the left. By

1948, the French socialists and communists were also irredeemably divided: there was no left alliance in France until the 1970s. In the sphere of foreign policy, the French hope of preserving national or at least European independence as against the two superpowers was crushed, and with the onset of the Cold War France was forced to take sides. As one of the major recipients of Marshall aid, France had in reality no choice: aligning itself with the Western alliance, in 1949 it allowed General Eisenhower to set up his NATO headquarters in Paris.

In this political context, Beauvoir's voice was that of a left-wing intellectual, deeply critical of the bourgeoisie in her own country and firmly committed to the socialist ideal of a just, classless society without exploitation, oppression, violence and hunger. She was not, however, a communist, and in the 1940s she kept a firm distance between herself and the PCF (the French Communist Party). Her main objection to communist policies, in France as elsewhere, was the authoritarianism and disregard for human rights displayed by Stalinism. Her distaste for the totalitarianism of communism found its counterpart in her scathing condemnation of the exploitative colonialism of the Western world. For throughout this period, French forces, with increasing US material assistance, were fighting to uphold French colonial dominance in Vietnam. As early as May 1945, after a nationalist riot in the Algerian town of Sétif in which 29 Europeans died, French troops massacred between 6,000 and 8,000 Algerian Muslims. In 1947 an uprising in Madagascar left 550 Europeans and 1,900 natives dead. In April 1948 a French expeditionary force proceeded to ruthless retaliation: according to official figures 89,000 Madagascans were killed.[14] In fact, at this time in France *Les temps modernes* was the only periodical consistently to publish critical reports on colonial conflicts. In *The Mandarins* (1954) Beauvoir herself makes several explicit references to the massacres in Madagascar and their aftermath. The riots in Sétif, on the other hand, were hushed up for years after the event. Caught up in the propaganda war between the superpowers, the rest of the French media paid little or no attention to colonial questions before the Algerian War of Independence (1954–62) finally forced the issue to the top of the French political agenda.

From Beauvoir's viewpoint, the political tragedy of the post-war period was the loss of French independence, which forced even non-aligned left-wingers like herself and Sartre to choose between the Soviet Union and the United States. In the 1940s Sartre's political engagement (for it must be said that at this time Beauvoir was happy to leave political initiatives to him) moved from an immediate post-war belief in a united socialist front, to a short-lived attempt to set up a neutralist, non-communist socialist party of his own (1948–9). At the outbreak of the Korean War (1950–2) Sartre found himself unable wholeheartedly to defend either side, and temporarily withdrew from politics. His increasing political isolation is nowhere more evident than in what Beauvoir in *Force of Circumstance* calls their 'farcical and unpleasant' trip to French West Africa in the spring of 1950, where his isolation from the communists made him *persona non grata* to the colonial resistance movements (FC230; FCa303). Sartre's sense of powerlessness and isolation finally pushed him into an alliance with the PCF. In the summer of 1952 he published his massive essay on the communists and peace, broke with Camus, and took up his new position as a semi-official fellow traveller of the Communist Party.

On the material level, France remained devastated by war and Occupation for many years after 1944. According to the French historian Jean-Pierre Rioux, the French economy reached crisis levels in 1947. Many essential foods were still rationed, and when the bread ration was reduced to 200 grammes (a little over 7 ounces) per person in 1947 – lower than it ever was under the Nazi Occupation – there were riots in many towns in France. Scarcity led to extreme price rises, wages were low, and strikes were widespread throughout the country. Industrial output was below the level reached in 1929, and the French government had neither foreign currency with which to import food, nor the equipment needed to rebuild industry. The housing crisis was the worst in French history. By the end of 1947, it was clear that only a massive influx of US dollars could pull France out of a potentially revolutionary political situation: from 1948 to 1952 France received from the United States $2,629 million, of which $2,122 million were free grants. The woman who was writing *The Second Sex* was poorly dressed, badly nourished, and lived in squalid hotel rooms on the Left Bank before moving, in October 1948, to a leaky room in a rundown building near Notre Dame. At the same time, however, her own and Sartre's increasing fame guaranteed them an income far beyond that of an ordinary member of the intelligentsia at the time: in spite of her harsh living conditions, Beauvoir was privileged indeed.

On the emotional level, Beauvoir's situation was difficult too. In January 1945 Sartre met Dolorès Vanetti in New York, and immediately embarked on what may have been the most passionate love affair of his life. In spite of her best efforts, Beauvoir felt threatened and undermined by Sartre's passion for Vanetti. In 1947 Beauvoir met Nelson Algren in Chicago, and threw herself wholeheartedly into an affair which lasted until 1951; by far the greater part of *The Second Sex* was written during Beauvoir's liaison with the American novelist.

There are a number of points to be gathered from this brief account of Beauvoir's situation from 1946 to 1949. First of all, there is the startling originality of *The Second Sex*. While the actual situation of women in France at the time may in itself be considered bad enough to explain Beauvoir's indignation, the fact remains that in France in 1949, women's issues were not central to the political agenda of any major party or faction, nor was there an independent women's movement outside the established parties; in this historical situation, *The Second Sex* is nothing short of unique. Seen in the context of her increasing political disillusionment after 1947, Beauvoir's originality may appear as the outcome of a vast effort to forge a new field of intervention for herself, one in which her passionate desire for change would not immediately be dragged into the increasingly sterile polarities of the Cold War.

The very fact of raising the question of women, of course, immediately placed Beauvoir on an intellectual terrain not dominated by Sartre. By providing exhaustive discussions of the difficulty of uniting love and freedom under current patriarchal conditions, Beauvoir was also – more or less unwittingly – expressing many of the insights gained from her relationship with Nelson Algren. In so doing, she infused her political discourse with personal concerns: while I would have preferred her to do so more openly, there is no doubt in my mind that the power of her sexual passion for Algren helped Beauvoir to place sexuality firmly at the centre of her agenda. The result was a radical breakthrough in feminist analysis: Beauvoir is the first thinker in France explicitly to politicize sexuality.

Neglected by dominant political discourses, the subject of women's oppression was, if anything, even more marginal in France than questions of colonialism and racism. It is not a coincidence that throughout her essay Beauvoir makes frequent comparisons between the situation of women and that of Jews and blacks. As we shall see, there is much to be gained by relating her political analysis to that of Frantz Fanon, whose *Black Skin, White Masks* was published in Paris in 1952, only three years after *The Second Sex*.

PATRIARCHAL FEMININITY

In the first volume of *The Second Sex*, Beauvoir sets out to assail and destroy patriarchal myths of femininity. According to *Force of Circumstance*, the decisive impulse to write *The Second Sex* came when she discovered how deeply she herself had been shaped by patriarchal mythology: 'This world was a masculine world, my childhood had been nourished by myths forged by men, and I hadn't reacted to them in at all the same way I should have done if I had been a boy. [. . .] I went to the Bibliothèque Nationale to do some reading, and what I studied were the myths of femininity' (FC103; FCa136). What Beauvoir in 1949 calls 'myth' is close to Lévi-Strauss's use of the concept in *Les structures élémentaires de la parenté*, the manuscript of which she studied before finishing her own essay.[15] Her critical, ironic and often very witty dissection of patriarchal mythology also points forward to the essays collected in Roland Barthes's *Mythologies*, which started to appear in 1954. For Beauvoir, myths are fundamentally false representations of reality, not because they always get the facts wrong, but because they proclaim the existence of eternal, immutable and non-contingent essences. If we internalize and identify with such myths, we are 'mystified', in Beauvoir's terms, that is to say, victims of false consciousness. Myths, then, have real effects on people's lives: mythology is a crucial weapon in the patriarchal armoury. Compared to more sophisticated theories of ideology and language, Beauvoir's understanding of mythology and mystification leaves much to be desired.[16] This does not prevent her, however, from producing a devastating analysis of the falsehood and lies invoked to shore up patriarchal power structures.

In one of the most important passages in *The Second Sex*, she elegantly summarizes the effect of patriarchal mythology:

> Thus, as against the dispersed, contingent, and multiple existences of actual women, mythical thought opposes the Eternal Feminine, unique and changeless. If the definition provided for this concept is contradicted by the behaviour of flesh-and-blood women, it is the latter who are wrong: we are told not that Femininity is a false entity, but that the women concerned are not feminine. The contrary facts of experience are impotent [*ne peuvent rien*] against the myth (SS283; DSa395).

Contrasting the fixed essence of mythical femininity with the diversity of women's actual lives, Beauvoir seeks to expose the fictionality of patriarchal thought. This polemical project also provides the overall structure for *The Second Sex*, in which the patriarchal myths of the first volume are deliberately and provocatively contrasted with the 'lived experience' of women described in the second volume. Although Beauvoir herself tends to use the term 'woman', *The Second Sex* does in fact distinguish quite carefully between *three* categories of women: traditionally oppressed women, independent women and the free women of the future. None of these groups of women is presented as socially or ideologically homogeneous. By far the greater part of her essay is devoted to the first category, or what Beauvoir labels the 'traditional destiny of woman' (SS31; DSb9). As a social problem, patriarchal mythology obviously concerns the first two categories only.

The construct of patriarchy, mythological femininity exists in two different modes: imposed on women through the process of alienation, it becomes one aspect of the very structure of their subjectivity; perceived as part of patriarchal ideology, 'femininity' becomes an external set of rules for how to dress, behave, etc: 'Precisely because the concept of femininity is artifically shaped by custom and fashion,' Beauvoir writes, 'it is imposed upon each woman from without. [. . .] The individual is still not free to do as she pleases in shaping the concept of femininity' (SS692; DSb601). Either way, such 'femininity' is the result of slavery: for Beauvoir, it is the antithesis of freedom. It ought to be clear by now that the 'femininity' discussed by Beauvoir is quite different from other, more positive notions of femininity that have become current in feminist theory since the 1970s. In order to avoid confusion, I shall call Beauvoir's concept *patriarchal femininity* from now on.

Since there can be no question of showing solidarity with the *condition* of slavery, Beauvoir would argue, there can be no question, either, of valorizing its consequences: on this logic, patriarchal femininity becomes the very signifier of oppression. The struggle between the sexes will last until women are free, she writes, and for women to be free, patriarchal femininity must go: 'The quarrel will go on as long as men and women fail to recognize each other as equals [*semblables*]; that is to say, as long as femininity is perpetuated as such' (SS727–8; DSb646–7). What Beauvoir opposes, then, is any effort to *define* or *fix* women or, in other words, any attempt to impose a given, pre-existing standard of femininity on the divergent and different experiences of real women.

Detesting patriarchal femininity in all its manifestations, the author of *The Second Sex* nevertheless demonstrates deep sympathy with women's plight under patriarchy. Women, she writes, have no home in this world; they live in perpetual exile, they are foreign to a world which ought to belong to them as much as it belongs to men: 'Overburdened, submerged, she becomes a stranger to herself because she is a stranger to the rest of the world' (SS353; DSb91). The paradox of women's situation, Beauvoir argues, is that 'they belong at one and the same time to the male world and to a sphere in which that world is challenged; shut up in their world, surrounded by the other, they can settle nowhere in peace' (SS608–9; DSb484).

Beauvoir's indignation and outrage at the damage done to women is everywhere apparent. The education received by the little girl alienates and divides her against herself; the adolescent girl is forced to accept as her own a destructive and degrading body image fashioned by patriarchy, and to identify with a concept of femininity that can only hurt her: on the threshold to adult life, the young woman is already damaged, split and mutilated by patriarchal oppression: 'Since all roads are closed to her, and since she can only *be*, not *act*, she is under a curse', Beauvoir writes (SS381; DSb130; TA); 'so she moves towards the future, wounded, shameful, anxious, culpable' (SS351; DSb88; TA).[17]

When the young girl realizes what is in store for her, Beauvoir writes, she rightly revolts against her destiny. But patriarchal ideology has already done its work: often she is no longer capable of true resistance: 'She does not accept the destiny assigned to her by nature and by society; and yet she does not repudiate it completely; she is too much divided against herself to join battle with the world; she limits herself to a flight from reality or a symbolic struggle against it. Each of her desires has its corresponding anxiety' (SS375; DSb122). Struggling to reconcile the contradictory demands of patriarchal mythology, Beauvoir writes, women often develop the finest qualities of authenticity and transcendence. Exposed as they are to men's double moral standards, for instance, women develop greater moral imagination than men (see SS557; DSb411). Young girls, as a rule, also develop much greater subtlety than young boys:

> The young girl is secretive, disturbed, the victim of severe conflicts, but this complexity enriches her, and her inner life develops more profoundly than that of her brothers; she is more attentive to her feelings and so they become more subtly diversified; she has more psychologic insight than boys turned towards external aims. She can give weight to revolts that set her against the world. She avoids the snares of over-seriousness and conformism. The deliberate lies of her associates encounter her irony and clairvoyance. She feels daily the ambiguity of her position: beyond sterile protests, she can bravely put in question offical optimism, ready-made values, hypocritical and cheerful morality (SS382–3; DSb133; TA).[18]

An excellent example of Beauvoir's passionate and clear-eyed analysis of women's contradictory situation under patriarchy is to be found in her account of the hypocritical treatment of prostitutes. Towards the end of last century, Beauvoir writes, the French police raided a brothel where they found two girls aged 12 and 13. In the ensuing court case the girls testified, and mentioned the number of important customers they had. One little girl, Beauvoir writes, opened her mouth to name one of them:

> The prosecutor stopped her at once: 'You must not befoul the name of a respectable man!' A gentleman decorated by the Legion of Honour is still a respectable man when deflowering a little girl; he has his weaknesses, as who does not? Whereas the little girl who does not have access to the ethical realm of the universal[19] – who is not a magistrate, or a general, or a great Frenchman, nothing but a little girl – stakes her moral value in the contingent realm of sexuality: she is perverse, corrupted, vicious, fit only for the reformatory (SS625; DSb504–5; TA).

Profiting from the woman's 'immoral' actions, the man keeps his dignity and public standing. If the woman threatens to reveal his little games, she takes all the blame:

> Woman plays the part of those secret agents who are left to the firing squad if they get caught, and are loaded with rewards if they succeed; it is for her

to shoulder all man's immorality: all women, not only the prostitute, serve as sewer to the shining, wholesome edifice where respectable people have their abode. When, thereupon, to these women one speaks of dignity, honour, loyalty, of all the lofty masculine virtues, it is not astonishing if they decline to 'go along' (SS625–6; DSb505; TA).

Sexism, for Beauvoir, consists in refusing women – and little girls – access to the universal. As long as women continue to be defined as the particular, she argues, men and women will tend to develop different sets of values and attitudes, even when it comes to intellectual and philosophical choices.

Beauvoir, then, does not seek to deny that women sometimes develop valuable qualities in response to patriarchal oppression. Moral imagination, psychological insight, authenticity, lucidity, awareness of the ambiguity of existence: under patriarchy, these are values more likely to be found in women than men. For Beauvoir, however, the values of freedom – generosity, lucidity, realism, reciprocity, authenticity and autonomy – are neither masculine nor feminine, but simply *human*; to abandon them to the patriarchal opposition is to sustain the myths that universalize masculinity. On this point, *The Second Sex* recalls Mary Wollstonecraft's passionate distaste for 'prejudices that give a sex to virtue' (*Vindication*, p. 83).

It would also be a mistake to assume that Beauvoir seeks to outlaw any specific action or activity normally associated with patriarchal femininity: that would precisely be to grant intrinsic meaning to individual acts. For Beauvoir, any action may be carried out freely or as part of the coercive structures of oppression. In themselves, having children, cleaning floors, getting married or communing with Nature are neither 'good' nor 'bad' activities.[20] Any act can be carried out in good or bad faith: only a more general interpretation of the situation in which they are performed will tell us what meanings such acts acquire in individual contexts. If there is one point ceaselessly repeated in *The Second Sex*, it is the fact that under oppressive social conditions women are never truly free to choose: Beauvoir's utopia consists in the vision of a society where no choice would be unfairly constrained by social conditions. What Beauvoir is against, then, is not so much any particular activity as the desire to *produce essences*, to attribute intrinsic meanings and values to activities or persons: for her, the most execrable aspect of patriarchal ideology remains its persistent harping on the theme of 'eternal femininity'.

THERE HAVE BEEN NO GREAT WOMEN WRITERS

An instructive example of Beauvoir's anti-patriarchal polemics can be found in her discussion of women's so-called creative inferiority. As an *agrégée* of philosophy and an established writer, she clearly found the patriarchal litany of women's cultural inadequacy particularly galling. Her riposte to such mythology is, first of all, to refuse the comparison. Under patriarchy, she argues, women and men create from such different positions that every comparison is vain: 'all comparisons are idle which purport to show that woman is superior, inferior, or equal to man,' she writes, 'for their situations are profoundly different' (SS638; DSb521). On this logic, it makes no sense, for instance, to compare *The Second Sex* to *Being and Nothingness*, at least not in terms of 'pure' philosophical value. Beauvoir, then, takes the *fact* of women's difference under patriarchy as the starting point for her discussion.

Until women's situation becomes equal to that of men, Beauvoir claims, the concrete products of female creativity will, as a rule, be inferior to those of men. This discrepancy is entirely due to the advantage of men's situation under patriarchy: 'he has many more opportunities to exercise his freedom in the world. The inevitable result is that masculine accomplishment is far superior to that of women, who are practically forbidden to *do* anything' (SS638; DSb521).[21] Beauvoir's argument here is statistical: given the far higher number of males with access to cultural expression, the likelihood of finding excellent work produced by men is obviously higher than for women.[22]

Beauvoir, then, accepts that there have indeed been few great women philosophers, painters, sculptors and composers. But her insistence that there have hardly been any great women writers either is particularly disturbing. What about George Eliot? Virginia Woolf? Lady Murasaki? Madame de Staël? Madame de Lafayette? On the evidence of *The Second Sex* it is clear that Beauvoir does not imagine challenging the criteria for 'greatness' dominant in her intellectual field. For Beauvoir, women's writing under patriarchy remains less 'universal' than that of men. On this point, her uncritical Kantian use of the word 'universal' is curiously at odds with her general political critique of abstract Enlightenment universals; the result is a total disregard for the historicity of value judgements. Where *The Second Sex* in general provides an exhaustive catalogue of patriarchal crimes against women, there is not a single reference to the fact that, more often than not, the reception of women's works has been cruelly sexist and unjustly dismissive. Ironically, this has proved to be no less true for *The Second Sex* itself than for other books by women. Radically contradicting her general political analysis, Beauvoir's aesthetics remain abstract and universalist. It is as if, having struggled to politicize subjectivity and sexuality, the author of *The Second Sex* now balks at having to politicize aesthetics too.

To take Beauvoir to task for her aesthetic conservatism as if it were some individual flaw of hers would nevertheless be anachronistic: on this point, her blindness is characteristic of the French intellectual field as a whole. Apart from the proponents of Stalinist socialist realism, I doubt that anybody criticized the traditional canon of French literature in 1949. Sartre's summary of French literary history in *What Is Literature?* (1948), for instance, remains wholly traditional in its selection of texts and authors. In my experience, intellectuals who attempt to challenge dominant aesthetic and philosophical canons in France are few and far between. In spite of considerable recent efforts to promote text by women and francophone authors, the French in the 1990s remain overwhelmingly committed to a Jacobin notion of a centralized and universal aesthetic canon.[23] It is no coincidence that the three major French feminist theorists in the 1970s and 1980s (Cixous, Kristeva, Irigaray) never stray from that canon in their selection of literary and philosophical texts either, just as it is not entirely fortuitous that every major French theoretical trend since the 1960s (*Tel Quel*, deconstruction, postmodernism) has been perfectly content to remain within the confines of the accepted literary tradition.

Beauvoir, then, is not out to produce an alternative canon of female greatness. Her point is not that there have in fact been many female Mozarts or Michelangelos, but rather that *there will be*: 'How would women ever have had genius when they were denied all possibility of accomplishing a work of genius – or just a work?', she asks (SS723; DSb641). Under current social conditions, women's concrete freedom is so restricted that the only authentic behaviour available to them is revolt (see SS639; DSb522). In Beauvoir's opinion, women cannot fully devote themselves to creative endeavours until they have achieved the necessary social conditions of freedom. If there have not been any great women poets, Beauvoir argues, that hardly proves that women cannot write, but simply that their historical situation may be compared to that of the French proletariat, or of the United States as a nation in the 1790s, or that of blacks in the 1940s:

> The free woman is just being born; when she has won possession of herself perhaps Rimbaud's prophecy will be fulfilled: 'There shall be poets! When woman's unmeasured bondage shall be broken, when she shall live for and through herself, man – hitherto detestable – having let her go, she too, will be a poet! Woman will find the unknown!' (SS723; DSb641).

It is impossible to say whether women's 'world of ideas' will be all that different from that of men, Beauvoir writes, since she can only free herself by becoming more like them, that is to say, by becoming a free subject in her own right. By now, every reader surely recognizes Beauvoir's persistent tendency to idealize the male in such statements. For Beauvoir, 'behaving like a man' normally means 'behaving freely and authentically'. I have discussed the shortcomings of that position in my previous chapter. It does not follow, however, that her intention is to devalue women. On the contrary, her almost boundless belief in female capacities is evident on every page of her discussion: 'What is certain is that hitherto woman's possibilities have been suppressed and lost to humanity, and that it is high time she be permitted to take her chances in her own interests and in the interest of all' (SS724; DSb641). When it comes to the free woman of the future, then, Beauvoir has no preconceptions: some current sexual differences may remain, others may disappear, new ones may appear; the only self-evident point is that it is impossible for us to foretell which differences will remain, and which – if any – will be socially significant.

The freshness and optimism of Beauvoir's vision of the future are breathtaking. Yet it follows from her own argument that she herself is writing as a figure arrested on the threshold of a new world: if the free woman was only just being born in 1949, Simone de Beauvoir is not a free woman. On her own judgement she is, at most, an 'independent woman': a woman caught in a painful conflict between the old and the new, between patriarchal femininity and female freedom: 'The woman of today is torn between the past and the future. She appears most often as a "true woman" disguised as a man, and she feels herself as ill at ease in her flesh as in her masculine garb. She must shed her old skin and cut her own new clothes' (SS734; DSb655).

INDEPENDENT WOMEN

For Simone de Beauvoir, economic independence is the *sine qua non* of women's liberation. As long as women are prevented from earning their own living, they will always be dependent on others. Women actually seeking paid work, however, are confronted with class exploitation and sexist oppression at every turn. Oppressed at home, they find themselves exploited, underpaid and alienated at work. Under capitalism, Beauvoir writes, there is nothing liberating in factory work: no wonder many working-class women would rather be housewives if only they could afford it, particularly since they usually have to do the housework anyway.[24] Under such conditions, women are caught in an infernal double bind: without paid work they are delivered up to male exploitation, with paid work they find themselves working a double shift, with very little money to show for it at the end of the week. While some women heroically struggle to change their condition by becoming politically active in trade unions or various socialist parties, most – quite understandably – do not have the energy to spare.

A painful paradox thus emerges: only work can emancipate women, yet nothing enslaves them more completely. For genuine freedom to be possible, the social conditions of women's lives must be radically transformed. What is required, Beauvoir writes, is what the Bolshevik revolution promised but never delivered:

> Women reared and trained exactly like men were to work under the same conditions and for the same wages. Erotic liberty was to be recognized by custom, but the sexual act was not to be considered a 'service' to be paid for; woman was to be *obliged* to provide herself with other ways of earning a living; marriage was to be based on a free agreement that the contracting parties could break at will; maternity was to be voluntary, which meant that contraception and abortion were to be authorized and that, on the other hand, all mothers and their children were to have exactly the same rights, in or out of marriage; pregnancy leaves were to be paid for by the State [*la collectivité*], which would assume charge of the children, signifying not that they would be *taken away* from their parents, but that they would not be *abandoned* to them (SS733–4; DS653–4).[25]

Until such utopian conditions prevail – for this is the most complete description of Beauvoir's social utopia to be found anywhere in *The Second Sex* – women will remain economically and professionally disadvantaged.[26] While economic independence remains the fundamental starting point for liberation, Beauvoir is far from arguing that money alone guarantees happiness and freedom. This becomes particularly evident in her discussion of the status of 'independent women', that is to say, the 'fairly large number of privileged women who find social and economic autonomy in their professions' (SS691; DSb600). Beauvoir herself, of course, is an outstanding example of just such a woman.

Independent women are not free. 'As yet they are only halfway there', Beauvoir writes: 'The woman who is economically emancipated from man is not for all that in a moral, social, and psychological situation identical with that of man. [. . .] The fact of being a woman today poses peculiar problems for an independent human being' (SS691; DSb600; TA). Theirs is a particularly contradictory situation, one in which they are, as it were, trying to live the future before the objective conditions are ripe. It is not surprising, then, that such women tend to be even more torn by conflicts and contradictions than their more traditional sisters.

'The independent woman of today is torn between her professional interests and the problems of her sexual life [*les soucis de sa vocation sexuelle*]', Beauvoir claims (SS705; DSb618). Whole, autonomous human beings are sexual beings: 'Man is a human being with sexuality; woman is a complete individual, equal to the male, only if she too is a human being with sexuality', she writes. 'To renounce her femininity, is to renounce a part of her humanity' (SS691–2; DSb601). Sacrificing their sexual needs and desires to the pressures of social conventions, women mutilate themselves, since freedom includes the right to sexual expression. For independent women in France in 1949, however, such freedom was hard to find. As we have seen, contraception and abortion were illegal. To give birth out of wedlock usually amounted to professional suicide, while marriage, on the other hand, might well mean the end of any real independence for the woman. Even assuming that the woman somehow solved the problem of contraception, she could not simply pick up a man in the street without fear of venereal disease and violence. In smaller, more provincial towns, such behaviour would in any case be out of the question. Given the prevalence of patriarchal mythology, a truly successful woman might alien- ate potential sexual partners looking for more conventional incarnations of patriarchal femininity. An independent woman engaged in a stable rela- tionship, on the other hand, might more or less unconsciously wish to avoid too much professional success, in order not to appear dominating in relation to her partner: 'split between the desire to assert herself and the desire for self-effacement,' Beauvoir writes, 'she is torn and divided' (SS703; DSb616; TA).

Arising from the woman's wish not to repress her own sexual needs, such conflicts are profoundly painful. But they also signal the presence of a will to struggle, and may produce great lucidity: an independent woman is likely to be more aware of her difficulties than a woman who buries her projects and her desires, but she is nevertheless infinitely better off.[27] Precisely because of her lived experience of the ambiguity of oppression, the independent woman becomes more authentic – but not more free – than most men. On this point, then, Beauvoir's political analysis rejoins her philosophical understanding of women's condition: as long as they are consciously experienced and accepted, women's contradictions and con- flicts make them more acutely human than men.

For Beauvoir, lesbians make up one important category of independent women. Lesbianism, she writes, 'is one way, among others, in which woman solves the problems posed by her condition in general, by her erotic situation in particular (SS444; DSb218).[28] According to *The Second Sex*, then, lesbianism may be understood as an existential choice like any other. Heterosexuality, one may add, is also a choice.[29] If anything, Beauvoir suspects lesbianism of being more, not less 'natural' than hetero- sexuality: 'And if nature is to be invoked, one can say that all women are naturally homosexual', she writes (SS427; DSb195). Lesbians may live their sexuality authentically or inauthentically: *per se* they are neither inferior nor superior to other women: 'Like all human behaviour, homosexuality will lead to make-believe, disequilibrium, frustration, lies, or, on the contrary, it will become the source of rewarding experiences, depending on how it is lived – whether in bad faith, laziness, and falsity, or in lucidity, generos-

ity, and freedom' (SS444; DSb218; TA). While Beauvoir does not absolutely exclude the idea, often advanced by patriarchal discourse, that
hormonal or anatomical factors may in some cases contribute to lesbian
object choice, she resolutely rejects the idea that anatomy alone can
determine sexual orientation: 'But anatomy and the hormones only define
a situation and do not set the object towards which the situation is to be
transcended' (SS425; DSb193; TA).

A number of lesbian feminists have been disappointed by the fact that
Beauvoir fails to provide a theory of lesbian identity. Claudia Card, for
instance, complains that Beauvoir 'assesses lesbian relationships simply as
human relationships, not as specifically lesbian' (p. 213), and Ann Ferguson
is unhappy with the fact that Beauvoir fails to 'make the historical distinction between lesbian practices and a lesbian identity' (p. 207). The question
of whether it is in fact desirable to have a strong theory of lesbian identity
will not be discussed here. Given Beauvoir's general application of the
maxim that 'existence precedes essence' to every form of sexuality and
identity, however, her understanding of lesbianism as an existentialist *act*
expressed in a specific object choice is consistent with her general theoretical framework. Identity, for Beauvoir, does not precede but *follows from* our
acts in the world. In so far as different women have different reasons for
choosing to 'make themselves lesbian', to use a Beauvoirean expression,
they will not all develop the same understanding of what it means to be a
lesbian. Just as there is no general 'female essence' shared by all women, *The
Second Sex* implies, there can be no common 'lesbian nature' either.

Beauvoir's discussion of lesbian life displays all the rhetorical and philosophical contradictions I have analysed in chapter 6. There is the same
insistence on the passivity of female sexuality (on this point Beauvoir makes
no difference between heterosexual and homosexual women), and the
same tendency to take the masculine to be the universal, in spite of her own
explicit warnings against that particular fallacy. In fact, her relatively brief
chapter on lesbianism is exceptionally confused, structurally as well as
thematically. Moving from trousers for women (now usual on beaches,
Beauvoir notes) to the outlandish story of an aristocratic bisexual cross-
dresser in Austria, taken from the notoriously unreliable Wilhelm Stekel's
'study' of frigidity in women, Beauvoir also throws in glancing references
to Radclyffe Hall, Sarah Ponsonby, wild jealous rages, and 'butch' and
'femme' behaviour and, finally, ascribes lesbian object choice to anything
from a need for relaxation or a predilection for softness of skin (natural to
all women, according to Beauvoir), to a desire to avoid being reduced to
an object for men *or* a desire to compete with men on their own terrain.

The theoretical and rhetorical confusion of this chapter is indicative of
deeper difficulties: it is as if the very subject of lesbianism makes Beauvoir
incapable of organizing her thought. The revelation of Beauvoir's own

homosexual practices in the posthumously published *Letters to Sartre* (1990) opens new perspectives on Beauvoir's troubled response to the subject. In this context, however, it is crucial to remember that she never considered herself a lesbian: the definition of lesbianism provided in *The Second Sex* also applies to her own case. According to Beauvoir, lesbians are not simply women who enjoy sexual relations with women; the decisive point is that is *all* they enjoy: '[The lesbian] is distinguished not by her taste for women but by the exclusive character of this taste', she insists (SS427; DSb196). Or in other words: lesbians are women who *never* consider men potential objects of pleasure. On this definition, everybody else, including herself, is heterosexual.

There may be more than a touch of bad faith in this: Beauvoir's definition was after all formulated well after her major lesbian or, rather, bisexual period in the late 1930s and early 1940s. Perhaps it suited her to define lesbians as different from herself. Perhaps she simply could not face labelling herself as anything other than heterosexual, regardless of what her own sexual practices might be. Perhaps – and in the *Letters to Sartre* there is much evidence for this – she considered her own lesbian practices as purely 'supplementary' to heterosexual sex. Whatever her reasons may have been, the fact is that the author of *The Second Sex* answered every inquiry about her own sexual relationships to women in the negative for the rest of her life. In 1982, for instance, Alice Schwartzer asked her whether she had ever had a sexual relationship with a woman, and Beauvoir replied: 'No. I have had some very important friendships with women, of course, some very close relationships, sometimes close in a physical sense. But they never aroused erotic passion on my part' (pp. 112–13).[30]

There is a touch of Jesuitical casuistry about Beauvoir's answer here. But it is also true that it probably never occurred to her that a woman who also related to men might be thought of as a lesbian. This is confirmed by the curious episode in the *Letters to Sartre* where she denies that Nathalie Sorokine is a lesbian, in spite of the fact that she herself carried on an unusually tempestuous affair with the very same Sorokine in 1939 and 1940. Under the morally repressive Vichy regime, in 1943 her affair with Sorokine even cost Beauvoir her job.[31] This is what Beauvoir writes to Sartre in her letter of 28 August 1950:

> When Sor. had left, Algren told me that his friends had been struck by her lesbian side. It has to be said, she does caress and kiss me in front of people in a way that must appear odd. But Christine had thought her a lesbian simply from hearing her voice on the telephone, and Algren says she made the same impression on him as soon as she got out of the taxi. She isn't one, though – she had one ludicrous, failed experience with a professional lesbian, that's all – she's above all sexually infantile (LS475; LSb392).

After 1944, if the information currently in the public domain is anything to go by, there is not much evidence of lesbian practices in Beauvoir's own life. Sylvie Le Bon de Beauvoir – Beauvoir's adoptive daughter and the editor of the *Letters to Sartre* – does nothing to dissuade the reader from the idea that her life-long relationship with Beauvoir was also a sexual one: '[It was] love between Castor [Beauvoir] and myself', she insists. 'What made it complicated is that neither one of us was prepared, especially me, to love someone who was a woman. But that's what it was, love, that's all' (Bair, p. 509). Asked to specify whether they were in fact having a sexual relationship, Le Bon de Beauvoir would just say that, in public, Beauvoir always insisted 'that we were good friends because I didn't want her to say anything more, for many reasons, many bad reasons' (Bair, p. 510).[32]

What, then, does Beauvoir have to say about lesbian sexuality? Is it truly an escape from the objectification imposed on women in a patriarchal world? In many ways, the answer would seem to be yes. It is in her discussion of lesbianism that Beauvoir produces one of the most positive descriptions of sexual relations to be found anywhere in *The Second Sex*: 'Between women love is contemplative; caresses are intended less to gain possession of the other than gradually to re-create the self through her; separateness is abolished, there is no struggle, no victory, no defeat; in exact reciprocity each is at once subject and object, sovereign and slave, duality becomes mutuality' (SS436; DSb208). On this account, lesbians would seem actually to achieve the existentialist ideal of reciprocity. The contrast to Françoise's heroic struggle to seduce Gerbert in a reciprocal mode is significant. Françoise found herself caught in a web of social hierarchies; here, on the other hand, the master–slave dialectics is undone, the struggle between the sexes plays no role: this is a true relationship of equals. This does not prevent Beauvoir from finding even more exciting values in *ideal* heterosexual sex:

> When woman finds in the male both desire and respect; if he lusts after her flesh while recognizing her freedom, she feels herself to be the essential in the very moment she makes herself object; she remains free in the submission to which she consents. [. . .] Under a concrete and carnal form there is mutual recognition of the other and the ego. [. . .] Alterity has no longer a hostile implication; it is this sense of the union of truly separate bodies that makes the sexual act so moving; it is the more overwhelming as the two beings, who together passionately deny and assert their boundaries, are similar [*semblables*] and yet different (SS422; DSb189; TA).

As we have seen in chapter 6, Beauvoir's philosophical idealization of the male body leads her to find 'defeat' for women even in the most perfect instance of heterosexual intercourse. In this passage, it is as if the very difference between the two bodies adds intensity to the sexual encounter.

True reciprocity, Beauvoir implies, presupposes difference: too much similarity reduces sexual interaction to a narcissistic mirroring of the other: it is not a coincidence that she speaks of the 'miracle of the mirror' (SS436; DSb207) precisely in the context of lesbian sexuality. Overall, then, Beauvoir apparently believes that homosexual relations are preferable to the vast majority of heterosexual relations available to women under patriarchy. At the same time, however, she also comes dangerously close to equating lesbianism with narcissism. Ultimately, it would seem, Beauvoir stakes her sexual hopes on truly reciprocal sex with men: it is hard not to perceive the traces of Nelson Algren in Beauvoir's glowing praise of ideal heterosexual sex.

For Beauvoir, the advantage of her theoretical position is that it explains her own sexual practices in the 1930s and 1940s.[33] The disadvantage is that it is more than a little illogical. For if homosexuality truly represents one existential choice among others, and if such relations may potentially be lived in complete authenticity, as Beauvoir clearly believes, then there can be no reason to define lesbian relations as overwhelmingly narcissistic. For, as we have seen in chapter 6, narcissism for Beauvoir is one specific mode of female alienation, one that always leads to bad faith: it is no coincidence that she devotes a whole chapter to narcissism as a false solution to women's dilemmas under patriarchy. Nor should it be forgotten that for existentialists, *every* subject is an Other: if the master – slave dialectics may be acted out in the encounter between two men, a point taken for granted by Sartre as well as by Hegel, then there can be no reason to assume that the tension of alterity would be absent between two women either. As Beauvoir suspects, under patriarchy, true reciprocity may in fact be easier to achieve between women than between women and men. There is no justification for assuming that women are somehow so marked by their sameness that instead of respecting – or fighting – each other's difference they simply proceed to a harmonious, symbiotic merger with the Other.

In spite of its confusion, Beauvoir's chapter on lesbianism does make a number of valuable political points. In France in 1949, it took courage even to raise the subject. There can be no doubt that Beauvoir in fact sees lesbianism as a perfectly valid existential choice; she is clearly radically opposed to any kind of discrimination against women who choose to lead lesbian lives. A strong point of her chapter is her generous mapping of the many different ways of being a lesbian; the confusion of her writing is partly caused by the profusion of idiosyncratic examples jostling for space on her pages. Just as Beauvoir explicitly refuses to generalize about women's identity, she also, in principle, refuses to generalize about lesbian identity. Acutely sensitive to the difficulties encountered by lesbians and other independent women trying to protect their autonomy under patriarchy, Beauvoir describes their dilemmas – which are also her own – with sympathy and insight. The obstacles placed in the way of real freedom remain daunting, yet Beauvoir refuses to abandon the struggle. For her, everything remains possible: women's potential is unlimited; the future remains wide open.

NARRATIVES OF LIBERATION

How, then, does Beauvoir envisage the future? What would count as liberation for the author of *The Second Sex*? In order to answer such questions, it is useful to consider *The Second Sex* in the context of Sartre's 'Black Orpheus' (1948) and Frantz Fanon's *Black Skin, White Masks* (1952). There can be no doubt that Beauvoir read Sartre's famous essay on *négritude*, published only a year before *The Second Sex*. To claim that *Black Skin, White Masks* can help to illuminate *The Second Sex* may be more surprising, yet the parallels between the two texts are striking. Just like *The Second Sex*, Fanon's epochal study of racism and colonialism explicitly invokes Lacan's theory of alienation in the mirror stage. Where Beauvoir draws on Lacan and Sartre to construct a highly complex theory of female alienation under patriarchy, Fanon mobilizes the same thinkers to theorize black alienation in a racist society. Centrally concerned with the question of the subjectivity of the oppressed, both theorists turn to a whole range of psychoanalytic writers in order to develop their own perspectives. Moreover, as we shall see, the authors' personal experience of oppression and marginality makes the question of *style* particularly important – and particularly problematic – for them.

Fanon himself makes absolutely no reference to *The Second Sex*. Nor does he seem even remotely interested in the question of women's liberation. Writing his essay as a medical student in Lyons, Fanon was influenced by existentialism, and – judging by his footnotes – clearly an assiduous reader of *Les temps modernes*. In 1948 and 1949 the existentialist journal published many excerpts from *The Second Sex*, yet Fanon fails to mention any of them. Nor does he refer to the full-length book, although he could hardly have been unaware of its publication and the outraged response it provoked in France in 1949 and 1950.[34] Unfortunately, Fanon's explicit invocation of Sartre and his total neglect of Beauvoir exemplify the usual response of male intellectuals to existentialism. In spite of the obvious historical connections between Fanon and Beauvoir, it would seem that present-day colonial and post-colonial critics have done nothing to change this unhappy state of affairs.[35]

In *The Second Sex* Beauvoir often draws parallels between women's liberation and black liberation struggles. Her reaction to *Black Skin, White*

Masks is not recorded. As far as I know, she never remarked on the Martiniquan theorist's neglect of her own work. In *Force of Circumstance* she gives a glowing account of her own meeting with Fanon shortly before his death in 1961.[36] In the late 1950s and early 1960s Beauvoir travelled extensively, and was constantly meeting some of the world's most influential politicians and intellectuals: Fidel Castro, Nikita Khrushchev, Albert Camus, Alberto Moravia, Jorge Amado, Nicolas Guillén and many others defile through her pages. The only person truly to stand out in this glittering array, however, is Fanon, who by the late 1950s had become an important figure in the Algerian revolution. When Beauvoir met him, he was marked by illness, yet she found him 'intensely alive'. Praising Fanon's 'wealth of knowledge, his powers of description and the rapidity and daring of his thought', Beauvoir testifies to his intellectual stature (FC611; FCb427). 'He was an exceptional man', she writes. 'When one was with him, life seemed to be a tragic adventure, often horrible, but of infinite worth' (FC611; FCb427).

Since Fanon's essay directly engages with Sartre's positions, it is necessary first to consider 'Black Orpheus'.[37] In order to free itself, Sartre argues, the working class must develop a consciousness of itself as a class, and then go on to oppose itself to its capitalist oppressors. The process of reaching the necessary proletarian class consciousness, however, is purely objective: it is simply a matter of recognizing the historical situation of the proletariat, and in no sense involves the subjectivity of the individual worker. Forced by racism to face their colour every day, blacks, on the other hand, realize that the first step towards liberation is to affirm and vindicate their very blackness: 'The final unity which will bring all the oppressed together in the same struggle, must be preceded in the colonies by what I shall call the moment of separation or negativity: this antiracist racism is the only road that will lead to the abolition of racial differences' (*Situations III*, p. 237). For Sartre, the ultimate aim of the antiracist struggle is a 'society without privileges in which skin pigmentation will be considered purely accidental' (*Situations III*, p. 236). Such 'antiracist racism' must necessarily produce a language of racial essentialism radically at war with its own ultimate goals. If racism alienates blacks from themselves, liberation requires them to recuperate their own blackness, to take it over for themselves, one might say. This is true even though the blackness recuperated is in no sense a 'pure' or 'essential' blackness, but the contradictory product of racism and colonialism. For Sartre, the 'antiracist racism' of *négritude* is an absolutely necessary ingredient in a process which will ultimately transform the abstract notion of universal humanity into a concrete reality. Or to put it differently: under truly non-racist conditions race will no longer carry *political* implications. Sartre's model of black liberation, one might say, represents a utopian vision of the ultimate *depoliticization* of identity: his point, however, is that the way to this goal necessarily goes through the radical *politicization* of racial identity, however contradictory and conflictual the latter may be.

If we now turn to *Black Skin, White Masks*, the first and most striking aspect of it is its style. No doubt partly as a consequence of his marginal position in the French intellectual and cultural fields, Fanon's essay is deeply personal in tone. Shifting between poetic prose, irony, anecdote and relatively technical psychiatric and philosophical analysis, the multiplicity of voices in his text is such that the whole essay tends towards the centrifugal, only to be reined back by the intense staging – *mise en scène* – of the narrative and experiencing 'I'. The very plurality of Fanon's discourse enacts his complex relationship to his own experience and political situation. It also enables him to stage his arguments on a multiplicity of different levels: in *Black Skin, White Masks* the contradictions of black alienation and identity in a racist society are examined through narrative, literary criticism, polemics, personal experience and poetic musings. As a result, the reader grasps not only the contradictions of black subjectivity under colonialism, but also the pain, confusion and disillusionment which are part of the experience of blackness under such conditions. In this way, the very subjectivity at stake in Fanon's debate with Sartre is rhetorically enacted and placed at the centre of the text.

Through his highly idiosyncratic – and, to me, quite admirable – *écriture*, Fanon manages at once to signal his distance from and endorsement of Sartre's positions. Reflecting and refracting his theoretical investments, his rhetorical practice represents a radical break with the prevalent form of the philosophico-political essay in France at the time. If the Sartre of the late 1940s is the incarnation of French 'philosophy', Fanon's stylistic raids on that poetry of *négritude* which he clearly feels more than a little ambivalent about spell a subtle opposition to the very voice of the French master thinker. Deeply aware of the social and political implications of Sartre's distinguished speaking position, Fanon sees Sartre at once as a highly valuable political ally for the *négritude* movement, and as a crushingly condescending theorist. Objecting to Sartre's high-handed reduction of his own experience to a mere moment in the dialectics of liberation, Fanon shows that the existentialist thinker completely fails to grasp the emotional and experiential implications of black discourse:

> *Orphée noir* is a date in the intellectualization of the *experience* of being black. [. . .] Jean-Paul Sartre, in this work, has destroyed black zeal. In opposition to historical becoming, there had always been the unforeseeable. I needed to lose myself completely in negritude. One day, perhaps, in the depths of that unhappy romanticism . . . [. . .] The dialectic that brings necessity into the foundation of my freedom drives me out of myself. It shatters my unreflected position (*Black Skin, White Masks*, pp. 134–5).

Fanon's point, then, is not that *négritude* ('that unhappy romanticism') is a flawless theoretical position, but that it corresponds to an emotional and political need. In the very act of declaring his support for *négritude*, Sartre fails to understand that subjectivity and the body are inseparable. The result is that the *embodied* nature of black experience entirely escapes him: 'Not yet white, no longer wholly black, I was damned', Fanon writes. 'Jean-Paul Sartre had forgotten that the Negro suffers in his body quite differently from the white man' (p. 138).

The need for *négritude*, then, is not simply an abstract moment in the dialectics, but rather an inescapable aspect of the weave of black subjectivity, anchored as deeply in Fanon's body as is his need to partake of that general humanity where colour is only one variable among others: 'My black skin is not the wrapping of specific values,' Fanon writes at the end of his essay, 'I do not have the duty to be this or that.' (p. 227 and p. 229). Echoing fundamental existentialist themes, Fanon goes on to declare that 'No attempt must be made to encase [*fixer*] man, for it is his destiny to be set free [*lâché*]' (p. 230), and to insist on his desire to liberate himself from the burdens of the past: 'I do not have the right to allow myself to be mired in what the past has determined. [. . .] The Negro is not. Any more than the white man' (pp. 230–1). Fanon, then, does not object to the ultimate depoliticization of identity; his point is rather that Sartre's final utopia would seem to hold no space for black identity at all. While Fanon's critique of Sartre stops short of an explicit rejection of dialectics, his very *écriture* tends towards the non-dialectical. It is as if he is grasping for a way to theorize subjectivity in which the dialectical moments outlined by Sartre would all be constantly in movement, so that every element would ceaselessly cross the paths of others in new and unpredictable combinations. My point is that although Fanon's theory does not offer such a postmodern elaboration of the problem, his discourse comes close to enacting it.

What position, then, does Beauvoir occupy in this picture? The oppression of women, Beauvoir argues, is in some ways similar to the oppression of other social groups, such as that of Jews or blacks. Members of such groups are also treated as objects by members of the ruling caste or race. Yet women's situation remains fundamentally different, above all because women are scattered across *all* social groups: 'The bond that unites her to her oppressors is not comparable to any other', Beauvoir insists in the introduction to *The Second Sex* (SS19; DSa19).[38] As a result, women tend to feel solidarity with men in their own social group rather than with women in general. Under patriarchy there are no female ghettoes, no female compounds in which to organize a collective uprising: 'Women', Beauvoir writes in 1949, 'do not say "We" [. . .] they do not authentically posit themselves as Subject' (SS19; DSa19). Opposing themselves to whites, blacks may posit blackness as a dialectical moment of revolutionary negation, in a way that women simply cannot do in relation to men who are their sons, brothers and fathers when they are not their husbands or lovers. 'Women lack concrete means for organizing themselves into a unit which would posit itself in the act of opposition', Beauvoir writes (SS19; DSa19; TA).[39]

Precisely because the great majority of women have never lived in their own communities, segregated from men, women's alienation is much more ambivalent than that of other oppressed groups. The complex and contradictory outcome of patriarchal socialization, female subjectivity is an ambiguous mixture of transcendence and freedom. No other oppressed group experiences the same kind of contradiction between freedom and alienation.[40] *The Second Sex* in fact establishes an exact parallel between women's subjective and objective (social) positions. In both cases, their situation is characterized by the absence of a clear-cut opposition between the two first moments of the dialectic. It follows that women's liberation cannot be squeezed into the classically Hegelian narrative of freedom provided by Sartre.

What, then, is Beauvoir's alternative to Sartre's Hegelian narrative? On this point, *The Second Sex* becomes somewhat vague. On my reading of Beauvoir, the ambiguity of female subjectivity under patriarchy appears to be at once a political strength and a weakness. It is a strength in so far as it potentially enables women to achieve freedom with less violent struggle than other groups: in this scenario, change becomes a matter of seizing upon the multiple contradictions of patriarchal ideology and using them to undermine the system from within. It is a weakness in so far as it prevents women from constructing a revolutionary movement in which they clearly and squarely oppose themselves to men.[41] On this logic, women's very ambiguity makes the revolutionary option – which is precisely the development Sartre imagines for blacks as well as for the working class – impossible. Instead, women will have to keep up a continuous struggle against the contradictory manifestations of patriarchal ideology, as well as against outright violence and callous exploitation. On such a reading of *The Second Sex*, women's struggle for liberation emerges as a slow and contradictory process, the one truly non-violent revolution in history.

What, then, is the aim of this process? Remarkably clear and coherent, Beauvoir's utopia presupposes that the material conditions described above (p. 198) have been achieved. Firmly linking freedom to brotherhood, the last sentence of *The Second Sex* has often seemed problematic to feminists: 'Man must establish the reign of liberty in the world of the given. To gain the supreme victory, it is necessary, for one thing, that by and through their natural differentiation men and women unequivocally affirm their brotherhood' (SS741; DSb663; TA). In spite of appearances, this sentence cannot be reduced to a simple betrayal of the values of sisterhood.[42] Rhetorically as well as thematically, the last word of *The Second Sex* represents Beauvoir's final utopian gesture. 'All oppression creates a state of war', she writes (SS726; DSb645). Only when oppression ceases will genuine solidarity be possible between men and women: Beauvoir's final *fraternité* must be imagined as situated in a space where patriarchy no longer rules, for only then can the word be given the truly universal meaning it ought to have had all along. In such a political space the word *sisterhood* will finally be taken to be just as universal as *brotherhood*.[43]

There is here, of course, a deliberate allusion to the French Revolution: her utopia, Beauvoir is saying, would consist in a world in which the ideals of freedom, equality and brotherhood would finally be translated into reality. Equality here does not mean sexual *sameness*: hers is not a theory of a sexless society, in any sense of the word. For Beauvoir, political equality presupposes social and economic equality. Together, these three elements make up the *sine qua non* of ethical equality between the sexes. Ethical equality implies the mutual recognition of the other as a free, acting subject, and in *The Second Sex* this is usually called *reciprocity*, not *brotherhood*.[44] It may be necessary to add that what Beauvoir has in mind is *concrete* equality, not the purely *abstract* equality invoked by traditional bourgeois humanism. Concrete equality encompasses difference: maternity leave, for instance, signals the social recognition of women's specific role in procreation, but it also demonstrates the social will to ensure that such difference is not turned into a professional and economic liability. Or in other words: for concrete equality to be established, difference must be recognized.[45]

Much like Marx, Beauvoir dreams of a society in which the ostensibly universal values of the Enlightenment tradition will finally become available to all. Today, she writes, 'man [. . .] represents the positive and the neutral – that is to say the male and the human being, whereas woman is only the negative, the female' (SS428; DSb197). As long as women are denied access to the universal, sexual difference is used against them. In Beauvoir's utopia, women would no longer be constantly reminded of their difference, no longer made to feel deviant from the patriarchal norm:

> When at last it will be possible for every human being to set his pride beyond sexual differentiation, in the difficult glory of free existence, then only will woman be able to let her history, her problems, her doubts, her hopes merge with those of humanity; then only will she, in her life and her works, be able to reveal the whole of reality and not merely her own person. As long as she still has to struggle to become a human being, she cannot become a creator (SS722–3; DSb640; TA).

Torn between their existence as women and their existence as human beings, women under patriarchy are obliged either to deny their specificity, or obsessively to focus on it. For Beauvoir, either option is unacceptable. To desire access to the universal, however, is not to deny difference. What Beauvoir wishes to escape is patriarchal femininity, not the fact of being a woman: 'What woman essentially lacks today for doing great things is forgetfulness of herself; but to forget oneself it is first of all necessary to be firmly assured that now and for the future one has found oneself' (SS711; DSb626). There is in *The Second Sex* a recognition that women will never be free unless they establish a sense of themselves as female, as well as human. Beauvoir's insistence on women's right to full sexual expression points in the same direction.

Agreeing on the fact that oppression entails exclusion from the universal, Sartre, Beauvoir and Fanon differ markedly when it comes to the value they accord to the subjectivity of the oppressed. Inspired by Léopold Sédar Senghor's *Anthologie de la nouvelle poésie nègre et malgache*, Sartre insists that 'black subjectivity' must be explored for political purposes (*Situations III*, p. 238), but casts this as a purely negative moment of 'antiracist racism'. Embracing *négritude*, Fanon argues, Sartre imprisons it in negativity. Stressing the profoundly interconnected roots of body and subjectivity, Fanon, on the other hand, warns that blackness will not simply wash away in the inexorable movement of the dialectics ('Not yet white, no longer wholly black, I was damned', p. 138). For Fanon, then, liberation consists in gaining access to the universal *as a black human being*.

What political role, then, is to be assigned to female subjectivity in the transition from patriarchy to freedom? In their different ways, Sartre and Fanon both agree that the way to the ultimate, utopian depoliticization of identity goes through its radical politicization. Compared to their strong defence of the political uses of the subjectivity of the oppressed, Beauvoir's position remains curiously hesitant. In *The Second Sex*, there is no mention of a purely negative need for an 'anti-sexist sexism'. Nowhere does she explicitly posit the necessity of reaffirming the value of female contradictions under patriarchy, or of singing the praises of *féminitude* as a necessary step on the way to liberation. This does not prevent her, however, from developing one of the most ambitious theories of female – not 'universal' – subjectivity ever produced. Nor does it stop her from recognizing that women, in order to be free, must be able to assert themselves as women. Ultimately, however, she recoils from drawing the political consequences of such insights. It is as if Beauvoir finds herself uneasily suspended between her own pioneering recognition of the political importance of female subjectivity under patriarchy and an equally marked reluctance to cast that subjectivity as a *necessary* element in women's political struggle for freedom. In order to avoid having to confront the gap in her own thought, Beauvoir seeks refuge in Marxism: placing all her hopes in a socialist revolution, in 1949 she simply assumes that the demise of capitalism would spell the end of patriarchy as well.

In the end, then, the deepest political flaw of *The Second Sex* consists in Beauvoir's failure to grasp the progressive potential of 'femininity' as a political discourse. More than forty years after the publication of her epochal essay, it is easy to see that she vastly underestimated the potential political impact of an independent women's movement, just as she failed to provide an adequate analysis of female sexuality. Fanon may not have produced a fully developed alternative to Sartre's Hegelian dialectics, yet his rhetoric, at least, gestures towards an alternative story. By remaining unable to face the issue explicitly, whether on the level of style or on the level of theory, Beauvoir finds herself in a tighter theoretical impasse than Fanon. It is tempting to conclude that in the historical moment of France in 1950 it was not yet possible fully to reach beyond the confines of classical Marxist or traditionally bourgeois narratives of emancipation: Beauvoir's and Fanon's achievement consists in having demonstrated the impossibility of using such paradigms to theorize sexism and racism alike.

Beauvoir's failure explicitly to oppose Sartre's Hegelian narrative of liberation may not be surprising. From a purely personal perspective, the fact that she does not explicitly endorse it either is actually far more startling. Beauvoir's silence on the issue, however, is heavily over-determined. At one level, her hesitations on the question of the political value of female subjectivity reflect her own position as an independent woman, a transitional figure arrested on the threshold of a new world. Having experienced the degradations of patriarchal femininity, Beauvoir is understandably reluctant to proclaim its world historical necessity. Her failure to posit femininity as a potentially positive force for change also springs from her excessively negative analysis of female sexuality. As such it is linked to her persistent tendency to overestimate the freedom of men, and to underestimate the power of traditional women. An even more important factor, however, is the historical situation of women in France in the 1940s. While the struggle against colonialism was gaining momentum throughout the decade, there was no sign of the future explosion of the women's movement. In 1949 it was far easier to envisage the necessity of an autonomous movement for blacks than for women. It would be un-charitable indeed to take Beauvoir to task for having failed fully to think through an issue not even broached by anybody else.

When she joined the women's movement in November of 1971, Beauvoir herself was quick to recognize some of her earlier mistakes:

> At the end of *The Second Sex* I said that I was not a feminist because I believed that the problems of women would resolve themselves automatically in the context of socialist development. By feminist, I meant fighting on specifically feminine issues independently of the class struggle. I still hold the same view today. In my definition, feminists are women – or even men too – who are fighting to change women's condition, in association with the

class struggle, but independently of it as well, without making the changes they strive for totally dependent on changing society as a whole. I would say that, in that sense, I am a feminist today, because I realised that we must fight for the situation of women, here and now, before our dreams of socialism come true. Apart from that, I realised that even in socialist countries, equality between men and women has not been achieved. Therefore it is absolutely essential for women to take their destiny in their own hands. That is why I have now joined the Women's Liberation Movement (Schwartzer, p. 32).

In the 1970s, then, Beauvoir came to realize the necessity of independent feminist mobilization of women *as* women, both with and against the general socialist movement of which she considered herself a part. For her, however, such separatism remained wholly strategic: her general vision of liberation never changed.

In an interview from 1976, Beauvoir stresses the positive nature of certain 'feminine' qualities, such as lack of self-importance, the absence of vanity and arrogance, a sense of humour, disrespect for hierarchies and so on:

These 'feminine' qualities are a product of our oppression, but they ought to be retained after our liberation. And men would have to learn to acquire them. But we shouldn't go to the other extreme and say that a woman has a particular closeness with the earth, that she feels the rhythm of the moon, the ebb and flow of the tides . . . Or that she has more soul, or is less destructive by nature etc. No! If there is a grain of truth in that, it is not because of our nature, but is rather the result of our conditions of existence. [. . .] One should not believe that the female body gives one a new vision of the world (Schwartzer, pp. 78–9).

Sceptical of the tendency to idealize reified images of 'women's culture' or 'women's tradition', the author of *The Second Sex* understands such phenomena as the contradictory products of patriarchy.[46] For Beauvoir, female sexuality does not have the wide-ranging cultural implications often asserted by later generations of feminists. Many of the qualities (openness, generosity, spontaneity, fluidity) considered by the proponents of *écriture féminine*, for instance, as grounded in feminine sexuality, Beauvoir does not consider particularly sexual at all.[47] Even in the 1970s, then, her position remained wholly antagonistic to those feminists who chose to focus on women's difference, often without regard to other social movements, and certainly with distinct distaste for the 'old-fashioned' ideal of equality she herself incarnated.[48]

While Beauvoir is right to question the historical and theoretical value of feminist identity politics, I believe that she seriously underestimates the *strategic* value of a politics of difference. That is not to say, however, that I disagree with her ultimate vision of liberation. In the political and theoretical space of the 1990s, a real conflict remains between those who accept the strategic use of intellectual and political separatism in order to achieve a new, truly egalitarian society, and those who are convinced that women's interests are best served by the establishment of an enduring regime of sexual difference in every social and cultural field. What is at stake in current feminist debates, in other words, is different visions of liberation.

By casting the question in such terms, I am already doing homage to Beauvoir. In my view, the strongest legacy of *The Second Sex* is the fact that all its analyses and polemics are placed within a powerful narrative of liberation. By taking as her point of departure a story of historical and social transformation, or in other words: by giving feminism an end, by imagining a society in which there would no longer be any need to *be* a feminist, Beauvoir provided women all over the world with a vision of change.[49] This is what gives her essay such power and such a capacity to inspire its readers to action, and it is also the reason why *The Second Sex* remains the founding text for materialist feminism in the twentieth century.[50]

Historically, narratives of freedom have been remarkably effective in producing social change: we abandon them at our peril. To raise the question of liberation in a postmodern intellectual field, however, is immediately to expose oneself to accusations of teleology and other metaphysical crimes: no wonder many feminists are rapidly losing faith in the future of feminism. But to deprive feminism of its utopias is to depoliticize it at a stroke: without a political vision to sustain it, feminist theory will hit a dead end.[51] The result will be a loss of purpose, a perfect sense of futility, and the transformation of feminism into a self-perpetuating academic institution like any other. Deprived of narratives of liberation, feminist theory becomes anaemic, theoreticist and irrelevant to most women. The great virtue of narratives is that they come to an end: *The Second Sex* helps me to remember that the aim of feminism is to abolish itself.

PART III

PART III

8

The Scandal of Loneliness and Separation: The Writing of Depression

When I love thee not, chaos is come again.

(*Shakespeare*, Othello)

My sorrow is the hidden face of my philosophy.

(*Julia Kristeva*, Black Sun)

BEAUVOIR'S DEATH'S HEAD

'Every woman in love recognizes herself in Hans Andersen's little mermaid who exchanged her fishtail for a woman's legs for love, and then found herself walking on needles and burning coals', Beauvoir claims in *The Second Sex* (SS664; DSb561–2; TA). *Every* woman? Even Simone de Beauvoir? Beauvoir hesitates to draw that particular conclusion: 'It is not true that the loved man is absolutely necessary,' the paragraph continues, 'and the woman is not necessary to him; he is not really in a position to justify the woman who devotes herself to his worship, and he does not permit himself to be possessed by her' (SS664; DSb562; TA). But in spite of her efforts to maximize the distance between the cool narrator of *The Second Sex* and the *amoureuse*, the effects of that unguarded 'every woman in love' still linger in the air. The little mermaid, one may remember, suffers agonies of pain for the love of her prince and, in the end, gives up her very soul for him. The quintessential *amoureuse*, the speechless mermaid is absolutely dependent on the feelings of the beloved man.[1] Is the little Danish mermaid to be written off as a mere illustration of false consciousness, as Beauvoir implies, or does her casual appearance in *The Second Sex* signal the presence of more fundamental preoccupations?

Beauvoir readily admits that the spectre of the *amoureuse* haunts her own fiction: in a throwaway line in *The Prime of Life* she points to Elisabeth in *L'Invitée*, Denise in *The Blood of Others* and Paule in *The Mandarins* as particularly relevant examples. These characters, she writes, are representations of her own personal 'death's head' (*tête de mort*); they are incarnations of 'the woman who sacrifices her independence for love' (PL80; FA94). Her novels and short stories obsessively return to harrowing descriptions of depressive passivity and more or less suicidal outbreaks of madness: think of the ultra-narcissistic Régine in *All Men are Mortal*, the jealous and depressed Monique in 'The Woman Destroyed', the paranoid Murielle in 'Monologue', the anorexic Laurence in *Les Belles Images,* or the extravagant Paule in *The Mandarins*. The radically ex-centric woman in love is fascinating, fearsome and, ultimately, deadly; in Beauvoir's fiction the little mermaid turns out to be not only witch, but mother and Medusa as well.

In my view Beauvoir's writing – *The Second Sex* as much as the fiction and the memoirs – represents a constant effort to fight off the death-dealing mermaid. By conjuring up the image of an autonomous, centred and balanced woman – Françoise, Anne, the 'independent woman' of *The Second Sex* – Beauvoir attempts to disarm the Medusa, to ensure that the snake-haired monster remains at a safe remove from any character that resembles herself. This struggle is not successful. In spite of her efforts, in Beauvoir's fiction it is not only the 'dependent' characters who suffer neurotic paralysis and passivity. In *L'Invitée*, for example, the emotional reality of suffocating anxiety and depression is brilliantly captured in the active – but creatively blocked – Françoise, and, at the end of *The Mandarins*, it is the level-headed and professionally competent Anne – not Paule – who, suicidal with despair, goes to her bedroom to pick up the vial of poison she confiscated from Paule's handbag.

The ideal of the autonomous woman is always present in Beauvoir's autobiographies: *Memoirs of a Dutiful Daughter* reads as a sustained effort to write the *Bildungsroman* of an independent woman; the story of the young Simone is explicitly intended to counter that of Maggie Tulliver in *The Mill on the Floss*, and yet, even here, the death-dealing Medusa rears her ugly head: it is not Simone's triumph at the *agrégation* or her meeting with Sartre that ends the book, but her account of the death of Zaza, who dies for love at the hands of a selfish and petty-minded mother. In Beauvoir's version of the story, Zaza becomes the ultimate little mermaid; her mother the Medusa incarnate. Simone's independence is paid for by Zaza's dependence and ultimate death; Simone's brilliant career is built on Zaza's dead body: *Memoirs of a Dutiful Daughter* weaves its tale of success and happiness across the shadows of disappointment, dependence and death.

When she chooses to dramatize the conflict between her own need to assert herself as an independent woman and the guilty wish to yield to the seductions of dependence, Beauvoir nevertheless comes close to acknowledging that the death-dealing Medusa also hides within her own psyche. In her autobiographies she tends to be at once devastatingly honest about her experience of the temptation to 'abdicate', and somewhat disingenuous in her dismissal of its significance. In the first chapter of *The Prime of Life*, for instance, she readily informs us that she experienced the siren call of dependence during her first two years with Sartre. In the very last lines of that chapter, however, at the moment when she has refused Sartre's offer of marriage and is about to demonstrate her autonomy by leaving Paris to take up a teaching position in Marseille, she completely denies that it had been a danger at all: 'Today,' she writes (in 1960), 'I ask myself how much, in fact, such a risk ever existed' (PL80; FA94). After all, she continues: 'The only sort of person in whose favour I could ever wish to surrender my autonomy would be just the one who did his utmost to prevent any such thing' (PL80; FA94). Sartre had no wish to dominate her in any way, she claims, nor could she possibly have fallen in love with a conventionally patriarchal male: 'If any man had proved sufficiently self-centred and commonplace to attempt my subjugation, I should have judged him, found him wanting, and left him' (PL80; FA94). Quietly slipping from one meaning of the word 'dependence' to another, her analysis shifts from the idea of *alienating oneself in* the other to that of *being dominated by* the other. Affirming that *Sartre* had no taste for domination, Beauvoir in fact hopes to dispel any lingering suspicions about *her own* tendencies to alienation, merger and dependence.

The woman in love, the *amoureuse*, is an overdetermined figure in Beauvoir's writing, a nodal point where a number of interwoven affects and positions converge: she represents at once the temptation to sacrifice one's sense of individuality for love, the need for merger with the beloved Other, a desperate yearning for emotional intensity and an equally anguished fear of abandonment. In the *amoureuse*'s experience of love, moreover, moments of ecstatic jubilation are juxtaposed with moments of absolute dejection at the loss, real or imagined, of the beloved: staggering from depression to elation, the *amoureuse* knows no middle ground.

SARTRE'S PACT OF FREEDOM; BEAUVOIR'S MYTH OF UNITY

In the first chapter of *The Prime of Life* Beauvoir describes her life in Paris from September 1929 until the summer of 1931. Following her success at the *agrégation*, she was able to make a meagre living as a part-time teacher in Paris, and finally found herself free to move out of her parents' flat. For the first time in her life she had a room of her own, that is to say, a door she could close against intruding glances: 'To have a door that I could shut was still the height of bliss for me' (PL12; FA16). In addition to all this, she was in love: when Sartre returned to Paris after the long vacation, Beauvoir comments, 'my new life really began' (PL13; FA17). For the rest of their lives Beauvoir and Sartre were to refer to the date of 14 October as their 'wedding anniversary'.[2]

According to Beauvoir's recollections, it did not take many weeks for Sartre to propose the two 'pacts' that were to regulate their life for the next fifty years. First, he insisted, they were not to be monogamous. The memorable passage in which Beauvoir sets forth the first of their pacts deserves to be quoted in full:

> Sartre was not cut out for monogamy;[3] he took pleasure in the company of women [. . .]; he had no intention, at twenty-three [sic!], of renouncing their tempting variety.[4] 'What we have,' he explained to me in his favourite terminology, 'is an *essential* love; but we should also know *contingent* loves.' We were two of a kind [*d'une même espèce*]; our understanding would endure as long as we did; but it could not make up for the fleeting riches to be had from encounters with different people. How could we deliberately forego that gamut of emotions — astonishment, regret, pleasure, nostalgia — which we were also capable of feeling (PL22; FA28; TA)?

Beauvoir was not immediately swayed by Sartre's appeal to the Gidean theme of sexual availability (*disponibilité*). One day, however, he decisively furthered his case by proposing that they should sign a 'lease' (*un bail*) of two years. The two years would be spent 'in the closest possible intimacy' (PL23; FA29), and during that time they would not make use of the sexual freedom they had given each other. When the two years were up, he would go off to teach in Japan, and they would not see each other for two or three years. There would be nothing terrifying in this, however, since they would never *truly* separate: 'We would never become strangers to one another, and neither would appeal for the other's help in vain; nothing would prevail against this alliance of ours. But it must not be allowed to degenerate into mere duty or habit; we had at all costs to preserve it from decay of this sort' (PL23; FA29). It was only at this point that Beauvoir acquiesced in his plan: the famous 'pact of freedom' had become a reality.

While Sartre in effect was trading two years of monogamy for a lifetime of infidelity, Beauvoir would seem to have been willing to pay just about any price for the promise of two years of immediate intimacy and absolute monogamy. Although the very thought of separation provoked anxiety in her, the future was simply going to have to wait: 'The separation which

Sartre envisaged did frighten me; but it lay well in the future [. . .]; in so far as I still felt a flicker of fear, I regarded it as mere weakness and made myself subdue it' (PL23; FA29; TA). In this effort she was greatly assisted, she adds, by Sartre's absolute reliability: if he made a promise, he always kept it.

But this is not all: 'In a more general way I knew that no harm could ever come to me from him – unless he were to die before I died' (PL23; FA29). There is in this sentence strong echoes of her adamant insistence, at the end of *Memoirs of a Dutiful Daughter*, that after spending a week with him in August 1929, she *knew* that Sartre would never disappear from her life ('When I left him at the beginning of August, I knew that he would never go out of my life again' – MDD345; MJF482). Only the benefit of hindsight – that is to say the existence, both in the reader's and the author's mind, of a powerful myth of the Sartre–Beauvoir couple – can make such statements appear as simple descriptions of facts. It is obvious, moreover, that in sentences such as this, there is no distance at all between the perspective of the mature Beauvoir and her younger self: what we are witnessing here is at once the enactment and the construction of the fundamental Beauvoirean myth of unity between herself and Sartre.[5]

A page further on, Beauvoir reinforces the theme of unity by insisting on the 'identical sign [*ces signes jumeaux*] on both our brows' (PL25; FA31–2), which made more humdrum commitments, such as living under the same roof, superfluous. In the attempt to explain the extraordinary nature of their unity, Beauvoir's discourse strains against the very limits of intelligibility: 'One single project fired us: to embrace everything, to bear witness to everything; [. . .] so that in the very moment we divided, our wills were as one. That which bound us freed us [*nous déliait*]; and in that freedom [*déliement*] we found ourselves bound in our deepest selves' (PL25–6; FA32; TA).

The fact that Beauvoir fantasizes an indestructible union precisely at the moment where she describes her own anxiety at the thought of separating from Sartre is no coincidence: only her own profound belief in the reality, however transcendent, of that unity makes Sartre's pact of freedom bearable for her. Crucial to her own sense of identity, the myth of unity enables her to resolve a number of conflicts. First of all, it bridges the gap between her own fear of separation and Sartre's wish for unlimited emotional and sexual freedom. In its stubborn denial of the ordinary and the everyday, it locates the essence of their relationship at a transcendental level which by definition cannot be degraded by any particular action in the world. Beauvoir's myth permits her to continue to idealize Sartre regardless of what he actually does or says. By placing Sartre in a sphere inaccessible to reality, however, she also prevents herself from recognizing him as a human being with ordinary human needs and desires. If Sartre's role is to provide her with absolute protection against loss, it remains unclear what she sees herself as providing for him. It is as if by turning him into a godlike figure she also dispenses herself from the task of recognizing and responding to his needs: the idea of Sartre as the good, all-providing mother is certainly one of the operative elements in Beauvoir's founding fantasy of their couple. For Sartre, one might say, the price of Beauvoir's idealization is a certain degree of dehumanization.[6]

In Beauvoir's own case her Romantic idealism clearly serves as a defence against the anxiety provoked by loneliness and separation, but the price she pays is steep indeed. By taking their unity as axiomatic, she sets up a situation in which she will never be able to define herself *against* Sartre without opening herself up to the threat of absolute separation and loss. If her needs conflict with his, she will simply repress her own desires. Such self-abnegation is different from an emotionally more self-reliant response to another's needs: where the former allows its victims no freedom and no choice, the latter entails the possibility of refusing or negotiating with the other. The fact that Beauvoir acquiesces to Sartre's pact of freedom in the first place illustrates my point: since he desires it, she cannot voice her own anguish; instead of opposing his wishes she compensates for her frustration by producing a fantasy of transcendental presence. In so far as it owes its very existence to the emotional subordination of the woman, the famous pact can hardly figure as an exemplary case of existential freedom.[7]

The same structure, incidentally, may be seen at work in the episode of the trio, at the moment when Sartre decides to seduce the young Olga Kosakiewicz, Beauvoir's student and intimate friend, away from her. Although Beauvoir experiences both jealousy and rage, she can only acquiesce: 'There was no question of fighting him for her, since I could not bear any dissension between us' (PL255; FA293). Perfect communion, in other words, means that when he insists, she gives way. As with Françoise and Pierre in *L'Invitée*, the two may well be one, but *he* is the one they are.

THE PACT OF OPENNESS

The pact of freedom was immediately followed by another: 'We made another pact between us: not only would we never lie to one another, but neither of us would conceal anything from the other' (PL23; FA29). In *L'Invitée* Beauvoir gives a vivid description of the delights as well as the horrors of such a pact. In *The Prime of Life*, however, she deliberately dwells on its positive aspects:

> I no longer needed to worry about myself: all my actions were subjected to a kindly enough scrutiny, but with far greater impartiality than I could have

achieved myself. The picture I thus received I regarded as objective; and this system of control protected me against all those fears, false hopes, idle scruples, fantasies and minor brain-storms which can so easily breed in conditions of solitude. The absence of solitude did not bother me; on the contrary, I was delighted to have got away from it. Sartre was as transparent to me as I was to myself: what peace of mind (PL24; FA30; TA)!

In *The Prime of Life* this pact is represented as a mere supplement to the pact of freedom: dwelling on the potential disadvantages of too much openness, Beauvoir speculates that this pact may only be suitable for couples as deeply united as herself and Sartre. For Beauvoir herself, however, there is nothing optional about the pact of openness or transparence. By guaranteeing maximal access to the other's mind, the second pact works to minimize the distance established by the first; Sartre's freedom would not be bearable without the guarantee of transparence. If Sartre is to have affairs with other women, at least she will be witnessing his emotions from within, as it were. In its attempt to merge their two consciousnesses, the promise of total sincerity becomes the very cornerstone of the fantasy of unity that structures Beauvoir's relationship to Sartre.

Focusing exclusively on her own experience of the second pact, Beauvoir leaves us to guess at its importance for her companion. 'I wasn't interested in myself at all', Sartre writes, referring to the period from 1925 to 1940. 'I was curious about ideas and the world and other people's hearts. [. . .] I couldn't stand diaries and I used to think that man wasn't made to look at himself. [. . .] After the war, I won't keep this diary any longer [. . .]. I don't want to be haunted by myself until the end of my days' (*Carnets*, pp. 174–5). If it was truly the case that he did not share Beauvoir's intense need to have her image reflected back to her by the other, the pact of sincerity would have carried much less emotional weight for him than for her. In his memoir of his life with the 'little family', Olivier Todd claims to have asked Sartre how he managed to cope with so many women at the same time:

> – How do you do it?
> – I lie to them, Sartre said. It is easier, and more decent.
> – Do you lie to all of them?
> He smiles.
> – To all of them.
> – Even to the Beaver?
> – *Particularly* to the Beaver (*Un fils rebelle*, p. 116)![8]

If Todd is right, Sartre never considered the famous 'pact' as more than a casual concession to yet another woman in love: in one light-hearted aside he deals Beauvoir a devastating blow.[9] For Beauvoir, on the other hand, their agreement had dramatic consequences. A textbook illustration of

Lacan's theory of alienation in the mirror stage, the pact of transparence turns her own self into an effect of the subjectivity of the other. While the specular image gives the baby a sense of its psychic unity, Lacan writes, what the baby sees in the mirror is not itself, but the 'ideal imago of the double' (*Les complexes familiaux*, p. 44): 'The characteristic world of this phase is narcissistic. [. . .] It is a world [. . .] which contains no others' (pp. 44–5). Unable to distinguish between love and identification, the narcissistic self can only love its double, but that double is not an other: in the very moment of alienation the narcissistic subject remains profoundly alone. In accepting the pact of transparence, Beauvoir trades her sense of identity for a shaky bulwark against loneliness.

ABSOLUTE HAPPINESS, ABSOLUTE DESPAIR

Explicitly comparing her 'fundamental understanding' with Sartre (PL26; FA32; TA) to her relationship with Zaza and, before that, to the 'poignant pleasures when my father smiled at me' (PL26; FA33), Beauvoir insists on the complete happiness produced by her communion with Sartre. In fact, she tells us, in Sartre she found not only the companionship provided by Zaza, but all the emotional security of her earliest childhood; Sartre takes the place of God: 'My trust in him was so complete that he supplied me with the sort of absolute unfailing security that I had once had from my parents, or from God' (PL27; FA33). In this early period of their relationship, she reports, she was in a constant state of 'triumphant bliss' (PL27; FA33), the intensity of which was such as almost to wipe out the pain of Zaza's tragic death in November 1929.

It is at this precise moment in her narrative that Beauvoir chooses to expand on her own unique capacity for happiness. 'I have never met anyone, in the whole of my life,' she writes, 'who was so well equipped for happiness as I was, or who laboured so stubbornly to achieve it. No sooner had I caught a glimpse of it than I concentrated upon nothing else' (PL28; FA34). The intensity of her happiness is clearly caused by the experience of overwhelming unity with a dominant other: Sartre is Zaza, God and her parents rolled into one, he alone guarantees her security. But if her bliss rests on a fantasy of merger with a dominant other, the slightest threat to that profoundly satisfying and exhilarating sense of unity might produce an equally violent experience of desolation and abandonment.

And this is in fact what happens. Throughout her life, Beauvoir writes, profound distress penetrates her shield of happiness. In *Memoirs of a Dutiful Daughter*, Beauvoir paints an idyllic picture of her early childhood, only to be puzzled by her own attacks of violent rage. In *The Prime of Life*, she draws our attention to a similar phenomenon:

Guilt and fear, far from cancelling one another out, attacked me simultaneously. I surrendered to their assault, in accordance with the dictates of a rhythmical pattern that has governed almost the entire course of my life. I would go weeks on end in a state of euphoria; and then for a few hours I would be ravaged by a kind of tornado that stripped me bare. To justify my condition of despair yet further, I would wallow in an abyss compounded of death, nothingness, and infinity. When the sky cleared again I could never be certain whether I was waking from a nightmare or relapsing into some long sky-blue fantasy, a permanent dream world (PL65–6; FA76).

Recurrent in Beauvoir's writings, such imagery of emptiness, death and engulfment always signals an experience of profound emotional distress.[10] Linked to the figure of Xavière, in L'Invitée the very same imagery conveys the fear of a hostile, intrusive and overpowering maternal imago. In her novel Beauvoir chooses to gloss Françoise's experience of desolation in the terms of existentialist philosophy. In The Prime of Life, on the other hand, she carefully avoids comments of any kind: on this point, Beauvoir's narrative repeats and reinforces the position of her younger self, who, in spite of her eagerness to explore everything, simply refuses to consider these particular experiences as potentially meaningful phenomena. 'I did not often succumb to these crises', Beauvoir writes; 'normally I reflected but little on my own behaviour, being too preoccupied with the world at large. Nevertheless,' she brusquely concludes, 'many of my experiences were coloured by this malaise' (PL66; FA78).

In the spring of 1931 it became clear that in October of that year Beauvoir would have to take up a teaching position in Marseilles, more than five hundred miles away from Paris. According to Deirdre Bair, the news brought on months of anxiety attacks often witnessed by friends and acquaintances. In general, the attacks progressed according to a set pattern which Beauvoir, referring to her years in Rouen in 1934 and 1935, describes as follows:

There were occasions when I slipped from my Mount Olympus. If I drank a little too much one evening I was liable to burst into floods of tears, and my old hankering after the Absolute would be aroused again. Once more I would become aware of the vanity of human endeavour and the imminence of death; I would reproach Sartre for allowing himself to be duped by that hateful mystification known as 'life.' The following day I would still be suffering from the effects of this revelation (PL207; FA239).[11]

Having interviewed Beauvoir and many of her friends, Deirdre Bair provides the following description of a typical 'crisis':

These episodes usually occurred in a public place, generally a café. She would drink silently and steadily, consuming remarkable quantities of liquor which seemed to have little effect on her sobriety until she started to cry, silent tears at first, then audible sobs that grew in strength and volume until they racked her body. Suddenly, as if some inner safety valve warned her that she had vented quite enough for the moment, everything stopped. She would dry her tears, powder her face, straighten her clothes and rejoin the conversation as if nothing had happened (p. 169).

Beauvoir's absolute refusal to discuss her attacks of 'melancholia' on any but the most superficial level deprives her of a language in which to work through her experiences and leaves her defenceless against the void that threatens to engulf her very sense of subjectivity. Oscillating between radical absorption in Zaza or Sartre, and a sense of absolute emptiness, the young Beauvoir appears incapable of establishing a solid sense of identity. This, in fact, is the conclusion she herself draws:

> Perhaps it is hard for anyone to learn to coexist with others: certainly I had never been capable of it. Either I reigned supreme or sank into the abyss. During my subjugation by Zaza I plumbed the black depths of humility; [with Sartre] the same story repeated itself, except that I fell from a greater height, and my self-confidence had been more rudely shaken. In both cases I preserved my peace of mind; fascinated by the other, I forgot myself to the point where there was nobody left to say to herself: I am nothing (PL61; FA72–3; TA).

Echoing Françoise's 'for many years now she had ceased to be an individual; she no longer even possessed a face [. . .] never did she say "I" ' (SC173; I216), Beauvoir, like her protagonist, reacts to the experience of 'abdication' by blaming herself: 'It's my fault', Françoise insists (SC173; I216). 'I reproached myself with [. . .] the over-easy tenor [la trop grande facilité] of my life', Beauvoir writes (PL60; FA72); 'I felt myself at fault' (PL62; FA73).[12] Beauvoir's sense of duty and responsibility, the intellectual vocation instilled in her by her education, her own social image of herself as a promising young woman, her father's expectation that she become a writer – every super-egoic structure in her, one might say – enters into violent conflict with her yearning for harmonious merger with the beloved. In this conflict everything that matters to her is at stake: if she abandons herself to her narcissistic yearnings, her super-ego punishes her atrociously for her 'abdication', and Beauvoir feels guilty, loses her self-esteem and sinks into self-loathing and depression. At the same time, the bliss of amorous happiness turns out to be unreliable: at the slightest sense of separation from Sartre, she is invaded by emptiness, anxiety and depression. Her emotional survival, it would seem, comes to depend on her power to satisfy the demands of the super-ego – to assert herself as a strong, self-reliant and creative woman – without exposing herself to more separation and loneliness than she can tolerate. In this context, her firm belief in her fundamental unity with Sartre turns out to be the cornerstone of a highly elaborate – and remarkably effective – defensive strategy.

SCHIZOPHRENIA AND REALITY

Upset by Beauvoir's emotional crises, Sartre proposed marriage, above all because marriage would have meant the certainty of getting teaching posts in the same town. Beauvoir refused. Distressed by what she saw as her own childish dependence on Sartre, she was determined to go to Marseilles, to overcome her 'weakness', and to recuperate a sense of identity. Given the apparent depth of her despair, this must have been one of the hardest decisions Beauvoir ever made. Her own text bears this out:

> In the whole of my life I have experienced no special moment that I can label 'decisive'; but certain occasions have retrospectively become so charged with significance that they emerge from my past with all the brilliance of great events. I remember my arrival in Marseilles as if it marked an absolute turning point in my life (PL88; FA103; TA).

In order to cope with the solitude of Marseilles, Beauvoir became a fanatic walker. Systematically exploring every village, hill and mountain around the Mediterranean city, she felt charged with a mission: 'My curiosity gave me no respite. [. . .] With tenacious perseverance I rediscovered my mission to rescue things from oblivion' (PL90; FA106). There was something driven, even obsessional, about Beauvoir's mania for mountain hikes at this time. When her sister came to visit her, she did not even consider deviating from her walking schedule. Bravely accompanying her, Hélène suffered from blisters and exhaustion, but never complained. One day, in the middle of a long walk, she developed a temperature: 'I told her to rest in the hospice, have some hot toddy, and wait for the Marseilles bus, which was due a few hours later. Then I finished my trek alone' (PL91; FA107; TA). In the evening, Hélène took to her bed with flu. Truly puzzled by her own behaviour, Beauvoir asks herself how she could have treated her sister so callously:

> Sartre often used to tell me that I was a schizophrenic, that instead of adapting my schemes to reality I pursued them in the teeth of circumstances, regarding reality as a mere detail. [. . .] I was prepared to deny my sister's existence rather than deviate from my programme. [. . .] This 'schizophrenia' seems to me an extreme and aberrant form of my particular

brand of optimism. I refused, as I had done when I was twenty, to admit that life contained any wills apart from my own (PL91; FA107; TA).

For a long time Sartre would tease Beauvoir about her 'schizophrenia.' And there is, to be sure, something quite mad about her desperate refusal to let reality impinge on her projects; her carefully worked out timetables and planned walks; her belief that her happiness depended on the strict observance of her own rules. In her very obsession with her own rigid schedules it is hard not to glimpse a fear of emptiness, or rather of the emotional chaos that might ensue were she to deviate, even by an inch, from her own plans. Pitting her own will against reality, she enacted in adult life the narcissistic childhood fantasy Freud labels 'omnipotence of thought': Beauvoir, we might say, had a hard time coming to terms with the reality principle.[13]

In *The Prime of Life* Beauvoir often returns to her 'schizophrenia': 'My schizophrenic obsession with happiness blinded me to political reality', she claims at the outbreak of the Munich crisis (PL363; FA415; TA).[14] It took a world war to release her from such aberrant selfishness: 'What Sartre used to call my "schizophrenia" had finally yielded to the implacable opposition of reality', she asserts in the summer of 1941 (FA555; PL484; TA).[15] And at the Liberation of France in August 1944, she claims, her 'schizophrenic delirium' disappeared for good:

> Never again would I slip back into the schizophrenic delirium that for years had contrived to bend the universe to serve my will. [. . .] My life ceased to be a game, I knew what my roots were, and I no longer pretended I could escape my own situation. Instead I endeavoured to assume it. Henceforth I took reality at its proper weight and valuation (PL600; FA686; TA).[16]

If *Memoirs of a Dutiful Daughter* is the *Bildungsroman* of an intellectual woman, *The Prime of Life* is a narrative of lost illusions: it is the story of how Simone de Beauvoir lost her 'schizophrenia' and finally faced reality. The existentialist doctrine of political and existential commitment apparently saved her from having to continue to erect her old manic defences against emptiness.[17] In this context, it is interesting to note that the British psychoanalyst Donald Winnicott explicitly links existentialism to a defence strategy he calls the search for personal non-existence:

> In the religions this idea [the wish for non-existence] can appear in the concept of one-ness with God or with the Universe. It is possible to see this defence being negatived [sic!] in existentialist writings and teachings, in which existing is made into a cult, in an attempt to counter the personal tendency towards a non-existence that is part of an organised defence ('Fear of Breakdown', p. 95).

Winnicott's remarks brilliantly illuminate an essential aspect of Beauvoir's conflicts: on the one hand there are her teenage experiences of ecstatic communion with nature, later to be displaced into the experience of unity with Sartre; on the other, there is the fear of loss of love and an obsession with rigid schedules (her 'schizophrenia') which slowly gives way to an investment in the category of existence. It is as if Beauvoir oscillates, philosophically as well as psychologically, between the siren song of non-existence and the bracing challenge of existence, as she herself acknowledges in *Force of Circumstance*, where she speaks of the 'basic confrontation of being [*existence*] and nothingness that I sketched at the age of twenty in my private diary, pursued through all my books and never resolved' (FC283; FCa370). Her various other conflicts – between dependence and independence, loneliness and communion, despondency and happiness – are in many ways variations on and displacements of this basic theme.

It was not only Beauvoir's experience of historical reality, however, that contributed to breaking down her 'schizophrenia': it is clear that the eventful period of the trio also forced her to face reality – Sartre's desire for Olga – in its most unpleasant aspects. In 1935, Sartre turned 30 and discovered that he was nothing but a provincial philosophy teacher with no significant publications. His feelings of frustration led to a veritable crisis of boredom and depression, culminating in hallucinations of being persecuted by lobsters. 'Sartre could not resign himself to going on to "the age of reason" ', Beauvoir wryly comments (PL211; FA243). In a desperate attempt to hold on to his youth, Sartre threw himself into the experience of passion. 'I placed [Olga] so high', he writes in his wartime diaries, 'that for the first time in my life I felt humble and disarmed before another person' (*Carnets*, p. 102). With Olga, Beauvoir noted with considerable apprehension, Sartre experienced 'feelings of alarm, frenzy, and ecstasy such as he had never known with me' (PL261; FA299).

Desperately trying to safeguard her fundamental union with Sartre, Beauvoir dutifully entered into a triangular relationship. Forced to confront the existence of real emotional disunity between the two of them, she experienced an agony 'which went far beyond mere jealousy', she writes; 'at times I asked myself whether the whole of my happiness did not rest upon a gigantic lie' (PL261; FA299). Confronted with the spectacle of Sartre's passion for another woman, Beauvoir had to face her illusions: 'When I said we are one,' she writes, 'I was cheating. Harmony between two individuals is never given, it must be worked for continually' (PL260; FA299; TA). Such voluntaristic reflections did little to ease the tension, however, and in the end she fell seriously ill with pulmonary inflammation. When she discovered that she was being carried out of her hotel on a stretcher, the stupefied Simone de Beauvoir suddenly realized that disaster had actually struck *her*: this time, her 'schizophrenia' foundered against the implacable reality of her own body. One thing is certain, however: it was only when Beauvoir's 'schizophrenia' started to fall apart that she truly came to writing: 'From now on, I always had something to say' (PL 606; FA694).

FILLING THE VOID

In *The Prime of Life* World War II represents the completion of a painful process of awakening to reality which started with the experiment of the trio. The trio marked the end of Beauvoir's uncomplicated happiness with Sartre. It also marked the end of a certain kind of frankness in her memoirs: from this point her text tends to conceal rather more of the sexual truth than before. Beauvoir's letters and wartime diaries (published in 1990) confirm the idea that the trio inaugurated a new era in Beauvoir's relationship with Sartre. Before 1937 neither Sartre nor Beauvoir had more than occasional affairs. After that time, however, they would seem to have been continuously involved in tortuous and sometimes rather shabby relationships with others. As we have seen in chapter 5, Beauvoir herself started a sexual relationship with Bost, Olga's lover, in July 1938. This marked the beginning of a long-lasting affair between the two of them (it certainly lasted until the late 1940s). Sartre, for his part, moved from Olga to her younger sister Wanda, with whom he carried on a relationship for the rest of his life. During the phoney war, much to Beauvoir's alarm, he even proposed marriage to Wanda. In addition to this, he got himself involved in a seemingly endless number of more or less scandalous affairs with other women, all meticulously chronicled in his letters to the 'Beaver'. Beauvoir herself took up with a number of younger women, sharing some – but not all – of them with Sartre.[18] Why did Beauvoir want to live in this way? Did it make her happy? And did she feel free to choose otherwise?

In September 1939, Sartre and Bost were mobilized. Left to her own devices, Beauvoir had to cope with their absence as best she could. This is what she writes to Sartre on 10 November 1939:

> Most dear little being
>   I received your [*votre*] letter this morning. I shan't file this one in the big yellow folder at school, I'll keep it in a secret pocket in my bag and I think I'll read it every day. I love you. I love you, and feel your love as strongly as I feel my own: we are one [*on ne fait qu'un*]. You can't imagine how calm and strong that makes me. I'm happy. Never, never, have I felt so fully merged with you and alone with you in the world.

Yesterday, after writing to you, we went to Agnès Capri's place. I've charged Bienenfeld with telling you all about that – it was very entertaining. Then we went back to the hotel and she slept in my room (without letting on to the Kos. sisters). We had a passionate night – the strength of that girl's passion is incredible. Sensually I was more involved than usual, with the vague and brutish idea (I think) that I should at least 'profit' from her body. There was a hint of depravity that I can't quite put my finger on, but which I think was simply the absence of affection. It was the awareness of having a sensual pleasure without affection – something that has basically never happened to me. [. . .] Now that Bienenfeld has taken charge of me and is oppressing me, Kos. is taking on something of the attraction of forbidden fruit – and I found her seductive and charming. [. . .] I'd restart a life with you by making a clean sweep of everything – Paris, money, everything – with joy. I need nothing but you and a bit of freedom. I love you. [. . .] And I am so happy, because I've nothing to tell you about my love that you don't know as well as I do, my dear love.

Your charming Beaver (LS154–6; LSa247–50; TA).

An ex-student of Beauvoir's, Bianca Bienenfeld (who is called 'Louise Védrine' in the French edition of these letters) was also Sartre's lover at the time, and many of Beauvoir's letters are taken up with complaints about Bienenfeld's attempts to claim parity with Beauvoir in the trio: 'Flushing with anger, I told her I couldn't understand how she envisaged our relations; that she seemed to see the threesome as an exact tripartite division, which astonished me. [. . .] For a moment there was a real, sharp quarrel' (LS160; LSa253). This did not prevent her from going to bed with the offending Bienenfeld: 'A pathetic and passionate night. I felt quite sickened by passion – like foie gras, and poor quality into the bargain', she reports to Sartre on 12 November (LS161; LSa255).

Commenting on Beauvoir's version of events, Bianca Lamblin (née Bienenfeld) accuses Beauvoir of deliberatedly undermining her (Bianca's) relationship with Sartre in a manner worthy of a Mme de Merteuil. All through the autumn and winter of 1939–40, Beauvoir fills her letters with negative references to Bianca, who has committed the crime of wanting to have an equal share in Sartre. At the end of February 1940 her work bears fruit: 'At the end of the month, without any warning, I suddenly received a letter from Sartre that announced that everything was over between him and me', Bianca Lamblin writes. 'The shock was all the more cruel, since it was totally unexpected: all his previous letters were warm, tender and loving' (*Mémoires d'une jeune fille dérangée*, p. 80). Judging by the evidence in Beauvoir's correspondence, Lamblin is right to accuse Beauvoir of perfidious behaviour in this case. Sartre, on his part, hardly comes across as a model of probity either. One of the most appalling passages in Lamblin's *Mémoires d'une jeune fille dérangée* is her chilling account of how she lost her virginity. On their way back to the hotel Mistral where the epochal event was to happen, the 34-year-old Sartre could not prevent himself from boasting about his other exploits. 'The chambermaid will be really surprised,' he casually told the 18-year-old Bianca, 'you see, only yesterday I took the virginity of another young girl' (pp. 54–5). When it came to the act itself, Sartre behaved with unexpected brutality: 'No erotic warmth, no truly spontaneous gestures made the situation easier. I got the impression that this man was following a set of instructions learned by heart. It was like the preparations for a surgical operation' (p. 57). Unlike Sartre, Lamblin writes, Beauvoir was capable of true physical enjoyment: 'Our physical relationship enchanted me, and gave me much pleasure' (p. 59).[19]

Writing to Sartre, Beauvoir nevertheless claims not to enjoy her sexual relations with women very much. When she finally 'gave in' to Nathalie Sorokine, it was with a sense of reluctance: 'We began to kiss, and without any desire – but from a sense of scruple – I asked her if she wanted us to have "complete relations"' (LS243; LSb18). Yet she was moved by Sorokine's obvious inexperience ('She couldn't be more of a virgin' – LS243; LSb19), and occasionally even admits to wanting to sleep with her (see for instance the letter dated 11 January 1940). This does not prevent her from claiming that when it comes to giving women sexual pleasure, men are invariably superior. In December 1939 she complains in her diary (also written for Sartre to read) about Bienenfeld's approach in bed:

> [It is] economical, rational, sensible [. . .] a mechanical reaction. I feel this mechanical aspect as long as we are in bed, and I *hate* Bienenfeld ferociously, and take pleasure in hating her while she is ecstatically going on about my tenderness. [. . .] Under her murderous hands, I wonder about the clumsiness of women precisely where men are so expert (JG208).

Writing to Sartre, Beauvoir returns to her lament: 'I asked myself why it should be women rather than men who are clumsy in localized caresses (since Kos., R. and Bienenfeld have put me through equal tortures). [. . .] There is a little mystery here' (LS2289; LSa377). The real mystery, of course, is why she regularly submitted to the female caresses in which she claimed to take so little pleasure. Written to and for Sartre, the *Lettres à Sartre* consolingly imply that sexual relations between women do not count: *real* sex is elsewhere, as every patriarch knows.

But there is more. In these passages, Beauvoir also reveals the ferocious intensity of her feelings for these women: she *hates* Bienenfeld, she was *tortured* by Olga, and she literally comes to blows with Sorokine. 'When Sorokine came along at 7 and I thought how I was going to spend 4 hours with her, I started to hate her', she writes in July 1940, after the fall of France (LS325; LSb170). When Sorokine refused to leave at the curfew,

Beauvoir flew into a rage, Sorokine tried to beat her up, and Beauvoir threw her out. Sorokine rang the doorbell, and Beauvoir was beside herself with fury: 'I went to open the door, trembling with rage – I wanted to be alone, have some peace, and sleep. I frankly hated her' (LS330; LSb175). The next evening, there was physical violence: 'Amid shouts, blows, clinches and threats, I eventually threw her out' (LS331; LSb177; TA). Reconciliation followed, until the next crisis flared up. Such scenes of fury and distaste *never* occur in Beauvoir's relationship with men: with men she is reasonable, friendly and nice; with women she is petty-minded, angry, disdainful, slightly sadistic and deeply ambivalent: 'I understood [. . .] those huge, reprehensible, but irresistible fits of rage which sometimes grip you in the face of weak, defenceless little individuals', she sighs to Sartre (LS180; LSa293).

On the evidence of her letters, Beauvoir treated her female lovers with all the fury, passion and intensity that Françoise mobilizes against Xavière in *L'Invitée*. In many ways, Beauvoir cast her female lovers as exact carbon copies of her own mother. In *A Very Easy Death*, for instance, she castigates her mother for spying on her daughters: 'She could not bear to feel left out' (VE34; UM54). She also insists on her mother's 'heavy-handed intrusions' and her 'outbursts of self-consequence' (VE35; UM55).[20] With her women friends, she acted out a veritable obsession with spying and intrusion. Constantly worried about where to hide her personal papers, she kept Sartre's letters under lock and key at work and received all her mail from Bost poste restante (although her sexual relationship with Bost dated from 1938, by 1941 Olga had apparently still not been told – or found out). Sometimes she was overcome by terror at the very thought of Olga reading them. Then there was the problem of Wanda who disliked Beauvoir – and who lived in the same hotel as Beauvoir and Olga. At times, Beauvoir was not above reversing the roles of intruder and intruded upon, and frankly admits to sneaking into Wanda's room to read *her* diary (see LS361; LSb220).

When the two men in her life visited Paris, Beauvoir orchestrated a complex scenario of subterfuge and lies. Pretending to visit her sister in the provinces, as soon as Sartre arrived in Paris she slipped off to the Right Bank to spend four clandestine days in his company. Staging his 'official' arrival, Sartre then saw Beauvoir for two days, Wanda for four days, and Beauvoir secretly again for another four days. Sartre's mother also got a few days in the general mêlée of women. The same scenario was acted out when Bost came on leave, except that then Beauvoir got no 'official' days at all. Whenever Bienenfeld arrived in Paris, Sorokine became insanely jealous. Even Olga, whose own passionate affair with Beauvoir and Sartre was essentially over, suffered from jealous fits when Beauvoir spent too much time with Bienenfeld. Congratulating Sartre on one of his more treacherous letters to the latter, Beauvoir contentedly purrs: 'All in all, lies and truth correct one another admirably, and you and I have done good work' (LS184; LSa301). Lying to Olga about Bost, to Bienenfeld about Sorokine and Sartre, to Sorokine about Bienenfeld, to Wanda about Sartre, all with the full complicity and understanding of Sartre: in these sordid transactions Beauvoir hardly cuts a heroic figure.

However much she complained about her 'charming vermin' (LS231; LSa383), Beauvoir never took the obvious way out: it did not even occur to her simply to sever her relationships with the various women surrounding her. Reading her letters, it is not hard to see why: for all her complaints, and all her dramatic insistence on her need for solitude and time to work, she actually thrives on the emotional intensity of her female relationships. Perhaps she really did not like the sex; she most certainly enjoyed the thrilling sense of *presence* produced by all the tearful scenes, dramatic quarrels and high drama of physical struggle. Her anxiety about other women reading her letters never made her burn them, or refrain from keeping a diary in the first place: others may require their fix; Beauvoir required her daily dose of anxiety. Without her 'vermin', the emptiness hidden beneath her games of hide-and-seek would have been harder to keep at bay.

The price to be paid for such emotional back-up, however, was her friends' demands on her time and affection. In her letters she sounds as if she constantly felt invaded, even polluted, by her own female lovers: 'I am so happy that Bienenfeld couldn't come,' she writes to Sartre on a skiing holiday in Mégève at Christmas 1939, 'it is so restful to be alone and not be the prey of anybody, to have to think only of myself' (LSa382).[21] Back in Paris in early January, she starts complaining again: 'My charming vermin are beginning to devour me again, and I'm finding it a bit overwhelming – I *so much* want to work, you can't imagine' (LS241; LSb15). Yet in the very next sentence she admits that 'Seeing Sorokine at lunch gave my heart a pleasing little jolt – so much so that I offered her my evening (I'm writing to you while waiting for her)' (LS241; LSb15). In Beauvoir's Parisian life her time became her bargaining chip: thirty minutes for discussion of Descartes with Sorokine (who was studying philosophy), thirty minutes for caresses in bed. Her diaries and letters are filled to the brim with precise timetables, careful counting of hours spent working, eating and sleeping. Whether it was mountain hikes in Marseilles or restaurant outings in Paris, Beauvoir exhibited the same rigid obsession with her plans. 'You're nothing but a clock in a refrigerator!', sobs Sorokine (PL476; FA546).

In one sense then, Beauvoir needed her female lovers desperately: filling her life, they helped her hide the terrifying emptiness that always haunted her: encouraging their affection, needing their admiration, she loved feeling adored by and superior to these young women who, unlike the professionally successful Beauvoir, led precarious existences on the edges of down-and-out Paris. Sharing her own and Sartre's salary with many of them, Beauvoir never complained about the drain on her fairly meagre financial resources.[22] Since all of them were young, socially marginal or professionally inferior to Beauvoir, she found it easy to feel autonomous and reasonably successful, in spite of the fact that she still had not published a line. (As we shall see, when she did become a published writer, she became less dependent on such relations with women.) Surrounding herself with her own coterie of dependent women, Beauvoir balanced her precarious emotional equation: in this way she managed to feel autonomous *and* loved; love no longer excluded independence.

It did not take much, however, to disrupt that precarious semblance of harmony. In February 1940, Sartre was on leave in Paris. During the days he spent with Wanda, Beauvoir fell into the blackest depression. 'It is not the fact that Sartre is with Wanda that weighs me down,' she notes in her diary, 'it would be the same if he were with his family – it's a suffering full of not seeing him' (JG275). However that might be, it is clear that when Sartre was with other women, Beauvoir's world was drained of affect: 'His consciousness is such an absolute for me, and this morning the world seems utterly empty, as if I had been thrown into the loneliness of stones', she continues. 'It makes me sick to think of the surrogates: Kos., Bienenfeld.[23] Right now I'd rather like to think of myself as absolutely alone; it's a real burden to have to see them today' (JG276).

When Sartre or Bost were there, however, happiness, freedom and joy reappeared: 'Sartre is here, Bost is almost here, my work this year has been really good, Paris is beautiful. This is a strong, full and free moment with happy repercussions' (JG272). A week later, immediately after Sartre's departure, she still felt 'all enfolded and sustained by [his] love' (LS274; LSb82): a striking contrast to the 'absolutely pure distress of absence' experienced when he was with Wanda (JG276). With Sartre at the front – that is to say, away from other women – she felt less lonely, and much less depressed than when he was in Paris with Wanda, or Bianca or some other mistress. What Beauvoir feared, it would seem, was not being alone, but the loss of Sartre's love.[24]

There is much evidence in her letters and diaries from 1939 and 1940 that she was seriously in love with Bost. She spends much time trying to prove to herself that his relationship with her is 'essential' (as opposed to 'accidental') and therefore superior to his relationship with Olga. The parallel to Sartre's distinction between 'necessary' and 'contingent' loves is surely no coincidence. There is something rather touching about her efforts to discard the impression, gathered from their last pre-war meeting in Marseilles (in July 1939), that in relation to Bost *she* was no more than 'an affair among others, perfectly pleasant, but a bit cumbersome from time to time, and a little *accidental* – that's what made me cry so much at Juan-les-Pins, that was the disappointment that left me dejected for the duration of the holidays' (JG287). When Bost leaves her to see Olga, Beauvoir records a feeling of emptiness: 'I want to see Bost, this is a simple desire and no distressing anguish, but it does make it empty around me' (JG290).

Whether they are friends or lovers, women rarely manage to replace the sexual and emotional fulfilment produced by Bost, and they can only put up a futile struggle to fill the gap left by the absolute presence of Sartre. A manic defence against depression and loneliness, Beauvoir's desperate timetables, her frenetic efforts to leave no hole unplugged, her immense need for emotional *filling up*, made her turn for comfort to the *petite famille*, the little clan of people who looked up to Sartre and Beauvoir as gurus and breadwinners. The transferential links between the members of the clan and the parent–teacher couple were intense, always encouraged, never broken. During the war it was Wanda, Olga, Bost, Sorokine, Bienenfeld; later some dropped out, others were added (Michèle Vian, Claude Lanzmann, Arlette Elkaïm, Sylvie Le Bon): this little group of people squabbled and fought, fell out and made it up again; their lives may not have been admirable, their sense of authenticity and moral responsibility may not have been quite what existentialist philosophy claims it should be, but none of this mattered. What truly mattered to Simone de Beauvoir is that *they were there*: filling the void, they were her very own anti-depressants.

OLD AGE, DEATH AND DEPRESSION

Many critics have noted Beauvoir's obsession with death. In her perceptive study of the theme, Elaine Marks points out that, for Beauvoir: 'The self [is] engaged in a losing combat to preserve itself from annihilation and from the intrusion of others. Death for Simone de Beauvoir is nothingness, absence' (*Simone de Beauvoir*, p. 7). For an existentialist, death is at once absurd and that which gives meaning to life. Trying to do justice to this paradox, Beauvoir on the one hand emphasizes the *scandal* of death: 'There is no such thing as a natural death', she writes at the end of *A Very Easy Death*: 'All men are mortal: but for every man his death is an accident and, even if he knows it and consents to it, an unjustifiable violation' (VE92; UM152; TA). On the other hand, however, she also tries to persuade herself and her readers that death is indeed that which gives life its value. Thus she writes a whole novel, *All Men Are Mortal*, devoted to the plight of the immortal Count Fosca. Describing himself as 'a phantom [without] a living heart'

(AMM249; TH385), Fosca laments the absence of affects in his life. Even when he is thinking of his beloved Marianne, who died in the eighteenth century, he cannot feel anything: 'Embalmed in my heart, in the depths of that freezing cellar, she was as dead as in her tomb', he sighs (AMM320; TH491). Fighting on the barricades of the February revolution, he still feels disengaged: 'My heart was buried under cold lava' (AMM322; TH494). Encouraged to live in the present, he replies: 'But words dry up in my throat. [. . .] Desires dry up in my heart and gestures at the tips of my fingers' (AMM329; TH505). In a striking metonymical move, Beauvoir describes Fosca's living death by endowing him with all the symptoms of depression: Fosca feels empty and lonely; his words seem meaningless; he is unable to invest his affects in people or causes; all activities come to seem equally futile; his only wish is to die.

For Beauvoir, death evokes the spectre of non-existence, whereas old age is above all associated with the loss of sexual attractiveness, and therefore – according to her beliefs – the loss of love.[25] In The Second Sex, published when Beauvoir herself was 41, she asserts that women reach their highest pitch of sexual desire at the age of 35, precisely at the point where they have to confront their own inevitable decline. While she may 'deceive her mirror' for some time, as menopause approaches the woman has to confront death: 'But when the first hints come of that fated and irreversible process which is to destroy the whole edifice built up during puberty, she feels the fatal touch of death itself' (SS588; DSb457). 'As an elderly woman', Deirdre Bair reports, Beauvoir 'still held the view that people in their forties were too old for sex' (p. 625, note 16). In All Said and Done, Beauvoir also notes this point: 'Even when I was thirty-five it shocked me when I heard older people referring to the amorous side of their married life: there comes a time, thought I, when one should in decency give up that sort of thing' (ASD43; TCF52). In Force of Circumstance, however, it is with considerable irony that she refers to her own former opinion:

> When I was thirty I made the same sort of resolution: 'Certain aspects of love, well, after forty, one has to give them up.' I loathed what I called 'harridans' [les vieilles peaux] and promised myself that when I reached that stage, I would dutifully retire to the shelf.[26] All of which had not kept me from embarking upon a love affair at thirty-nine. Now, at forty-four, I was relegated to the land of shades; yet, as I have said, although my body made no objection to this, my imagination was much less resigned. When the opportunity arose of coming back to life, I seized it gladly (FC291; FCb9).

The chance that she grasped so eagerly was the opportunity to start a relationship with Claude Lanzmann, a member of the editorial committee of Les temps modernes, and seventeen years her junior (Lanzmann was later to gain fame as the director of Shoah).

But if the 'ageing' woman turns out to want – and to get – sex after all, Beauvoir still does not find it easy to accept the fact. In *The Mandarins* (published in 1954, when Beauvoir was 46), the 40-year-old heroine, Anne, is invited to a high society party where she immediately turns down an invitation to dance because she feels 'too old', before giving vent to her disgust at 'older' women's bodies:

> Glass mirrors are too indulgent; the faces of these women of my own age, that flabby skin, those blurred features, those drooping mouths, those bodies so obviously bulging under their corsets – these were the true mirrors. 'They're old, worn-out hags [*de vieilles peaux*],' I thought, 'and I'm the same age as they (M666–7; LMb371).

Obvious self-loathing, repulsion, even abjection: Anne's image of the bodies and desires of women over 40 could not be more negative. The same touch of cruelty surfaces in *The Second Sex*, in a passage describing the sexual subterfuges of 'ageing' women:

> One and all, they declare that they never felt so young.[27] They want to persuade others that the passage of time has never really touched them; they begin to 'dress young'; they assume childish airs. [. . .] [The ageing woman] exaggerates her femininity, she adorns herself, she uses perfume, she makes herself all charm, all grace, pure immanence. She babbles to men in a childish voice and with naïve glances of admiration, and she chatters on about when she was a little girl; she chirps instead of talking, she claps her hands, she bursts out laughing (SS589–90; DSb459–60).

According to *The Second Sex*, the only thing such women can do is to accept their destiny, that is to say, to abandon all thought of sexual desire or sexual pleasure: 'From the day a woman consents to growing old, her situation changes. [. . .] She becomes a different being, unsexed but complete: an old woman' (SS595; DSb466–7).[28]

In Beauvoir's memoirs, her obsession with old age surfaces at a remarkably young age: it is already evident in the crises she experienced as a young teacher in Rouen: 'If I drank a little too much one evening I was liable to burst into floods of tears,' she writes, '[. . .] once more I would become aware of the vanity of human endeavour and the imminence of death' (PL207; FA239). After ascribing her crises to general existential anguish, she adds that she had another cause for concern:

> I had another worry besides this: I was getting old. Neither my general health nor my face were deteriorating, but from time to time I complained that everything was going grey and colourless around me: 'I can't feel anything any longer,' I lamented. I was still capable of going into one of my

'trances,' but I nevertheless had a feeling of irreparable loss. [. . .] Even so this depressed mood [*cette mélancolie*] did not seriously disturb my life (PL208; FA239–40; TA).

When life comes to seem repetitive, colourless, drained of vitality and significance, Beauvoir – who was 27 at the time – immediately leaps to the conclusion that all this happens because she is growing old. Clearly recognizing her mood as one of 'melancholia', she refuses to consider other reasons why she might be suffering from a feeling of 'irreparable loss'. It is not a coincidence, however, that the anxiety crises in Rouen actually occurred exactly at a time when Sartre was looking around for new experience, only to find it in the shape of a young girl named Olga. Depression, loss of sexuality, loss of love, fear of death, anguish at the void of non-existence: all these elements cluster together in the heavily overdetermined descriptions of Beauvoir's 'crises'.[29]

Not surprisingly, similar reactions are brought on by situations where she is threatened by or actually experiences loss of love: Sartre's serious involvement with Dolorès Vanetti; the break-up of the affair with Nelson Algren; the end of her liaison with Claude Lanzmann. According to her memoirs, Sartre's affair with Vanetti, which started in January 1945, reached paroxysmic intensity in the summer of 1947. Arriving back in Paris from the United States, Beauvoir discovered that Vanetti was still in Paris, refusing to leave the scene to her returning rival. Fleeing to the suburbs, Beauvoir hardly set foot in the city for two months. Confined to a small hotel, deprived of the company of her friends, longing for Algren, pained and upset by Sartre's obsession with Vanetti, she suffered two horrendous months of anxiety, depression and something that sounds like a complete nervous breakdown:

[I experienced] an anxiety that bordered on mental aberration. To calm myself, I began to take orthedrine. For the moment, it allowed me to regain my balance; but I imagine that this expedient was not entirely unconnected with the anxiety attacks I suffered from at the time. [. . .] They were in fact accompanied by a physical panic that my greatest fits of despair, even when enhanced by alcohol, had never produced. [. . .] Perhaps, too, these crises were a last revolt before resigning myself to age and the end that follows it; I still wanted to separate the shadow from the light. Suddenly I was becoming a stone, and the steel was splitting it: that is hell (FC137; FCa181).

Sartre finally put Vanetti back on the boat to New York, but Vanetti, who much to her credit, refused to play the role of compliant victim of Sartre's seductive ploys, kept complaining that 'he was doing violence to her.'[30] Sartre, who could not stand female recriminations of any kind, felt unusually ill at ease. Dragging themselves through a trip to Scandinavia,

Sartre and Beauvoir were distraught with depression and doubt: 'I wondered in terror if we had become strangers to one another', Beauvoir writes (FC142; FCa188).

As for her own affair with Algren, she resumed it in 1948, but when it became clear that she remained truly committed to her life with Sartre in Paris, Algren felt justifiably hurt and rejected.[31] The relationship slowly disintegrated, and after the final, sad and frustrating summer of 1951, Beauvoir (now aged 43) again told herself that her sex life was over: ' "I'll never sleep again warmed by another's body." Never: what a knell! When the realization of these facts penetrated me, I felt myself sinking into death. [. . .] It was like some brutal but inexplicable amputation' (FC266; FCa349). When Claude Lanzmann first asked Beauvoir out, she shed tears of joy: 'After two years in which the universal marasma had coincided for me with the break-up of a love affair and the first warnings of physical decline, I leapt back enthralled into happiness' (FC297; FCb17). Lanzmann, then, became her bulwark against the fear of growing old. He also protected her from her own moods:

> Lanzmann's presence beside me freed me from my age. First, it did away with my anxiety attacks. Two or three times he caught me going through one, and he was so alarmed to see me thus shaken that a command was established in every bone and nerve of my body never to yield to them; I found the idea of dragging him already into the horrors of declining age revolting (FC297; FCb17).

In spite of the evidence – she had after all had such attacks since childhood – Beauvoir here succeeds in persuading herself that they can be explained by fear of old age alone.

In 1958 political and personal distress converge in Beauvoir's narrative. This was the year in which the Fourth Republic collapsed, De Gaulle seized power, and the war in Algeria reached the point of no return. When she learned that over 80 per cent of the French voted in favour of De Gaulle in the September referendum, she burst into tears: 'I'd never have believed it could affect me so much', she writes in her diary: 'I still feel like crying this morning. [. . .] Nightmares the whole night. I feel as if I have been put through a grinder. [. . .] It's a sinister defeat. [. . .] A repudiation by eighty per cent of the French people of all that we had believed in and wanted for France. [. . .] An enormous collective suicide' (FC460-1; FCb228–9). But 1958 was also the year in which Beauvoir turned 50 and her relationship with Lanzmann came to an end. To compound her distress, the final break-up with Lanzmann coincided with a serious decline in Sartre's health. When Sartre barely escaped a stroke in 1954, Beauvoir had already felt the chill of her own mortality: 'Sartre recovered. But something irrevocable had happened; death had closed its hand around me. [. . .] It was an intimate presence penetrating my life, changing the taste of things, the quality of the light, my memories, the things I wanted to do: everything' (FC319; FCb45). When he fell ill again in 1958, it was as if her whole future had been erased: 'Henceforth [death] possessed me. [. . .] Basically, there was nothing for us to look forward to except our own death or the deaths of those close to us' (FC465–6; FCb236).

Politically isolated because of her stance on the war in Algeria, personally isolated because of her fame, Beauvoir was thrown back on the dwindling resources of the 'little family'. In the 1950s, however, tensions built up in this circle, and the protective closeness so eagerly sought by Beauvoir was no longer so easy to find. However intimate, however incestuous, in the end even the little clan of the *petite famille* could not protect her against the hollow emptiness she found at the heart of all things. In the 1950s even the old sense of unity with Sartre became increasingly elusive. The fruits of fame turned out to be rather bitter: recognized in the streets, Sartre and Beauvoir had to change their way of life. Old friends disappeared, and new friendships were hard to find: '[Sartre] seemed further away from me than ever before. [. . .] I had the feeling that he had been stolen from me' (FC267; FCa350).

As she grew older, Simone de Beauvoir's depression caught up with her: 'I have lost my old power to separate the darkness from the light, to produce, at the price of a few thunderstorms, a radiant sky', she writes at the end of *Force of Circumstance*: 'Death is no longer a brutal event in the far distance; it haunts my sleep; in my waking hours I sense its shadow between the world and me: it has already begun' (FC673; FCb507; TA). The darkness of death and depression produces the famous final sentence of *Force of Circumstance*. Looking back at herself as a credulous young girl, Beauvoir's bitterness is obvious: 'I realize with stupor how much I have been swindled' (FC674; FCb508; TA).[32] The bourgeois girl setting out in life in the late 1920s was promised the world: now that she has it, she is finding the misery of it hard to bear.

When she finished *Force of Circumstance*, Beauvoir was 54. Her autobiographies were best sellers in France; she enjoyed international success as a writer; she was certainly one of the most famous women in the world. Yet she tirelessly insisted that her life was over:

> Yes, the moment has come to say: Never again! It is not I who am saying good-bye to all those things I once enjoyed, it is they who are leaving me; the mountain paths disdain my feet. Never again shall I collapse, drunk with fatigue into the smell of hay. Never again shall I slide down through the solitary morning snows. Never again a man. Now, not only my body but my imagination too has accepted that (FC673; FCb506).

In 1962 the social convention concerning women in their fifties probably differed from those current in the 1990s. It is quite likely that they were expected to behave in a more resigned, more passive, less sexual way than their counterparts today.[33] Even so, Beauvoir's renunciation of life remains puzzling: why is she is so eager to embrace death and decline at such an early age? What is it that drives her headlong into renunciation and an obsession with death? In my view, the answer is clear: every time she is overcome by depression, she ascribes her feelings of absurdity, loss of vitality and increasing sense of desolation to her horror of old age or death. Such a strategy of displacement in fact allows her to acknowledge feelings of depression without ever labelling them as such, and without ever having to reflect on the other anxieties that also express themselves in her sadness: her constant fear of solitude and separation. In her texts, the massive and explicit discussions of old age and death block a closer investigation of the fear of emptiness and loss of love.

In 1962 Beauvoir's disappointment in her life would seem to have been total: at once philosophical, political and personal, her dejection seemed destined to last; old age and death were just around the corner; her life was over. Ten years later, however, in *All Said and Done* (1972), she had regained her tranquillity: 'I was mistaken [. . .] in the outline of my future', she notes with evident relief. 'I had projected the accumulated disgust of the recent years into it. It has been far less sombre than I had foreseen' (ASD132; TCF165).[34] The reason for this change of mood is not hard to spot: 'I was wrong in 1962 when I thought nothing significant would happen to me any more, apart from calamities; now once again I was given a great chance' (ASD69; TCF84; TA), Beauvoir writes in 1972, referring to her encounter with Sylvie Le Bon, thirty-three years her junior.[35] With its emphasis on the idea of repetition ('now once again'), this sentence contains a deliberate echo of her meeting with Sartre: 'I had been given a great chance: I suddenly didn't have to face [the] future alone' (MDD345; MJF481; TA).[36] Sartre protected her against solitude in her youth, Sylvie Le Bon was to do so in her old age.

Just as Sartre is represented as Beauvoir's double and twin in *Memoirs of a Dutiful Daughter*, in *All Said and Done* Le Bon is consistently represented as her double. She has the same fraught relationship to her mother; the same sense of revolt, she has also been accused of lesbian relationships in her past;[37] she is torn between passionate affirmation of life and happiness and violent crises of rage and depression, and she is an intellectual; she even gets appointed to teach philosophy in the very same *lycée* in Rouen where Beauvoir had taught in the 1930s: 'All this gave me a certain feeling of being reincarnated', Beauvoir comments (ASD75; TCF92). Their way of life also mirrors that of Sartre and Beauvoir:

I told her about my past in detail, and day by day I keep her in touch with my life. [. . .] We can see one another every day. She is as thoroughly interwoven in my life as I am in hers. I have introduced her to my friends. We read the same books, we see shows together, and we go for long drives in the car. There is such a reciprocity between us that I lose the sense of my age; she draws me forward into her future, and there are times when the present recovers a dimension it had lost (ASD75–6; TCF92; TA).

'It was love between [us]', says Sylvie Le Bon (Bair, p. 509). 'You can explain my feeling for Sylvie by comparing it to my friendship with Zaza', Beauvoir told Deirdre Bair: 'Since she died, I have often desired to have an intense, daily, and total relationship with a woman. [. . .] It did not work with Olga, it did not work with Natasha, but now I have Sylvie, and it is an absolute relationship, because from the beginning we were both prepared to live in this way, to live entirely for each other' (Bair, p. 509). 'Beauvoir often told me, "My relationship with you is almost as important as mine with Sartre" ', Le Bon informs us (Bair, p. 510). Whether Beauvoir and Le Bon's relationship was sexual or not, both women certainly considered it committed, life-long and loving.[38]

Providing emotional stability and closeness, Le Bon enabled Beauvoir to throw herself into a renewed encounter with fiction: her 1960s best sellers *Les Belles Images* and *The Woman Destroyed* read as if she has finally decided to write her depression and her rage against evil and intrusive mothers out of her body once and for all. Eventually, even age was turned into a source of creativity: *Old Age* (1970) represents Beauvoir's triumphant settling of scores with her old enemy. Now she can face her age with equanimity: 'In short, I see myself as settled into old age', she comments in *All Said and Done* (ASD40; TCF48). Sylvie Le Bon and Simone de Beauvoir remained close until Beauvoir's death on 14 April 1986.

THE WRITING OF DEPRESSION

How, then, do these emotional structures affect Beauvoir as a writer? Commenting on the reception of *Force of Circumstance*, she expresses astonishment at the reactions it provoked: 'There were even some psychiatrists who put the end of my book down to an access of depression [*une crise dépressive*]', she exclaims (ASD133–4; TCF167). Categorically denying the charge, the author of *All Said and Done* insists that depression has nothing to do with writing: 'A person who is psychologically torn to pieces, who is shattered and desperate, does not write anything at all: he retreats into silence' (ASD134; TCF167). Yet the young woman struggling to write her first novel in 1930 felt convinced that happiness prevented her from writing: 'My work lacked all real conviction. [. . .] But in any case there was no hurry. I was happy, and for the time being, that was enough' (PL60; FA71). The author of *L'Invitée* concurs: 'Literature is born when something in life goes slightly adrift. [. . .] My strict work routines remained futile till the day came when [my] happiness was threatened, and I rediscovered a certain kind of solitude in anxiety' (FA417; PL365; TA). At the end of *The Prime of Life* Beauvoir again asserts that her own writing stems from a certain experience of unhappiness: 'Misfortune and misery had erupted into the world, and literature had become as essential to me as the very air I breathed. I am not suggesting that it constitutes a remedy against absolute despair; but I had not been reduced to such extremeties' (PL606; FA694).

It is as if writing is called upon to help and sustain the writer in all but the most extreme distress. I believe that this is exactly the function of Beauvoir's *personal writing*. I use this term to designate writing carried out for personal purposes, as opposed to writing undertaken with a view to publication. In Beauvoir's *oeuvre*, the bulk of her personal writing is made up by her letters and diaries, but I also include in the same category the (fairly heavily edited) fragments and excerpts of her diaries reprinted in her memoirs. 'At those times when my life has been hard for me, jotting words down on paper – even if no one is to read what I have written – has given me the same comfort that prayer gives to the believer', Beauvoir writes in *All Said and Done* (ASD135; TCF168–9). It was no coincidence that her reaction to the separation from Sartre in September 1939 was to start a diary: 'It was now, in an agony of loneliness, that I began to keep a diary' (PL378; FA433). When Sartre is not there to 'process' her experiences for her, letters and diaries help her to produce a coherent image of herself.[39]

In *The Prime of Life* she reprints two long and much edited excerpts from her diaries from 1 September 1939 to 14 July 1940; in *Force of Circumstance* there are two major diary sequences (30 April to some time in late May 1946; and the period from 25 May to 28 October 1958, which covers the political débâcle of the Fourth Republic as well as various personal crises). In addition to these major excerpts, shorter diary fragments abound. During her ill-fated trip to Scandinavia with Sartre in 1947, for instance, she suffered from nightmares and suicidal thoughts: 'I tried to conjure these crises away with words', she comments before quoting a few lines of what she wrote at the time: 'The birds are attacking me – must drive them away; it's such an exhausting struggle, keeping them off, day and night: death, our deaths, solitude, vanity; at night, they swoop down on me; in the morning, they take their time flying away. [. . .] Ah! let's put an end to it! I'll pick up a revolver, I'll shoot' (FC143; FCa189). Another example dates from a night in June 1944. Overcome by one of her anxiety crises, she writes: 'I suppose I was a little drunk: in that room, decorated in red, Death suddenly appeared to me. I wrung my hands, and wept, and banged my head against the wall, as vehemently as I had done at the age of fifteen' (PL602–3; FA689). Her reaction is to write in order to 'exorcize death with words' (PL603; FA689). What she writes is that writing is the supreme antidote to death: 'I have written the beginning of the book which is my supreme recourse against death' (PL603; FA690). Death here, she adds, is to be considered not simply as non-existence, but also as the 'scandal of loneliness and separation' (PL695; FA695; TA). We recognize in these passages the usual cluster of Beauvoirean depressive themes: death, anxiety, emotional loneliness, loss of love. It is not by coincidence that these themes constantly occur in her personal writings: in Simone de Beauvoir's works the very appearance of the form or genre of the diary signifies emotional anguish.

To criticize her letters and diaries, as some have done, for not displaying a greater interest in culture, or politics, or even philosophy, is therefore to misunderstand the nature and purpose of Beauvoir's personal writings.[40] In order to write with passion about topics other than herself, Beauvoir would have had to be able to invest her affects in the world. But it is precisely when she feels the absurdity of existence most keenly – that is to say, when she is anxious, frightened and depressed – that she undertakes personal writing. When she feels more receptive to the outside world, she gets on with her other writing, leaving her journal aside. Such swings of mood often happen within very short spaces of time: two hours of writing for publication often give way to headaches, lack of inspiration and diary writing during one and the same morning. In my view, then, her letters and diaries represent Beauvoir in her most vulnerable psychological state: it is a mistake to take them to reveal the essence of the whole woman.

Bearing this in mind, it is easy to understand why her memoirs include diary excerpts from 1939–40 and 1958, or why the journal mode surfaces, however briefly, during the deep emotional turmoil of 1947. But why revert to the genre to report on the seemingly perfectly insignificant month of May 1946? On 12 December 1945 Sartre left for his second visit to New York, undertaken above all because he wanted to see Dolorès Vanetti again (they first met during Sartre's trip to the United States in January 1945). In February 1946 he writes to Beauvoir that he was delaying his departure: he would now leave by plane on 15 March. Apart from that, he reports that 'Dolorès [. . .] is a charming and poor little creature, really the best there is after you' (LCb334), and declares that he was 'exhausted [tué] by passion and lectures' (LCb335). After his return Sartre could not stop talking about the new woman in his life. According to Sartre, Vanetti 'shared completely all his reactions, his emotions, his irritations, his desires. [. . .] Perhaps this indicated a harmony between them at a depth – at the very source of life, at the wellspring where its very rhythm is established – at which Sartre and

I did not meet, and perhaps that harmony was more important to him than our understanding' (FC77–8; FCa102). If Vanetti was *more* like Sartre than Beauvoir was, then *she* would be his real twin and double: no wonder Beauvoir took her to be the first serious threat to her relationship with Sartre. For the first time in her life, Beauvoir felt obliged to ask the classic question: 'She or I?'. Sartre's reply was a masterpiece of ambiguity – and of cruelty: '[Dolorès] means an enormous amount to me,' he said, 'but I am with you' (FCa102; FC78). Beauvoir was stunned: 'I understood it to mean: "I am respecting our pact, don't ask more of me than that." Such a reply put the whole future in question' (FC78; FCa102). According to her account, Sartre cleared up the 'misunderstanding' the very same day, and Beauvoir closes the discussion with a terse 'I believed him' (FC78; FCa102).[41] A paragraph later, she decides to reproduce her diary from this period, apparently only because she wants to share with her readers the 'daily dust [*poussière*] of my life' (FC78; FCa102).[42]

The position of the diary excerpts in the text – immediately after the crucial 'She or I' conversation – points to the cause of her dejection.[43] Trying to finish *The Ethics of Ambiguity*, Beauvoir was disturbed by headaches, fatigue and nightmares. On 5 May she felt 'like those dabfish which have used all their energy spawning [*qui ont trop baisé*] and get washed up onto the rocks, dying and drained' (FC84; FCa110). She also complains about her persistent 'strange anxiety' and a 'sort of chill around my heart' (FC84; FCa110). On 18 May she was due to leave for Switzerland with Sartre, and obviously decided to pull herself together: 'For three weeks now I've scarcely left my room and seen almost no one except Sartre and Bost. It was restful and fruitful' (FC95; FCa125). Her depressed mood, however, was not that easily cast off: in Switzerland she still felt separated from Sartre, resenting their official lunches and engagements as yet another series of interruptions of their tête-à-tête: 'I find this sort of thing even more painful when I am with Sartre. Alone, as in Portugal or Tunis, it's bad enough, but when he's there I always think of the time we could spend together, without the others' (FC97–8; FCa129; TA). However much she tries to persuade herself that she really is having a good time, there is in her text less evidence of 'fruitful rest' than of the unnerving effects of the 'scandal of loneliness and separation'. It is not so much *what* she says, however, as the *genre* in which she says it – that of the diary – that signals the presence of anxiety and distress during this month of her life.

On 13 May Beauvoir re-reads her diary:

I notice as I re-read bits here and there that already it evokes nothing for me. And why should one hope that these words would be different from any others, that they should have the magic power of retaining life within themselves and resuscitating the past? No. For myself the last two weeks are already merely sentences written down, nothing more. Or I would really have to pay attention to how I tell the story [à la façon de raconter]. But that would become a real work [une oeuvre], and I haven't time (FC90; FCa119; TA).[44]

It is as if Beauvoir feels that language is failing her, that it is refusing to signify, and that nothing short of an aesthetic working through of her text would help restore it to life, to make experience seem significant again. What, then, is a 'work' (une oeuvre) for Beauvoir? The word certainly refers to fiction as well as autobiography.[45] For her, the essay has a slightly different status: attempting to communicate through knowledge (par le savoir), she writes, it nevertheless has a 'style, composition, a sense of writing. [. . .] It follows that certain essays may be literary works' ('Mon expérience', pp. 441–2). While the essay sets out to communicate the writer's convictions or insights as precisely and clearly as possible, fiction and autobiography communicate through 'non-knowledge' (par le non-savoir); they seek to capture an existential moment, to 'render a lived experience in its ambiguity and contradictions' ('Mon expérience', p. 442). Although Beauvoir much appreciates the form of the essay, as a writer she ultimately prefers to engage with the nuances and complexities of fiction and autobiography (see 'Mon expérience', p. 455).[46] Given her own understanding of these terms, Beauvoir's greatest essay – The Second Sex – most certainly counts as a 'work', not only because it carries the mark of her own style, but because it does in fact set out to render the nuances and complexities of women's condition in the patriarchal world, not simply through the clear communication of a 'knowledge', but through its acute – and often autobiographical – awareness of the ambiguities and contradictions of women's lived experience in a patriarchal world.

Whether she writes novels or autobiographies, however, Beauvoir writes her 'works' for love. Crying for hours at the death of Maggie Tulliver, the 14-year-old Simone de Beauvoir identified at once with Maggie and with George Eliot: 'one day another adolescent girl would bathe with her tears a novel in which I would tell my own story' (MDD140; MJF195; TA). By the time she was 30, she had not changed in that respect:

I passionately wanted the public to like my work; therefore like George Eliot, who had become identified in my mind with Maggie Tulliver, I would myself become an imaginary character, endowed with necessity, beauty, and a sort of shimmering transparent loveliness. It was this metamorphosis that my ambition sought. [. . .] I dreamed of splitting into two selves, of becoming a shadow that would pierce and haunt people's hearts (PL366; FA418; TA).

At the fantasmatic level writing is to endow the writer with a lovable *alter ego*; fixing the alienated image of the writer for all posterity, writing will allow her to remain in the imaginary forever.

But writing for Beauvoir also has another, slightly different function. Writing, she repeatedly insists, helps writers to break out of their isolation, and to 'go beyond their pain, their anguish, their sadness' ('Mon expérience', pp. 456–7). The essential task of literature, she declares, is to 'speak of our most intimate experiences such as solitude, anguish, the death of people we love, our own death: it is [. . .] a way to get closer to each other, to help each other and to make the world less dark' ('Mon expérience', p. 457). In the 1940s and 1950s the success of *L'Invitée*, of *The Blood of Others* and the *Mandarins* helped Beauvoir to gain a stronger sense of herself as a writer, as an intellectual and as a woman. Towards the end of her life, her readers took over some of the functions the 'little family' once had: granting her an idealized image of herself, in the very act of declaring their love and admiration they also confirmed her status as an autonomous and highly successful woman: in the encounter with her readers Simone de Beauvoir truly balanced her fundamental emotional equation.

For Beauvoir, then, language would seem to be the author's most reliable ally; a faithful workhorse which never fails to convey the desired message.[47] Her understanding of fiction is more interesting: 'Sometimes I thought that words only catch reality after having murdered it; that they let the most important aspect of it – its presence – escape', she writes in *The Prime of Life* (PL40; FA48; TA).[48] Lecturing in Japan in 1966, she returned to this theme: 'To write a novel is in some way to demolish [*pulvériser*] the real world, holding on only to the elements one could introduce in the re-creation of an imaginary world: then everything can be much clearer, much more significant' ('Mon expérience', p. 443). Destroying lived experience, the novel seeks to communicate a meaning that is never present to us *in* that experience. For Beauvoir as for Sartre experience is never 'full': even in the most ecstatic moments of our life, we are always projecting ourselves into the future. The novel, for Beauvoir, is an attempt to *produce* the fullness of experience that always escapes us: 'Personally, one of the reasons why I write is the *inadequacy* of real, lived experience: it haunts my horizon, it beleaguers me, I never quite manage to grasp it' ('Mon expérience', p. 443). Proceeding through the total destruction of experience, the novel succeeds in reconstructing it as more fully significant than it ever was: the seduction of the novel resides precisely in the movement from nothing to everything, from emptiness to fullness.[49] Or – in more psychoanalytic terms – filling the existential void, representing plenitude and significance, the novel becomes the very object that covers up lack: for Beauvoir the novel is a fetish.

A fetish, Freud writes, 'remains a token of triumph over the threat of castration and a protection against it' ('Fetishism', p. 155). The function of the fetish is to mask the absence of the maternal phallus – to plug the gap, one might say; to engage in fetishism is to engage in a certain disavowal of reality.[50] In so far as the fetishist wants to maintain his or her belief in the existence of a phallic mother, this is a highly narcissistic fantasy, yet one that can only arise once the child starts to doubt that the mother does indeed possess the phallus.[51] The ambivalence of the fantasy is striking: the child both sees and does not want to see that the mother is castrated; in so far as it has perceived her lack, it is already in the symbolic order; in so far as it denies the reality of that lack, it refuses to give up its imaginary relationship with the mother. The structure of the fetishistic disavowal displays the same ambivalence in relation to the maternal imago as the ambivalently 'hysterical stage' on which Françoise moves in L'Invitée: in Beauvoir's relationship to writing there is always the same oscillation between plenitude and emptiness, where both poles are inscribed under the sign of the phallic mother who cruelly withdraws or generously extends her breast at will.

In her autobiographical writings Beauvoir's emotional structures are strikingly dualistic: plenitude (life, existence, love, communion, unity) opposes emptiness (death, non-existence, age, loneliness, separation, anguish); on the fantasmatic level, she clearly writes for the one, specular Other that is to hold the narcissist's alienated image together: this is a writing marked by the Imaginary. But fetishism is defined precisely by its ambiguous relationship to signification. In so far as it is marked by fetishistic disavowal, then, Beauvoir's writing is necessarily invested in the pleasures of the symbolic order: representation, transcendence, difference. However much the writing subject indulges in fetishistic fantasies, the text is never simply a fetish: it is also signification, symbolic creation, social action.[52]

This ambiguous relationship to signification is reflected in Beauvoir's remarkable range of tone. As a writer, she is quite unable to conceal the slightest oscillation in her belief in the power of language to signify: her ironic accents, the way she attacks her phrases, the energy she brings to the structuring of her narrative, the intensity of her imagery – these and other elements ceaselessly fluctuate across a spectrum stretching from the mournful and meaningless depths of depression to the jubilant – perhaps cathartic – affirmation of victory over death. At its best her writing lets her affects – joy, anxiety, depression – flow freely through language; at its worst it becomes a lifeless simulacrum of representation in which the only affect conveyed to the reader is that of boredom. It is as if the very texture of Beauvoir's writing displays all the moodiness – and all the incitement to interpretation – embodied in the woman murdered in L'Invitée: in this sense, Xavière becomes a representation of Beauvoir's own écriture.

I now want to take a closer look at the links between this kind of writing and the structures of depression and anxiety that I have studied in this chapter. 'There is no imagination that is not, overtly or secretly, melancholy', Julia Kristeva writes in *Black Sun: Depression and Melancholia* (p. 6).[53] If the artistic imagination is always melancholic, it is because it arises from a desperate sense of exile and separation, caused above all by the unmourned loss of the archaic mother. When we succumb to that mother's hold on our imagination, language ceases to signify: it becomes flat, toneless, it loses its rhythm and its savour; in the end it disappears altogether. But when we succeed in expressing our protest against her absence, expression becomes not only possible, but healing: once we admit that she is lost, the mother can finally be re-presented in language: ' "I have lost an essential object that happens to be [. . .] my mother," is what the speaking being seems to be saying. "But no, I have found her again in signs, or rather since I consent to lose her I have not lost her [. . .], I can recover her in language" ' (*Black Sun*, p. 43).

The depressive subject is nevertheless not constantly locked in the depths of despair: 'When we have been able to go through our melancholia to the point of becoming interested in the life of the signs,' Kristeva writes, 'beauty may also grab hold of us' (*Black Sun*, pp. 99–100). Artistic beauty holds out the promise of reparation, of forgiveness, of healing. By desiring beauty – by writing for the aesthetic, one might say – the depressive imagination sublimates its loss and suffering; fabricating an imaginary object, the melancholic imagination lifts itself out of its own attachment to the death-dealing mother. In so far as such beauty inscribes the traces of the loss and separation that gave rise to it in the first place, it succeeds in *naming* the unspeakable experience of depression, and therefore also opens up a 'space of a necessarily heterogeneous subjectivity', as Kristeva puts it (*Black Sun*, p. 100). The writing subject is, as it were, lifted out of its imaginary dualisms by the connecting – metonymic – powers of the signifier.

If the work ends up *denying* or *erasing* sorrow, however, it loses its significance; for Beauvoir, such writing does not conquer death. The power of Beauvoir's writing, I would argue, is directly dependent on the degree of disavowal she engages in.[54] When she refuses to confront – to *name* – the sources of her pain, her texts read like laundry lists. It is when unspoken suffering blocks Beauvoir's creativity that her language grows flat and her accents lifeless, and her syntax loses its bite.[55] For all their descriptions of sadness, depressive monotony and grandiose breakdowns in bars, her letters and diaries hold back from searching for the deeper causes of her own conflicts. As a result they read as one long disavowal of the pain they so explicitly describe: on every page of her letters to Sartre she complains about her loneliness and emotional neediness *and* assures him that she is perfectly happy, totally satisfied with his love for her, and that she cannot wish for a better life. But this is precisely what Freud understands by disavowal: just as the fetishist both sees and does not see that the mother is castrated, Beauvoir both sees and does not see her own sorrow.

In her published memoirs, such 'writing of disavowal' is particularly noticeable in *All Said and Done*. Written specifically to counter the impression of melancholia left by *Force of Circumstance*, the introduction to the fourth volume of her autobiography seeks not only to present her life as a success story – which of course it was – but specifically to deny the existence, in that story, of loneliness and anxiety. So much disavowal turns the volume into a lifeless ghost of an autobiography, a mere chronicle of official duties, rather than an exploration of lived experience. The same is true for *Adieux: A Farewell to Sartre*, where Beauvoir's bleak and devitalized prose conveys not only her inability to lift herself out of her sorrow, but also her resolute determination not to mention her conflicts with Sartre. For it is not only Sartre's death that pains Beauvoir, it is also his lack of loyalty to her during their final years, his betrayal of what she took to be their common ideals, and his cavalier disregard for her feelings in his dealings with other women. The price she pays is an almost complete blockage of affect in her language: on the pages of *Adieux*, her prose is dry as dust. The contrast to *A Very Easy Death* could not be greater: when Beauvoir finally forces herself to confront her long-buried feelings for her mother, she produces the most vibrant, energetic and moving prose she ever wrote.

Beauvoir's most disturbing and most challenging works – *L'Invitée*, *The Second Sex*, *The Mandarins*, *Memoirs of a Dutiful Daughter* and *A Very Easy Death* – all testify to her ability to convey – and transcend – her sorrow in her writing.[56] Bearing witness to the grandeur of her ceaseless effort to write against death, these texts show her as the acutely original and deeply perceptive writer and intellectual woman she always wanted to be. In some respects, however, I feel that *The Prime of Life* and *Force of Circumstance* remain her most interesting works, not because they always offer the best plots or the most energetic writing, but because they are so profoundly contradictory in tone and style. Veritable battlegrounds for the struggle between self-insight and disavowal, they are not short of passages providing all the interest of an official court calendar: when it comes to boredom, the eighty-seven pages recording the existentialist couple's official visit to Brazil are hard to beat. But at the same time, these volumes contain an extraordinarily honest chronicle of the making of an intellectual woman in mid-century France. Setting out to analyse her own condition with all the precision and courage of a surgeon, Beauvoir's nerve sometimes fails her. But the very instability of her style – the monotonous, disaffected passages, the lacklustre moroseness of her diary excerpts, the vibrant accounts of her writing, or of happy days with Sartre or Algren – tell their own story:

through the oscillations in her tone Beauvoir poignantly conveys to us what it cost her to become a woman admired by a whole world for her independence.

Afterword

'[There is a] question every thinking woman in the Western world must have posed herself one time or another', Angela Carter once wrote: 'Why is a nice girl like Simone wasting her time sucking up to a boring old fart like J.-P.? Her memoirs will be mostly about him; he will scarcely speak of her' (p. 135). At times, I have certainly shared Carter's exasperation with the existentialist womanizer, yet I wonder whether she is right to write him off quite as firmly as she does here. First of all, it needs to be acknowledged that an intellectual woman who values her mind usually wants to be loved for her thinking powers as much as for her sweet temper or sexy legs. Assuming she is heterosexual, intellectual men will always seem attractive to her: they, at least in theory, hold out the promise of intellectual understanding and support. No wonder, then, that the erotico-theoretical dynamics flourished between Simone and Jean-Paul in the Luxembourg Gardens.

To explain why Beauvoir fell in love with Sartre, however, is not the same thing as to explain why she never left him. What possible good did the relationship with Sartre do her after the first seven or ten years? Is Beauvoir not to be faulted for remaining emotionally subservient to her companion? On the one hand, Beauvoir's attempt to forge a new kind of alliance with Sartre has many admirable aspects to it. Her commitment to freedom made her eschew the limitations of traditional, bourgeois marriage. In so doing she inspired countless other women to strike out for freedom in their own lives. It is clear, moreover, that Beauvoir saw her 'necessary love' as a life-long project. One does not abandon a founding project without abandoning the very meaning of one's life, she often says in *Old Age*: there is something heroic about her cast-iron determination to make that central relationship work in spite of everything.

Yet it is equally clear that Beauvoir paid a high emotional price for her commitment to Sartre. It is as if she was under a compulsion to repeat her cycles of depression, anxiety and fear of abandonment throughout her life. So much pain, so much jealousy, and all for the sake of a man? In this book I have used terms such as hysteria and primary narcissism to describe certain psychic structures exhibited by Beauvoir. After reading my manuscript, Julia Kristeva pointed to the masochism of Beauvoir's emotional responses. Nothing, apparently, could make her break out of the vicious emotional circle that led her from emptiness to imaginary fullness to new loss and suffering. Perhaps the presence of pain, in the end, felt more comforting to her than the fearsome emptiness of existential freedom? Yet, however much she suffered, she never abandoned her struggle to incarnate precisely that freedom: it is in that tension that I find the fundamental paradox of Beauvoir's life.

For me, the most striking aspect of Beauvoir's choices is the fact that she consistently refused to examine her own emotional strategies with anything like the discernment she mobilized to analyse those of other women. What would have happened to Simone de Beauvoir had she taken psychoanalysis seriously from the start? But this, clearly, is an anachronistic question. Beauvoir was born into a pre-analytical age: in France in the 1920s, 1930s and 1940s there was little incentive for her or any other intellectuals to consider psychoanalysis as a major influence on their thought or personal lives.

Full of the wisdom of hindsight, some present-day readers confidently recommend alternative lives for Beauvoir: a clean break with Sartre, emigration to Chicago, marriage and motherhood (whether with Sartre or somebody else), open lesbianism. But who are we to say what choices would have been 'better' for Simone de Beauvoir? For all its conflicts and difficulties, the life she chose did in fact make her one of the most influential women in the world. So why is there so much disappointment in the air? Why, after the publication of her letters and diaries, are so many critics voicing their disapproval of Beauvoir's relationship with Sartre? Beauvoir herself is partly to blame for this reaction. Although she never explicitly set her own relationship with Sartre up as an ideal for others to follow, her writing is in fact filled with narcissistic longings for absolute emotional fulfilment. In so far as she also writes in order to make her readers identify with her, on her own terms her memoirs can only be successful if they inspire the same longing in her readers. At the same time, however, readers desperately looking for perfect (as opposed to 'good enough') role models are only too ready to fall into the psychological trap set by Beauvoir. Wanting her to be ideally happy with Sartre, such readers project their own narcissistic ideals onto her: the pain of having to abandon that position is what causes the recent outbursts of disappointment, anger and rejection. The discovery of what Beauvoir's sexual and emotional life was 'really' like makes it difficult to continue to imagine that perfect satisfaction is to be had in this world: perhaps it is not only Simone de Beauvoir who has some difficulty in coming to terms with the reality principle, but her readers as well.

Whether we approve or disapprove of Beauvoir, however, our intense interest in her love life is not fortuitous. More than that of any other woman in this century, her life invites us to consider the question of love and the intellectual woman. Ever since Mary Wollstonecraft first asked her readers to suspend their disbelief and imagine that fiction could be made out of the existence of the 'mind of a woman, who has thinking powers' (*Mary*, p. xxxi), thinking women have worried about their capacity to inspire love. In 1788 Wollstonecraft satisfied all her own daydreams when she made Mary, inspired by the very latest philosophical ideas of the time, launch into a long tirade on the nature of the soul and of human feelings, only to enjoy the moment when the chosen man, Henry, whispers ecstatically: 'Dear enthusiastic creature, [. . .] how you steal into my soul' (*Mary*, p. 40). His soft exclamation is not intended to interrupt her, however, and Mary is allowed to hold forth on the immortal soul for another page and a half. For Wollstonecraft as for Beauvoir, the thinking woman wants to seduce by her *thought*, not simply by her virtue or beauty.

For our foremothers to imagine that such an enterprise could be successful under patriarchy was to indulge in daydreams. In this respect no daydream could be more splendid than that of Madame de Staël, who makes the irresistible Lord Nelvil fall in love with Corinne as she is being crowned on the Capitol of Rome, that is to say, in the very moment of public recognition of her talents: Corinne at least will not have to pretend to be a dumb blonde for ever after. Of course it does not work. Henry dies of consumption, Corinne languishes alone and Lord Nelvil marries the fair Lucile. Given her conviction that an unhappy end is always in store for the intellectual woman, Maggie Tulliver simply refused to finish Mme de Staël's novel: 'As soon as I came to the blond-haired young lady reading in the park, I shut it up and determined to read no further. I foresaw that that light-complexioned girl would win away all the love from Corinne and make her miserable. I'm determined to read no more books where the blond-haired women carry away all the happiness' (*The Mill on the Floss*, p. 312). Maggie's own destiny, which made such a profound impression on Simone de Beauvoir, is an excellent illustration of the conflicts experienced by the intellectual woman in love. Intellectually compatible with Philip Wakem, Maggie knows that she does not love him; caught up in a highly sensual passion for Stephen Guest, she cannot come to terms with the overwhelming physicality of her feelings and prefers to renounce the body altogether. The problem of the intellectual woman's relationship to love – and sexual love at that – is one that George Eliot never ceased to work through: after imprisoning her most accomplished female intellectual, Romola, in a disastrous marriage with the perfidious – but disturbingly sexy – Tito, she makes Dorothea Brooke in *Middlemarch* literally fall in love with Casaubon's mind, only to realize that it takes more than the love of pure minds to satisfy an intellectual woman.

Deploying a pernicious imagery of ugly bluestockings and dried-up spinsters, patriarchal ideology seeks to enforce the split between body and mind with particular rigour in the case of intellectual women. More than any other category of women they have been enjoined to choose between their thoughts and their wish for emotional and sexual happiness. Dorothea Brooke's choice of Casaubon wonderfully illustrates the power of the intellectual woman's desire not to sacrifice her mind for marriage, but also her capacity to divorce her body from her intellectual passions. As long as women were deprived of formal education, they were rarely taken seriously as intellectuals: Dorothea never even considers an intellectual career for herself. In this respect, she is more representative of nineteenth-century women than George Eliot herself.

Simone de Beauvoir's case was different: like many women today, she found herself educated on a par with men and competing with them in their professional sphere. As a result, her erotic and emotional choices were fraught with new complications. The emblematic conversation in the Luxembourg Gardens represents at once Beauvoir's philosophical undoing and her version of Corinne's crowning on the Capitol. Just as Lord Nelvil admired Corinne's poetry, Sartre admired Beauvoir's intellect: discussing her ideas with her for three hours, he earned the right to be her lover. In this context, the fact that he out-argued her does not matter: what matters is that he took her seriously enough as a philosopher to deploy all his usual intellectual passion and skill in order to do so. Unlike Corinne or Maggie, the dark-haired Simone got the chance to construct a life with her lover without having to renounce her intellect: it is easy to see why we so passionately wish for her to be blissfully happy ever after.

Simone de Beauvoir now belongs to a past generation. Her pioneering example has opened the way for women to be taken seriously – and loved – as intellectuals and as women. On the threshold of the twenty-first century, she still makes it easier for us to live our lives as we wish, without regard to patriarchal conventions. My awareness of the complexities and contradictions of her life has added depth to my admiration for Simone de Beauvoir. Her persistent and patient efforts to become an independent woman, to build a literary career for herself, and to devote herself to the solitary task of writing testify to her courage, patience and fortitude. Her absolute insistence, in the face of patriarchal prejudice, on her self-evident right to emotional and sexual happiness is truly exemplary: one could hardly expect her to have done it all without displaying the slightest trace of pain or psychological conflict. It ought not to surprise us that, like the rest of us, she too was torn by the contradictions of a patriarchal society. Reading her autobiography, I am struck at once by her strength, energy and vitality, and by her helplessness and fragility. When I realize how hard it was for her to gain a sense of autonomy and independence, I find her achievements all the more admirable. To admire, however, is not to worship. We do not need to be perfect, Simone de Beauvoir teaches us, we simply need never to give up. To me, that is both a comforting and an utterly daunting prospect.

Notes

Notes to the Introduction

1. Simone de Beauvoir was a white, bourgeois woman brought up in the capital of one of the great European cultural nations. This is precisely my point: given the historical situation of women in the twentieth century, only such a woman could embody the situation of the woman intellectual in its purest form. Given the changing global situation as well as the rapid expansion of women's access to education, there is every reason to hope that the twenty-first century will find that its emblematic intellectual women emerge from quite different circumstances.

2. In addition to *The Second Sex* (1949), one might mention Alva Myrdal and Viola Klein's *Women's Two Roles* (1956), Åse Gruda Skard, *Kvinnesak: tredje akt* (1953); Mary McCarthy, *The Group* (1963; it is worth noting that several chapters of this book were drafted and/or published in the 1950s). Margaret Mead and Hannah Arendt considered questions concerning women well before the war. Mead published *Coming of Age in Samoa* in 1928, *Growing Up in New Guinea* in 1930, and *Sex and Temperament in Three Primitive Societies* in 1935. Arendt started her most 'woman-centred' work, the biography *Rahel Varnhagen*, as early as 1932, finished it in 1939, but did not publish it until 1958. (My information is taken from Engelstad et al., Dahl et al., May, Bok, and Gelderman.)

3. This is hardly due to female stupidity. At the School of English at Birmingham University, 80 per cent of the students are women. 'In 1991, one woman and four men were awarded Firsts; in 1992, five women and one man', Viner writes. 'What made such a difference? In 1992, for the first time, scripts were numbered and anonymous.'

4. The actual figures show $4,915 in median monthly income for men, $3,162 for women. (See table in *The New York Times*, 28 January 1993, p. 11.)

5. See Le Doeuff's 'Long Hair, Short Ideas' in *The Philosophical Imaginary*.

6. I do not mean to say that one *has* to write about *The Second Sex* whenever

one writes about Beauvoir. My point is simply that anybody pretending to produce a reasonably full account of her significance cannot overlook her path-breaking essay.

7. The published English translation of this novel is entitled *She Came to Stay*. The translation itself is excellent, but I find it impossible to use the English title. Here and throughout my book I therefore refer to this particular novel as *L'Invitée*, not as *She Came to Stay*.

8. Biddy Martin, in her study of Lou Andreas Salomé, *Woman and Modernity: The (Life)styles of Lou Andreas Salomé*, shares my impatience with the generic limitations of biography and literary criticism, without quite marking out an alternative position. In practice, I note that my own approach leads me to place a far greater emphasis on the impact of educational institutions on the intellectual woman than does Martin. In the context of modern intellectual women, I find Martin's analysis of the multiple sexual identifications of Salomé extremely interesting, particularly since my own work shows that Simone de Beauvoir demonstrates a fundamental instability or ambiguity in this respect (see, for instance, my analysis of Françoise's 'hysterical stage' in chapter 4, and its re-emergence in *The Second Sex*, as well as the discussion of fetishism in chapter 8).

9. I take this image from Roland Barthes's famous essay 'The Death of the Author'. In my imagination I nevertheless give Barthes's image a Freudian twist: a weave is flat, the Freudian dreamtext is dynamic, shifting and multidimensional.

10. See Saint Martin, 'Les "femmes écrivains" et le champ littéraire,' p. 53. She is referring to Christophe Charle, *Naissance des 'intellectuels' 1880–1990*.

11. I am grateful to Bernard Aresu for drawing the case of Breton to my attention.

Notes to chapter 1

1. Michèle Le Doeuff's reading of the encounter in the Luxembourg Gardens first drew my attention to the passage. Le Doeuff also quotes the entry for Beauvoir in the *Petit Larousse* which I have used as the epigraph for this chapter (see *Hipparchia's Choice*, pp. 135–9). Her work on Beauvoir and Sartre in general (and not least the early essay entitled 'Operative Philosophy'), as well as her pioneering essay 'Long Hair, Short Ideas', have been major sources of inspiration for my own work. To raise the question of Beauvoir's self-image as second to Sartre is not necessarily to concur in her self-assessment. For me as for Le Doeuff, the question of Beauvoir's philosophical and theoretical importance remains to be argued. Beauvoir herself never ceased to insist on her own lack of originality (see for instance the interview entitled 'Being a woman is not enough', p. 109). Some feminists have argued for her originality and influence on Sartre. In 'Simone de Beauvoir: Between Sartre and Merleau-Ponty', Sonia Kruks claims that Sartre sometimes took his cue from her, particularly when it comes to

recognizing the importance of social constraints on individual freedom. Margaret Simons also emphasizes Beauvoir's philosophical independence in her 1986 essay 'Beauvoir and Sartre: The Philosophical Relationship'. My own view is that although Beauvoir remained philosophically dependent on Sartre throughout her life, *The Second Sex* nevertheless represents a surreptitious break with early existentialism. Such covert divergence is presumably what Le Doeuff has in mind when she talks about Simone de Beauvoir being a 'tremendously well-hidden philosopher [*une philosophe formidablement cachée*]' (*Hipparchia's Choice*, p. 139).

2. In her autobiography Clara Malraux furnishes a striking illustration of Beauvoir's analysis of the violence of logical arguments between a husband and wife. Although Clara Malraux does not come across as a particularly reliable narrator, there is no reason to doubt her account of her own *experience* of logical defeat at the hands of the young André Malraux. According to Clara Malraux then, discussions between herself and André took an acrimonious turn before the end of their honeymoon: 'I spoke, not without confusion, of social inequality, of a future revolution in western Europe. The reply I got astonished me – it still astonishes me: "You belong to the kind who wants to kill everybody for the good of the few." But no, it was precisely the opposite that I wanted. As usual, when my views seem to me at once to be important and under attack, I wanted to say everything, got angry, stammered, mixed everything up, and finally finished by a phrase that later I was to have more than ample opportunity to use: "You appear to be right, but I know you are wrong." At the time this phrase made both of us laugh. Later it annoyed him, understandably enough' (*Nos vingt ans*, p. 46).

3. I use the terms 'subjective' and 'objective' here much as Pierre Bourdieu does. 'Subjective' must not at all be taken to mean 'unreliable' or 'unverifiable'. For Bourdieu, anything that is *made public* is an 'objective' factor. For further discussion of this point, see my 'Appropriating Bourdieu: Feminist Theory and Pierre Bourdieu's Sociology of Culture'.

4. For a study of jealousy in the short story 'The Woman Destroyed', see my *Feminist Theory and Simone de Beauvoir*. For a reading of *L'Invitée*, see chapter 4.

5. Anne D. Cordero focuses on this passage as an example of the shortcomings of James Kirkup's translation of *Mémoires d'une jeune fille rangée* (pp. 50–1). My translation differs from hers: I am simply aiming to render the metaphoric connotations of the original as closely as possible in English.

6. I am not at all implying that Simone de Beauvoir simply *was* a heterosexual woman, whatever that might mean. Her complex relationships to women are discussed in chapters 7 and 8. Here, however, I am trying to explore her own *representation* of herself at the time she met Sartre. And in that context, she casts herself as heterosexual.

7. For a detailed analysis of the way in which femininity interacts with various forms of social, educational, intellectual and literary capital, see my 'Appropriating Bourdieu'.

8. I have restored Sartre's emphasis on the word *taste*, which appears in the

original French, but not in the English translation.

9. As one of my students once pointed out, this turns the whale and not Jonah into the subject of knowledge. When Sartre then goes on to refer to the 'Jonah complex' as constitutive of the experience of knowledge, the confusion of subject and object is complete (see BN740; EN640).

10. Lurking under the image of knowledge as undigested incorporation is the ultimate human dream: that of the for-itself which remains for-itself without ceasing to be in-itself. For Sartre, this is the desire to be God: to be at once consciousness *and* that of which one is conscious. Our most fundamental passion, this desire is nevertheless deeply contradictory, and ultimately useless: 'Man', Sartre writes, in the famous last sentence of *Being and Nothingness*, 'is a useless passion' (BN784; EN678).

11. The specific images used here are particularly evident in *L'Invitée*. Through a closer study of such representations of anguish, it is possible to gain a better understanding of the nature of the *crises de larmes* which continued to haunt Simone de Beauvoir throughout her adult life. For a reading of Beauvoir's writing of depression, see chapter 8.

12. Other reference books are not necessarily any better. The Larousse *Dictionnaire de la littérature française et francophone* from 1987 gives Beauvoir one column and a half as opposed to over seven pages on Sartre. The entry for Beauvoir mentions Sartre four times, the entry for Sartre does not mention Beauvoir once. As for Beauvoir, the entry ends by emphasizing the 'contradictions of a person [*un être*] who never found the point of balance between her condition as a woman and as an intellectual'. What annoys me so intensely about that statement, incidentally, is the smugness of tone, the bland assumption that it is *possible* to be a harmonious mixture of woman and intellectual under patriarchy, and, most of all, the arrogant belief that any little writer of dictionaries has the right to accuse women of inferiority if they somehow fail to 'balance' their emotional life under such conditions.

13. From 1935 to 1937 she wrote a third book, quickly rejected by several publishers. That manuscript finally appeared in 1979 under the title *Quand prime le spirituel*.

14. See Jean-Louis Fabiani, *Les philosophes de la république*, particularly the introduction (pp. 7–18), for a discussion of this opposition. Those who read Beauvoir in English should bear in mind that 'teacher' is an imperfect translation of the French *professeur*, which covers everything from university professors to secondary schoolteachers, but excludes primary schoolteachers (*instituteurs*).

15. In *Sartre et 'Les temps modernes'*, Anna Boschetti points to Gide, Proust and Valéry as typifying the *créateur*: 'Gide, Proust and Valéry correspond to the image of the "creator" as much by their social characteristics as by the slowness of their careers. They come from bourgeois or high bourgeois families. [. . .] They are not particularly brilliant students. Early on all three of them frequent literary salons, still decisive for the mutual knowledge and the success of writers' (p. 29). In his 'Normaliens et autres enseignants à la Belle Époque', Victor Karady bears out Georges de Beauvoir's hypothesis

about the somewhat undistinguished class background of secondary schoolteachers at the time.

Notes to chapter 2

1. The psychological aspects of this story are discussed in chapter 1.
2. I am not at all trying to argue that nineteenth-century intellectual women did not produce excellent work: my point is that however original and perceptive they were, their marginalized social and intellectual position made it highly unlikely that their ideas would become influential in society at large. Given the odds against them, the fact that some women nevertheless made themselves heard signals quite exceptional talent and willpower. In her excellent study *Intellectual Women and Victorian Patriarchy*, Deirdre David, while documenting the relative influence and prestige of Harriet Martineau and Elizabeth Barrett Browning, leaves us in no doubt that only one woman, George Eliot, achieved a position of true intellectual influence: 'Martineau was a political journalist and travel writer, Barrett Browning was an intellectual poet, but Eliot was *the* woman intellectual of the Victorian period', David concludes (p. 229).
3. Figures extrapolated from Table XXI, opposite p. 200, in Edmée Charrier, *L'évolution intellectuelle féminine*.
4. The information on Simone de Beauvoir's family background presented here is taken from Francis and Gonthier's biography. Deirdre Bair's more recent, and in general far better biography adds little new information on this specific subject. Bair's account of Beauvoir's university education, in particular, is fairly superficial, and sometimes quite confused.
5. *Daughters of de Beauvoir*, BBC 2, 22 March 1989.
6. I would like to signal the fact that there are considerable – unmarked – differences between the French and English editions of Francis and Gonthier's biography of Beauvoir. On the whole, the English version is far more critical, deleting laudatory terms included in the French edition, and adding hostile passages omitted in French. The difference in tone may have something to do with the fact that the French text appeared in 1985, well before Simone de Beauvoir's death in April 1986, whereas the English version did not appear until 1987. Simone de Beauvoir herself objected violently to what she saw as the inaccuracies of Francis and Gonthier's work, as well as to their persistent tendency to glamorize her life: 'Really, everything from the most insignificant to the most important things is false', she complained in an interview with *Le matin* on 5 December 1985: 'One would think that they were talking about the life of, I don't know, a starlet' ('Simone de Beauvoir: le désaveu'). Francis and Gonthier's reply, where they accuse Beauvoir of 'intellectual imperialism', as well as Beauvoir's rejoinder, may be consulted in *Le matin* 16 December 1985.
7. Francis and Gonthier present a dismal picture of the finances and life-style of

the Beauvoirs after 1919. They tend to cast the family as 'poor', and talk about the 'state of near deprivation in which the family struggled' (p. 35). This is surely an exaggeration: the Beauvoir family seem to have spent what limited resources they had on keeping up a semblance of refined habits, such as ladies' teas, fee-paying schools for their daughters, summers in the country houses of their family connections and so on. This is not a working-class, let alone a 'deprived' upbringing. In her *Souvenirs*, Hélène de Beauvoir makes this point with conviction: 'We lived in straitened circumstances [*la gêne*], but not in destitution [*la misère*]. [. . .] But one had to maintain one's standing, my parents had a maid, their daughters went to an expensive private school, [. . .] my mother was "at home" for ladies' teas and still gave a dinner party from time to time' (p. 26).

8. In the French school system there was a considerable gap in status and prestige between primary and secondary schoolteaching. Whereas primary schoolteaching was considered a lowly and non-intellectual task, secondary schoolteaching was a perfectly acceptable career for an intellectual.

9. The first ENS for women was not Sèvres but Fontenay-aux-Roses (at the same desirable distance from Paris), founded in 1880. In its early days this school was not part of higher education, in that it was primarily intended to educate teachers for the teachers' training colleges that educated primary schoolteachers across the country. Its 'male' counterpart was St Cloud. Both these schools were integrated into the tertiary educational system in France in 1937. For more information on Fontenay-aux-Roses see Yvonne Oulhiou, *L'ENS de Fontenay-aux-Roses à travers le temps 1880–1980*.

10. See Marguerite Cordier, 'Le difficile accès', p. 11, for information on the female *agrégations*.

11. Another important factor was that graduates of modern languages had to spend a considerable time abroad, often studying at foreign universities. Françoise Mayeur argues that, above all, it was these women's prolonged exposure to foreign educational institutions that made them suspect in the eyes of the French academic officials deciding on their careers (p. 133). The information in this and preceding pararagraphs is derived from Mayeur's illuminating study.

12. It is interesting to note that it was far harder for women to gain equal access to the *agrégation* that it was for them to be allowed to study medicine. Already in 1871, the first woman – the American Mary Corinna Putnam – received a medical degree from the Ecole de Médecine in Paris. For more information on women's access to medical education, see Thomas Neville Bonner, *To the Ends of the Earth: Women's Search for Education in Medicine*.

13. It is not surprising, then, that Colette, with her petty bourgeois rural background, did pass this exam. Her account of her experiences of this education is to be found in *Claudine à l'école*.

14. For a list of the rapidly increasing number of Catholic girls' schools in Paris from 1903 to 1916, see Langlois, 'Aux origines de l'enseignement secondaire catholique des jeunes filles', p. 88. There was also a non-religious private academy preparing girls for the *bac*, the so-called Collège Sévigné, founded

by Mathilde Salomon in 1905 (see Mayeur, p. 388).

15. The quotation in the subheading is taken from MDD168; MJF234.

16. In *Madame le Professeur: Women Educators in the Third Republic,* Jo Burr Margadant provides a fascinating account of the personal and professional lives of the first generation of women to be educated at Sèvres (the classes entering from 1881 to 1890).

17. If they declared their intention to return to the independent sector, they would need special ministeral authorization to be allowed to enter the school (Gibon, pp. 189–90).

18. The information in this paragraph is taken from Charrier, pp. 222–3. The number of women at the ENS has been calculated from the *Annuaire de l'ENS* from 1986. From 1926 to 1939 inclusive 746 students entered the school; 37 of these or about 5 per cent were women. If one studies the figures for letters and sciences separately, there is only a slight difference in the proportion of women: 23 women out of 441 students of letters (5.2 per cent) and 14 women out of 305 students of sciences (4.6 per cent).

19. In his voluminous study of students at the Ecole Normal Supérieure and in 'khâgnes' and 'hypokhâgnes' (preparatory classes for ENS entrance exams) throughout France in the 1920s and 1930s, Jean-François Sirinelli includes an interesting discussion of the trajectories of the first women to enter the ENS (see *Génération intellectuelle*, pp. 208–15). It is nevertheless disappointing to discover that these seven pages apparently contain *all* Sirinelli has to say about the specific problems of aspiring women intellectuals in this period. In a book that runs to over 720 pages one might have expected a little more.

20. Interview with Mme Martinet (née Keim) in Paris in June 1988.

21. Mme Danielou was the mother of the cardinal who was to die in somewhat unfortunate circumstances. She was born in 1880 as Madeleine Clamorgan, did the 'licence de Sèvres' and was classed as number one in the female *agrégation* in letters in 1903 (see Jeanne Caron, 'Les débuts de Sainte-Marie', pp. 123–4). It is not correct, as Francis and Gonthier claim, that she 'became the first woman *agrégée*, in literature, in 1903' (p. 49); as we know, women had been sitting the *agrégations féminines* since the early 1880s.

22. Readers of the English translation of *Mémoires d'une jeune fille rangée* should bear in mind that, faced with the impossible task of translating the various French university exams mentioned in the text, the translator tends to use terms such as 'diploma', 'thesis', 'doctorate' or 'degree' without much consistency.

23. Two women passed their *doctorats d'Etat* more or less simultaneously in the spring of 1914. The other pioneer was Jeanne Duportal, who submitted a thesis entitled 'Etude sur les livres à figures édités en France de 1601 à 1660' and a supplementary thesis entitled 'Contribution au catalogue général des livres à figures du XVIIe siècle (1601–1633)'.

24. All quotations in this paragraph are taken from Rocheblave, p. 6.

25. It is difficult to find much material on Léontine Zanta. Françoise d'Eaubonne in her book of reminiscences on Simone de Beauvoir, *Une femme nommée Castor,* claims that Zanta was a household name among educated women in

France in the 1920s: 'All the feminists used to brandish her name like a flag' (footnote, p. 85). Zanta's major publications are as follows: *La renaissance du stoïcisme au XVIe siècle* (doctoral thesis); *La science et l'amour: Journal d'une étudiante* (Paris: Plon, 1921, novel); *Psychologie du féminisme*, Préface de Paul Bourget (Paris: Plon, 1922, essays), *La part du feu* (Paris: Plon, 1927, novel), *Sainte Monique et son fils*, Préface du R. P. Sertillanges (Paris: Plon, 1941, essay). Zanta's supplementary thesis is entitled 'La traduction française du Manuel d'Epictète d'André de Rivaudeau au XVIe siècle, publiée avec une introduction'. In her essays on feminism she argues that women's nature is more idealistic, purer and more absolute than that of men. In an interview in *La Française* on 29 October 1927 she is quoted as saying that 'it seems to me that women have a moral sense, a thirst for the ideal and the absolute, which is lacking in most of their male friends, and this is true for all areas of life.' In the same interview she argues that ideas are not convincing if they remain abstract: it is necessary to give them 'a body, an activity'. The novel *La science et l'amour* shows how young and ardent women students of philosophy at the Sorbonne during World War I become disappointed with the arid and soulless teaching they receive there and finally decide to emigrate to the Institut catholique in search of more spiritual wisdom. Zanta worked as an editor for the *Echo de Paris*, and was a member of the jury for the Fémina prize, one of the more prestigious literary prizes in France (see Marthe Bertheaume, 'L'activité féminine' in *Forces nouvelles*, the journal of a feminist group called 'Comité de propagande féministe'. This specific cutting in the 'Dossier Zanta' at the Bibliothèque Marguerite Durand is unfortunately undated, but must have been published in the late 1920s). Zanta was active in the Conseil national des femmes françaises, founded in 1901, and gave the keynote address to their 'Etats-Généraux du féminisme' in 1929 (reprinted in *La Française* on 23 February 1929).

26.   The first woman *agrégée* in philosophy in France was Mlle Baudry, ranked as number two in 1905 (see Cordier, p. 11).

27.   See Table III in Charrier, p. 113; Cohen-Solal, p. 115. According to Charrier's figures, up to and including 1928 there were eight women *agrégées* in philosophy in France. They qualified in the following years: 1905–1; 1920–1; 1921–2; 1922–1; 1923–1; 1925–1; 1926–1; 1929–4.

28.   See Cordier, p. 11.

29.   I owe some of my anecdotal evidence to Siân Reynolds, who generously provided much useful commentary on an early draft of this chapter, as well as photocopies from the 'Dossier Zanta' at the Bibliothèque Marguerite Durand.

30.   If this sounds like a confusing case of multiple allegiances, I should stress the fact that in Paris *only* the Sorbonne had the right to organize exams for the various university degrees mentioned in this chapter (*licence, diplôme, agrégation*). All students therefore registered at the Sorbonne and had the option of going to lectures there. Since there was no compulsory attendance requirement, candidates were nevertheless free to prepare for the Sorbonne exams in any way they found suitable. This is why the Institut catholique

could prepare its students for Sorbonne exams, and why students from the ENS sometimes attended Sorbonne lectures and sometimes preferred to attend the ENS's own, separate seminars.

31. Sartre, then, was never officially taught by Alain, but given their brilliance, Sartre and Nizan were allowed to sit in on some of his classes at Henri IV while they were still studying for their *bac*.

32. In a late interview with Margaret Simons, Beauvoir discusses her educational experience (see 'Two interviews', particularly pp. 35–6).

33. Sartre suffers from a lapse of memory here. Due to his failure at the *agrégation* in 1928, he actually spent *five* years at their ENS.

34. For examples of Sartre's sexual and sexist metaphors, see chapter 2, part IV ('Faire et avoir'), in *L'être et le néant* and chapter 1 of *Qu'est-ce que la littérature?*. Margery Collins and Christine Pierce ('Holes and Slime') were the first to document Sartre's rhetorical sexism, further illustrated and analysed by Le Doeuff in *Hipparchia's Choice*, 'Operative philosophy' and 'Sartre: l'Unique Sujet parlant'.

35. The affair took place in the mid-1930s: 'After all, I had a serious love affair, a long adventure with Jean Giraudoux. I was very much in love with him; he had the most winsome charm. But he turned out to be extremely or even annoyingly prudent. He was so afraid of being surprised that he never went out with me, but came to see me secretly with a thousand precautions. When one has a lover, one ought to dare to show her in public. In the end I had had enough of these mysterious meetings, and I told him that our secret adventure had come to an end' (Hélène de Beauvoir, *Souvenirs*, p. 122).

36. The 'academy at the end of life' is presumably a reference to the *Académie française*; Giraudoux's fantasy trajectory obviously takes him from consecration at the rue d'Ulm to ultimate glory *sous la Coupole* – under the dome of the Academy.

37. The bulk of this essay has now been incorporated into Bourdieu's major study of the transmission of power in France, *Noblesse d'etat*.

38. Quoted in Cohen-Solal, p. 103.

39. Student rag from the 1920s quoted in Pierre Jeannin, *Ecole Normale Supérieure: livre d'or*, p. 140.

40. This section and the next are endebted to Pierre Bourdieu's analysis of the educational and intellectual field in France. For a full account of the advantages and difficulties of using Bourdieu for feminist purposes, see my 'Appropriating Bourdieu'.

41. Sartre's opposition to all other camps in the French intellectual field signals his self-confidence in taking on all comers at once: he never doubts his legitimacy. Given his supreme consecration by the educational system, there is no reason why he should do so. In the very act of contesting his opponents, he shows his supreme grasp of the rules of the game. The influence of the educational system on the future writer is noticeable even in highly specific rhetorical moves. In 'Modèles scolaires dans l'écriture sartrienne', Geneviève Idt shows how certain rhetorical *topoi* inclucated in French schools, particularly the '*description*', surface in Sartre's *Nausea*. Her point is that Sartre

at once profits from his command of a well-known topos and derives even higher intellectual prestige from his playful subversion of it.

42. See Bourdieu and Saint Martin, 'Les catégories de l'entendement professoral', for an analysis of such teacherly rhetoric.

43. In *Sartre et 'Les temps modernes'*, Anna Boschetti emphasizes Beauvoir's peculiar status as at once richly endowed in intellectual capital of her own, and a simple mirror image of Sartre: 'Her sucess and her trajectory are inseparable from her relationship to Sartre. She is a valuable *alter ego* for him, and her presence on the editorial board would alone be sufficient to indicate Sartre's absolute dominance in the undertaking, since he is the only one to have a "double" at his disposal' (p. 228).

44. I do not mean to say that Beauvoir herself *was* a *petite bourgeoise*. Her *déclassé* social status combined with her intellectual and educational capital makes her a typical member of the 'dominated fractions of the dominant classes', to use a Bourdieuican expression.

Notes to chapter 3

1. This chapter is not intended as a full-scale reception study. A full exploration of the North American reception of Simone de Beauvoir is forthcoming from Nathalie Duval, who kindly let me read her *Maîtrise* dissertation, 'Etude de la réception littéraire du *Deuxième Sexe* de Simone de Beauvoir au Québec francophone et au Canada anglophone' (Nanterre, 1989), as well as her DEA dissertation, 'Simone de Beauvoir: rejets, controverses et légitimation ou la réception de Simone de Beauvoir en Amérique du Nord francophone et anglophone (Québec, Canada et Etats-Unis)' (Nanterre, 1990). I have also learned much about the reception of Simone de Beauvoir in personal conversations with Nathalie Duval.

2. Drawing on magazine and newspaper articles as well as academic research, I do not limit myself to criticism in the academic sense. In order to avoid awkward repetitions, in this chapter I sometimes use the term 'criticism' as a near-synonym to 'reception'.

3. In her fascinating essay on the reception of Marguerite Duras, Jane Winston documents the sexism of responses to Duras's work. On Winston's evidence Duras's critics come across as more overbearing but considerably less vicious than Beauvoir's.

4. In 1992 Bair's biography was followed by Margaret Crosland's *Simone de Beauvoir: The Woman and Her Work*, which adds little to Bair's account.

5. The reason why Le Doeuff does not figure in my list of authors in note 8 is that she has never written a book exclusively devoted to Beauvoir.

6. For a more detailed discussion of this point, see chapter 7.

7. Keefe (see note 8) is an exception to this rule.

8. In my own reading of full-length studies on Beauvoir published in French or English from 1958 to 1992 I found it useful to divide my material into the following rough groups (I have included the year of publication in order to

help the reader identify the emergence and disappearance of the various trends):

Catholic: Henry 1961, Hourdin 1962, Gagnebin 1968.

Existentialist/Socialist: Jeanson 1966, Julienne-Caffié 1966.

Scholarly: Gennari 1958, Berghe 1966, Jaccard 1968, Lasocki 1970, Moubachir 1971, Cayron 1973, Marks 1973, Cottrell 1975, Audet 1979, Bieber 1979, Whitmarsh 1981, Keefe 1983, Marks (ed.) 1987, Hibbs 1989, Brosman 1991.

Popular: Descubes 1974, Madsen 1977, Armogathe 1977, Francis and Niepce 1978, Francis and Gonthier 1985, Eaubonne 1986, Appignanesi 1988, Winegarten 1988, Bair 1990, Crosland 1992.

Feminist: Lilar 1969, Leighton 1975, Ascher 1981, Zéphir 1982, Hatcher 1984, Evans 1985, Okely 1986, Fallaize 1988, Heath 1989, Forster and Sutton 1989, Patterson 1989, Lundgren-Gothlin 1991.

These categories are fairly rough and ready. The division between 'scholarly' and 'popular' is particularly impressionistic. The substantial biographies by Gonthier and Francis and by Bair, for instance, are scholarly, popular and feminist at one and the same time. This list does not encompass books where important chapters or sections are devoted to Beauvoir. I would nevertheless like to mention Nahas 1957 as an important early study partly devoted to Beauvoir. I also consulted Barnes 1959, Fitch 1964, Huvos 1972 and Celeux 1986, all highly scholarly works containing one or more chapters on Beauvoir. A pioneering feminist study is Ophir 1976, which contains a systematic reading of Beauvoir's *The Woman Destroyed*. Evans 1987, Sankovitch 1988, Hewitt 1990 and Sage 1992 also contain interesting feminist readings of Beauvoir.

9. Since I discuss the feminist reception of Simone de Beauvoir in greater detail in the context of my account of *The Second Sex* in chapter 7, this chapter focuses on other political responses to Beauvoir.

10. 'Jeune fille de la ville, simple et frivole'. The example which follows is: 'Goûts, lectures de midinette'.

11. He has competition, however. The obituary in *Minute* after Beauvoir's and Genet's death was entitled 'Deux morts sans importance' ('Two deaths of no importance'), and concluded that now that they are dead, 'this world seems a little bit cleaner [*un peu plus propre*] to us.

12. The great exception here is Francis Jeanson's study of *Memoirs of a Dutiful Daughter*, where he brilliantly demonstrates the way in which serious philosophical concerns underpin the text.

13. It does happen, however. In his *Croquis de mémoire*, Sartre's ex-secretary, Jean Cau, claims that: '"The milk of human kindness" is not only undrinkable, but unknown to him. If he swallowed as much as a mouthful of it, he would think he was taking a drug. He would no longer be, and I'll pronounce the word, free' (p. 251).

14. See for instance pp. 50, 55, 111, 123, 137.

15. The last sentence is awkward to translate. The original reads: 'Et cette oeuvre

d'une ambition toute masculine suscite plus de curiosité qu'elle n'exerce d'influence vraie.'

16. I agree with Marks that Beauvoir is haunted by a sense of emptiness. I also agree with her that Beauvoir's works display remarkable oscillations in tone. But I cannot see that this has much to do with Beauvoir's political commitments, one way or the other. It is simply not true that every 'political' passage in Beauvoir's works displays a 'journalistic' style, as Marks says. Beauvoir's accounts, in *Force of Circumstance*, of the agonies of the war in Algeria are as powerful and energetic as anything she wrote. The variations in Beauvoir's style cannot be explained by positing a clear-cut opposition between history and death; rather, they must be considered fluctuations across a depressive range (see chapter 8 for further discussion of this point). For me, it is not death *per se* but depression that exerts pressure on Beauvoir's prose. Marks is nevertheless the only critic I have come across who really tries to make sense of Beauvoir's style.

17. All references from Reuillard. Unfortunately page numbers were not provided on the cuttings in the Bibliothèque Marguerite Durand.

18. 'Simone de Beauvoir ou le corps enseignant', quips *Carrefour*, 'Une épouvantable donneuse de leçons', complains Jacques Henric.

19. I am indebted to Culler's discussion of irony in his *Flaubert*, pp. 185–207.

Notes to chapter 4

1. I should perhaps remind my readers that the English title of *L'Invitée* is *She Came to Stay*, and that I find it hard to use that title in my own work.

2. Karen McPherson ('Criminal Passions') shares my interest in the *raison d'être* of the final murder, as well as in the excess of Beauvoir's language in *L'Invitée*. Although I do not enter into extensive dialogue with other critics of *L'Invitée*, I would like to signal my appreciation of Elizabeth Fallaize's fine reading of the novel (in *Simone de Beauvoir*), and of Jane Heath's valuable effort to read the text from the point of view of psychoanalytically inspired poststructuralism. Feminists such as Mary Evans, Martha Noel Evans and Jean Leighton have provided highly critical accounts of Beauvoir's first novel: in many cases my readings differ sharply from theirs.

3. Feminist film critics have contributed decisively to our understanding of the melodramatic mode. I am convinced that all of Simone de Beauvoir's fiction may profitably be read from such a perspective. A useful introduction to feminist readings of melodrama can be found in Christine Gledhill's anthology *Home is Where the Heart Is*.

4. Mary Lydon's essay on 'Hats and Cocktails' gives a witty account of the textual vicissitudes of cocktails in Beauvoir's *oeuvre*.

5. The English translation of *Being and Nothingness* has 'slimy' for *visqueux*. In some cases this is an excellent translation, in others it comes across as far too repulsive. Some of Sartre's examples of 'viscosity', such as tar, glue and honey, are not 'slimy'. I do not think my own translation of 'stickiness' is

generally superior to Hazel Barnes's 'sliminess' (one cannot talk about a 'sticky' fellow, for instance), but it suits the examples I use here somewhat better.

6. For an analysis of this phenomenon in philosophy, see Michèle Le Doeuff, *Hipparchia's Choice*. See also chapter 6 below for a discussion of the sexist effects of certain existentialist metaphors.

7. Sartre's turn of phrase ('if one knows how to question them'), alluding to the superior insight of the confident explorer of tastes, reminds me irresistibly of Freud's proud confidence in his own psychoanalytic capacity to detect the secrets of Dora: 'He that has eyes to see and ears to hear may convince himself that no mortal can keep a secret. If his lips are silent, he chatters with his finger-tips; betrayal oozes out of him at every pore. And thus the task of making conscious the most hidden recesses of the mind is one which it is quite possible to accomplish' (*Fragment of an Analysis of a Case of Hysteria*, pp. 77–8).

8. James Kirkup's English translation misunderstands Beauvoir's reference to the *petits camarades* (she even puts the expression in inverted commas to signal its specific slang usage, where it means 'fellow students at the ENS'), and translates 'left-wingers'. The same passage also has 'betrayal' for *mauvaise foi*. This makes it almost impossible for the English-language reader of Beauvoir to grasp the double reference – to the all-male intellectual hothouse of the Ecole Normale and to Sartre's philosophy – implicit in Beauvoir's description of their 'pact' of total openness to each other. For further discussion of the shortcomings of Kirkup's translation see Anne D. Cordero's 'Simone de Beauvoir Twice Removed'. Although I agree with much of Cordero's assessment of Kirkup's version of Beauvoir, her conviction that a British translation must always be unsuitable for American readers (and *vice versa*) strikes me as rather strange.

9. I am aware that the Sartrean morality expressed in *L'existentialisme est un humanisme* is more simplistic than the general philosophy in *Being and Nothingness*. This is particularly obvious when it comes to Sartre's Kantian invocation of the necessity to choose as if one were choosing for everybody else as well, an idea which is nowhere to be found in *Being and Nothingness*.

10. If anything, Simone de Beauvoir, particularly in early texts such as *Pyrrhus et Cinéas*, *L'existentialisme et la sagesse des nations* and *The Ethics of Ambiguity*, is even more starkly moralistic than Sartre. In *L'Invitée*, for example, the character of Elisabeth, Pierre's sister, is given short shrift from the start. Xavière perceives her as false, Françoise realizes that she simply cannot tell Elisabeth her *true* opinion of Elisabeth's lover Claude, and Elisabeth herself is shown to be ruled entirely by the desire to build up an image. Hopelessly inauthentic, Elisabeth takes her values from other people; she is a classic case of bad faith.

11. Andrew Leak (*The Perverted Consciousness*) and Josette Pacaly (*Sartre au miroir*) have produced interesting psychoanalytic readings of Sartre's *oeuvre*. The project I am gesturing towards here is methodologically close to that of Michèle Le Doeuff, who has shown how Sartre's implicit sexism sometimes

destroys the logic of his own arguments (see particularly her entertaining discussion of Sartre's account of the bad faith of frigid women who nevertheless exhibit 'objective signs of pleasure,' in *Hipparchia's Choice*, pp. 64–8).

12.   This highly philosophical epigraph has unfortunately been omitted from the English translation.

13.   In a brief discussion with Xavière, the 30-year-old Françoise tells us that it deals with her youth: 'I want to explain in my story why people are so often misfits [*disgracié*] when they're young' (SC134; I170).

14.   In his perspicacious reading of *L'Invitée*, Merleau-Ponty sees this as a piece of good fortune for Françoise: 'By an extraordinary piece of luck, even love has not made her realize her limits. Doubtless Pierre has come to be more to her than an object in her own particular world, a backdrop for her life as other men are. But for all that, he is not an Other' ('Metaphysics and the Novel', p. 34).

15.   In her study of *The Second Sex* Eva Lundgren-Gothlin stresses the fact that Beauvoir does not remain wedded to this view, but instead strongly affirms the possibility of reciprocity between consciousnesses. I discuss the way Beauvoir sets up reciprocity as a utopian ideal for relationships in chapter 7 below.

16.   See for instance *Lettres au Castor*, vol. 1, pp. 359–60 and p. 391; as well as vol. 2, p. 70. See also chapter 8 below for further discussion of this problematic sense of 'unity'.

17.   Beauvoir's *Letters to Sartre* also demonstrate her cool relationship with Wanda in 1939–40. Whereas Olga by this time had become simply a close and often cheerful friend, Wanda would seem to have felt considerable hostility and jealousy towards Beauvoir.

18.   *Grouiller* literally means to swarm, teem, crawl or to be alive with, and is often – but by no means exclusively – used in connection with vermin, worms and the like.

19.   The whole section on knowledge in *Being and Nothingness* (see BN737–40; EN638–41) is illuminating reading for feminists, with its bizarre insistence on metaphors of rape and penetration of virgins on the one hand and eating, swallowing and digestion on the other.

20.   Françoise's first real perception of Xavière as a sexual woman takes place well before this paroxysmal scene, when Françoise is still in hospital: 'Françoise looked at her a little uneasily; it seemed sacrilegious to think of this virtuous little madam as a woman, with the desires of a woman. But how did she think of herself? What dreams of sensuality and amorous passion made her nose and mouth quiver? What picture of herself, concealed from the eyes of the world, was she smiling at with mysterious connivance? Xavière, at this moment, was aware of her body, she knew herself to be a woman, and Françoise felt that she was being duped by an ironical stranger hiding behind familiar features' (SC183; I228–9).

21.   'If at least nothing had remained of her!', Françoise exclaims: 'Yet there remained a faint phosphorescence hovering over the surface of things'

(SC293; I365; TA). My translation of the first sentence is quite different from the published English version ('Had she perchance become a complete void!'). The original French reads, 'Si au moins plus rien n'était demeuré d'elle.'

22. For a detailed reading of the seduction scene, see chapter 5.

23. From a psychoanalytic perspective, there is perhaps some entertainment to be derived from the fact that the key is stolen out of the innermost *pocket* of Françoise's *bag*. In Beauvoir's writing there is an interesting parallel between Xavière's stealing of the key from Françoise's bag, and Anne's confiscation of a small vial of poison from Paule's handbag in *The Mandarins*.

24. The term 'family romance' may be slightly imprecise here. Strictly speaking, Freud takes the child's 'family romance' to be the fantasy of having different parents (see his 1909 paper 'Family Romances'). Here I use it simply to refer to a fantasy of any family constellation. Nor does my usage here converge with the literary fantasy explored by Marthe Robert. It is not easy to read *L'Invitée* as a literary family romance in the sense indicated by Robert. Her models tend to fit either straightforwardly pre-Oedipal plots ('the foundling fantasy') or male Oedipal ('the bastard fantasy') plots. It is difficult to fit the highly ambivalent Oedipal position of a girl into either one of the two categories proposed by Robert.

25. It is also quite striking to note that she names the heroine of her second novel, *The Blood of Others*, Hélène. Presumably she had not forgotten that her only sister was called Hélène.

26. This is not by any means to be taken as a general theory of homosexuality in women. As far as I can see, Chasseguet-Smirgel only wants to indicate that this may be one among many other ways to arrive at a homosexual object choice. On my reading of psychoanalytic theory there is nothing self-evident about the route to a heterosexual object choice either.

27. In her study of Beauvoir, Jane Heath argues that while Xavière represents femininity, Françoise is, however problematically, masculine: 'In Xavière, [the text] represents a dynamic and subversive femininity which exceeds all masculine efforts at containment and control. It is so threatening that it must, ultimately, be eradicated, killed off', Heath writes; 'Xavière's murder [is] the justifiable and legitimate act of the forces of law and order – a fatal phallic backlash' (p. 43). While I agree with much of Heath's reading (in particular with the fact that the text exceeds a simple Oedipal scenario), I do not think it is helpful to cast Françoise simply as 'masculine' or even as 'phallic'. I hasten to add that Jane Heath is by no means the worst offender in this respect: far too many readers of Beauvoir seem only too happy to argue in terms of the most traditional notions of femininity and masculinity, a theoretical choice which more often than not forces the critic to declare Beauvoir or her heroines 'masculine' as soon as they express the slightest taste for mastery or control. When it comes to *L'Invitée*, the whole point, after all, is that Françoise is a *woman* occupying a specific psychic position which must be described in some detail. When a man and a woman occupy the *same* psychic position, their positions are – necessarily – *different*. For a man to be 'phallic'

is not the same thing as for a woman to be so. It is unhelpful to say, as Heath does, that 'Pierre and Françoise are inscribed within the phallic economy. They are both masculine' (p. 42). Even if this were true, it does not make the two protagonists equal. As a woman under patriarchy Françoise would have travelled quite a different route to get to the 'same' point as Pierre. That is true sociologically as well as psychologically: when Beauvoir and Sartre sit the same exam in 1929, this event has widely different significations for them. It is also relatively useless to cast Xavière as 'femininity' without adding that she represents a historically specific and highly patriarchal construction of femininity. I can see no reason to valorize Xavière over Françoise on the grounds that the one is so much more 'feminine' than the other. To me, Françoise's psycho-social position – that of the daughter struggling to separate from the mother – is no more and no less 'feminine' than the extreme case of secondary narcissism represented by Xavière.

28.   It is quite possible to go on to analyse many of Beauvoir's major texts (including the autobiographies) as *hysterical* in this sense. Freud's Dora is not at all unrelated to Beauvoir's existential heroines.

29.   For an attempt to provide this kind of reading of Dora, see my 'Representation of Patriarchy: Sexuality and Epistemology in Freud's Dora'.

30.   For a discussion of a fairly similar case of idealization of men in *The Second Sex*, see chapter 6.

31.   On this point my reading rejoins that of Alice Jardine, who in her 'Death Sentences' argues that in *A Very Easy Death* and *Adieux: A Farewell to Sartre*, Sartre represents a phallic mother-figure for Beauvoir (see Jardine, p. 215).

32.   For an interesting exploration of the modernism of these heroines see Susan Rubin Suleiman, 'Nadja, Dora, Lol V. Stein'.

33.   This observation might lead to a theorization of Beauvoir's writing in terms of Julia Kristeva's notion of the relationship between depression, loss of the mother, and creativity, as developed in *Black Sun*. Françoise's anxiety crises – and Beauvoir's own, for that matter – can usefully be read in the light of Kristeva's views on depression as the source of a certain kind of creativity. I return to these matters in chapter 8. In a private communication, Julia Kristeva stresses the death-dealing nature of the plot of *L'Invitée*. In so far as it seems to be marked by the death drive, Kristeva suggests, the killing of Xavière would be more than just a melodramatic scenario, it would also reveal the psychosis of the female narrator.

Notes to chapter 5

1.   'Beauvoir [. . .] recognized earlier than did Sartre the limiting effects of the social-historical context, including one's personal history and childhood, upon an individual's choice,' Margaret Simons writes ('Beauvoir and Sartre,' p. 169).

2.   In *Hipparchia's Choice* Michèle Le Doeuff was the first to draw attention to the curious politics of Sartre's accounts of bad faith. According to Le Doeuff,

there is in Sartre's writings a tendency to attribute bad faith primarily to women and subordinate or marginal males such as waiters, students and homosexuals (see pp. 70–4).

3. In French: *Je vous admire tant*. The English translation here has 'I find you so attractive,' which is already an interpretation, precisely of the kind Sartre would want the woman to have.

4. Hazel Barnes's translation of *le désir cru et nu* is, strangely enough, 'the desire cruel and naked.' While there may well be some cruelty in 'crude' male desire, I doubt that Sartre intended to say so.

5. The dictionary actually claims that these relations take place 'between persons of different sex', but I can see no reason why persons of the same sex should not engage in flirtation, or seduction for that matter.

6. Or in other words: every flirtation contains an element of danger. This is surely why apparently 'innocent' flirtations may provoke strong feelings of jealousy in the flirtatious person's partner, and why, in many historical periods, 'true' decency in a woman has been considered incompatible with even the mildest flirting.

7. The very ambiguity of the idea of flirtation guarantees that there will be all sorts of intermediate positions between flirting and seduction. My aim here is not to provide a general analysis of such activities, but simply to sketch out some definitions which would seem to be operative in Sartre's text.

8. I am not, of course, claiming that women never cynically seduce unsuspecting young men; I am simply saying that under patriarchy, power relations between the sexes tend to favour male attempts at seduction.

9. Perhaps the relationship between flirtation and seduction may be conceived of as a continuum, in which the extreme positions are represented by an exchange of smiles in the grocer's shop on the one hand, and Valmont's cynical debauching of Cécile de Volanges on the other. In the middle of this sliding scale there will be a large grey area in which subtle shades of seduction and flirtation will be acted out. This area will certainly allow abundant misunderstandings to take place.

10. As Michèle Le Doeuff has shown in *Hipparchia's Choice*, Sartre's account of frigidity in women (BN95–6; EN89–90) provides an even more striking example of his belief in his own epistemological superiority (see pp. 64–8).

11. I am not assuming that everything Sartre says in the section on bad faith in *Being and Nothingness* is compatible with his post-war essay. In *Being and Nothingness*, for instance, bad faith is more specifically seen as the refusal to choose between facticity and transcendence, between thinking of oneself as a mere thing in the world (as an *en-soi*, Sartre would say) and thinking of oneself as a transcendent consciousness (as a *pour-soi*). Affirming the identity of such mutually exclusive concepts, yet all the while insisting on the differences between them, bad faith posits the non-contradiction of contradictory positions (see BN98; EN92). Every attempt to give oneself a stable definition falls under the notion of bad faith. If I claim to be sincere, for instance, I am turning my transcendence into facticity just as much as if I claim that my hand is an inert thing on a café table: bad faith is inherent in

the very structure of human consciousness, which always strives to coincide with itself. In this sense, we are all in bad faith, or rather, as Sartre puts it in a footnote, it is 'indifferent whether one is in good or in bad faith' (BN111; EN107). This does not prevent Sartre's actual description of bad faith in this woman from slipping from the austerely technical towards psychological moralizing. In *A Preface to Sartre*, Dominick LaCapra gives a useful account of the discrepancies and difficulties of Sartre's concept of bad faith, particularly on pp. 130–4.

12. I discuss Beauvoir's account of the male body at some length in chapter 6.

13. See Chabrol's film *Une affaire de femmes* (*A Story of Women*) for an unsettling reconstruction of Marie-Jeanne Latour's life.

14. I am not, of course, arguing that *I*, unlike Sartre, *know* that the woman has a project of her own. After all, this 'woman' is nothing but a philosophical illustration intended to prove Sartre's point. My intention is rather to point to the limitations of Sartre's philosophical imagination: the scandal is that Sartre never even stops to *consider* alternative explanations of the woman's behaviour.

15. In *What is Literature?* Sartre explicitly opposes the freedom and generosity of the acts of reading and writing to the idea of being *obliged* to do something. When it comes to readers and writers, to be free is to act generously and with confidence in the other's freedom; when it comes to men and women, apparently, it is not quite that simple (see pp. 61–2).

16. In a brief discussion of this scene Lorna Sage interestingly notes that 'Beauvoir's woman [. . .] is a lot sadder than Sartre's' (p. 6).

17. In a footnote in *The Literature of Possibility* Hazel Barnes also draws attention to the man's bad faith: 'What strikes me as odd', she writes, 'is that neither Sartre nor de Beauvoir points out that there is some bad faith on the man's side as well. His choice of ambiguous words is explicitly designed to allow him to retreat rapidly to the plane of polite friendship in case he has misjudged the situation' (p. 52).

18. In his paper 'Le mort saisit le vif', Bourdieu gives a brilliant analysis of Sartre's other famous example of bad faith, the café waiter who plays the role of a café waiter. For Bourdieu, Sartre's account should be read as an anthropological document which says a lot more about Sartre than it does about café waiters: 'empowered by his exemplary use of the phenomenological *I*,' Bourdieu writes, '[Sartre] projects an intellectual's consciousness into the practice of a cafe waiter, producing a kind of social chimera, a monster with the body of a waiter and the head of an intellectual' (p. 9).

19. I will return to the question of whether this *is* a scene of seduction.

20. In *The Prime of Life* Beauvoir calls her 'Cécilia Bertin'. Given this profusion of names, it is hard to know which one to use. I have opted for the one that is used more frequently, and have settled for 'Martine Bourdin', in inverted commas. Sartre's letters are not always dated, but comparing them to Beauvoir's carefully dated letters, it is not hard to reconstruct the chronology of these events.

21. Apparently, 'Martine Bourdin' (alias 'Cécilia Bertin,' alias Colette Gibert)

had believed that she was having a serious affair with Sartre. At one point she showed Sartre's letters to her to Moloudji, and rumours that Sartre was still seeing 'Bourdin' sent Wanda into a jealous fit. Outraged by 'Bourdin's' attempt to spread her version of the story, Sartre writes an open letter to 'Bourdin', which he asks Wanda to pass on to her. Beauvoir receives a copy of everything and instructions to make quite sure that Sartre's version of events prevails. His letter to 'Bourdin' would make Valmont pale with envy: 'I never loved you,' he writes, 'I found you physically attractive, although a bit vulgar, but your very vulgarity appealed to my own sadistic tendencies' (*Lettres au Castor*, vol. 2, p. 90). As for his letters to her, they were nothing but 'practice in passionate literature: how the Beaver [Beauvoir] and I laughed!' (p. 91). After having attacked the poor woman's sexuality as well as her sentimentality, he also dismisses her intelligence ('Martine Bourdin' was a philosophy student): 'And then, on top of everything, I had to listen to your pretentious chit-chat, your philosophical galimatias', he complains (p. 91). In her review of Sartre's *Lettres au Castor* Michèle Le Doeuff gives a fine analysis of the sexual and discursive politics of this scene ('Sartre: l'Unique Sujet parlant').

22. In the last chapter of *The Second Sex* Beauvoir also discusses the sexual situation of the independent woman at great length.

23. I can think of two near precursors. Rachilde's *Monsieur Vénus*, first published in 1887, offers a fascinating description of the aristocratic heroine, Raoule de Vénérande's, sexual desire for the young and poor Jacques Silvert. As a whole Rachilde's text is ruled by a logic of reversal: the high point of the plot being reached when Jacques notices Raoule's breast in bed and cries out in utter frustration: 'So you are not a man, Raoule? You really can't be a man?' (p. 198). While the breast here seems to have acquired the castrating effect normally ascribed to the phallus, such sexual confusion in Rachilde's text leads to social isolation and suicide. Rachilde's main preoccupation, however, is desire and sexual ambiguity, not freedom, and she tends to write as if her heroine exists for the sake of sexuality alone. The other woman writer relevant in this context is of course Colette. But while Colette often describes the relationship of an older woman and a younger man, they are either described from the young man's point of view (*Le blé en herbe*), or start *in medias res*, after the initiation of the relationship (*Chéri*). In these books the older women are never professional women. In one sense, the novel by Colette closest in spirit to the problematics raised by Beauvoir here is *La vagabonde*, where Renée Néré struggles to make a living as an independent woman, and where her rich lover's money is experienced as a threat to her freedom.

24. In *The Second Sex*, Beauvoir returns to the question of the 'woman who takes'. To believe that a woman can 'take' in this sense, she argues, is false. Men are not seduced by an active woman, Beauvoir claims; the 'woman who takes' must still *offer* herself to the man: 'Woman, therefore, can take only when she makes herself prey: she must become a passive thing, a promise of submission', she concludes (SS698; DSb610). Here as everywhere else in the

second volume of *The Second Sex*, Beauvoir is referring to the situation in France in 1949 (see SS31; DSb9). It is striking to notice that Françoise in 1943 is allowed more activity and more freedom than the 'woman who takes' in *The Second Sex*. The difference is probably caused by two factors: first, Beauvoir identifies with Françoise but feels no kinship with the hypothetical woman in *The Second Sex*. Secondly, *The Second Sex* focuses on the role of the body, whereas *L'Invitée* erases the body from the scene of seduction. As we shall see, it is not so difficult for Beauvoir to represent Françoise's *consciousness* as free: the question is whether the female *body* can ever be free.

25. In her letter of 27 July 1938, Beauvoir gives the following account of this exchange: 'In the end I laughed foolishly and looked at him, so he said: 'Why are you laughing?' and I said: 'I'm trying to picture your face if I suggested that you sleep with me' and he said: 'I was thinking that you were thinking that I wanted to kiss you but didn't dare.' After that we floundered on for another quarter of an hour before he made up his mind to kiss me' (LS21; LSa62–3; TA).

26. It is interesting to note that Beauvoir herself admits to a certain penchant for sentimental and vaguely romantic texts. In 1930 she started work on a novel inspired by Alain-Fournier's *Le Grand Meaulnes* and Rosamond Lehmann's *Dusty Answer*. (Translated into French under the title *Poussière*, Lehmann's novel remained one of Beauvoir's favourite texts: there is an interesting study to be done on the implications of Beauvoir's lifelong admiration for the British writer.) 'I became vaguely aware that enchantment [*le merveilleux*] didn't do much for me, though this didn't prevent me from chasing it stubbornly, and for a long time. I still have a touch of 'Delly' about me; it is very noticeable in the first drafts of my novels' (PL60; FA71; TA). 'Delly' was the pseudonym of Jeanne and Frédéric Petitjean de la Rosière, whose sentimental novels long dominated the market for popular romances in France. When it comes to the end of the seduction chapter in *L'Invitée*, one has to conclude that the 'Delly' side of her imagination remained evident even in the final version.

27. 'All popular romantic fiction', Radway writes in *Reading the Romance*, 'originates in the failure of patriarchal culture to satisfy its female members. Consequently, the romance functions always as a utopian wish-fulfilment fantasy through which women try to imagine themselves as they often are not in day-to-day existence, that is, as happy and content' (p. 151). Ultimately, Radway argues, the 'ideal romance' gives women a representation of an 'exclusive and intense emotional relationship with a tender, life-giving individual', that is to say, with the pre-Oedipal mother (p. 151). In her interesting essay 'Resisting Romance: Simone de Beauvoir, "The Woman Destroyed" and the Romance Script', Elizabeth Fallaize discusses the relationship between Beauvoir's text and the romance plot.

28. I discuss this point in greater detail in chapter 6.

29. In his short paper entitled 'Sartre', Pierre Bourdieu makes this point with conviction.

30. Such a bridging is made possible precisely because existentialist philosophy is

so crucially concerned not only with fundamental human situations but also with the interpretation of everyday events. See chapter 4 for a more detailed account of Sartre's and Beauvoir's quest for existential meaning in everyday life.

Notes to chapter 6

1. Raising the question of the relationship between freedom and the individual's situation, Sartre writes: 'All these questions, which refer us to a pure and not an accessory reflection, can find their reply only on the ethical plane. We shall devote to them a future work' (BN798; EN692). His notes and drafts from this period were published in 1983 under the title *Cahiers pour une morale*.

2. According to Beauvoir, the specific historical situation of France in the years when the Cold War took hold of Europe made a preoccupation with ethics almost inevitable: 'So soon after a war which had forced us to re-examine all our ideas, it was natural enough to attempt to reinvent rules and reasons. France was crushed between two blocs, our fate was being decided without us; this state of passivity prevented us from taking practice as our law; my moralism doesn't surprise me' (FC76; FCa100; TA). Sartre too worked on ethics throughout the 1940s. His 1946 lecture, *L'existentialisme est un humanisme*, has a much more explicitly 'moral' slant than *Being and Nothingness*, and all his post-war plays are primarily concerned with moral issues. Already in *Pyrrhus et Cinéas* (1944), Beauvoir raised the question of the ethical uses of freedom. In 1945 and 1946 she wrote several essays on specific questions of ethics (the punishment of collaborators, the role of engagement in literature, and so on) for *Les temps modernes*. These essays were republished in 1948 under the title *L'existentialisme et la sagesse des nations*. In June 1946 Beauvoir published the first draft of some of the introductory sections of *The Ethics of Ambiguity*, in a paper entitled 'Introduction à une morale de l'ambiguïté', which appeared in *Labyrinthe* 20 (1 June 1946). The text is reprinted in Francis and Gonthier, *Les Ecrits de Simone de Beauvoir*, pp. 337–43.

3. Here and throughout this chapter I run up against a linguistic and ideological difficulty. Sartre and Beauvoir normally write 'man' [*l'homme*] for 'human beings', and Beauvoir often writes 'woman' where I would prefer 'women'. In many contexts, I cannot bring myself to adopt their usage. In others, the context and syntactical structure of the argument makes it impossible not to imitate them. In general, however, I try neither to change my own style nor to amend theirs.

4. According to Beauvoir, it is when I fully accept this tension, the fundamental ambiguity of my mode of being in the world, that I act morally – or 'authentically'. This positive acceptance of failure is what Beauvoir calls *conversion*: at a stroke our failure to be is converted into the positive source of our existence. Her point is, I think, that we have to live the contradiction

between the negativity of being and the positivity of existence precisely as a contradiction, as an ever-present conflict producing the paradoxical ambiguity of our lives.

5. In *The Ethics of Ambiguity* Beauvoir already makes a similar claim: 'The negro slave of the eighteenth century, the Mohammedan woman enclosed in a harem have no instrument, be it in thought or by astonishment or anger, which permits them to attack the civilization which oppresses them' (EA38; MA56). Since their situation prevents them from realizing their original freedom in the world, she argues, they are not guilty of bad faith.

6. Beauvoir's concern for the social situation of the subject was always greater than Sartre's. Many feminists have produced excellent readings of this aspect of Beauvoir's work. See particularly Simons, 'Beauvoir and Sartre', and Lundgren-Gothlin.

7. I define metaphor as a figure based on the principle of likeness or similarity.

8. I take metonymy to be a figure based on the principle of contiguity or proximity. Synecdoche (also known as *pars pro toto*) is one particular kind of metonomy where the part is taken for the whole.

9. I would like to stress the fact that Beauvoir is hardly the only philosopher in the Western tradition to be caught in this specific figural trap. When it comes to mistaking consciousness for the whole of the human being, Sartre and Beauvoir are deeply indebted to Descartes. In both cases, the effect of the figure is to cast consciousness as radically disembodied.

10. My argument differs sharply from that of Moira Gatens in *Feminism and Philosophy*, who holds that the very act of appropriating existing theories for feminism necessarily presupposes the belief that 'these theories are *essentially* sex-neutral tools that become sexist [. . .] in the hands of a Rousseau or a Freud' (p. 2). I do not assume any such thing: in my view, every theory *is* its language, and no language can ever be said to be socially 'neutral'. By analysing the old metaphors, and suggesting new ones, I am transforming – not totally rejecting – the theory. If I suggest metaphors which are relatively unmarked by sexual difference, it is because they are intended to further a specific feminist project: they are no more politically 'neutral' than Sartre's or Beauvoir's. In my view, Gatens's study of sexism in philosophy loses much of its interest precisely because she fails to consider the *language* of philosophy. She also underestimates the impact of personal and institutional factors on any act of writing: as I am attempting to show in this book, the personal and social unconscious of the author tends to leave its traces on every text, even the text of philosophy.

11. I take this information from Lundgren-Gothlin, p. 324. See too Lundgren-Gothlin, pp. 322–40, for a thorough discussion of the opposition between transcendence and immanence in *The Second Sex*. Lundgren-Gothlin also points out that in *The Second Sex* Beauvoir tends to substitute the term 'immanence' for that of 'bad faith'.

12. I return to this theme in chapter 8.

13. In this crucial phrase, the Folio edition reads 's'assumer *contre* l'Autre' (DSa31). Introducing a wholly erroneous idea of opposition, this misprint

may give rise to many misunderstandings. Fortunately the original *édition Blanche* correctly prints 's'assumer *comme* l'Autre' (p. 31).

14. Since I do not go on to discuss the subject/object division in *The Second Sex* in any detail, I would like to stress that Beauvoir – like Sartre – at times conflates the idea of objectification as a value-neutral state of being other to a subject (in this, rather Hegelian sense, we are all objects for each other, and there is nothing particularly distressing about that); and as a morally and politically degraded state of *reification* and *alienation*. Again, the slippage from fact to value is obvious.

15. At this point one may well ask why it is not the other way round: could one not argue that the ontological ambiguity mirrors the social conditions of existence? Taking ontology – the general theory of human freedom – as the starting point for her analysis, Beauvoir herself would clearly not condone such a reversal. Given what I call the metaphorical structure of her argument – the fact that she never spells out the exact relationship between the two levels of the argument – nothing prevents the reader from preferring such a reading to that of Beauvoir herself.

16. The fact that Beauvoir explicitly rejects Freudian psychoanalysis in the first part of *The Second Sex* does not prevent her from producing a relatively psychoanalytical account of women's psychosexual development. As far as I can see, her rejection of psychoanalysis is based on the Sartrean grounds that the unconscious does not exist, and that to claim that human dreams and actions have sexual signification is to posit the existence of essential meanings. When it comes to the phenomenological description of women's fantasies or behaviour, however, Beauvoir is perfectly happy to accept psychoanalytical evidence.

17. Beauvoir met Lacan during the Occupation, at a series of rather wild parties organized by Picasso, Camus and Leiris among others. Deirdre Bair claims that when writing *The Second Sex*, Beauvoir 'went sporadically to hear Jacques Lacan lecture' (Bair, p. 390), but this is not very likely. According to Elisabeth Roudinesco, Lacan's earliest seminars were held at Sylvia Bataille's apartment from 1951 to 1953 (see Roudinesco, p. 306). In his essay 'De nos antécédents' ('About our Antecedents'), Lacan himself claims that he started his teaching in 1951: 'No real teaching other than that routinely provided saw the light of day before we started our own in 1951, in a purely private capacity' (*Ecrits*, p. 71). According to David Macey, the subject of that first seminar was Freud's *Dora* (see Macey, p. 223). If Beauvoir ever attended Lacan's seminars, then, it must have been well after finishing *The Second Sex* in 1949.

18. I do not mean to suggest that Lacan's concept of alienation is radically original or that it is the only source of Beauvoir's development of the concept. Eva Lundgren-Gothlin makes a plausible case for the influence of Kojève on Beauvoir (see pp. 89–94). Beauvoir herself tells of a drunken afternoon in 1945 spent discussing Kojève with Queneau (FC43; FCa56–7). Given that Lacan's concept of the mirror stage also displays the traces of Kojève's reading of Hegel, Beauvoir's own readings of Hegel may well have

predisposed her to feeling particular affinities with this aspect of Lacanian theory. Nor should it be forgotten that Lacan himself – as every other intellectual in post-war France – was influenced by Sartre. In her study of Beauvoir's concept of alienation, Lundgren-Gothlin breaks new ground not only by focusing on Beauvoir's reading of Hegel, but by being the first to consider Beauvoir's use of the concept of alienation as an original intellectual development.

19.   I do not think, as some have argued, that this is an effect of conscious sexism on the part of the translator. Rather it demonstrates the fact that he was utterly unfamiliar with existentialist philosophical vocabulary. The general effect of Parshley's translation of *The Second Sex* is to divest the book of the philosophical rigour it has in French. When Beauvoir consistently uses the phrase *s'affirmer comme sujet*, for example, Parshley translates vaguely and variably 'assume a subjective attitude', or 'affirm his subjective existence' (see SS19 and SS21). The word *situation*, heavy with philosophical connotations for Beauvoir, is not perceived as philosophical at all by Parshley, who translates *condition* as 'situation,' and *situation* interchangeably as 'situation' or 'circumstances', and so on. The same tendency to turn Beauvoir's philosophical prose into everyday language is to be found in the English translations of her memoirs, particularly *The Prime of Life* and *Force of Circumstance*. The effect is clearly to divest her of philosophy and thus to diminish her as an intellectual. The sexism involved in this process has more to do with the English-language publishers' perception and marketing of Beauvoir as a popular woman writer, with all the stereotypes that implies, than with the sexism of individual translators.

20.   At this point Beauvoir inserts a footnote quoting Lacan's *Complexes familiaux*. It is interesting to note that Lacan's essay introduces the notion of alienation in the other, not in relation to the mother, but in the context of a discussion of jealousy as a fundamental social structure. Beauvoir's actual quotation is slightly inaccurate: 'The ego retains the ambiguous aspect [*figure*] of a spectacle', she quotes (SS297; DSb15), whereas Lacan actually refers to the 'ambiguous *structure* of the spectacle' (*Les complexes familiaux*, p. 45).

21.   Beauvoir also uses the term 'phallus'. In general, she tends to use 'penis' and 'phallus' as interchangeable terms, mostly in the sense of 'penis'.

22.   This is true for Sartre too. When I claim that their metaphors of transcendence are phallic, they would claim that it is the phallus that is transcendent, not the other way round. For my argument, however, it does not very much matter which way round the comparison goes: my point is that, in their texts, projection and erection get involved in extensive metaphorical exchanges.

23.   Similar in many respects to Freud's analysis of femininity, Beauvoir's account differs in its explicit denial of *lack*, and in its emphasis on the tactile rather than the visual. For Freud, girls experience themselves as inferior because they *see* the penis and conclude that they themselves are lacking; for Beauvoir they are different (not necessarily inferior) because they have nothing to *touch*.

24. Beauvoir's extraordinary claim that erection, in some sense at least, is *voluntary*, owes more to her own metaphors than to the facts of biology.

25. Vigdis Songe-Møller helped me to appreciate the comic aspects of Beauvoir's use of Hegel.

26. It follows from this analysis, and from the rest of this chapter, that I cannot agree with Moira Gatens's claim that for Simone de Beauvoir the 'female body and femininity quite simply *are* absolutely Other to the human subject, irrespective of the sex of that subject' (p. 58). I also think it is rather too easy simply to assert, as Gatens does, that the inconsistencies and difficulties in *The Second Sex* simply reveal Beauvoir's 'intellectual dishonesty' (p. 59).

27. Beauvoir herself would certainly disagree with my value judgement here. As I go on to show, she idealizes the male configuration, perhaps precisely because she perceives it as more 'neatly' philosophical.

28. Interestingly enough, the same belief in the transcendent qualities of any form of movement makes her recommend sports and other forms of physical training as an excellent way to help girls develop a sense of themselves as subjects.

29. There is something circular about Beauvoir's argument here. For if 'equivalents of the phallus' are what is required to become an authentic subject, it is hard to see why women would want them *after* they have managed to become subjects in their own right anyway.

30. My discussion of Françoise's sexual project in chapter 5 raises some of these questions from a different perspective. In that chapter I am concerned with Beauvoir's understanding of consciousness; here I am turning the equation upside down in order to look at her theory of the body.

31. As Charlene Haddock Seigfried puts it in her instructive analysis of biology in *The Second Sex*, there can be no doubt that '[Beauvoir's] descriptions of biological data incorporate value judgements' (p. 308). On the other hand it is hard to imagine an utterly 'value-free' description of anything.

32. Beauvoir goes on to claim that older women, in this sense, are neither male nor female, but a third sex. In general, her account of post-menopausal women is strikingly ambivalent. On the one hand she sees them as finally free from the servitudes of the body, on the other she casts them as unusually neurotic and alienated (see the contrast between the chapter on biology in volume 1, and the one entitled 'From Maturity to Old Age' in volume 2).

33. Parshley's translation of this passage is particularly misleading. Translating the French *aliénée* as *being beside herself*, his version reads as follows: 'Being more profoundly beside herself than is man because her whole body is moved by desire and excitement, she retains her subjectivity only through union with her partner' (SS417). Here as elsewhere, the general tendency of Parshley's version is to lose sight of the philosophical aspect of Beauvoir's arguments.

34. In my account, I follow Beauvoir's chapter on 'The Sexual Initiation' quite closely. In that chapter she deals exclusively with heterosexual relations. I will return to her account of lesbianism in chapter 7, and discuss her own lesbian relationships in chapter 8.

35. I do not intend to pursue this question here. See chapter 4 for a detailed

discussion of the ambivalent relationship to the mother imago in *L'Invitée*, and chapter 8 for a discussion of Beauvoir's relationships with other women.

36. I rarely amend Hazel Barnes's excellent translation of *Being and Nothingness*. In this case, however, I have chosen to do so. Emphasizing the general – what he takes to be the 'philosophical' – in his description, Sartre confidently writes *chacun* and *on* in this passage: 'Il n'est pour chacun que de consulter son expérience: on sait que dans le désir sexuel la conscience est comme empâtée', he claims (EN438). Sensitive to the absurdity of this *chacun*, Hazel Barnes translates: 'Let any man consult his own experience; he knows how consciousness is clogged, so to speak, by sexual desire' (BN504). (I take her 'man' to refer to males and not to human beings.) As I see no reason to rescue Sartre from his own style, I have chosen to restore Sartre's original *chacun* and *on*.

37. Beauvoir's relationship to Merleau-Ponty is more interesting than this short account implies. Beauvoir met Merleau-Ponty when she was studying philosophy at the Sorbonne, and it was through her that he met Zaza, Beauvoir's best friend. Represented under the name of 'Pradelle' in *Memoirs of a Dutiful Daughter*, Merleau-Ponty was the young man with whom Zaza fell violently in love. As a result of her family's implacable opposition to the match, Zaza fell ill and died at the age of 21. Her moving correspondence was finally published by her family in 1991 (Elisabeth Lacoin, *Zaza: correspondance et carnets d'Elisabeth Lacoin 1914–1929*). As the editor of *Les temps modernes*, in the period from 1945 to 1952 Merleau-Ponty was Sartre's and Beauvoir's closest collaborator. In the politically beleaguered position in which the existentialists found themselves at this time, she would be highly unlikely to signal any kind of public disagreement with him. In the 1950s, the situation changed. Deciding to align himself with the Communist Party in the summer of 1952, Sartre alienated Merleau-Ponty, who quietly withdrew from *Les temps modernes*. When Merleau-Ponty published *Les aventures de la dialectique* in 1955, it was Simone de Beauvoir, not Sartre, who published a scathing reply in *Les temps modernes* (republished in the collection of essays entitled *Privilèges*, or *Faut-il brûler Sade?*). In 1952 Sartre had left it to Francis Jeanson to attack Camus's *The Rebel*; this time Simone de Beauvoir did not hesitate to do his dirty work for him: 'Merleau-Ponty et le pseudo-sartrisme' is, from every point of view, Beauvoir's most deplorable piece of writing. In *Force of Circumstance* (1963) Beauvoir stresses her old friendship with Merleau-Ponty, notes their personal differences, and ends on a slightly critical note: 'I had great respect for his books and essays, but it seemed to me that he didn't understand Sartre's thinking very well' (FC70; FCa91). In the light of her own attack on him in 1955, this is quite an understatement. Her conciliatory tone is no doubt the effect of Merleau-Ponty's premature death in 1961.

38. Christina Howells puts it nicely when she says that for Sartre 'flesh and agency are incompatible.' (p. 7).

39. In the 1950s and early 1960s the problem of female frigidity was much discussed among doctors and psychologists of various kinds, mostly as a problem for men. It is striking to note that in their major philosophical essays

Sartre, Beauvoir and Merleau-Ponty *all* quote the less than reputable *Frigidity in Woman* by Wilhelm Stekel, ex-student of Sigmund Freud's, and very much a renegade in Viennese psychoanalytic circles. Despite its title, Stekel's essay comes across as a semi-pornographic collection of stories of female orgasm, loosely organized around the theme of the struggle between the sexes. Comparing *Frigidity in Woman* to Stekel's autobiography, it is impossible not to suspect him of disguising as a case history the story of his own courtship of his second wife. Not surprisingly, in that particular story the understanding analyst literally provides the 'frigid' woman with earth-moving orgasms (see Stekel, *The Autobiography of Wilhelm Stekel*). The 'Stekel connection' in existentialism would be well worth exploring in greater detail.

40. In her essay on the Marquis de Sade in *Privilèges* (a book later republished under the title *Faut-il brûler Sade?*) Beauvoir unambiguously affirms that arousal (*le trouble*) produces 'immediate communication with the other' (p. 35). Suddenly sexual desire produces intimacy and communion, patriarchy or no patriarchy. It would seem that she produces such an uncomplicated version of 'normal' desire in order to contrast it more effectively with what she sees as Sade's radical emotional 'isolationism'.

41. On this point, she is faithful to *Being and Nothingness*, where Sartre argues that the three categories of being, having and doing can all be reduced to the category of *having* (see the fourth part of his treatise, entitled 'Having, Doing and Being').

42. I am of course not trying to argue that philosophy is the *only* discourse marked by the unconscious, nor am I trying to establish that philosophical texts are *more deeply* haunted by the unspoken than, say, literary or historical writings.

43. I will return to these issues in chapter 7.

44. The translation of this particular punchline is unusually misleading: 'La femme a d'elle-même une expérience plus authentique', Beauvoir writes (DSb191). 'Woman lives her love in a more genuine fashion', Parshley translates (SS423).

45. I briefly discuss the reception of *The Second Sex* in chapter 7. Beauvoir herself gives a good account of French reactions in *Force of Circumstance* (FC195–203; FCa258–68).

46. Politically, the existence of a large and militant women's movement made this a feasible option in the early 1970s. Intellectually, the increasing challenge of psychoanalysis provided the impetus to explore questions of sexuality and sexual difference.

Notes to chapter 7

1. Judith Okely, for instance, quotes positive responses to *The Second Sex* from women from the Middle East and India (pp. 3–4). 'I was fortunate', Okely writes, 'in receiving the testimony of some women from the Third World, not just from the west' (p. ix). Her work indicates that serious

anthropological and theoretical research on the *experience* of reading *The Second Sex* would yield fascinating insights into the way texts both influence and are constructed by their readers.

2. The English translation here is fairly misleading. 'On m'offrait [. . .] d'assouvir mes appétits de goule', Beauvoir writes (FCa260). 'People offered to [. . .] temper my labial appetites', Richard Howard translates (FC197). But in French, *goule* is not only an old-fashioned slang word for 'mouth', but a female vampire of Oriental extraction.

3. Jacqueline Rose's *The Haunting of Sylvia Plath* and Diane Wood Middlebrook's *Anne Sexton* both document the traumatic pain experienced by two exceptionally creative young women trying to come to terms with the role assigned to them by patriarchal ideology in the 1950s and early 1960s.

4. For a more detailed discussion of the significance of the absence of Beauvoir's name in 'The Laugh of the Medusa', see my 'Appropriating Bourdieu', pp. 1040–3.

5. In 'Stabat mater', Kristeva explicitly disagrees with Beauvoir's interpretation of Piero della Francesca's nativity in the National Gallery in London (see 'Stabat mater', p. 171). When I chose that particular painting for the cover of *The Kristeva Reader* (1986), it was very much because it alluded to a rare encounter between two pioneering intellectual women.

6. Claire Duchen's *Feminism in France* as well as Duchen's edition of text from the women's movement in France, *French Connections*, contain invaluable information on the social and political constellation of the French feminist field in the 1970s and 1980s. The editorial of the first issue of *Questions féministes* is translated under the title 'Variations on Common Themes' in Marks and Courtivron, pp. 212–30. Some of Christine Delphy's central texts, including her pioneering essay 'For a Materialist Feminism' from 1975, are collected in *Close to Home*. *French Connections* contains a text by Colette Guillaumin entitled 'The Question of Difference'. Monique Plaza's critique of Irigaray's *Speculum of the Other Woman* was translated in *Ideology & Consciousness* in 1978. Monique Wittig's theoretical essays have now been collected in *The Straight Mind*. Other texts from this materialist branch of the French women's movement can be found in *French Feminist Thought*, edited by Toril Moi. In an essay from 1990, Rose-Marie Lagrave draws an intriguing panorama of current intellectual trends among French feminists.

7. Arguing that for Beauvoir, the body itself is an effect of choice, Judith Butler's original and thought-provoking essay 'Sex and Gender in Simone de Beauvoir's *Second Sex*' takes Beauvoir's radical anti-essentialism in new and unexpected directions.

8. To be quite precise: in *The Second Sex*, Beauvoir never uses the word 'feminist' about her own position. That had to wait until she joined the women's movement in France in November 1971.

9. I should perhaps stress that for me, as for a whole tradition of socialist thinkers, the word 'utopian' has no negative connotations. Every revolutionary or reformist movement is informed by a utopian ideal,

however implicit or badly formulated it may be.

10. The first volume was published in Paris in June 1949, the second in November of the same year. Excerpts from the first volume were published in *Les temps modernes* in May, June and July 1948, and in February 1949, and excerpts from the second volume appeared in the May, June and July issues of 1949.

11. In chapter 2 I provide a detailed analysis of what I see as Beauvoir's legitimate *and* marginal speaking position.

12. The information in this paragraph comes from Huguette Bouchardeau, *Pas d'histoire, les femmes . . .*, and Eva Lundgren-Gothlin, *Kön och existens*. Claude Chabrol's film *Une affaire de femmes* (*A Story of Women*, 1988) tells the story of Marie-Jeanne Latour (Isabelle Huppert in the film).

13. The information in this paragraph is based on Albistur and Armogathe's study of feminism in France.

14. I take these figures from Jean-Pierre Rioux's magisterial study of the Fourth Republic.

15. In fact, Beauvoir reviewed Lévi-Strauss's study in the November 1949 issue of *Les temps modernes*. In her review, Beauvoir stresses the different roles of the sexes. In Lévi-Strauss's account of kinship, there are no relations of exchange and reciprocity between men and women, she writes, such relations being 'established between men, *by means of women*' (p. 945). Turning it into a close relation to *The Second Sex*, Beauvoir also finds Hegelian, Marxist and existentialist influences in Lévi-Strauss's book (see p. 949).

16. For an overview of theories of ideology, see Eagleton, *Ideology*. For further comments on the limitations of Beauvoir's understanding of ideology and language, see chapters 5 and 6.

17. The published translation of the first sentence quoted here has little to do with the original text. 'Du fait que tous les chemins lui sont barrés, qu'elle ne peut pas *faire*, qu'elle a à *être*, une malédiction pèse sur sa tête', Beauvoir writes (DSb130); 'and to ask what is the truth of her nature means little in her situation since she can only *be*, not *act*', Parshley translates (SS381). The whole passage from which this quotation is taken reads more like a fairly rough summary of Beauvoir's original prose than like a translation.

18. Beauvoir's examples are Maggie Tulliver in *The Mill on the Floss*, Olivia in Rosamond Lehmann's *Invitation to the Waltz*, Judy in Lehmann's *Dusty Answer* and Tessa in *The Constant Nymph* by Margaret Kennedy.

19. On this point, the published translation is misleading. The little girl 'n'accède pas à [. . .] l'universel', Beauvoir writes (DSb504−5); she 'has no aspirations towards [. . .] the universal', Parshley translates (SS625). But Beauvoir's point is that these little girls are exploited and mistreated precisely because they are cast as less than universal by the patriarchal establishment that judges them. If the men in power had been capable of recognizing the universal humanity of the girls, Beauvoir implies, they could not have treated them in such a callous way *without being obliged to face their own moral duplicity*. In this context it hardly matters whether the girls themselves 'aspire' to universality.

20. *The Second Sex* provides both a negative and a positive account of the pleasures of nature: 'Any woman who has preserved her independence through all her servitudes will ardently love her own freedom in Nature', Beauvoir writes (SS631; DSb512). As we have seen in chapter 6, Beauvoir's own emotional investments leave their mark on her text: her problematic relationship to motherhood, for instance, is constantly evident. This does not prevent her from giving a highly positive evaluation of 'authentic' motherhood. On this point, Lundgren-Gothlin's discussion of motherhood and authenticity in *The Second Sex* is particularly acute (see pp. 308–22). In general, Beauvoir insists on almost every page on the 'ambiguity' and 'ambivalence' of women's attitudes under patriarchy: such ambiguity may lead either to authenticity or to bad faith: for Beauvoir, the outcome is never given in advance.

21. In her 1966 lecture in Japan, entitled 'Women and Creativity', Beauvoir still insists that there have been no truly great women writers. Even Lady Murasaki's *Tale of Genji* is downgraded as somehow not truly 'universal' enough.

22. 'There is a statistical law which states that the larger the group, the more likely it is that one of its members will be exceptional', Beauvoir writes in her lecture in Japan ('Women and Creativity', p. 19).

23. In this context one notes that Pierre Bourdieu's felt the need to publish his anti-Kantian diatribe, *Distinction*, as late as 1979.

24. Claire Etcherelli's novel *Elise ou la vraie vie* (1967) gives a moving account of the situation of women and North African immigrant workers at the Citroën factories during the war in Algeria. As a result of her admiration for Etcherelli's novel, Beauvoir invited her to join the editorial board of *Les temps modernes*.

25. It is interesting to note that this passage is written entirely in the past conditional tense, just like Françoise's final 'direct' proposition to Gerbert. It is as if Beauvoir's very style signals the fact that, for her, at least in the 1940s, direct and unambiguous expression of female desire, whether social or sexual, remained impossible.

26. In 1949, Beauvoir considered herself a socialist. In the English translation of *The Second Sex*, the extent to which she relies on Marxist and socialist thought is not always obvious to the reader. As Margaret Simons has shown, almost every reference to socialist feminism has been deleted from the English text (see her 'Silencing', p. 562).

27. Beauvoir's account of the sexuality of independent women suffers from all the problems discussed in chapter 6. Allusions to women's necessary passivity in sexual intercourse, for instance, are to be found throughout her discussion of women's sexual dilemmas. In spite of my misgivings about her analysis of sexuality in general, Beauvoir's discussion of women's *concrete* sexual dilemmas in France in 1949 still strikes me as sound.

28. Beauvoir also writes that: 'Woman's homosexuality is one attempt among others to reconcile her autonomy with the passivity of her flesh' (SS426–7; DSb195). While this statement unfortunately reiterates Beauvoir's belief in

the fundamental passivity of female sexuality, it also casts lesbianism as one potential way forward for women reluctant to sacrifice their autonomy in exchange for sex.

29. I disagree with Claudia Card, who argues that 'Beauvoir seemed not to see that if "homosexuality" is a choice, heterosexuality is likewise a choice' (p. 209). Card forgets that within Beauvoir's existentialist framework, *everything*, including sexual orientation, is subject to choice. Choice *is* the use we make of our freedom, we might say. While Sartre's study of Jean Genet, for example, emphasizes his choice of homosexuality, his study of Flaubert stresses the latter's choice of heterosexual bachelorhood. Given her own existentialist premises, it is quite unlikely that Beauvoir would take heterosexuality somehow to be given and not chosen.

30. Discerning lesbian readers of *L'Invitée* nevertheless suspected that the truth was more complex. Focusing on the need for role models among lesbians, Jean Carlomusso's video *L Is For The Way You Look* has a short sequence where one woman describes her reaction to the relationship between Françoise and Xavière: 'I didn't know what it was,' she comments, 'but it was so damned attractive.' As revealed in the *Letters to Sartre*, Beauvoir and Olga Kosakiewicz, the model for Xavière, did in fact have a sexual relationship at the time of the 'trio' with Sartre (1935–7).

31. A number of the relevant bureaucratic dossiers are quoted in Gilbert Joseph's otherwise highly sensationalist, historically inaccurate and thoroughly malicious *Une si douce Occupation* . . . (pp. 197–222).

32. Margaret Simon's 1992 essay 'Lesbian Connections: Simone de Beauvoir and Feminism' contains a useful summary of available information on Beauvoir's lesbian relationships.

33. I can think of no other chapter in *The Second Sex* where the political and the philosophical are so clearly involved with the personal – and I can think of no other chapter where Beauvoir's censorship of the personal aspects of her discourse is more massive.

34. In her study of Fanon, Irene L. Gendzier stresses the importance of *Les temps modernes* for Fanon in the period from 1947 to 1952: '[*Les temps modernes*] carried articles on the subjects that Fanon was to concern himself with as time went on: communism and terror, the politics of the oppressed, black–white relations, the third world and the European left' (pp. 20–1).

35. I base this claim on information from the following sources: Bhaba, Caute, Feuchtwang, Gates, Gendzier, Mudimbe and Taylor. I am grateful to Faith Smith and José Muñoz for their bibliographical assistance on this matter. Although my discussion here will focus on the effects of reading Beauvoir with Fanon, I think it is high time finally to establish *The Second Sex* as a major intertext for *Black Masks, White Skin*, or in other words, to go on to read Fanon with Beauvoir. To do so would be one way to follow up Henry Louis Gates's suggestion that it is time to start '*reading* [Fanon], with an acknowledgement of his own historical particularity' ('Critical Fanonism', p. 470).

36. Her resolutely positive account of Fanon is clearly overdetermined. Although

there can be no doubt of Beauvoir's personal admiration for him, the fact that she was writing immediately after his death obviously influenced her tone. Nor should it be forgotten that Beauvoir and Sartre's pro-Algerian stance forced them into a beleaguered minority position in France: it would have been out of the question for Beauvoir to undermine a political ally such as Fanon in print. (Published in 1963, *Force of Circumstance* was finished in the summer of 1962, only a few months after the Evian agreements.)

37. At about the same time (1947–8) as he was writing 'Black Orpheus', Sartre also drafted another text on black liberation, particularly in the context of slavery in the United States. Published in 1983 under the title 'La violence révolutionnaire', this paper now constitutes the second appendix to Sartre's *Cahiers pour une morale*.

38. To argue, as Elisabeth Spelman does in her *Inessential Woman*, that Beauvoir's comparison of women with blacks and Jews is sexist because it implies that Beauvoir excludes the existence of black and Jewish women from her categories is to make the mistake of taking a statement about *oppression* (that is to say, about power relations) for a statement about *identity*. What Beauvoir is saying is that the relationship of men to women may in some ways (not all) be seen as homologous to that of whites to blacks, anti-semites to Jews, the bourgeoisie to the working class. In such a statement there is absolutely no implication that these other groups do not contain women, nor that all women are white and non-Jewish: nothing prevents us from arguing that the position of a black Jewish woman, for instance, would form a particularly complex intersection of contradictory power relations. In her chapter on Beauvoir, Spelman also confuses the idea of otherness and the idea of objectification. Spelman's book in general is an excellent example of the consequences of treating the word *identity* as if it represented a simple logical unit, and of mistaking the opposition of *inclusion* and *exclusion* for a theory of power relations. Such strategies tend to backfire: while criticizing Beauvoir's 'exclusivism', Spelman herself excludes women who are not citizens of the United States from her categories. Thus the figures intended to illustrate different categories of people all have the suffix 'American' appended to them ('Afro-American', 'Euro-American', 'Hispanic-American', 'Asian-American' and so on; see Spelman, pp. 144–6).

39. In this sentence Parshley's translation entirely fails to capture the Hegelian flavour conveyed by Beauvoir. 'Elles n'ont pas les moyens concrets de se rassembler en une unité qui se poserait en s'opposant', Beauvoir writes (DSa19). 'Women lack concrete means for organizing themselves into a unit which can stand face to face with the correlative unit', Parshley translates (SS19).

40. Beauvoir is not interested in producing a competitive hierarchy of oppression. Her point is not that women are necessarily *more* or *more painfully* oppressed than every other group, but simply that the oppression of women is a highly specific *kind* of oppression.

41. In this sense, Monique Wittig's utopian novel, *Les guérillères*, is an excellent – and highly dialectical – commentary on *The Second Sex*: by imagining

outright warfare between a society of women and a society of men, ending with the celebration of a new solidarity – *fraternité* – between men and women, Wittig shrewdly posits a truly utopian solution to Beauvoir's dilemma. After all, Wittig seems to say, this would be the *easy* way out of the patriarchal quagmire.

42. English-language readers should note that, in French, the word *sororité* never took on the political and feminist connotations achieved by *sisterhood* in English in the late 1960s and early 1970s. To argue that Beauvoir *ought* to have written *sororité* in 1949 is absurd: since Beauvoir truly dreams of a society marked by solidarity – not struggle – between men and women, she could hardly end her book on a term which in 1949 would have been perceived as exclusively pertaining to females.

43. Only under such utopian conditions, I would add, would the word 'he' be a true universal. Under current social conditions, 'he' remains a false universal. As long as current patriarchal conditions prevail, my own usage is to use 'she' as a gender-neutral pronoun in order to signal my (utopian) desire to construct a society in which the feminine finally would be as universal as the masculine.

44. Reciprocity in fact represents for Beauvoir the incarnation of the highest human value: 'Authentic love', she writes, 'ought to be founded on the mutual [*réciproque*] recognition of two freedoms; the lovers would then experience themselves both as self and as other: neither would give up transcendence, neither would be mutilated; together they would reveal values and aims in the world' (SS677; DSb579; TA).

45. Beauvoir's own position is influenced by the socialist tradition, but one hardly needs to be a Marxist to accept the argument for maternity leave. Most Europeans find the widespread American equation of equality with abstract equality quite shocking. When I first discovered that American women do not have an automatic, legal right to maternity leave – let alone to maternity leave on full pay – my reaction was one of profound disbelief. Only the most abstract idea of equality can allow such blatant discrimination against women. Taking equality to mean abstract equality, the ultra-conservative feminist Elisabeth Fox-Genovese gleefully accuses the great majority of other US feminists of cynical and self-serving manipulation of logic, since they refuse to see maternity leave and social equality as mutually exclusive concepts (see pp. 56–7). Positions such as Fox-Genovese's obviously have nothing to do with Beauvoir's point of view – or indeed with my own.

46. To argue that women's development under patriarchy should be valorized as the norm and standard for free femininity, one may add, is to generalize from the particular case by turning the experience of one group of women into the norm for others.

47. For a useful collection of essays illustrating the basic tenets of *écriture féminine*, see Wilcox et al. Morag Shiach provides an excellent account of Cixous's own positions.

48. For a perspicacious analysis of the French women's movement in the 1970s and 1980s, including dominant accounts of Simone de Beauvoir, as seen

from the perspective of a young Frenchwoman in the 1990s, see Sandrine Garcia's 'Le féminisme, une révolution symbolique?'. Garcia particularly emphasizes the intellectual excitement provoked by the 'sexual difference' faction, even among women who did not share the political analysis of that group.

49.   For Beauvoir, then, post-feminism presupposes post-patriarchy. In my paper on 'Feminism, Postmodernism and Style', I argue a very similar case against certain forms of postmodern feminism. In an interview from 1980, Antoinette Fouque, the leading light of *Psych et Po* and the Editions des femmes, takes a diametrically opposite view: '[In the 1970s] it was important to us to stress that we are not feminist', she says to Catherine Clément. 'That was − is − to say: feminism isn't the final destination of our revolution. We are neither pre-feminist, nor antifeminist, but "postfeminist": we work for heterosexuality, for the arrival of the other, just as Senghor worked for *négritude*, and he wasn't working against whites' (p. 13). Fouque's invocation of *négritude* to defend her own, depoliticized position is theoretically significant, but politically highly disingenuous. It is absurd to imply that Beauvoir, for instance, saw feminism as the *aim* of feminism.

50.   My analysis of the current situation in feminism is close to Edward Said's impatience with the 'depoliticization of knowledge' occurring in the postmodernist rejection of every great narrative ('Representing the Colonized', p. 222).

51.   Although I argue for the production of feminist utopias, I do not feel obliged to *endorse* them all. I have no quarrel with Margaret Whitford, for instance, who stresses the utopian aspects of Luce Irigaray's thought (see Whitford, pp. 9−25). I too see Irigaray as a truly utopian thinker, offering a powerful political vision to contemporary feminism. Unfortunately, however, I shudder to think what it might be like to live in the fully 'sexuate' culture which makes up the stuff of Irigaray's dreams (see *Je, tu, nous*, pp. 101−15). Whether I am right or wrong to feel this way remains to be seen. My point is simply that unless we are willing openly and forcefully to *debate* questions of utopia and liberation, feminist theory will lose sight of the political.

Notes to chapter 8

1.   In order to have her fishtail transformed into legs, the little mermaid has to sacrifice her tongue. In selfless devotion she accepts her own total extinction: if the prince does not marry her, she will become mere foam upon the sea; she is never to have an immortal soul. Like many of us, Beauvoir may have forgotten that Andersen actually rewards the little mermaid for her loving heart by turning her into a 'daughter of the air', an aerial being animated by the very spirit Beauvoir so deplores: 'You have striven, poor little mermaid, with all your heart for the same as we [the daughters of the air] have striven for; you have suffered and borne, and have raised yourself up into the world of the aerial spirits. Now through your own good deeds, you can create an

immortal soul for yourself in three hundred years' time' (Andersen, p. 35).

2. See for instance Beauvoir's letter to Sartre dated 10 October 1939: 'Saturday's precisely our anniversary: 14 October' (LS109; LSa175), or the entry for 10 October 1939 in her *Journal de guerre*: 'I got two letters from Sartre, one talks about our anniversary, our tenth anniversary, the one we were going to celebrate so splendidly' (JG82). The actual entry for 14 October also comments on the date: 'A sad anniversary of our morganatic marriage' (JG92).

3. In French: 'Sartre n'avait pas la vocation de la monogamie.' Peter Green translates the phrase as: 'Sartre was not inclined to be monogamous by nature.' The word 'nature' here has led some suspicious feminists to claim that Beauvoir believed in essences after all.

4. In the autumn of 1929 Sartre was in fact 24.

5. I discuss the production and function of this myth in *Memoirs of a Dutiful Daughter* in chapter 1, and its fictional elaboration in *L'Invitée* in chapter 4.

6. My topic is not Sartre, and I hesitate to speculate on his emotional reactions in this context. The one entry in his *Carnets de la drôle de guerre* referring to the famous pact nevertheless remains absolutely fascinating: 'On one occasion I was caught in my own game', Sartre writes on 1 December 1939. 'The Beaver accepted my freedom and kept it. It was in 1929. I was foolish enough to be upset by it: instead of understanding the extraordinary luck I'd had, I fell into a certain melancholy' (*Carnets*, p. 99).

7. In an unpublished lecture, given in Berlin in 1990, Michèle Le Doeuff points to the potential contradiction between the idea of a freely chosen pact and Sartre's declared intention to 'take Beauvoir under his wings'.

8. Todd, who married Paul Nizan's daughter in a ceremony where Sartre gave the bride away, situates this conversation towards the end of Sartre's life. As this particular passage shows, Todd is not afraid of hurting Beauvoir's feelings. While professing to admire her, he never loses an opportunity to put the boot in: Beauvoir 'often reminds one of a teacher, an inspector of schools, an examiner' (p. 115); she is the most traditional of women: 'Because she knew that she would outlast them all, in relation to Sartre Simone de Beauvoir made me think of the woman, the perfect wife in a 19th century bourgeois couple' (p. 116).

9. Beauvoir's reaction to Todd's casual demolition of her most cherished beliefs was predictable enough. In *Adieux: A Farewell to Sartre*, published only a few months after Todd's *Un fils rebelle*, Beauvoir rejects his claim to have been a kind of surrogate son to Sartre and adds: 'Sartre was all the less eager to have Todd for his son since he did not like him at all and had only a very superficial relationship with him, which is the contrary of what Todd tries to insinuate in his book' (AF30; CA48).

10. See particularly my discussion of the imagery surrounding Xavière in *L'Invitée* in chapter 4, the imagery of childhood distress in *Memoirs of a Dutiful Daughter* in chapter 1, and the imagery relating to female sexuality in *The Second Sex* in chapter 6.

11. This passage refers to her life in Rouen in 1934, at the age of 26. In the same

context Beauvoir refers to these crises as her 'depressed mood' (*ma mélancolie*) (PL208; FA240).

12. This experience of loss of identity, one might add, receives its ultimate gloss in Beauvoir's searching analysis, in *The Second Sex*, of female alienation in general and of the alienation of women in love in particular.

13. Beauvoir recognized the maniacal dimension of her leisure pursuits, and readily conceded that she 'elevated [her] pleasures to the level of sacred obligations' (PL92; FA108).

14. Peter Green's translation drops the crucial reference to Beauvoir's 'schizophrenia.' 'Mon entêtement schizophrénique au bonheur', Beauvoir writes (FA415); 'my emotionally ambivalent obsession with happiness', Green translates (PL363).

15. 'Ce que Sartre appelait naguère ma "schizophrénie"', Beauvoir writes (FA555); 'What Sartre used to call my "divided mind"', Peter Green translates (PL484).

16. In this quotation I have had to make considerable changes to the published text. 'Je ne devai jamais retomber dans mon délire schizophrénique', Beauvoir writes (FA686); 'Never again would I slip back into the fantasies of a divided mind', Green translates (PL600). Green also has 'human condition' where Beauvoir has *situation*, and prefers to translate the existentialist term *assumer* as 'to bear'.

17. After 1944, the only mention of her 'schizophrenia' that I can find relates to the break-up of Beauvoir's affair with Algren. Referring to her wild hopes that Algren might accept that she would spend nine months a year with Sartre, she wryly comments: 'I must have remained "schizophrenic" – in the sense that Sartre and I gave to that word – to imagine that Algren would accommodate himself to that state of things' (FC171; FCa225; TA).

18. That Beauvoir failed to tell this side of the story in *The Prime of Life* is not surprising. In 1960, almost all the people involved were still alive. To confess to lesbian relationships in pre-feminist France would have brought pain and difficulties not only to Simone de Beauvoir but to her partners as well.

19. However one judges Bianca Bienenfeld's own participation in the informal trio, there can be no doubt that the whole scenario was harmful to her. In later life Bianca Lamblin suffered grievously from anxiety attacks and depression. While it seems unlikely that Sartre and Beauvoir alone caused all of Bianca's psychological problems – the extreme anxiety she suffered as a Jewish woman living in Nazi-occupied France during the war also played a significant role – they certainly aggravated her condition. When Bianca Lamblin entered into psychoanalysis with Jaques Lacan, the latter made her see that she had cast Sartre and Beauvoir as her parents. Eventually she developed the following interpretation of the situation: 'I had been caught up in a rare psychological configuration: not only had I, like all human beings, unconsciously wished to have carnal relations with my parents when I was a small child, but in this case the wish had really come true. I had been in love with Sartre, and had transferred onto him the drives normally directed towards the father. Usually the child only dreams about it, but in our

relationship I had actual sexual relations with him. That was a serious transgression, linked to a strong identification with the Beaver [Beauvoir]: as with all little girls, my desire to replace her in Sartre's/the father's affections was based on this maternal identification. This is what she obscurely felt and that explains her jealousy and the violent quarrel over Sartre's leave. At the same time, the love that I felt for the Beaver, as for a mother, also had a physical reality. This is quite unusual and causes a regression to the earliest stages of childhood, to the primordial sensual bond between a little child and her mother. This double affective impregnation left deep and lasting traces in me. This is why I had a complete breakdown when the whole construction came cracking down' (pp. 204–5). Although Bianca Lamblin saw Beauvoir regularly until the latter's death, her final verdict on their relationship is harsh: 'In the end,' she writes, 'Sartre and Simone de Beauvoir did me nothing but harm' (p. 207).

20. See chapters 1 and 4 for specific examples. As late as 1972, in the otherwise far too sanguine introductory section of *All Said and Done*, Beauvoir calls her mother 'tactless' and 'oppressive' (*tyrannique*) (ASD24; TCF29), and complains that 'My mother was so timorous and at the same time so despotic she would never have known how to discover diversions for us and she would have disliked letting us amuse ourselves without her' (ASD25; TCF29).

21. This passage is not translated in the English selection of Beauvoir's letters.

22. Given Beauvoir's strong arguments in favour of female economic independence in *The Second Sex*, it seems somewhat contradictory that she never reflected on the wisdom of keeping so many women economically dependent on herself or Sartre.

23. 'Kos.' here is Olga Kosakiewicz.

24. Gerassi adds an interesting perspective on Sartre's very different investment in his emotional relationships: 'In all my adult life I have never shed a tear for a woman. I wish I had, I wish I still could', Gerassi quotes him as saying in 1973 (p. 104).

25. Beauvoir tends to assume that the sexually unattractive woman simply will not be *loved*. She does not discuss the possibility of being loved by men on less patriarchal terms, nor does she discuss the fact that the equation between heterosexual 'attraction' and love does not hold in the case of lesbian relationships.

26. The French text contains a fairly untranslatable pun on the word *peau* (skin): 'Je détestais ce que j'appelais "les vieilles peaux" et je me promettais bien, quand la mienne aurait fait son temps, de la remiser' (FCb9).

27. This is precisely Paule's reply to Anne in the scene quoted above: "Too old!" Paule said to me, sounding annoyed. "What an idea! I've never felt younger"' (M666; LMb371).

28. Again Beauvoir is only thinking of heterosexual pleasure. It is because the older woman is no longer pleasing to men, Beauvoir implies, that she loses her sexual powers. This leaves the question of lesbian relations between older women relatively open. She does assert that menopausal women often

change their lives dramatically – for instance by choosing lesbian relationships for the first time – simply to catch up with the pleasures of life before it is too late (see SS590–2; DSb460–2).

29. In her analysis of the theme of old age in Beauvoir's works, Kathleen Woodward makes a related point: 'Beauvoir associates old age in general with melancholia, a terrible solitude and loss, and specifically, with the death of Sartre, which for her would be catastrophic', she writes (p. 106). Woodward also analyses Beauvoir's 'crises' as anxiety attacks (see pp. 108–9).

30. In French: 'qu'il lui fît violence' (FCa187). The English translation has Vanetti 'complaining of the pain he was causing her' (FC142).

31. Deirdre Bair gives an excellent account of Beauvoir's relationship to Algren. I nevertheless disagree with her far too positive assessment of the virtues of that liaison. In an interview with Nathalie Duval, Bair says that Algren was 'a man who offered her a harmonious sexual life and a perfect intellectual life: he didn't force her to do anything, didn't ask her to clean his house or whatever, he only wanted her to be herself' (DEA dissertation, 1990, p. 38). But according to Algren's biographer, Bettina Drew, Algren's track record with women was far from reassuring. 'Algren's need to destroy love had to be accepted, finally, as a tragic but undeniable part of his personality', Drew writes (p. 324). He was also a compulsive gambler, given to excessive consumption of alcohol, and widely known for his moody and difficult personality. The sexism of his last, ferocious attacks on Beauvoir (after the publication of *Force of Circumstance* in English in 1964) cannot be explained simply by his justfiable anger at her publication of what he considered their private love affair. See Algren's 'I Ain't Abelard', 'The Question of Simone de Beauvoir', and also chapter 7 ('Paris and Friends') and chapter 11 ('Writers and Writing') in *Conversations with Nelson Algren*. In the latter, he claims that he did not know Beauvoir was a 'French feminist, femininist, feminist?' and that theirs was a 'relationship that assumed the secondary status of the female in relation to the male. [. . .] The irony of the title *The Second Sex* is a purely literary irony. In reality there was no irony. Second is where second belongs' (*Conversations*, pp. 266–7). These interviews and essays contrast sharply in tone with the far more friendly account of Beauvoir given in *Who Lost an American?*, published in 1963 (see particularly pp. 94–101, and also p. 118).

32. In French: 'jusqu'à quel point j'ai été flouée' (FCb508). Richard Howard translates: 'how much I was gypped' (FC674), whereas I – marginally – prefer 'cheated' or 'swindled'.

33. Even in *Old Age*, however, I can not find any cases where Beauvoir refers to healthy people under 60 as 'old' in a social or sociological sense.

34. The upbeat reassessment of her life provided at the beginning of *All Said and Done* is explicitly designed, in my view, to dispel the depressed mood so evident at the end of *Force of Circumstance*. 'What is certain is that I am satisfied with my fate and that I should not want it changed in any way at all' (ASD11; TCF13). 'Since I was twenty-one I have never been lonely', she insists (ASD39; TCF46); 'Until I was ten or twelve I had virtually no problems' (ASD16; TCF19), and so on.

35. Although they first met in 1960, Beauvoir and Le Bon only developed a
     closer relationship in the autumn of 1963.
36. In both cases the French text has 'une grande chance m'a été donnée.'
37. I am referring to Nathalie Sorokine's mother's accusations against Beauvoir,
     which led to Beauvoir's dismissal from her teaching position in 1943.
38. For further discussion of Beauvoir's relationship to Elisabeth Lacoin and
     Sylvie Le Bon, see Margaret Simons, 'Lesbian Connections'.
39. Her letters to Sartre also have a second purpose: to cater to his intense interest
     in all the latest Left Bank gossip.
40. In the British *Guardian*, Paul Webster claims that 'the correspondence will
     damage her reputation for anyone who considers her as an objective,
     intellectual, caring and dedicated feminist' (p. 3). In France, the publication
     of Beauvoir's letters and war diaries in 1990 divided the critics. In *Libération*
     Marianne Alphant laments their publication, taking Beauvoir to task for her
     narrowness of mind: 'There's a war going on. One hardly notices. [. . .] The
     proportion of frivolous and degrading tittle-tattle is nothing short of
     stunning.' At this time, Alphant concludes, Beauvoir lives 'like a hamster in
     a wheel' (p. 21). Taking an opposing view, Josyane Savigneau in *Le monde*
     reads the letters as bringing new evidence to show that Sartre and Beauvoir
     were in fact uniquely committed to each other, and that Beauvoir had a 'real
     taste for everything [fools] have accused her of lacking: the body, the strange
     ways of love, the freedom to talk about them, a sense of humour, and the
     daily invention of an extraordinary life for two' (p. 26).
41. Deirdre Bair insists that this conversation took place in mid-May 1945, rather
     than in March or April 1946 (see p. 304), but apart from accusing Beauvoir
     of failing to provide 'accurate chronology [and] textual unity' in her memoirs
     (p. 303), she offers no evidence for this claim. As far as I can see, it is based
     on psychological intutition: Bair somehow feels convinced that they must
     have discussed Vanetti in this way after Sartre's *first* trip to the United States.
     It would obviously make just as good psychological sense to assume that
     Beauvoir only truly considered Vanetti a danger after it turned out that
     Sartre's second trip increased his infatuation. Beauvoir's diary excerpts are
     dated May 1946, and mention a trip to Switzerland which undoubtedly
     took place towards the end of that month. On my reading, it was pre-
     cisely because Beauvoir was seriously upset about Sartre's relationship to
     Vanetti that she turned to her diary at this particular time. In the absence
     of concrete evidence to the contrary, I will assume that Beauvoir gets
     the chronology of these events more or less right, mostly because her dates
     seem credible enough, whereas Bair, on the other hand, turns out to be
     slightly confused about a number of other dates at this time. As we have
     seen, Sartre returned to Paris from his second trip to New York on 15 March
     1946. In April he fell seriously ill with mumps. Bair places the onset
     of mumps *after* a conversation about New York that Beauvoir in her
     diary dates to May 16. Again Bair offers no evidence for her dating, which
     forces her to place the trip to Switzerland in mid-June, when Sartre and
     Beauvoir in fact were in Italy. The conversation reported here must in all

probability have taken place some time in April: before Sartre fell ill –
Beauvoir says they were going to a lunch party at the time – but after he has
had the time to say more than enough about Vanetti to make Beauvoir
seriously worried.

42. *Poussière*, as I note in chapter 5, is the French title of one of Beauvoir's
favourite novels, Rosamond Lehmann's *Dusty Answer*, which dwells on loss
and unfulfilled love.

43. There is a highly confusing moment in these diary excerpts. On 7 May
Beauvoir writes that 'I also frightened M. who brought me some rather
uninteresting pieces on England' (FC87; FCa112; TA). The only person
called M. in her memoirs is Vanetti, and at this stage Beauvoir had never met
her. There is no reference to her arrival in Paris, nor to her eventual
departure. No biographer implies that Vanetti turned up in Paris in the late
spring of 1946, although Annie Cohen-Solal does say that Sartre, after his
return in March, told everybody that 'Dolorès was the most marvellous
woman on earth, and that she would soon come to join him' (p. 366). It
would not be uncharacteristic of Beauvoir to try to eliminate information
about her rival's presence from her memoirs: according to Deirdre Bair,
Beauvoir told her that originally she did not want to mention Vanetti at all:
'Sartre wanted me to write about her, but I said no. He said I was being
dishonest. I said they were my memoirs' (Bair, p. 302). Given that she edited
her own diairies meticulously before publication, one might imagine that this
one, casual reference to 'M.' is the result of an oversight: perhaps she simply
forgot to delete this one line. But Beauvoir is also notoriously sloppy with the
spelling of names and places: for all I know, 'M.' here is a simple mistake:
perhaps it should be 'N.' or 'P.' or whatever. (The French text is studiously
gender-neutral, but the English translation of *Force of Circumstance* takes it for
granted that 'M.' is a man and adds the pronoun 'he'.)

44. For some inexplicable reason Richard Howard's translation leaves out the
crucial reference to the 'work': 'Mais ça deviendrait une oeuvre', Beauvoir
writes (FCa119).

45. Her only play, *Les bouches inutiles*, would obviously also be a 'work'.

46. Martha Noel Evans argues not only that Beauvoir considers the novel a 'less
worthy genre of writing' than the essay, but also that she genders the essay as
'masculine' and the novel as 'feminine' ('Murdering *L'Invitée*', p. 69). I can
find no evidence at all for such claims. The one quotation mobilized by
Evans to support her views clearly refers to *other people's* preference for the
essay, not Beauvoir's own (see Alice Jardine's 1979 interview with Beauvoir,
p. 234).

47. In most respects Beauvoir's understanding of language and communication is
identical to Sartre's analysis of prose in *What Is Literature?*.

48. Taken from a 1930 conversation with Sartre, this phrase refers to their early
disagreement about the relationship between language and emotions. Struck
by the view from Saint-Cloud, Beauvoir is deeply moved: 'I reproached
Sartre for his indifference [. . .]. He talked about the forest and the river far
more eloquently than I did, yet they did not make him *feel* anything' (PL39;

FA47). According to Sartre, a writer needed to be sufficiently detached from his emotion to capture it in words; according to Beauvoir, such a 'discrepancy between things and words' was bound to kill the writer's capacity for ecstatic experience: 'I wanted to write books, yet not to give up my "trances": I was torn [. . .]' (PL40; FA47).

49.   As a young girl, Beauvoir writes, she was convinced that she had *everything* to say; as a young writer, she suddenly discovered that she had *nothing* to say (see 'Mon expérience', p. 440).

50.   Here I use *disavowal* in Freud's sense of the word, which is *Verleugnung*. This is the translation preferred by the *Standard Edition*. For the sake of consistency I will use the same term in reference to Julia Kristeva's *Black Sun*, where *Verleugnung* is translated as *denial*.

51.   For Freud, all fetishists are male. In 'Female Fetishism' Naomi Schor makes a persuasive case for the analysis of female fetishism as particularly marked by sexual ambivalence or bisexuality (see particularly pp. 367–9).

52.   I borrow this point from Julia Kristeva. In *Revolution in Poetic Language* she asks: 'In short, isn't art the fetish par excellence, one that badly camouflages its archaeology? At its base, isn't there a belief, ultimately maintained, that the mother is phallic, that the ego – never precisely identified – will never separate from her, and that no symbol is strong enough to sever this dependence?' (p. 65). While Kristeva finds that the writing *subject* may 'cling to the help fetishism offers' (p. 65), she nevertheless insists that the *text* is never simply a fetish: 'The text is completely different from a fetish because it *signifies*; in other words, it is not a *substitute*, but a *sign* [. . .]' (*Revolution*, p. 65).

53.   Kristeva's text also contains extensive discussions of depressive case histories, many of which contain potentially illuminating insights in relation to Simone de Beauvoir: the depressive woman's tendency to see an intrusive mother in her male partner, for instance: 'Many women know that in their dreams their mothers stand for lovers or husbands and vice versa [. . .]. Such a mother, who is imagined as indispensable, fulfilling, intrusive, is for that very reason death-bearing: she devitalizes her daughter and leaves her no way out' (*Black Sun*, pp. 77–8). Or the tendency to choose an unfaithful partner: 'Her favorite partner or her husband is a fulfilling although unfaithful mother. The woman in despair can then be dramatically, painfully, attached to her Don Juan. For, beyond the fact that he gives her the possibility of enjoying an unfaithful mother, Don Juan satisfies her eager thirst for other women. His own mistresses are her own mistresses' (*Black Sun*, p. 84; TA). I do not intend to pursue these themes here. There are two reasons for this: first, the fact that my subject here is Beauvoir's relationship to writing and art, and second, the fact that I have no particular wish to *translate* my own reading of her memoirs into *one* particular psychoanalytic narrative, whether it be that of a Julia Kristeva, or – say – that of an Alice Miller, Melanie Klein or André Green.

54.   I have tried to avoid dwelling on some of the technicalities of Kristeva's account. In her text, she uses the word *denial* (*déni*) for the Freudian *Verleugnung*. Since I started by quoting Freud on fetishism, I feel obliged to

stick to the same usage throughout my text. I will therefore speak of Beauvoir's writing of *disavowal*. This turn of phrase has the advantage of signalling that I am not simply talking about *denial* in the more everyday sense of 'outright denial' or 'evasion'.

55. I want to register here my admiration for Elaine Marks's 1973 study of Beauvoir: while I disagree with Marks's general aesthetic positions, and her harsh personal attacks on Beauvoir, I find her assessment of the various modes of Beauvoir's styles quite excellent.

56. As for her other fiction – *The Blood of Others*, *All Men Are Mortal*, *Les Belles Images*, *The Woman Destroyed* – they all display considerable oscillations across Beauvoir's register: from the most leaden prose to moments of extraordinary intensity. Personally, I find much power in 'The Woman Destroyed' and 'Monologue', and much less so in *All Men Are Mortal*.

Works Cited

I WORKS BY SIMONE DE BEAUVOIR

Works are listed in chronological order according to the date of the original French publication. In the text I give references to the editions listed here.

Books

In French

L'Invitée. Coll. Folio. Paris: Gallimard, 1943.
Pyrrhus et Cinéas. Paris: Gallimard, 1944.
Le sang des autres. Coll. Folio. Paris: Gallimard, 1945.
Les bouches inutiles. Coll. Le manteau d'Arlequin. Paris: Gallimard, 1945.
Tous les hommes sont mortels. Coll. Folio. Paris: Gallimard, 1946.
Pour une morale de l'ambiguïté. Coll. Idées. Paris: Gallimard, 1947.
L'existentialisme et la sagesse des nations. Paris: Nagel, 1948.
L'Amérique au jour le jour. Paris: Morihien, 1948; Paris: Gallimard, 1954.
Le deuxième sexe. Coll. Folio. Paris: Gallimard, 1949.
Les mandarins. Coll. Folio. Paris: Gallimard, 1954.
Privilèges. Paris: Gallimard, 1955. (Also published in the Collection Idées under the title *Faut-il brûler Sade?*.)
La longue marche. Paris: Gallimard, 1957.
Mémoires d'une jeune fille rangée. Coll. Folio. Paris: Gallimard, 1958.
La force de l'âge. Coll. Folio. Paris: Gallimard, 1960.
Djamila Boupacha. Avec Gisèle Halimi. Paris: Gallimard, 1962.
La force des choses. Coll. Folio. Paris: Gallimard, 1963.
Une mort très douce. Coll. Folio. Paris: Gallimard, 1964.
Les belles images. Coll. Folio. Paris: Gallimard, 1966.

La femme rompue. Coll. Folio. Paris: Gallimard, 1968.
La vieillesse. Coll. Folio. Paris: Gallimard, 1970.
Tout compte fait. Coll. Folio. Paris: Gallimard, 1972.
Quand prime le spirituel. Paris: Gallimard, 1979.
La cérémonie des adieux. Suivi de *Entretiens avec Jean-Paul Sartre.* Coll. Folio. Paris: Gallimard, 1981.
Lettres à Sartre. Vols 1 and 2. Paris: Gallimard, 1990.
Journal de guerre. Paris: Gallimard, 1990.

In English

She Came to Stay. Trans. Yvonne Moyse and Roger Senhouse. London: Fontana, 1984.
The Blood of Others. Trans. Yvonne Moyse and Roger Senhouse. Harmondsworth: Penguin, 1986.
Who Shall Die?. Trans. Claude Francis and Fernande Gontier. Florissant, Missouri: River Press, 1983.
All Men are Mortal. Trans. Leonard M. Friedman. Cleveland, Ohio: World Publishing, 1955.
The Ethics of Ambiguity. Trans. Bernard Frechtman. New York: Citadel Press, 1976.
America Day by Day. Trans. Patrick Dudley. London: Duckworth, 1952.
The Second Sex. Trans. H.M. Parshley. Harmondsworth: Penguin, 1984.
The Mandarins. Trans. Leonard M. Friedman. London: Fontana, 1986.
The Long March. Trans. Austryn Wainhouse. Cleveland: World, 1958.
Memoirs of a Dutiful Daughter. Trans. James Kirkup. Harmondsworth: Penguin, 1987.
The Prime of Life. Trans. Peter Green. Harmondsworth: Penguin, 1988.
Force of Circumstance. Trans. Richard Howard. Harmondsworth: Penguin, 1987.
A Very Easy Death. Trans. Patrick O'Brian. Harmondsworth: Penguin, 1983.
Les Belles Images. Trans. Patrick O'Brian. London: Fontana, 1985.
The Woman Destroyed. Trans. Patrick O'Brian. London: Fontana, 1987.
Old Age. Trans. Patrick O'Brian. Harmondsworth: Penguin, 1986.
All Said and Done. Trans. Patrick O'Brian. Harmondsworth: Penguin, 1987.
When Things of the Spirit Come First. Trans. Patrick O'Brian. London: Fontana, 1986.
Adieux: A Farewell to Sartre. Trans. Patrick O'Brian. Harmondsworth: Penguin, 1986.
Letters to Sartre. Trans. and ed. Quintin Hoare. New York: Arcade, 1991.

Essays, reviews, interviews referred to in the text

'*La phénoménologie de la perception* de Maurice Merleau-Ponty.' *Les temps modernes* 1.2 (November 1945): 363–7.
'Oeil pour oeil.' 1946. *L'existentialisme et la sagesse des nations* 125–64.

'Introduction à une morale de l'ambiguïté.' 1946. Francis and Gonthier, *Ecrits* 335–43.

'*Les structures élémentaires de la parenté* par Claude Lévi-Strauss.' *Les temps modernes* 5.40 (November 1949): 943–9.

'Merleau-Ponty et le pseudo-sartrisme.' 1955. *Faut-il brûler Sade?* 183–250.

'Mon expérience d'écrivain.' 1966. Francis and Gonthier, *Ecrits* 438–57.

'La femme et la création.' 1966. Francis and Gonthier, *Ecrits* 458–74. Trans. Roisin Mallaghan. 'Women and Creativity.' *Moi*, *French* 17–32.

'I am a feminist.' 1972. With Alice Schwartzer. Schwartzer 27–48.

'*The Second Sex*: thirty years on.' 1976. With Alice Schwartzer. Schwartzer 65–79.

'Interview with Simone de Beauvoir.' With Alice Jardine. *Signs* 5.2 (Winter 1979): 224–36.

'Being a woman is not enough.' 1982. With Alice Schwartzer. Schwartzer 108–20.

'Simone de Beauvoir: le désaveu.' With Cathy Bernheim and Antoine Spire. *Le matin* 5 Dec. 1985.

'Two interviews with Simone de Beauvoir.' 1982 and 1985. With Margaret Simons. Fraser and Bartky 25–41.

II OTHER WORKS CITED

Alain-Fournier. *Le Grand Meaulnes*. 1913. Paris: Le livre de poche, 1967.

Albistur, Maïté and Daniel Armogathe. *Histoire du féminisme français du moyen âge à nos jours*. Paris: des femmes, 1977.

Algren, Nelson. *Who Lost an American?* New York: Macmillan, 1963.

—— *Conversations with Nelson Algren*. With H. E. F. Donohue. New York: Hill and Wang, 1964.

—— 'I Ain't Abelard.' *Newsweek* 29 Dec. 1964: 58–9.

—— 'The Question of Simone de Beauvoir.' *Harper's Magazine* (May 1965): 134–6.

al-Hibri, Azizab Y. and Margaret Simons, eds. *Hypatia Reborn: Essays in Feminist Philosophy*. Bloomington: Indiana University Press, 1990.

Alphant, Marianne. 'L'album de la mère Castor.' Review of *Lettres à Sartre*. *Libération* 22 Feb. 1990: 19–21.

Andersen, Hans Christian. *Fairy Tales*. Trans. Reginald Spinks. London: Dent, 1958.

Annuaire de l'Association amicale des anciens élèves de l'Ecole Normale Supérieure. Paris, 1986.

Appignanesi, Lisa. *Simone de Beauvoir*. Harmondsworth: Penguin, 1988.

Armogathe, Daniel. *Le deuxième sexe: Simone de Beauvoir*. Paris: Hatier, 1977.

Ascher, Carol. *Simone de Beauvoir: A Life of Freedom*. Brighton: Harvester, 1981.

Atack, Margaret and Phil Powrie, eds. *Contemporary French Fiction by Women: Feminist Perspectives*. Manchester: Manchester University Press, 1990.

Audet, Jean-Raymond. *Simone de Beauvoir face à la mort*. Lausanne: L'âge d'homme, 1979.

Bair, Deirdre. *Simone de Beauvoir: A Biography*. New York: Summit Books, 1990.

Barnes, Hazel A. *The Literature of Possibility: A Study in Humanist Existentialism*. Lincoln: University of Nebraska Press, 1959.

Barthes, Roland. *Mythologies*. Paris: Seuil, 1957.

—— 'The Death of the Author.' 1969. *Image – Music – Text*. Trans. Stephen Heath. New York: Hill and Wang, 1983: 142–8.

Beauvoir, Hélène de. *Souvenirs*. Receuillis par Marcelle Routier. Paris: Séguier, 1987.

—— 'Entretien avec Hélène de Beauvoir à Trebiano, 22 juin 1986.' With Yolanda Astarita Patterson. *Simone de Beauvoir Studies* 5 (1988): 12–31.

—— Interview. *Daughters of de Beauvoir*. BBC 2. 22 Mar. 1989.

Benda, Julien. *La trahison des clercs*. 1927. Paris: Grasset, 1975.

Benstock, Shari, ed. *The Private Self: Theory and Practice of Women's Autobiographical Writings*. Chapel Hill: UNC Press, 1988.

Berghe, Chr. L van der. *Dictionnaire des idées dans l'oeuvre de Simone de Beauvoir*. The Hague: Mouton, 1966.

Bernheimer, Charles and Claire Kahane, eds. *In Dora's Case: Freud Hysteria – Feminism*. Second Edition. New York: Columbia, 1990.

Bertheaume, Marthe. 'L'activité féminine.' *Forces nouvelles*. Late 1920s.

Bhaba, Homi. 'What Does the Black Man Want?' *New Formations* 1 (Spring 1987): 118–24.

Bieber, Konrad. *Simone de Beauvoir*. Boston: Twayne, 1979.

Boisdeffre, Pierre de. *Une histoire vivante de la littérature d'aujourd'hui, 1938–58*. Paris: Le livre contemporain, 1958.

Bok, Sissela. *Alva. Ett kvinnoliv*. Stockholm: Bonniers, 1987.

Bonner, Thomas Neville. *To the Ends of the Earth: Women's Search for Education in Medicine*. Cambridge, Massachusetts: Harvard, 1992.

Boschetti, Anna. *Sartre et 'Les temps modernes'*. Paris: Minuit, 1985.

Bouchardeau, Huguette. *Pas d'histoire, les femmes . . . 50 ans d'histoire des femmes: 1918–1968*. Paris: Syros, 1977.

Bourdieu, Pierre. *Distinction. A Social Critique of the Judgement of Taste*. Trans. Richard Nice. London: RKP, 1984. Trans. of *La distinction. Critique sociale du jugement*. Paris: Minuit, 1979.

—— 'Le mort saisit le vif.' *Actes de la recherche en sciences sociales* 32–3 (Apr.–June 1980): 3–14.

—— 'Sartre.' *London Review of Books* 2.22 (20 Nov. 1980): 11–12.

—— 'Epreuve scolaire et consécration sociale: les classes préparatoires aux grandes écoles.' *Actes de la recherche en sciences sociales* 39 (1981): 3–70.

—— *La noblesse d'etat*. Paris: Minuit, 1989.

—— and Monique de Saint Martin. 'Les catégories de l'entendement professoral.' *Actes de la recherche en sciences sociales* 3 (1975): 68–93.

Bourdoiseau, Yannick. 'Sous les couvertures.' *Minute* 25 Apr. 1986.

Breton, André. *Nadja*. 1928. Paris: Gallimard, 1964.

Brooks, Peter. *The Melodramatic Imagination: Balzac, Henry James, Melodrama, and the Mode of Excess*. 1976. New York: Columbia, 1985.

Brosman, Catherine Savage. *Simone de Beauvoir Revisited*. Twayne's World Authors

Series 820. Boston: Twayne, 1991.

Butler, Judith. 'Sex and Gender in Simone de Beauvoir's *Second Sex*.' *Yale French Studies* 72 (1986): 35–49.

Campbell, James. 'Experiencing Egoism.' Review of *The Tongue Set Free*, by Elias Canetti. *Times Literary Supplement* 26 Aug. 1988: 926.

Card, Claudia. 'Lesbian attitudes and *The Second Sex*.' *Women's Studies International Forum* 8.3 (1985): 209–14. (Reprinted in al-Hibri and Simons.)

Carlomusso, Jean. *L Is For The Way You Look*. Videocassette. No date.

Caron, Jeanne. 'Les débuts de Sainte-Marie.' Mayeur and Godille 123–9. *Carrefour* 24 Oct. 1957.

Carter, Angela. 'Colette.' *London Review of Books Anthology One*. Ed. Michael Mason. London: Junction Books, 1981: 129–39.

Cau, Jean. *Croquis de mémoire*. Paris: Julliard, 1985.

Caute, David. *Fanon*. London: Fontana, 1970.

Cayron, Claire. *La nature chez Simone de Beauvoir*. Paris: Gallimard, 1973.

Celeux, Anne-Marie. *Jean-Paul Sartre, Simone de Beauvoir: Une expérience commune, deux écritures*. Paris: Nizet, 1986.

Chabrol, Claude. *Une affaire de femmes*. (English title: *A Story of Women*.) MK2 Productions, Films A2, Films du Camelia and La Sept, 1988.

Chaigne, Louis. 'Simone de Beauvoir: Prix Goncourt.' *Le Courrier Français* 11 Nov. 1954.

Charle, Christophe. *Naissance des 'intellectuels' 1880–1900*. Paris: Minuit, 1990.

Charrier, Edmée. *L'évolution intellectuelle féminine*. Paris: Mechelinck, 1931.

Chasseguet-Smirgel, Janine. 'Feminine Guilt and the Oedipus Complex.' *Female Sexuality: New Psychoanalytic Views*. Ann Arbor: University of Michigan Press, 1970: 94–134.

Cheverny, Julien. 'Une bourgeoise modèle: Simone de Beauvoir.' *Figaro magazine* 17 Feb. 1979: 57.

Chrestien, Michel. Review of *La force des choses*. *La nation française* 13 Nov. 1963. Julienne-Caffié 229–30.

Cixous, Hélène. 'The Laugh of the Medusa.' Marks and Courtivron 245–64.

Cohen-Solal, Annie. *Sartre 1905–1980*. Paris: Gallimard, 1985.

Colette. *Claudine à l'école*. 1900. Paris: Laffont, 1989.

—— *La vagabonde*. 1910. Paris: Le livre de poche, n.d.

—— *Chéri*. 1920. Paris: Le livre de poche, n.d.

—— *Le blé en herbe*. 1923. Paris: Garnier-Flammarion, 1964.

Collins, Margery and Christine Pierce, 'Holes and Slime: Sexism in Sartre's Psychoanalysis.' Gould and Wartofsky 112–27.

Cordero, Anne D. 'Simone de Beauvoir Twice Removed.' *Simone de Beauvoir Studies* 7 (1990): 49–56.

Cordier, Marguerite. 'Le difficile accès des femmes à l'instruction et aux carrières ouvertes par l'enseignement supérieur.' *Bulletin de l'association amicale des anciennes élèves de l'ENS de Fontenay-aux-Roses* 102 (1977): 3–15.

Cottrell, Robert. *Simone de Beauvoir*. New York: Ungar, 1975.

Crosland, Margaret. *Simone de Beauvoir: The Woman and Her Work*. London: Heinemann, 1992.

Culler, Jonathan. *Flaubert: The Uses of Uncertainty*. London: Elek, 1974.

Dahl, Hans Fredrik, Jon Elster, Irene Iversen, Siri Nørve, Tor Inge Romøren, Rune Slagstad and Mariken Vaa, eds. *Pax Leksikon*. Oslo: Pax, 1980.

David, Deirdre. *Intellectual Women and Victorian Patriarchy. Harriet Martineau. Elizabeth Barrett Browning. George Eliot*. London: Macmillan, 1987.

Dayan, Josée. *Simone de Beauvoir*. Transcript of soundtrack. Paris: Gallimard, 1979.

Delphy, Christine. *Close to Home: A Materialist Analysis of Women's Oppression*. Trans. and ed. Diana Leonard. London: Hutchinson, 1984.

DePalma, Anthony. 'Rare in Ivy League: Women Who Work as Full Professors.' *The New York Times*, 24 Jan. 1993: 1 and 11.

Descartes, René. *A Discourse on Method*. 1637. Trans. J. Veitch. Buffalo, New York: Prometheus Books, 1989.

Descubes, Madeleine. *Connaître Simone de Beauvoir*. Paris: Resma, 1974.

'Deux morts sans importance.' *Minute* 18 Apr. 1986.

Domaize, Pierre. Review of *La force des choses*. *La nation* 30 Jan. 1964. Julienne-Caffié 233.

Drew, Bettina. *Nelson Algren: A Life on the Wild Side*. London: Bloomsbury, 1990.

Duchen, Claire. *Feminism in France From May '68 to Mitterand*. London: Routledge, 1986.

—— trans. and ed. *French Connections: Voices from the Women's Movement in France*. London: Hutchinson, 1987.

Duportal, Jeanne. 'Etude sur les livres à figures édités en France de 1601 à 1660.' Thesis. Sorbonne, 1914.

—— 'Contribution au catalogue général des livres à figures du XVIIe siècle (1601–1633).' Thesis. Sorbonne, 1914.

Duras, Marguerite. *Le ravissement de Lol V. Stein*. Paris: Gallimard, 1964.

Duval, Nathalie. 'Etude de la réception littéraire du *Deuxième Sexe* de Simone de Beauvoir au Québec francophone et au Canada anglophone.' Maîtrise. Université Paris X Nanterre, 1989.

—— 'Simone de Beauvoir: rejets, controverses et légitimation ou la réception de Simone de Beauvoir en Amérique du Nord francophone et anglophone (Québec, Canada et Etats-Unis).' DEA dissertation. Université Paris X Nanterre, 1990.

Eagleton, Terry. *Ideology: An Introduction*. London: Verso, 1991.

Eaubonne, Françoise d'. *Une femme nommée Castor. Mon amie Simone de Beauvoir*. Paris: Encre, 1986.

Eliot, George. *The Mill on the Floss*. 1860. London: Dent, 1976.

—— *Romola*. 1863. Edinburgh: Blackwood, 1903.

—— *Middlemarch*. 1872. New York: Bantam, 1992.

Ellmann, Mary. *Thinking About Women*. New York: Harcourt, 1968.

—— 'The Dutiful Simone de Beauvoir.' Marks, *Critical Essays* 94–101.

Engelstad, Irene, Jorunn Hareide, Irene Iversen, Torill Steinfeld and Janneken Øverland, eds. *Norsk kvinnelitteraturhistorie*. Vol. 3. Oslo: Pax, 1990.

Etcherelli, Claire. *Elise ou la vraie vie*. Paris: Denoël, 1967.

Evans, Martha Noel. 'Murdering *L'Invitée*: Gender and Fictional Narrative.' *Yale French Studies* 72 (1986): 67–86.

—— *Masks of Tradition: Women and the Politics of Writing in Twentieth Century France*. Ithaca: Cornell, 1987.

Evans, Mary. *Simone de Beauvoir: A Feminist Mandarin*. London: Tavistock, 1985.

Fabiani, Jean-Louis. *Les philosophes de la république*. Paris: Minuit, 1988.

Fallaize, Elizabeth. *The Novels of Simone de Beauvoir*. London: Routledge, 1988.

—— 'Resisting Romance: Simone de Beauvoir, "The Woman Destroyed" and the Romance Script.' Atack and Powrie 15–25.

Faludi, Susan. *Backlash: The Undeclared War Against American Women*. New York: Doubleday, 1991.

Fanon, Frantz. *Black Skin, White Masks*. Trans. Charles Lam Markmann. New York: Grove Weidenfeld, 1967. Trans. of *Peau noire, masques blancs*. Paris: Seuil, 1952.

Ferguson, Ann. 'Lesbian Identity: Beauvoir and History.' *Women's Studies International Forum* 8.3 (1985): 203–8. (Reprinted in al-Hibri and Simons.)

Feuchtwang, Stephan. 'Fanonian Spaces.' *New Formations* 1 (Spring 1987): 124–30.

Fitch, Brian T. *Le sentiment d'étrangeté chez Malraux, Sartre, Camus et Simone de Beauvoir*. Paris: Minard, 1964.

Forster, Penny and Imogen Sutton, eds. *Daughters of de Beauvoir*. London: The Women's Press, 1989.

Foucault, Michel. *The History of Sexuality. Vol. 1: An Introduction*. Trans. Robert Hurley. New York: Vintage, 1980.

Fouque, Antoinette. 'Notre ennemi n'est pas l'homme, mais l'impérialisme du phallus.' Interview with Catherine Clément. *Le matin* 16 July 1980: 13. Trans. 'Interview with Antoinette Fouque.' Duchen, *Connections* 50–4.

—— Interview. *Libération* 15 Apr. 1986: 5.

Fox-Genovese, Elisabeth. *Feminism Without Illusions: A Critique of Individualism*. Chapel Hill: UNC Press, 1991.

Francis, Claude and Fernande Gonthier. *Les écrits de Simone de Beauvoir*. Paris: Gallimard, 1979.

—— *Simone de Beauvoir*. Trans. Lisa Nesselson. London: Sidgwick, 1987. Trans. of *Simone de Beauvoir*. Paris: Perrin, 1985.

—— 'Simone de Beauvoir et ses biographes. Polémique.' *Le Matin* 16 Dec. 1985.

Francis, Claude and Janine Niepce. *Simone de Beauvoir et le cours du monde*. Paris: Klincksieck, 1978.

Fraser, Nancy and Sandra Lee Bartky, eds. *Revaluing French Feminism: Critical Essays on Difference, Agency, Culture*. Bloomington: Indiana University Press, 1992.

Freud, Sigmund. *The Interpretation of Dreams*. 1900. *Standard Edition* 4 and 5.

—— *Fragment of an Analysis of a Case of Hysteria* ('Dora'). 1905. *Standard Edition* 7: 3–122.

—— *Jokes and their Relations to the Unconscious*. 1905. *Standard Edition* 8.

—— 'Creative Writers and Day-dreaming.' 1908. *Standard Edition* 9: 141–54.

—— 'Family Romances.' 1909. *Standard Edition* 9: 235–41.

—— 'On Narcissism.' 1914. *Standard Edition* 14: 69–102.

—— 'Fetishism.' 1927. *Standard Edition* 21: 152–7.

Friedan, Betty. *It Changed My Life: Writings on the Women's Movement*. New York:

Norton, 1985.

Gagnebin, Laurent. *Simone de Beauvoir ou le refus de l'indifférence.* Paris: Fischbacher, 1968.

Galey, Mathieu. 'Simone de Beauvoir: le temps vaincu.' *L'express* 4 Sept. 1972: 87–8.

Garcia, Sandrine. 'Le féminisme, une révolution symbolique? Etude des luttes symboliques autour de la condition féminine.' Thesis. Ecole des hautes études en sciences sociales, 1993.

Gatens, Moira. *Feminism and Philosophy: Perspectives on Difference and Equality.* Cambridge: Polity, 1991.

Gates, Henry Louis Jr. 'Critical Fanonism.' *Critical Inquiry* 17 (Spring 1991): 457–70.

Gelderman, Carol. *Mary McCarthy: A Life.* London: Sidgwick & Jackson, 1989.

Gendzier, Irene L. *Frantz Fanon: A Critical Study.* New York: Pantheon, 1973.

Gennari, Geneviève. *Simone de Beauvoir.* Paris: Ed. Universitaires, 1958.

—— Review of *Mémoires d'une jeune fille rangée. Arts* 8 Oct. 1958.

Gerassi, John. *Jean-Paul Sartre: Hated Conscience of His Century.* Chicago: University of Chicago Press, 1989.

Gibon, Fénelon. *L'enseignement secondaire féminin.* Paris: Société générale d'éducation et d'enseignement, 1920.

Girard, René. 'Memoirs of a Dutiful Existentialist.' Marks, *Critical Essays* 84–8.

Giraudoux, Jean. 'Sur l'esprit normalien.' Preface to Reignup, *L'esprit de Normale.*

Gledhill, Christine, ed. *Home is Where the Heart Is: Studies in Melodrama and Woman's Film.* London: BFI Publishing, 1987.

Gould, Carol C. and Marx W. Wartofsky, eds. *Women and Philosophy: Toward a Theory of Liberation.* New York: Putnam, 1976.

Greene, Naomi. 'Sartre, Sexuality, and *The Second Sex.*' *Philosophy and Literature* 4.1 (Fall 1980): 199–211.

Guillaumin, Colette. 'The Question of Difference.' Duchen, *Connections* 64–77.

Hardwick, Elizabeth. 'The Subjection of Women.' Marks, *Critical Essays* 49–58.

Hatcher, Donald L. *Understanding 'The Second Sex'.* New York: Peter Lang, 1984.

Hayman, Ronald. *Writing Against: A Biography of Sartre.* London: Weidenfeld and Nicolson, 1986.

Heath, Jane. *Simone de Beauvoir.* Brighton: Harvester, 1989.

Henric, Jacques. 'Pourquoi ces biographies aseptisées?.' *Art Press* 104 (June 1986): 3.

Henry, A. M., OP. *Simone de Beauvoir ou l'échec d'une chrétienté.* Paris: Fayard, 1961.

Hewitt, Leah D. *Autobiographical Tightropes.* Lincoln: University of Nebraska Press, 1990.

Hibbs, Françoise Arnaud. *L'espace dans les romans de Simone de Beauvoir: son expression et sa fonction.* Stanford French and Italian Studies 59. Saratoga, California: Anma Libri, 1989.

Hourdin, Georges. *Simone de Beauvoir et la liberté.* Paris: Cerf, 1962.

Howells, Christina. 'Sartre: Desiring the Impossible.' Unpublished manuscript.

Huvos, Kornel. *Cinq mirages américains.* Paris: Didier, 1972.

Idt, Geneviève. 'Modèles scolaires dans l'écriture sartrienne: *La nausée* ou la "narration" impossible.' *Revue des sciences humaines* 174 (1979): 83–103.

Irigaray, Luce. *Spéculum de l'autre femme*. Paris: Minuit, 1974.

——*Je, tu, nous: pour une culture de la différence*. Paris: Grasset, 1990.

Jaccard, Annie-Claire. *Simone de Beauvoir*. Zürich: Juris Druck, 1968.

Jannoud, Claude. 'L'oeuvre: une vulgarisation plus qu'une création.' *Le monde* 15 Apr. 1986.

Jardine, Alice. 'Death Sentences: Writing Couples and Ideology.' Marks, *Critical Essays* 207–18.

Jeannin, Pierre. *Ecole Normale Supérieure: livre d'or*. Paris: Office française de diffusion artistique et littéraire, 1963.

Jeanson, Francis. *Simone de Beauvoir ou l'entreprise de vivre*. Paris: Seuil, 1966.

Joseph, Gilbert. *Une si douce Occupation . . . : Simone de Beauvoir et Jean-Paul Sartre 1940–1944*. Paris: Albin Michel, 1991.

Julienne-Caffié, Serge. *Simone de Beauvoir*. Paris: Gallimard, 1966.

Karady, Victor. 'Normaliens et autres enseignants à la Belle Époque. Notes sur l'origine sociale et la réussite dans une profession intellectuelle.' *Revue française de sociologie* 13.1 (Jan.–Mar. 1972): 35–58.

Keefe, Terry. *Simone de Beauvoir: A Study of her Writings*. London: Harrap, 1983.

Kennedy, Margaret. *The Constant Nymph*. 1924. London: Virago, 1986.

Kohon, Gregorio. 'Reflections on Dora: The Case of Hysteria.' *The British School of Psychoanalysis: The Independent Tradition*. Ed. Gregorio Kohon. London: Free Association Books, 1986: 362–80.

Kristeva, Julia. *Revolution in Poetic Language*. Trans. Margaret Waller. New York: Columbia, 1984.

—— 'Stabat mater.' 1976. *The Kristeva Reader*. Ed. Toril Moi. Oxford: Blackwell, 1986: 160–86.

—— *Black Sun: Depression and Melancholia*. Trans. Leon S. Roudiez. New York: Columbia, 1989.

—— *Lettre ouverte à Harlem Désir*. Paris: Rivages, 1990.

—— 'Quand les Samouraïs répondent aux Mandarins.' Interview with Josyane Savigneau. *Le monde* 9 Mar. 1990: 19–20.

—— *Les Samouraïs*. Paris: Fayard, 1990.

Kruks, Sonia. 'Simone de Beauvoir: Between Sartre and Merleau-Ponty.' *Simone de Beauvoir Studies* 5 (1988): 74–80.

Lacan, Jacques. *Les complexes familiaux dans la formation de l'individu: essai d'analyse d'une fonction en psychologie*. 1938. Paris: Navarin, 1984.

—— *Ecrits*. Paris: Seuil, 1966.

LaCapra, Dominick. *A Preface to Sartre*. 1978. Ithaca: Cornell, 1987.

Laclos, Choderlos de. *Les liaisons dangereuses*. 1782. Paris: Classiques Garnier, 1961.

Lacoin, Elisabeth. *Zaza: correspondance et carnets d'Elisabeth Lacoin 1914–1929*. Paris: Seuil, 1991.

Lagrave, Rose Marie. 'Recherches féministes ou recherches sur les femmes?.' *Actes de la recherche en sciences sociales* 83 (June 1990): 27–39.

Lalou, Etienne. 'La raison n'a pas toujours raison.' *L'express* 12 Dec. 1966: 107–8.

Lamblin, Bianca. *Mémoires d'une jeune fille dérangée*. Paris: Balland, 1993.

Langlois, Claude. 'Aux origines de l'enseignement secondaire catholique des jeunes filles. Jalons pour une enquête 1896–1914.' Mayeur and Godille 81–94.

Lasocki, Anne-Marie. *Simone de Beauvoir ou l'entreprise d'écrire: essai de commentaire par les textes*. The Hague: Nijhoff, 1970.

Leak, Andrew N. *The Perverted Consciousness: Sexuality and Sartre*. London: Macmillan, 1989.

Le Doeuff, Michèle. 'Long Hair, Short Ideas.' *The Philosophical Imaginary*. Trans. Colin Gordon. London: Athlone, 1989: 100–28. Trans. of *L'imaginaire philosophique*. Paris: Payot, 1980.

—— 'Sartre: l'Unique Sujet parlant.' *Esprit* (May 1984): 181–91.

—— 'Operative Philosophy: Simone de Beauvoir and Existentialism.' Marks, *Critical Essays* 144–54.

—— *Hipparchia's Choice: An Essay Concerning Women, Philosophy, etc*. Trans. Trista Selous. Oxford: Blackwell, 1991. Trans. of *L'étude et le rouet: des femmes, de la philosophie, etc*. Paris: Seuil, 1989.

Lehmann, Rosamond. *Dusty Answer*. 1927. Harmondsworth: Penguin, 1991.

—— *Invitation to the Waltz*. 1932. London: Virago, 1982.

Leighton, Jean. *Simone de Beauvoir on Woman*. Rutherford: Fairleigh Dickinson, 1975.

Leiris, Michel. *L'âge d'homme*. Paris: Gallimard, 1939.

Levaux, Michèle. 'Simone de Beauvoir, une féministe exceptionnelle.' *Etudes* (Apr. 1984): 493–8.

Lévi-Strauss, Claude. *Les structures élémentaires de la parenté*. Paris: PUF, 1949.

—— *Tristes tropiques*. Paris: Plon, 1955.

Lilar, Suzanne. *Le malentendu du Deuxième sexe*. Paris: PUF, 1969.

Lundgren-Gothlin, Eva. *Kön och existens: studier i Simone de Beauvoirs Le Deuxième Sexe*. Gothenburg: Daidalos, 1991.

Lydon, Mary. 'Hats and Cocktails: Simone de Beauvoir's Heady Texts.' Marks, *Critical Essays* 234–46.

Macey, David. *Lacan in Contexts*. London: Verso, 1988.

Madsen, Axel. *Hearts and Minds: The Common Journey of Simone de Beauvoir and Jean Paul Sartre*. New York: Morrow, 1977.

Malraux, Clara. *Nos vingt ans*. Paris: Le livre de poche, 1966.

Margadant, Jo Burr. *Madame le Professeur: Women Educators in the Third Republic*. Princeton, New Jersey: Princeton University Press, 1990.

Marks, Elaine. *Simone de Beauvoir: Encounters with Death*. New Brunswick, New Jersey: Rutgers, 1973.

—— 'Transgressing the (In)cont(in)ent Boundaries: The Body in Decline.' *Yale French Studies* 72 (1986): 181–200.

——, ed. *Critical Essays on Simone de Beauvoir*. Boston: Hall, 1987.

Marks, Elaine and Isabelle de Courtivron, eds. *New French Feminisms*. Brighton: Harvester, 1980.

Martin, Biddy. *Woman and Modernity: The (Life)styles of Lou Andreas Salomé*. Ithaca: Cornell, 1991.

May, Derwent. *Hannah Arendt*. Harmondsworth: Penguin, 1986.

Mayeur, Françoise. *L'enseignement secondaire des jeunes filles sous la Troisième République*. Paris: Presses de la fondation nationale des sciences politiques, 1977.

—— and Jacques Godille, eds. *Education et images de la femme chrétienne en France au début du XXème siècle*. Lyon: L'Hermès, 1980.

McCarthy, Mary. 'Mlle. Gulliver en Amérique.' Marks, *Critical Essays* 44–9.

McPherson, Karen. 'Criminal Passions in Simone de Beauvoir's *L'Invitée*.' *Simone de Beauvoir Studies* 5 (1988): 32–9.

Merleau-Ponty, Maurice. *Phénoménologie de la perception*. Paris: Gallimard, 1945.

—— 'Metaphysics and the Novel.' Marks, *Critical Essays* 31–44.

Middlebrook, Diane Wood. *Anne Sexton: A Biography*. Boston: Houghton Mifflin, 1991.

Miller, Nancy K., ed. *The Poetics of Gender*. New York: Columbia, 1987.

Moi, Toril. 'Representation of Patriarchy: Sexuality and Epistemology in Freud's Dora.' 1981. Bernheimer and Kahane 181–99.

——, ed. *The Kristeva Reader*. Oxford: Blackwell, 1986.

——, ed. *French Feminist Thought*. Oxford: Blackwell, 1987.

—— 'Feminism, Postmodernism, and Style: Recent Feminist Criticism in the United States.' *Cultural Critique* 9 (Spring 1988): 3–22.

—— *Feminist Theory and Simone de Beauvoir*. The Bucknell Lectures. Ed. Michael Payne. Oxford: Blackwell, 1990.

—— 'Appropriating Bourdieu: Feminist Theory and Pierre Bourdieu's Sociology of Culture.' *New Literary History* 22 (1991): 1017–49.

Moubachir, Chantal. *Simone de Beauvoir*. Paris: Seghers, 1971.

Mudimbe, V. Y. *The Invention of Africa: Gnosis, Philosophy, and the Order of Knowledge*. Bloomington: Indiana University Press, 1988.

Nahas, Hélène. *La femme dans la littérature existentielle*. Paris: PUF, 1957.

Neuhoff, Eric. 'Jean-Paul, Tintin et Milou.' *Le Quotidien de Paris* 14 Dec. 1981.

Nizan, Paul. *Aden-Arabie*. 1932. Paris: Maspero, 1971.

—— *Les chiens de garde*. 1932. Paris: Maspero, 1960.

Okely, Judith. *Simone de Beauvoir*. London: Virago, 1986.

Ophir, Anne. *Regards féminins: Beauvoir/Etcherelli/Rochefort. Condition féminine et création littéraire*. Paris: Denoël/Gonthier, 1976.

Oulhiou, Yvonne. *L'ENS de Fontenay-aux-Roses à travers le temps 1880–1980*. Fontenay: ENS, 1981.

Pacaly, Josette. *Sartre au miroir. Une lecture psychanalytique de ses écrits biographiques*. Paris: Klincksieck, 1980.

Patterson, Yolanda Astarita. *Simone de Beauvoir and the Demystification of Motherhood*. Ann Arbor & London: UMI Research Press, 1989.

Peyrefitte, Alain, ed. *Rue d'Ulm: chroniques de la vie normalienne*. Paris: Vigneau, 1950; 3rd ed. Paris: Flammarion, 1977.

Peyrefitte, René. 'L'Ecole et les Sévriennes.' Alain Peyrefitte, 3rd ed. 334–9.

Pivot, Bernard. 'Simone de Beauvoir: une vraie femme de lettres (pour le courrier du coeur).' *Figaro littéraire* 30 Oct. 1967: 29.

Plaza, Monique. '"Phallomorphic Power" and the Psychology of "Woman".' *Ideology & Consciousness* 4 (Autumn 1978): 4–36.

Poulet, Robert. *La lanterne magique*. Paris: Debresse, 1956.

Questions féministes. Editorial. Marks and Courtivron 212–30.

Rachilde. *Monsieur Vénus*. 1887. Paris: Flammarion, 1977.

Radway, Janice. *Reading the Romance: Women, Patriarchy, and Popular Literature*. 1984. London: Verso, 1987.

Reignup, J. *L'esprit de Normale*. Paris: SPES, 1935.

Reuillard, Gabriel. 'Simone de Beauvoir – "papesse" de l'existentialisme.' *Paris-Normandie* 17 Feb. 1954.

Rimmon-Kenan, Shlomith, ed. *Discourse in Psychoanalysis and Literature*. London: Methuen, 1987.

Rioux, Jean-Pierre. *The Fourth Republic 1944–1958*. Trans. Godfrey Rogers. Cambridge: CUP, 1987.

Robert, Marthe. *Origins of the Novel*. Trans. Sacha Rabinovitch. Bloomington: Indiana University Press, 1980.

Rocheblave, Samuel. 'Mlle Zanta soutient sa thèse de philosophie en Sorbonne.' *Le temps* 27 May 1914: 6.

Rose, Jacqueline. *The Haunting of Sylvia Plath*. London: Virago, 1991.

Roudinesco, Elisabeth. *La bataille de cent ans. Histoire de la psychanalyse en France. 2: 1925–1985*. Paris: Seuil, 1986.

Sage, Lorna. *Women in the House of Fiction: Post-War Women Novelists*. London: Macmillan, 1992.

Said, Edward. 'Representing the Colonized: Anthropology's Interlocutors.' *Critical Inquiry* 15 (Winter 1989): 205–25.

Saint Martin, Monique de. 'Les "femmes écrivains" et le champ littéraire.' *Actes de la recherche en sciences sociales* 83 (June 1990): 52–6.

Sankovitch, Tilde A. *French Women Writers and the Book: Myths of Access and Desire*. Syracuse, New York: Syracuse University Press, 1988.

Sarraute, Claude. 'Féminisme = humanisme.' *Le monde* 6–7 Apr. 1975: 11.

Sartre, Jean-Paul. *La nausée*. Paris: Gallimard, 1938.

—— *Les mouches*. Paris: Gallimard, 1943.

—— *L'être et le néant: essai d'ontologie phénoménologique*. Paris: Gallimard, 1943. *Being and Nothingness*. Trans. Hazel E. Barnes. New York: Washington Square Press, 1966.

—— *L'âge de raison*. Paris: Gallimard, 1945.

—— *L'existentialisme est un humanisme*. Paris: Nagel, 1946.

—— *Morts sans sépulture*. 1946. In *La putain respectueuse*. Paris: Folio, 1988.

—— *What Is Literature? and Other Essays*. 1948. Ed. Steven Ungar. Cambridge, Massachusetts: Harvard, 1988.

—— *Les mains sales*. 1948. Paris: Folio, 1981.

—— 'Orphée noir.' *Situations III*. Paris: Gallimard, 1949. 'Black Orpheus.' Trans. John MacCombie. *What Is Literature?* 289–330.

—— 'Avant-propos.' *Aden-Arabie*. By Paul Nizan. 1960. Paris: Maspero, 1971.

—— *Les mots*. Paris: Gallimard, 1964.

—— *Cahiers pour une morale*. Paris: Gallimard, 1983.

—— *Les carnets de la drôle de guerre*. Paris: Gallimard, 1983.

—— *Lettres au Castor et à quelques autres*. Ed. Simone de Beauvoir. Paris: Gallimard, 1983.

—— *Vérité et existence*. Ed. Arlette Elkaïm-Sartre. Paris: Gallimard, 1989.

Savigneau, Josyane. 'Cher petit vous autre.' Review of *Lettres à Sartre*. *Le monde* 28

Feb. 1990: 21 and 26.

Schor, Naomi. 'Female Fetishism: The Case of George Sand.' Suleiman, *Female Body* 363–72.

Schwartzer, Alice. *Simone de Beauvoir Today. Conversations 1972–1982.* London: Chatto, 1984.

Seigfried, Charlene Haddock. '*Second Sex*: Second Thoughts'. al-Hibri and Simons 305–22.

Senart, Philippe. Review of *La force des choses. La table ronde* Dec. 1963. Julienne-Caffié 231–2.

Senghor, Léopold Senghar, ed. *Anthologie de la nouvelle poésie nègre et malgache de langue française.* Paris: Presses universitaires de France, 1948.

Shiach, Morag. *Hélène Cixous: A Politics of Writing.* London: Routledge, 1991.

Simons, Margaret A. 'The Silencing of Simone de Beauvoir: Guess What's Missing from *The Second Sex*.' *Women's Studies International Forum* 6.5 (1983): 559–64.

—— 'Beauvoir and Sartre: The Philosophical Relationship.' *Yale French Studies* 72 (1986): 165–79.

—— 'Lesbian Connections: Simone de Beauvoir and Feminism.' *Signs* 18.1 (Autumn 1992): 136–61.

Sirinelli, Jean-François. *Génération intellectuelle. Khâgneux et normaliens dans l'entre-deux guerres.* Paris: Fayard 1988.

Spelman, Elisabeth V. *Inessential Woman: Problems of Exclusion in Feminist Thought.* Boston: Beacon, 1988.

Staël, Madame de. *Corinne ou l'Italie.* 1807. Paris: Folio, 1985.

Stekel, Wilhelm. *Frigidity in Woman in Relation to her Love Life.* 2 vols. Trans. James S. Van Teslaar. New York: Liveright, 1946.

—— *The Autobiography of Wilhelm Stekel: The Life Story of a Pioneer Psychoanalyst.* Ed. Emil A. Gutheil, M.D. New York: Liveright, 1950.

Suleiman, Susan Rubin, ed. *The Female Body in Western Culture: Contemporary Perspectives.* Cambridge, Massachusetts: Harvard, 1986.

—— 'Nadja, Dora, Lol V. Stein: Women, Madness and Narrative.' Rimmon-Kenan 124–51.

Taylor, Patrick. *The Narrative of Liberation: Perspectives on Afro-Caribbean Literature, Popular Culture, and Politics.* Ithaca: Cornell, 1989.

Thibaudet, Albert. *La république des professeurs.* 1927. Paris: Ressources, 1979.

Todd, Olivier. *Un fils rebelle.* Paris: Grasset, 1981.

Viner, Katherine. 'In the Finals Analysis.' *Guardian* 8 July 1992: 19.

Webster, Paul. 'Second Sex in Person.' Review of *Lettres à Sartre. Guardian* 24 Feb. 1990: 3.

Whitford, Margaret. *Luce Irigaray: Philosophy in the Feminine.* London: Routledge, 1991.

Whitmarsh, Anne. *Simone de Beauvoir and the Limits of Commitment.* Cambridge: CUP, 1981.

Wilcox, Helen, Keith McWatters, Ann Thompson and Linda R. Williams, eds. *The Body and the Text. Hélène Cixous, Reading and Teaching.* Hemel Hempstead: Harvester, 1990.

Winegarten, Renée. *Simone de Beauvoir: A Critical View.* Oxford: Berg, 1988.

Winnicott, D. W. 'Fear of Breakdown.' *Psycho-analytic Explorations*. Ed. Clare Winnicott, Ray Shepherd and Madeleine Davis. Cambridge, Massachusetts: Harvard, 1989: 87–95.

Winston, Jane. 'Forever Feminine: Marguerite Duras and her French Critics.' *New Literary History* 24.2 (May 1993): 467–82.

Wittig, Monique. *Les guérillères*. Paris: Minuit, 1969.

—— 'The Mark of Gender.' Miller 63–73.

—— *The Straight Mind and Other Essays*. Boston: Beacon, 1992.

Wollstonecraft, Mary. *Mary*. 1788. *Mary and The Wrongs of Woman*. Oxford: Oxford University Press, 1988.

—— *A Vindication of the Rights of Woman*. 1792. Ed. Carol H. Poston. Second edition. New York: Norton, 1988.

Woodward, Kathleen. 'Simone de Beauvoir: Ageing and Its Discontents.' Benstock 90–113.

Zanta, Léontine. *La renaissance du stoïcisme au XVIe siècle*. Thesis. Sorbonne, 1914.

—— 'La traduction française du Manuel d'Epictète d'André de Rivaudeau au XVIe siècle, publiée avec une introduction.' Thesis. Sorbonne, 1914.

—— *La science et l'amour: journal d'une étudiante*. Paris: Plon, 1921.

—— *Psychologie du féminisme*. Préface de Paul Bourget. Paris: Plon, 1922.

—— *La part du feu*. Paris: Plon, 1927.

—— Interview. *La Française* 29 Oct. 1927.

—— 'Les Etats-Généraux du féminisme. Discours de Mlle Zanta.' *La Française* 23 Feb. 1929.

—— *Sainte Monique et son fils*. Préface du R. P. Sertillanges. Paris: Plon, 1941.

Zéphir, Jacques J. *Le néo-féminisme de Simone de Beauvoir: trente ans après Le deuxième sexe: un post-scriptum*. Paris: Denoël/Gonthier, 1982.

Zola, Emile. 'Tous des pions.' Alain Peyrefitte, 3rd ed. 368–9.

Index

Books without an author's name are by Simone de Beauvoir. Within entries Simone de Beauvoir's name has been abbreviated to SDB. For the sake of clarity entries under 'Beauvoir, Simone de' have been severely restricted. As far as possible, references to Beauvoir's own experiences have been indexed under the relevant headwords ('depression', 'education', etc.). With the exception of Beauvoir's close family, references to Sartre and Beauvoir's relationships to other people have been indexed under the relevant person's name.